Palaeolithic and Mesolithic Settlement in Wales

with special reference to Dyfed

Andrew David

BAR British Series 448
2007

This title published by

Archaeopress
Publishers of British Archaeological Reports
Gordon House
276 Banbury Road
Oxford OX2 7ED
England
bar@archaeopress.com
www.archaeopress.com

Archaeopress
10 years

BAR 448

Palaeolithic and Mesolithic Settlement in Wales - with special reference to Dyfed

ISBN 978 1 4073 0146 4

Printed in England by CMP (Ltd)

All BAR titles are available from:

Hadrian Books Ltd
122 Banbury Road
Oxford
OX2 7BP
England
bar@hadrianbooks.co.uk

The current BAR catalogue with details of all titles in print, prices and means of payment is available free from Hadrian Books or may be downloaded from www.archaeopress.com

PALAEOLITHIC AND MESOLITHIC SETTLEMENT IN WALES WITH SPECIAL REFERENCE TO DYFED

PREFACE

This monograph is a direct transcription of my doctoral dissertation (David, 1990). Despite the embarrassing lapse of time since the original was completed I have been reassured recently by readers that making it more widely available would be worthwhile. It includes a useful collation of a wide array of evidence, together with the presentation of the results of field survey (surface collection) and excavation, backed up with the illustration of a large corpus of artefacts. I am particularly conscious, too, of the need to make the results of excavations at The Nab Head (1979-1986), and Daylight Rock (1988), both in Pembrokeshire, more accessible. Aspects of the Lateglacial component have been published elsewhere (David 1990), and a relatively recent review of the Mesolithic in Wales (David and Walker 2004) drew heavily on the earlier work. To what extent the analysis and interpretation offered in 1990 has stood the test of time is for others to judge; but I hope it still has some currency and may contribute beneficially to future research agendas.

So as to delay no further in making the full dissertation available I have resisted any (rather fleeting) temptation to try and bring the text up-to-date to take account of research and publication since 1990. Be warned therefore that the text and bibliography remain unchanged since that time. Much work of direct relevance has taken place during the intervening years, and a few sources are offered below. There has of course been much additional and wide ranging research from further field which also has a bearing on the wider context, but I must offer my apologies for not attempting to marshal this here.

Full acknowledgements are made in the appropriate place to the very many people who assisted with my original research and its outcome – itself an over-prolonged process. My thanks to them remain as heartfelt as ever. For encouragement to go into print after the lapse of so many years, I would like to thank Roger Jacobi, and supportive referees, and Elizabeth Walker for additional references. I am especially grateful to Archaeopress for risking the venture, and for their patient help in its production. Not least, I am thankful to my daughter Maddy who digitised all the images for me.

Andrew David
October 2007

Notes:
(a) Age estimates are quoted in radiocarbon years Before Present (BP).
(b) The county designation of Dyfed is retained, as it then was in 1990, despite the welcome reinstatement since then of the former county boundaries of Pembrokeshire, Carmarthenshire and Cardiganshire.

CONTENTS

LIST OF PLATES:

ACKNOWLEDGEMENTS

This project has taken far longer than I ever imagined, although I should have known better. It has been an unsteady progress of fits and starts over many years and during which I have therefore accumulated a great many debts of thanks.

As will become obvious, the foremost of these is to my supervisor, Roger Jacobi, and if there is any sense in what follows, then this is in large part thanks to him. His enthusiasm and encouragement over the years have been inexhaustible, as has been his generosity in sharing a unique knowledge of British early prehistory. Any lapses in the presentation of this Welsh material are despite Roger's drive to make me write sense.

Of the many others who have helped directly and indirectly with this study little could have come of it were it not for the recent excavations at The Nab Head and Daylight Rock. For the success of these I am entirely in the debt of Don Benson and his staff with the Dyfed Archaeological Trust. Ken Murphy, Clare Marshall, George Williams and the late Charles Stenger have been amongst the most stalwart of these, but I would like to thank all the other members of the Trust who have helped so much. Terry James very kindly provided the aerial photographs of both sites used here.

The excavations at The Nab Head have been funded variously by CADW (then the Ancient Monuments Branch of the Welsh Office), The Society of Antiquaries of London, The Board of Celtic Studies, The Cambrian Archaeological Association, The Pembrokeshire Coast National Park, The Pembrokeshire Museums and The Friends of the Pembrokeshire Museums. The work at Daylight Rock was funded by The Royal Archaeological Institute. To all these I am most grateful.

Returning to the results presented here, I would like to thank Stephen Aldhouse-Green for his assistance at the National Museum of Wales and for sharing his results from the Tenby caves. For their essential help with the Caldey material I am indebted to Mel Davies and Brother James van Nédervelde. Both the Tenby Museum and the Pembrokeshire Museums have also gone out of their way to be helpful. Robert Kennedy, especially, has always been a champion of The Nab Head. Jill Cook of the British Museum (Quaternary Section) willingly released material for dating and supplied photographs. Joan Rees has kindly allowed me to document her flint collection from Palmerston Farm.

Peter Berridge, Edward Cloutman, Martin Lewis, George Smith, Tim Schadla-Hall and Mike Walker have all generously allowed me to make use of unpublished material, or have discussed their current research. I am most thankful to Joan Huxtable for her efforts to provide TL dates despite such unprofitable material. I would also like to warmly acknowledge the efforts of others without whose help parts of this thesis could not have been achieved: Alister Bartlett, Nick Balaam and Paul Linford have patiently helped me out with computing; Louise Woodman with photographs and Hazel Martingell with several drawings. My colleagues at the Ancient Monuments Laboratory, especially, have patiently endured my occasional preoccupation with matters of apparent irrelevance to archaeometry and geophysics. For conceding the use of facilities and some of my professional time, I thank English Heritage for indulging this trespass over the border.

I would like also to make a point of thanking the following amongst friends and colleagues who have at one time or another helped or encouraged me: Mike Allen, Mrs Bagley, Nick Barton, The Caldey Cistercian Community, Tony Clark, Andy Currant, Tim Darvill, Brian Davies, Michael Freeman, John Gater, Phil Greenwell, the late W. F. Grimes, David Gurney, David Haddon- Reece, Tony Hawes, Ivel Hornbrook, Chris Houlder, Dave Jordan, Carole Keepax, Robert Kruszynski, Susan Limbrey, Gerry McDonald, Trevor Martin, Mr. Mahlin, Simon Mays, Ray Passfield, Andy Payne, Toni Pearson, Clifford Price, Mr. Raymond, Alison Roberts, Alan Saville, Kate Scott, Ann Sieveking, Alan Smith, Tom Spittle, Vanessa Straker, Geoff Wainwright, Caroline Wickham-Jones and Owain Williams. There are many others. Jacqui Watson, especially, has had to put up with more than her fair share of lithic clutter about the house and, moreover, has patiently and without complaint given me the encouragement and leeway to see this through.

Finally, but far from least, I would like to thank my mother for coping and bearing with my 'flinting' from the earliest days.

It was my father, H. E. David, however, who started me off and this is therefore dedicated to his memory, and to that of T. C. Lethbridge.

'... and then they began a circuit of Dyfed; they hunted and enjoyed themselves, and for roaming the countryside they had never seen a more delightful land, nor a better hunting ground ...' (The Mabinogion: Manawydan Son of Llyr).

This account has arisen through the need to set down the results of the author's excavation and fieldwork in west Wales within the framework now emerging for British early prehistory. It has its origins at least some twenty years ago when he first started to collect flints from Mesolithic surface scatters in south-west Wales. This was later followed by excavations at three important Mesolithic sites and the implementation of a radiocarbon dating programme, which is still current.

Whilst much of the new data assembled here is thus relevant to the early Flandrian settlement of Wales, the coverage has been extended to include a consideration of the evidence for Late Pleistocene settlement as well. This arises not only from the author's interests but also from the fact that both Upper Palaeolithic and Mesolithic find-spots are co-located if not at the same find-spot then frequently in the same area. In chronological terms, the scope of the thesis therefore extends from c. 250,000 BP to c. 5,000 BP, but concentrates specifically on the Upper Palaeolithic and Mesolithic record. That such a wide span can be attempted, with an attention to detail that may seem disproportionate in places, is perhaps an indication of the relative imprecision of the data and that this is biased both towards stone tools and only to a very limited number of useful 'sites'.

Just before the publication of Garrod's *resumé* of the Upper Palaeolithic Age in Britain (1926), Mortimer Wheeler was able to open the first attempt at a full description of Welsh prehistory with a complete chapter devoted to this period (Wheeler, 1925). His account of 'cave-man' relied then, as now, only on meagre information available from caves in the Carboniferous limestone, such as Ffynnon Bueno and Cae Gwyn in north Wales, and, to the south, The Hoyle's Mouth, near Tenby, and the Gower caves, particularly Paviland. Although research and some fresh excavation has taken place since then (McBurney,1959; Savory, 1973; Nédervelde *et al.*, 1973; J. B. Campbell, 1977; Jacobi 1980a; Green, 1986a, 1986b; Davies, 1989a, 1989b), the material database has changed little. Since the last major review (Jacobi, 1980a) striking refinements have, however, been made in the understanding of this period – especially of the bio- and chronostratigraphy of the late Devensian Lateglacial or Late Upper Palaeolithic. Most important for the human record has been the application of accelerator (AMS) radiocarbon dating of prey animals and artefacts.

Chapter II sets out to summarize the Pleistocene archaeological record for Wales against what is known of the environmental background. Only after the late Devensian glacial maximum, does this record become in any sense prolific in Britain. Recent research, for example at Cheddar Gorge, Somerset, and Creswell Crags, Nottinghamshire, has much improved the understanding of the character and timing of human settlement at this time. The evidence from Wales is assessed against this new information with which it is found to be largely complementary. In particular, the lithic collection from The Hoyle's Mouth is fully examined for the first time and compared to the newly dated artefact assemblage from Gough's (New) Cave, Cheddar. Both collections typify the 'Creswellian' as defined by Garrod (1926, 194) and can now be linked specifically to occupation and hunting at a time close to the thermal maximum of the Lateglacial interstadial. Other find-spots from this part of south-west Wales, notably on Caldey Island, are also examined and evidence for occupation later in the Lateglacial reviewed.

In Chapter III the discussion moves on into the Flandrian to consider the early Mesolithic settlement of Wales. Although the term 'Mesolithic' recurs repeatedly from now on, this is only for convenience sake, and no particular significance is placed in the term itself (for the latter, see Zvelebil, 1986). Whilst acknowledging the time-transgressive nature of human adaptations usually referred to as 'Mesolithic', the term will be used here simply in reference to the timespan between the Devensian/Flandrian boundary at 10,000 BP and the local appearance of farming.

When writing his book on 'Prehistoric and Roman Wales' Wheeler had felt obliged to confess that '...at present the opening phases of the New Stone Age in Wales are lost in uncertainty' (1925, 46). Despite the formal recognition of a 'Mesolithic' to fill this gap in Wales (Clark, 1932) the evidence for this was not extensively reviewed until much later (Wainwright, 1963). A subsequent synthesis (Jacobi, 1980b) showed that the database had changed little. In particular, no reliable radiocarbon chronology existed which could place the many finds of lithic material within the apparent sequence of earlier and later phases of the Mesolithic seen to be emerging elsewhere in Britain and parts of Europe. A first consideration of this research, therefore, was to attempt to initiate the construction of a secure chronological framework. Chapter III, therefore, after defining an early Mesolithic 'broad blade' technology in its wider context, concentrates on an account of investigations at Daylight Rock, Caldey, a site chosen for the apparent integrity of its artefact collection (Lacaille and

Grimes, 1955) and its potential for AMS dating. Typological comparison, somewhat surprisingly, suggests a close parallel with Star Carr in North Yorkshire (Clark, 1954). Fresh excavations on the site are described and the AMS dates obtained are discussed with reference to other Welsh and English data.

In Chapter IV a further very important Mesolithic find-spot is introduced. This is the well-known flint 'factory' at The Nab Head on the clifftop of St. Brides Bay, west Wales, recognized since the last century as a prolific source of flint tools and chippings. In 1925 it had attracted the attention of a local clergyman and amateur flint collector, J. P. Gordon-Williams. The character of the flint and stone tools he excavated there gave him the impression of a 'decadent Upper Cave culture' (Gordon-Williams, 1926). There were many scrapers, 'points' and blades, and also a remarkable collection of shale beads and a carved shale amulet; the retouched component of this collection very closely resembles that from Daylight Rock. More recently, since it was recognized that parts of this site (The Nab Head Site I) remained intact but were threatened by continuing erosion, rescue excavations were undertaken there by the writer and the Dyfed Archaeological Trust in 1979 and 1980. Also, samples were submitted for AMS dating. The results of this new work are described in detail in the context of the preceding discussion of early Mesolithic technology and chronology. Confirmation that such 'broad blade' industries date to at least *c.* 9,200 BP is achieved. It was also possible to confirm a previous conclusion (Jacobi, 1980b) that, apart from an early Mesolithic component, there was also a later or 'narrow blade' phase of occupation on the headland.

Later Mesolithic technology in Wales is introduced and discussed in Chapter V and new AMS dates are presented for its notably early appearance at Prestatyn, Clwyd, at *c.* 8,700 BP. Additional chronological and environmental data are assessed followed by a description of some of the other important Welsh find-spots with 'narrow blade' material. Amongst the latter is a newly discovered site at The Nab Head (Site II) - described in Chapter VI - where the writer conducted excavations in 1981, 1982 and 1986. A large lithic sample was obtained of which the retouched component was found to be dominated by small and narrow microliths, with fewer denticulates, scrapers, 'becs' or other tools. A significant addition to the inventory were large numbers of pebble tools, mostly 'bevelled pebbles', but also including ground stone axes (or adzes) and a perforated stone 'mace-head'. Charcoal samples were submitted for AMS dating and the results indicate periodic re-use of the headland during the late Mesolithic and even during the early 'Neolithic'.

Using the results from the excavations at The Nab Head to predict the probable appearance of local late Mesolithic stone technologies, Chapter VII then discusses collections made by the author from the abundant lithic scatters along the coastal lowlands of north-west Dyfed. Some of these were first described by W. F. Grimes in 1932 and they extend the geographical range of a quite remarkable density of find-spots of very similar lithic composition documented even earlier for the coasts to either side of Milford Haven (Leach, 1913; Cantrill, 1915). Many of the latter find-spots including those from submerged foreshore exposures were included in Wainwright's 'Reinterpretation of the Microlithic Industries of Wales' (1963). In this he concluded that a coastal economy was responsible for the bulk of Welsh Mesolithic material, and that this was the result of an 'enforced dependence on the sea-shore for food and raw materials' (*ibid.*, 126). Jacobi's review of the evidence for coastal settlement, in the light of then current research (1980b) sought to place a greater emphasis on the high biotic potential of western coasts and the advantages of a combined exploitation of both terrestrial and marine economies.

This latter theme is taken up again here in the final part of Chapter VII, which assesses the economic resources potentially available during the late Mesolithic and speculates upon the exploitation and settlement patterns responsible for such apparently intensive coastal activity. The significance of coastal regimes to the emergence of farming at the end of the Mesolithic is also considered. Finally, a concluding Chapter briefly notes some of the more significant results of this research and ends by emphasizing the need both for more freshly excavated data and the further application of AMS dating throughout the periods covered.

CHAPTER II

THE PLEISTOCENE BACKGROUND

1. Introduction:

The British Pleistocene sequence, extending over most of the last 2 million years, is characterized by numerous climatic oscillations between cooler and more temperate conditions (West, 1977). The stratigraphic record for the latter part of this period (from *c.* 870 ka) has been most effectively observed in the fluctuations of oxygen isotope ratios through deep oceanic sediments (Emiliani, 1966; Shackleton and Opdyke, 1973, 1976). At least 23 major fluctuations, or Oxygen Isotope Stages, are recognized and are believed to correspond with equivalent fluctuations in the volume of global ice.

Correlation between the oceanic record and British terrestrial stratigraphy is as yet very poorly developed owing to the highly incomplete and complex nature of the latter. Also, absolute chronologies beyond the range of radiocarbon (*c.* 40 ka) have so far had very limited application. A summary of the Pleistocene framework for Britain, as currently understood, is shown in Table 2.1.

The earliest indications of a human presence in Britain are provided by flint artefacts whose faunal associations (Stuart, 1982) would appear to date to the Anglian glaciation or earlier. At Westbury-sub-Mendip (Bishop, 1975, 1982), badly corroded flints, some of which seem likely to be artefacts, are believed to belong to a stage intermediate between the Cromerian (OI Stage ?13) and Hoxnian (OI Stage ?9/11) and are perhaps 'inter-Anglian or earlier' (Roe, 1981). The associated fauna includes mammalian species such as bear (*Ursus deningeri*) and the sabre-toothed cat (*Homotherium latidens*).

Of broadly the same age as the finds from Westbury may be the occurrence of crude bifaces from a breccia at Kent's Cavern, Devon (Campbell and Sampson, 1971). A 'Cromerian' fauna including *Ursus deningeri* may likewise have been the contemporary of these artefacts.

Two further sites - Boxgrove in Sussex and High Lodge in Suffolk - are the subject of current investigations. At Boxgrove, the *in situ* manufacture of ovate bifaces appears to be associated with a fauna of 'Westbury' type and also includes the distinctive Cromerian rodent *Sorex savini*. Recent re-examination of the High Lodge site has suggested that the flood-plain sediments containing the 'Mousterian'-type flint industry might have been 'rafted' by Anglian ice. Here also, the sparse fauna includes voles and a single fossil of *Dicerorhinus etruscus*, unknown from Hoxnian or later stages.

No primary context sites are known from deposits of the Anglian, although an abundance of artefacts, mostly bifaces of Acheulian type, are found in gravels attributed to this stage in southern England. In the succeeding Hoxnian interglacial Clactonian core and flake industries are represented at Clacton, Essex and Swanscombe, Kent (Lower Loam and Lower Gravel), whilst towards the end of the stage bifaces occur amongst the Lower Industry at Hoxne itself, in Suffolk (Wymer, 1988).

At present there is some debate as to the sequence of climatic events occurring between the Hoxnian and the pen-ultimate, or Ipswichian, interglacial (Shotton, 1986; Rose, 1987; Gibbard and Turner, 1988). Wymer (1988) has pointed out the irony that the majority of the Palaeolithic evidence in Britain appears to belong to this part of the Pleistocene sequence, yet it is virtually all in a derived condition (for instance in most of the Thames gravel terraces). It is during this cold phase (the 'Wolstonian') or during an intermediate interglacial, that use of a Levallois technology is first observed.

Despite apparently favourable environmental conditions, there is no evidence for a human presence during the Ipswichian (*c.* 125 ka). Within the succeeding Devensian stage Levallois flakes and Mousterian-type bifaces are suggested as pre-dating about 40 ka, after which Upper Palaeolithic artefacts predominate.

2. The Early and Middle Pleistocene in Wales:

The Pleistocene history of Wales, and with it the first evidence for a hominid presence only begins to become clear towards the very end of the Middle Pleistocene. Before this time, successive ice sheets generated on the Welsh uplands, combined with those from Ireland and the Lake District, have obliterated much of the stratigraphic record. Such evidence as remains for these periods is restricted to a few localities on the margins of the Cambrian Massif and to eastern and south-west England and is suggestive of at least three glacial episodes preceding Oxygen Isotope Stage 7, at about 225,000 years ago (Bowen, *et al.* 1985; 1986).

It has been suggested that the isolated find of a handaxe at Pen-y-Lan, Cardiff, could be of Hoxnian age (Lacaille, 1954), but the nature of the find, entirely without context, cannot allow any chronological attribution. Equally uncertain must be the dating of the recently reported finds of four rolled palaeoliths (three ovate bifaces and a Levallois flake) from derived positions on the Severn Estuary Levels (Green, 1989, 194-8, figs. 2-3).

It is, however, to Oxygen Isotope Stage 7 (sub-phases 7b and 7c), about 250 ka ago, that it has been argued that the earliest record for Palaeolithic man in Wales belongs, at

Chronostratigraphy				Oxygen-Isotope Stage	Age (KaBP)
			Flandrian/Holocene		10
LATE PLEISTOCENE	LUP	Late Devensian	Transition	2	10.5
			Loch Lomond/Younger Dryas Stadial		11
			Transition		12
			Lateglacial Interstadial		13
			Transition		14
			Glacial Maximum		18
	EUP				24
	Middle Palaeolithic	Middle Devensian		3	59
		Early Devensian		4	71
				5a	80
				5b	
				5c	105
				5d	122
		Ipswichian (Wales: Pennard D/L Stage)		5e	128
MIDDLE PLEISTOCENE	Lower Palaeolithic	['Wolstonian']		6	186
		(Wales: Minchin Hole D/L Stage)		7	245
		Hoxnian		8	303
				9	339
				10	
				11	423
		Anglian		12	478
		Cromerian		13	524
				14 15	620
		Elster 1		16	659
					659

Table 2.1: British Mid-Late Pleistocene chronostratigraphy (after Campbell and Bowen, 1989, with modifications).

Pontnewydd Cave, Clwyd, in North Wales (Green, 1984a; Green *et al.*, 1989). Here, current excavations have recovered seven bone fragments attributable to at least three individuals comparable to early Neanderthal types (Stringer, 1986). The lithic technology apparently associated with these is characterized by bifaces, flakes, and clear evidence for the use of a prepared-core (Levallois) technique. Despite the probability of geological re- working of the cave deposits, Green (1986a) has suggested that two occupations are represented by the Intermediate and Lower Breccia (*c.* 250-230 ka), and that these are associated with an interglacial and then colder fauna, respectively.

Estuarine deposits possibly belonging to the same interglacial phase as Pontnewydd (but perhaps equally to Oxygen Isotope Stage 5), have been noted to overlie till (O/I Stage ?9) at West Angle, at the entrance to Milford Haven, Dyfed (Dixon, 1921; Stevenson and Moore, 1982; Bowen, *et al.* 1986), yet no archaeological finds from south or west Wales are certainly attributable to this phase.

3. The Late Pleistocene

The Late Pleistocene (after 132 ka: Bowen *et al.*, 1986) includes at its base the so-called Ipswichian interglacial, correlated with Oxygen Isotope Sub-stage 5e, which is represented in south Wales and south-west England by raised beaches and their associated deposits (Bowen and Sykes, 1988). There is however, no certain evidence for human activity in Wales at this time (when it is also seems absent in England) despite favourable climatic conditions and an abundant fauna (Evans, 1975; Wymer, 1981, 1988).

Claims for a human occupation at Bacon Hole, Gower, during the last interglacial based upon supposedly polished bones (Stringer, 1977) are now discounted (Cook, 1986, 159).

A small 'plano-convex' bi-face made on a pebble of flint found eroded from the cliff at Rhossili, Gower, is undateable. Its original context is not known, but it may possibly have been derived from Devensian outwash or periglacial deposits exposed in the cliff section (Green, 1981).

4

Other undateable finds from Wales, but which could possibly be of earlier Late Pleistocene age, are single unstratified artefacts of supposed 'Mousterian' appearance from Paviland (Grimes, 1951, fig. 2) and Chepstow (Savory, 1961; Roe, 1981), but neither of these is in any way informative.

The boundary between the Ipswichian and Devensian stages lies at *c.* 122 ka (Bowen *et al.* 1985). The latter can be subdivided into Early (122 - 59 ka), Middle (59 - 24 ka) and Late (24 - 10 ka) sub-stages (Campbell and Bowen, 1989, Table 1).

Within the Early Devensian of Wales, archaeological evidence continues to be extremely thin. At Long Hole, Gower, south Wales, Campbell (1977) apparently recovered a possible limestone flake and a worked bone from his layer A2b. These particular artefacts cannot now be recognised amongst surviving collections from the cave, rendering meaningless any debate concerning their real age (Campbell, 1977, 60, 102-3; Bowen *et al.* (1986), and Green (1984).

4. The Mid-Devensian and the Earlier Upper Palaeolithic in Wales
In cultural terminology, the few incidences of prehistoric activity so far described belong within the Lower and Middle Palaeolithic periods. From about 40 ka, after a period of both anatomical change and technological innovation, *Homo sapiens sapiens* appeared throughout Europe.

An indication of possible Middle Devensian human occupation of Wales is provided by a reported radiocarbon date of 38.68 +0.27/- 0.20 ka ago (BM 499) on charcoal from an artefact-bearing layer within Coygan Cave, Dyfed. This dating is, however, near the chronological limit of radiocarbon assay and could therefore only represent a *minimum* age. Two subrectangular bifaces (Coulson, 1986) alongside a cold climate fauna are recorded from the cave. Research on the evidence from past excavations and new Uranium Series dates on speleothem is currently in progress (Green, 1986a). The cave, which once looked out over the Bristol Channel and the approaches to the present estuaries of the Taf and Tywi, has been destroyed by quarrying.

Recent reviews of Upper Palaeolithic archaeology in Britain have tended to anchor the available chronological and artefactual evidence to models of episodic settlement during interstadial phases on either side of the Late Devensian glacial maximum (Campbell, 1977; Jacobi, 1980a; Wymer, 1977). The dry-shod movement of hunters across the North Sea plain and the exposed English Channel has resulted in the introduction of cultural markers into British cave deposits and open sites which are currently interpreted in terms of adjacent continental cultural packages (Jacobi, 1980a; Campbell, 1980, 1986). The ever-developing radiocarbon record is currently refining chronological schemes relevant to such pan-European models and the

recent introduction of Accelerator Mass Spectrometry dating (Gowlett, 1986) is already set to clarify some of the many remaining complexities in the available archaeological record.

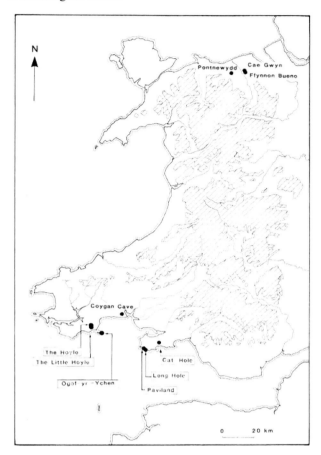

Figure 2.1: Distribution of caves in Wales from which artefacts of certain or possible pre-Devensian glacial maximum age have been recovered.

For Wales, the evidence for human exploitation in Mid and Late Devensian time far exceeds that for all of the foregoing Pleistocene, but the database is nevertheless pitifully imperfect. The terms 'Earlier' and 'Later Upper Palaeolithic' were introduced in Campbell's re-examination of the evidence in 1977, and served to divide so-called 'Aurignacian' and 'proto-Solutrean' technologies from those of the so-called 'Creswellian' and 'Cheddarian' (Garrod, 1926; Bohmers, 1956). The intervening glacial maximum, centred at about 18,000 BP, has generally been assumed to have forced a gap for human habitation which, in Jacobi's reappraisal of the radiocarbon data then available (1980), lasted from *c.* 27,000 to *c.* 11,500 BP. Campbell has more recently argued (1980, 1986) that there are grounds for believing man to have been much more tolerant of the harshness of extreme glacial conditions than previously credited, and that the 'hiatus' may consequently be unreal.

Employing lithic analogues from stratified and dated sites such as Ilsenhöhle (GDR), Spy and Maisières Canal (Belgium), Jacobi has suggested (1980a) that there may be

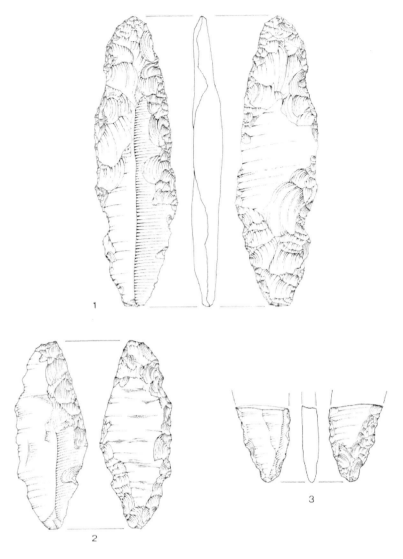

Figure 2.2: Leaf-points from Wales and Herefordshire: - 1, Ffynnon Beuno, Clwyd; 2, Paviland, W Glam; 3, King Arthur's cave, Herefordshire. Scale – 1:1.65.

three distinctive and chronologically discrete technological groupings of Early Upper Palaeolithic (EUP) age in England and Wales:

c. 38,000 BP	a 'leaf-point' technology
c. 32,000-30,000 BP	an 'Aurignacian' technology
c. 28,000 BP	a 'Gravettian' technology

'Leaf-point' technology:

Leaf points are flint blades whose outlines have been converted to an elongate lozenge form by an invasive surface retouch often concentrated on the ventral surface (Fig. 2.2). The resulting foliate point has a 'spear-head' appearance and can measure up to about 15 cms in length. Broadly equivalent tool forms on the continental mainland are *'Blattspitzen'* (Germany), 'Szeletian Points' (Central Europe) and *'pointes épaisses de forme lozangique'* (Belgium: Otte, 1977).

Referring to the stratigraphic sequence within Ilsenhöhle (GDR: Hulle, 1977), Jacobi (1980a) suggests that leaf points represent the earliest evidence for an Upper Palaeolithic presence and occur in a stratigraphic position below and distinct from characteristically Aurignacian lithic assemblages. Although this sequence is not demonstrable for either Belgian or British sites where Aurignacian and leaf-points have been found together, it is proposed (*ibid*) that such a separation may indeed have existed, only to escape the observation of early excavators. In support of this it has also been observed that specifically Aurignacian tool-forms are absent from a number of British 'leaf-point' find- spots.

The tentative dating of a 'leaf-point' technology to *c.* 32,000 - 38,000 BP, based on continental evidence, can now be supported by a single British radiocarbon determination. This is the recent AMS dating of a hyaena mandible found above and in contact with a leaf-point within cave sediments at Bench Cavern, near Brixham, Devon:

34,500 +1400 BP (OxA-1620)

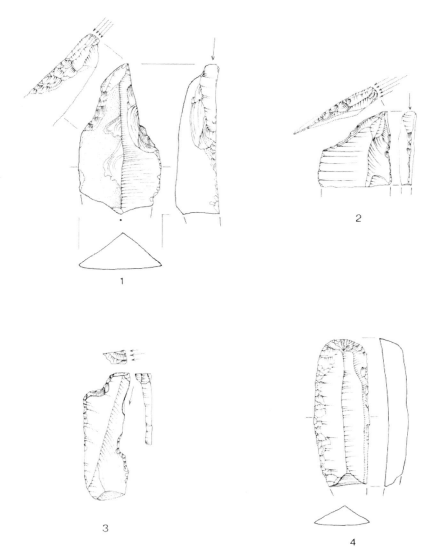

Figure 2.3: Early Upper Palaeolithic artefacts from Wales: - Burins busqué – 1, Ffynnon Beuno, Clwyd; 2, The Hoyle's Mouth, Dyfed; 3, Paviland, W Glam. Scraper – 4, Cae Gwyn, Clwyd. Scale – 1:1.46.

'Aurignacian' technology

It could be argued that any differences between the occurrence of leaf-points and Aurignacian artefacts might be a reflection of variation in the functional roles of such tools and/or the result of differing behaviour patterns of essentially contemporary human groups. This argument would not, however, appear to be supported by evidence from mainland Europe and it may be assumed that the few occurrences of clearly Aurignacian artefacts in Britain should be assigned, with the latter, to a time range of approximately 32,000 - 30,000 BP.

Perhaps the most characteristic of Aurignacian tool-types to be identified in Britain is the '*burin busqué*'. In this type the burin tip is formed by the oblique removal of several short spalls from the face of a preliminary lateral burin facet. The spalling is limited by a retouched notch, and the finished tool has a distinctive beaked and carinated appearance (see Fig. 2.3). Amongst other Aurignacian tool forms carinated and nosed scrapers and retouched blades are somewhat less confidently identifiable amongst the small and mixed

British cave collections.

At Kent's Cavern, Devon, a recent AMS determination on a human maxilla provides the earliest dating for a British hominid:

30,900 +900 (OxA-1621: Hedges *et al.*, 1989)

Although this date falls within the chronological brackets of the proposed 'Aurignacian', the maxilla was apparently recovered from below the level attributed to this phase (Jacobi, pers. comm.). Unfortunately, however, the only artefacts associated with the sample are four blade fragments which cannot allow of any close cultural diagnosis.

'Gravettian' technology:

Jacobi (*ibid*) has drawn attention to the similarity between finds of 'stemmed points' at seven British localities and the 'Font Robert' points of France, and their counterparts in Belgium and Germany. These tools are recognized by their long tang outlined by pronounced abrupt retouch to either side of the proximal end of a blade. The distal end of the tool is foliate in shape, often defined by partial surface retouch (Brezillon, 1968).

None of the British finds of these tools yet has the support of radiocarbon dating, although their equivalents at Maisières Canal (Belgium: de Heinzelen, 1973; Otte, 1976) are apparently dated to *c*. 28,000 BP.

All three of the technological groupings described above can be claimed to be recognizable amongst the stone tools from some five find-spots in or very near to Wales (Fig. 2.1). The evidence from these, along with other Welsh find-spots less certainly attributed to the earlier Upper Palaeolithic, is considered below, followed by a summary in Table 2.2.

King Arthur's Cave, Herefordshire (SO 547 157)

Excavated by: Anon; Symonds, 1871 (Symonds, 1871); Hewer and Taylor, 1925-27 (Hewer, 1926; Taylor, 1928); ApSimon 1952 (ApSimon, 1955). Plate 2.5.
Stratigraphy: a complex series of deposits appear to span a period from perhaps the early/mid-Devensian to the Flandrian. A single broken leaf-point was recovered from the same level as a small hearth (?Late Palaeolithic) in the Upper Cave Earth and Upper Red Loam within the cave passage (ApSimon, 1955; Campbell, 1977, 44).
Fauna: cave bear, brown bear, hyena, mammoth, woolly rhinoceros, horse, red deer and aurochs. *Artefacts*: the proximal fragment of a leaf-point (Fig. 2.2, No. 3).
Problems: intermittent excavations at the cave, some remaining unpublished, allow only an imprecise synthesis of stratigraphy and associated artefacts and fauna. Amongst the dozen or so flint artefacts described with the 'leaf-point' fragment are examples of Lateglacial-type backed blades (Hewer, 1926, fig. 3, 2). Fauna from this part of the cave appear to be mixed (K. Scott, pers. comm.) and the presence of hyaena and many gnawed bones suggests use of the cave as a hyaena den.
Radiometric dating: none relevant to the human occupation of the cave at this time has been attempted, and the surviving records and artefact collection are only a remnant, following war damage.

Ffynnon Beuno, Clwyd (SJ 0853 7242)

Excavated by: Hicks and Luxmoore, 1885 (Hicks, 1886; Garrod, 1926; Campbell, 1977).
Stratigraphy: the Pleistocene fauna and artefacts were recovered from 'cave earth' sealed beneath a stalagmitic breccia in the main cave chamber and an unbroken stalagmite floor in a side fissure.
Fauna: most of the extant faunal remains may not now be distinguished from those recovered from the nearby cave of Cae Gwyn. This collection includes lion, wild cat, hyena, wolf, fox, bear, badger, mammoth, woolly rhinoceros, horse, pig, giant deer, red deer, roe deer, reindeer and bovid.

Artefacts: 10 flints and a bone ?point (Campbell, 1977) are recorded. The latter would appear to be the corroded tip of an antler tine, rather than a genuine artefact (Jacobi, pers. comm.). The flints include the well known leaf-point and *burin busqué* (see Fig. 2.2, 2.3) both of which are clearly earlier Upper Palaeolithic tool forms. With the exception of a second burin, the remaining artefacts (scrapers (2), flakes (3) and the 'bone point') have not been seen by the author and their exact typological identification remains uncorroborated here.
Problems: excavation records are inadequate, and the stratigraphic record cannot now be satisfactorily reconstructed. The faunal collection is confused with that from another cave and includes species of Flandrian or even Ipswichian derivation, such as pig.

Cae Gwyn Cave, Clwyd (SO 0852 7244)

Excavated by: Hicks and Luxmoore, 1884-7 (Hicks, 1886, 1888; Garrod, 1926; Campbell, 1977).
Stratigraphy: the cave has two entrances, to the south and west respectively, the latter of which was covered by sediments said to include boulder clay and perhaps outwash deposits. A 'bone-earth' below these contained an unretouched blade and faunal material. Glacial sediments are also assumed to have covered the southern entrance where a flint end-scraper was found.
Fauna: the remaining collections from both Cae Gwyn and Ffynnon Beuno are inseparable. See above.
Artefacts: an end-scraper and a blade, both of flint, were found. The scraper (Fig. 2.3, No. 4) is of Upper Palaeolithic type but despite being frequently termed 'Aurignacian' is culturally undiagnostic. It was not observed to be in association with the early fauna.
Problems: as is the case for Ffynnon Beuno, excavation took place over a hundred years ago and those records and materials which survive lack sufficient detail for any exact reconstruction to be made. Neither artefact is specifically diagnostic of earlier Upper Palaeolithic workmanship. The archaeological occupation(s) is undated.
Radiometric dating: a determination was made on a mammoth carpal purporting to have come from this cave (but see comments on fauna, above), with the following result (Rowlands, 1971; Shotton and Williams, 1971):

18,000 +1400/-1200 (Birm-146)

Without any archaeological association, this date cannot have any bearing on the estimated timing of a human presence within the cave. If not a minimum date, it does, however, allow the assumption that this area of Wales was probably ice-free at a time when the Devensian ice was near its southern limits elsewhere in Britain (Penny *et al.*, 1969).

Long Hole, W. Glamorgan (SS 4512 8506)
Excavated by: Wood, 1861; Campbell, 1969 (Falconer, 1868; Garrod, 1926; Campbell, 1977). Plate 2.1.
Stratigraphy: the earlier excavations concentrated within cave and removed a thick deposit of 'cave earth' in which

Plate 2.1: Long Hole Cave, W. Glamorgan.

both 'warm' and 'cold' fauna were found, indicating either physical mixing or a failure on the part of the excavators to observe stratification. Campbell's trench in the cave entrance revealed a detailed stratigraphy (1977, figs. 18-22) in which he claimed to distinguish a sequence from the end of the last interglacial (Oxygen Isotope Stage 5) until the Flandrian, based on pollen and granulometric analyses. In layers A3a-b artefacts and fauna were recovered below sediments believed to be indicative of maximum glacial conditions and were therefore interpreted as of possible early Upper Palaeolithic age.

Fauna: from his investigations Campbell concluded that the following mammal species were the contemporaries of the earlier Upper Palaeolithic at the site: otter, brown bear, wolf, fox, ?arctic fox, mammoth, woolly rhinoceros, horse, giant deer, reindeer, bison and arctic hare.

Artefacts: a total of 16 flint and 6 ?chert artefacts are recorded from the cave. Of these, only the 5 blade and flake fragments recovered by Campbell have a secure provenance - none of these, however, are diagnostic forms. Amongst the earlier finds from the cave are a combined scraper/burin (Campbell, 1977, fig. 97, 5), a 'very rough keeled scraper' (Garrod, 1926, 69, and fig. 9, 9). The latter may perhaps be re-interpreted as a core. A fragment of leaf-point was apparently also found by Wood, but cannot now be re-located and may be a mis-identification. None of these latter pieces can be confidently assigned an early Upper Palaeolithic date on typological grounds alone.

Problems: the status of the cave deposits cannot now be evaluated owing to their removal in the last century. The attribution of an early Upper Palaeolithic presence rests only on Campbell's pollen and sediment studies of samples collected in 1969. These are unsupported by absolute dating or diagnostic artefact types.

Cathole, W. Glamorgan (SS 5377 9002)
Excavated by: Wood, 1860; McBurney, 1958-9; Campbell, 1968 (Garrod, 1926; McBurney, 1959; Campbell, 1977). Plate 2.2.
Stratigraphy: no record exists of the stratigraphy within the cave. The twentieth century excavations took place in the entrance area but did not find evidence for early Upper Palaeolithic occupation.

Fauna: Wood recovered the following: vole, ?cave lion, wild cat, bear, hyaena, wolf, mammoth, 'Rhinoceros [?tichorhinus], horse, reindeer, elk and red deer.

Artefacts: amongst the mixture of artefacts found by Wood are two fragmentary tanged points (Campbell, 1977, fig. 133, 2 and 3; Fig. 2.4, Nos. 1-2). Both Garrod (1926, 66) and Jacobi (1980a, 25) have drawn attention to the similarity of one or both of these to Font Robert points. A further retouched fragment (Fig. 2.4, No. 3) from the collection (NHM) may be the tang of a third point.

Problems: the designation of this cave as an early Upper Palaeolithic (?Gravettian) site depends only on the typological parallels of the two 'Font Robert points'. No other supporting data is available, and no evidence for related occupation was encountered in the later excavations outside the cave.

9

Plate 2.2: Cathole Cave, W. Glamorgan.

Nottle Tor, W. Glamorgan (SS 453 939, approx.)

Excavated by: Wood, *c.* 1869 (Garrod, 1926; Rutter and Allen, 1948; Campbell, 1977).
Stratigraphy: no record.
Fauna: no record.
Artefacts: there are 6 flints: 3 flakes, 2 scrapers and what has been described as a 'leaf- point'. The latter (Campbell, 1977, fig. 97, 7) is a short (55 mm) lozenge-shaped artefact with coarse surface flaking and a thick triangular section. Garrod figures a burin from the site (1926, fig. 9, 11), and Campbell lists a possible bone tool. The latter is not an artefact, however (Jacobi, pers. comm.).
Problems: this fissure has long since been quarried away and no records from the excavation survive. The so-called

'leaf-point' does not adequately fulfil this definition, and the find-spot should therefore be omitted from future listings of EUP locations.

Reynoldston, W. Glamorgan (SS 48 90 approx.)

Surface find of a single bi-facial 'leaf-point' (Green, 1984, 25- 26, fig. 7). Without context, and whilst resembling some Palaeolithic types, this implement cannot be reliably distinguished from those of Flandrian type.

Ogof-yr-Ychen, Caldey Island, Dyfed (SS 1465 9691)

The details of this cave are fully described in the listing of Lateglacial findspots (see below). Here, it need only be

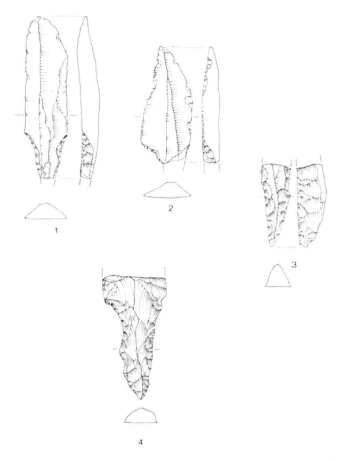

Figure 2.4: Font Robert points from Wales: - 1-3, Cathole, W Glam; 4, Paviland, W Glam. Scale – 1:1.86.

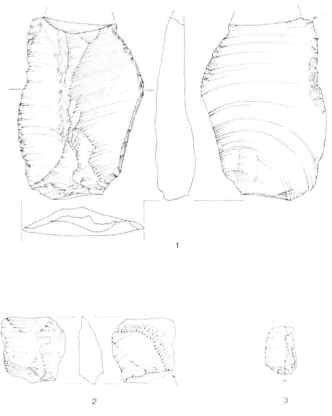

Figure 2.5: Artefacts from "The Pit" in Ogof-yr-Ychen, Caldey Island, Dyfed: - 1-2, "adinole" flakes; 3, flint flake.
Scale – 1:1.85.

noted that two flakes of adinole and one of 'chert' were found lodged, at a depth of about 5 metres, in the infill of a deep swallet (The Pit) within the cave system. Within the same infill were bones of hyaena and rhinoceros as well as many antlers of red deer. Radiocarbon dating of a rhinoceros scapula, found near the artefacts, gave the following result:

22,340 +620 BP (Birm-340: Van Nédervelde *et al.*, 1973)

Although there is no formal association between this date and the artefacts it nevertheless seems very probable that the latter are at least of Early Upper Palaeolithic age; indeed, the absence of blades or their fragments might imply an even earlier age. One of the flakes of adinole is very large, hard hammer struck, and apparently bears intentional as well as attritional chipping along parts of both lateral edges (Fig. 2.5, No. 1).

Little Hoyle (Longbury Bank Cave), Dyfed (SS 1118 9998)

Excavated by: Winwood, 1866; Smith, 1870; Power and Laws, 1877; Rolleston, Lane-Fox, Busk, Dawkins, Evans, Hilton-Price, 1878; McBurney, 1958-9, 1963; Green, 1984, 1986, 1990.
Laws (1878, 1888); Rolleston *et al.*, (1878); McBurney, 1959; Campbell, (1977); Green, (1986b); Rae *et al.*, (1987).
Stratigraphy: the recent investigations at the cave suggest that surviving deposits may span some 50,000 years, although those pre-dating the late Devensian are limited only to relict breccia overlain by stalagmite adhering in places to the cave wall.
Fauna: the excavations of the last century recovered a fauna including woolly rhinoceros and mammoth. The 1984 excavations also recovered bones of bear and reindeer the preservation of which suggested a dating previous to the apparently Late Devensian fauna within the same deposit (red sandy silt with limestone, in trench NC1, within the cave: Currant, 1986b).
Artefacts: those recovered prior to the 1984/6 work include an adinole scraper and bone 'bodkin' (Green, 1986b, fig. 28) listed by Campbell as Earlier Upper Palaeolithic, and two flint blades. Although the latter are certainly of Palaeolithic appearance, the scraper and 'bodkin' have no specific affinities and could even be later prehistoric. They were recovered by Laws (1878) 'from the surface of a probably Pleistocene deposit' (Green, 1986, 101), underlying material containing historic artefacts.
Radiometric dating: a Uranium-Series determination on the stalagmite overlying the breccia on the cave wall gave a result of:

47,500 +9,500/-8,500 BP (HUTH 2986: Rae *et al.*, 1987)

A further radiocarbon date has been obtained on a reindeer phalange from the North Platform with the following result:

29,000 +700 BP (OxA-1028: Hedges *et al.*, 1987)

Further dating evidence, relevant only to the late Devensian glacial maximum is discussed below (p. 16 and Table 2.11).
Problems: none of the above evidence can be used to argue for an early Upper Palaeolithic presence at the cave. The recent investigations at the site have yet to be fully published.

The Hoyle's Mouth, Dyfed (SN 1120 0033)

Excavated by: Smith, 1862; Winwood, Smith and Sandford, 1865; Lloyd Jones, 1878/9; Savory, 1968; Green, 1986, 1990.
Smith (1862); Winwood (1865); Boyd Dawkins (1874); Jones (1882); Garrod (1926); Savory (1973). Plate 2.8.
Stratigraphy: no adequate description of the deposits within the cave survive although most of the archaeological and faunal material seems to have been recovered from a breccia underlying stalagmite. Excavations within the cave entrance by H. S. Green and on the outer platform by Savory (1973) revealed mostly mixed deposits.
Fauna: the earlier reports describe finds of hyaena, cave bear, fox, wolf, mammoth, woolly rhinoceros, reindeer, red deer, giant deer and 'ox'. Additional wild fauna recovered by Savory include: field vole, badger, fox, cat, pig and *bos*/bison.
Artefacts: 361 chipped stone artefacts survive in various museum collections, but since the majority of these appear Lateglacial in date they are discussed later in this account (see below). Only one piece, an unambiguous example of a *burin busqué* (Fig. 2.3, No. 2), indicates an earlier human occupation of the cave, equivalent in time to a probable 'Aurignacian'.
Radiometric dating: there exists a single radiocarbon date, on an unidentified bone without stated archaeological association, of:

27,900 +600 BP (OxA-1024: Hedges *et al.*, 1987)

Problems: identification of an early Upper Palaeolithic presence at this site rests upon the typological integrity of the *burin busqué* alone. There are no supporting chronostratigraphic or chronometric data. Further work and/or publication by H. S. Green is awaited.

Paviland Cave, West Glamorgan (SS 4372 8588)

Principal excavators: Buckland, 1823; Sollas, 1912 (Buckland, 1824; Sollas, 1913). Plate 2.3.
Stratigraphy: no significant stratification was either observed or recorded.
Fauna: hyaena, cave bear, mammoth, horse, woolly rhinoceros, reindeer, giant deer and *bos*.
Inhumation: the partial skeleton of a *c.* 25-year old human male was found in 1823. The burial was accompanied by ivory rods, fragments of circlet(s) of ivory, and shells. All the grave contents were encrusted with ochre.
Artefacts: a total of 5,069 stone, bone and ivory artefacts survive in museums. The flaked stone collections cover a

wide spectrum of raw materials and forms amongst which are many likely to be of early Upper Palaeolithic date (Campbell, 1977). These include 'leaf-points' (11: eg Fig. 2.2, No. 2), stemmed ('Font-Robert') points (1: Fig. 2.4, No. 4), *burins busqués* (30: Fig 2.3, No. 3), nosed and keeled scrapers (111). These latter identifications cannot be confirmed in detail by the author who has only examined a sample of the now dispersed collections. Study of material housed in the University Museum (Oxford) suggests, however, that detailed re-examination would be repaid, and would result in significant revision of the 'Aurignacian' contribution to the cultural inventory from the cave.

Organic artefacts, in addition to those found with the inhumation, include perforated teeth of wolf and reindeer (7), ivory and bone points (2), bone spatulae (3), an ivory pendant and other items.

Radiometric dating: the following relevant radiocarbon dates have been obtained from bone material:

human bone from inhumation	:	18,460 +340 BP	(BM-374)	1
human bone from inhumation	:	26,350 +550 BP	(OxA-1815)	2
bone 'spatula'	:	23,670 +400 BP	(OxA-1790)	2
charred animal bone	:	29,600 +1900 BP	(OxA-365)	3
humic acids from OxA-365	:	28,000 +1700 BP	(OxA-366)	3
bone (uncharred)	:	38,000 +8000/-4000 BP	(OxA-140)	3
bone of *Bos primigenius*	:	27,600 +1300 BP	(BM-1367)	4

References:

1: Barker *et al.*, 1969
2: Housley, pers. comm.
3: Gowlett *et al.*, 1986a
4: Molleson, 1978

Plate 2.3: Paviland Cave, W. Glamorgan.

Problems: these have been widely debated and centre around the dating of the inhumation (eg. Oakley, 1968; Bowen, 1970; Campbell, 1977; Molleson, 1978; Jacobi, 1980a). This would now appear to have been resolved with the recent and more reliable determination provided by OxA-1815. Although radiocarbon dating would now suggest that there might have been several Earlier Upper Palaeolithic occupations, the lack of adequate excavation records invites little prospect of linking these to the abundant stone tool assemblages from the cave. Paviland is discussed further, below.

The Earlier Upper Palaeolithic in Wales - Summary

Having thus assembled the few instances in Wales for which an early Upper Palaeolithic (*c.* 40,000 - 24,000 BP) presence has been claimed, this evidence can briefly be summarized. Table 2.2 lists the findspots and gives to each a simple score based on an assessment of the contribution of each category of evidence. The limitations of such an attempted rationalization are only too apparent when it is re-stated that only at Paviland have these suggested instances of activity been radiometrically dated, and in each case, chronostratigraphic data is either totally absent or minimal. The presence of fauna such as woolly rhinoceros and hyaena, thought to be part of the mammalian biota until the glacial maximum, cannot, on their own, be used as evidence for a human presence.

Table 2.2: Summary of evidence for the Earlier Upper Palaeolithic exploitation of Wales.

Find-spot	Artefacts				Stratigraphy	Fauna	C14
	L-Ps	BBurins	FRPs	Other			
King Arthur's Cave	*	-	-	?	-	*	-
Ffynnon Beuno	***	***	-	?	?	*	-
Cae Gwyn	-	-	-	?	?	*	-
Long Hole	-	-	-	?	**	*	-
Cathole	-	-	**	?	?	*	-
Nottle Tor	-	-	-	?	-	-	-
Reynold-Stone	-	-	-	-	-	-	-
Ogof-yr-Ychen	-	-	-	?	-	*	22,340 BP
Little Hoyle	-	-	-	?	?	*	-
Hoyle's Mouth	-	***	-	?	-	*	29,000 BP
Paviland	***	**	**	?	-	*	23,670 BP
							26,350 BP
							27,600 BP
							28,000 BP
							29,600 BP
							38,000 BP

KEY:

?	=	uncertain
*	=	possible
**	=	probable
***	=	certain
L-Ps	=	leaf-point
Bburins	=	*burins busqués*
FRPs	=	F-Robert Points

Much of the confidence, therefore, that exists in the belief in a Welsh early Upper Palaeolithic still rests, as it did in Dorothy Garrod's time, in the recognition of *fossiles directeurs* already known from, and confined within, Pleistocene sequences on the continental mainland.

Perhaps most distinct of these 'type fossils' are the *burins busqués* the certain equivalents of which have been retrieved from Ffynnon Beuno, Paviland and The Hoyle (Fig. 2.3). Attention is drawn to the latter find, noted here for the first time (but illustrated and labelled as 'Creswellian' in Foster & Daniel, 1965, plate 2, no. 10). This burin, typical of Aurignacian II assemblages dated to *c.* 30,000 - 32,000 BP in south-western France (Laville *et al.*, 1980), therefore identifies a probable 'Aurignacian' location hitherto unrecognized. The heavily patinated flint is very slightly different in surface texture to the majority of others from the cave. Amongst the latter there are no certainly early forms but it must nevertheless now remain a possibility that potentially 'Aurignacian' artefacts are present here but indistinguishable alongside apparently Lateglacial pieces.

Of all the sites under discussion, the wealthiest archaeological material, if not stratigraphic detail, has been obtained over sixteen decades of sporadic excavation from the Goat's Hole, Paviland. The lithic collection from Paviland contains elements of all three of the typological groupings recognizable in the British Early Upper Palaeolithic. There is also the exceptional circumstance of the recovery, and now radiocarbon dating, of a human burial of this period.

The first dating obtained for the 'Red Lady of Paviland' - 18,460 ±340 BP (BM 374; Barker *et al.*, 1969) - aroused doubt owing to its implication of the use of the site far to the north of its Continental contemporaries and at a time when the Devensian ice front was only a few miles away. However, subsequent dating of charred bone from the cave by Accelerator Mass Spectrometry (AMS), with a result of *c* 28,000 ±1,700 BP (OxA-681) (Gowlett *et al*, 1986a), is fully in keeping with an Earlier Upper Palaeolithic occupation in the cave. If the human interference (charring) and the age of the bone are contemporary, then this occupation took place when local environmental conditions would have been less severe and at a time equivalent to the Aurignacian II or earliest Gravettian of southern France. This, in turn is in agreement with a previous determination of 27,600 ±1300 (BM-1367; Molleson, 1978) on a bone of *Bos primigenius* also from the cave, but without archaeological association.

Early doubts cast (Oakley, 1968, 307) on the adequacy of the sample used to date the Red Lady (BM-374) were strengthened by this new result and can now be confirmed following re-dating of the human remains by AMS. This latter determination (26,350 +550 BP: OxA-1815) firmly places the inhumation before the Late Devensian glacial maximum and within the proposed 'Gravettian' exploitation of the country. Taken with the dating of the bone 'spatula' (23,670 +400 BP: OxA-1790), there is perhaps evidence for human use of the cave on at least three occasions:

c. 28,000 BP : Aurignacian II/early Gravettian
c. 26,000 BP : Gravettian
c. 24,000 BP : Gravettian

The accompaniment of the burial by ivory rods and ring fragments, together with other signs of ivory-working (Jacobi 1980a, 31), has led Dennell (1983) to propose that the use of the cave at that time was possibly related to the exploitation of mammoth ivory. This proposition might be in keeping with Jacobi's more recent arguments that lowland Britain was continuous with the 'mammoth steppe' of the North European Plain across which hunters and hunted ranged over vast distances. In the unconstrained conditions of the open steppe where survival depended on considerable adaptive mobility, populations or groups of hunters would disperse widely, leaving material indicators of diverse cultural origins in widely separate geographic locations. The archaeological record might then consist of a series of 'unexpected punctuations' rather than a simple model of technological evolution of only local or regional significance (Jacobi, 1986a). Evidence now accumulating would suggest that the artefacts within Paviland represent just such a catchment of the various cultural traits of hunters roving the cooling steppelands of northern Europe.

5. The Late Devensian and Lateglacial in Wales

i) Introduction
After the few demonstrable instances of Early Upper Palaeolithic activity in Wales, and excepting the uncertain initial dating (BM-374) of the Red Lady of Paviland, there would appear to have been a gap in human residence over some nine millennia (22,000 - 13,000 BP) during the onset and decline of severe glacial conditions. There are, however, several instances where mammalian fauna have been dated to within this period of apparently severe climate:

Table 2.3: Radiocarbon determinations for human and faunal remains dating close to the Devensian glacial maximum.

Ogof-yr-Ychen, Dyfed

Woolly rhinoceros	:	22,350 +620 BP	(Birm-340)	ref. 1

Cae Gwyn, Clwyd

Mammoth	:	18,000 +1400/-1200 BP	(Birm-146)	ref. 2

Little Hoyle, Dyfed

Barnacle goose	:	22,800 +300 BP	(OxA-1027)	ref. 3
Bear	:	20,050 +900 BP	(ANU-4347)	ref. 4
Bear	:	17,800 +950 BP	(ANU-4348)	ref. 4
Reindeer	:	17,350 +850 BP	(ANU-4349)	ref. 4
Bear	:	19,950 +650 BP	(ANU-4350)	ref. 4

[*Paviland*, W. Glamorgan]

[Human	:	18,460 +340 BP	(BM-374)]	ref. 5

References:

1	:	Shotton and Williams (1973)
2	:	Shotton and Williams (1971); Rowlands, (1971)
3	:	Hedges *et al.* (1987)
4	:	Rae *et al.* (1987)
5	:	Barker *et al.* (1969)

With the exception of BM-374, the above dates cannot be shown to have any valid association with humanly derived deposits or artefacts. Those from Cae Gwyn and Ogof-yr-Ychen date isolated fossils: at Cae Gwyn the former location of the sample is unknown, and at Ogof-yr-Ychen the rhinoceros scapula concerned cannot be allocated any discrete association with the few undiagnostic artefacts from elsewhere within its varied filling (above, p. 15; Jacobi, 1980a, 28). At the Little Hoyle, the dated bones of bear and reindeer, from the 'Red Sandy Silt' within the cave, show no signs of human modification, and cannot at present be related to the 'Creswellian' artefacts reported from the 'Upper Scree' located on the cave platform (McBurney, 1959; Green, 1986b). Further publication of the recent work at the Little Hoyle and details of the context of the dated specimen of Barnacle goose (OxA-1027) are awaited with interest.

If these determinations cannot actually prove that Palaeolithic hunters were exploiting Wales at this time, the very presence of such prey animals is at least suggestive that this could have occurred. The proposal of an 'hiatus' in exploitation this far north ignores the possibility that hunters may have been more resilient in coping with severe climate than has hitherto been believed (Campbell, 1986). It has already been suggested that hunters and prey may have scattered widely over the European tundra-steppe, perhaps encroaching even to within a few kilometres of the ice front - as was formerly argued for Paviland. Such a thin and dispersed exploitation cannot be expected to leave the substantial archaeological residues that characterize the more favourable southerly latitudes of the Perigord. Equally, there is little evidence so far that lithic residues

from more northerly hunting and settlement need necessarily be homogenous in character or typologically distinctive. Jacobi has suggested (pers. comm.) that artefact combinations known elsewhere to be contemporary with the Late Devensian glacial maximum, may also be present in Britain but undifferentiated from other artefact groupings: just such a situation may exist amongst the large mixed lithic collection from Paviland, or from below the 'black band' at Kent's Cavern.

Following the fullest extension of the late Devensian ice sheets environmental conditions returned to interstadial status (the Lateglacial Interstadial) before the final pulse of bitter cold, or Younger Dryas or Loch Lomond Stadial, which immediately preceded the Flandrian. The range of these climatic fluctuations, from *c.* 14,000 BP to *c.* 10,000 BP comprises the Lateglacial as defined and sub-divided by Lowe and Gray (1980). It is during this period that indications of Upper Palaeolithic hunters become, if not actually abundant, more tangible and widespread. Their remains are known from several Welsh sites, and may be argued to date, along with equivalent sites in England, at the earliest to *c.* 12,800 BP. Before describing these remains, however, it is necessary to try and fill in details of contemporary changes in geography and environment.

ii) Lateglacial vegetation and climate:

The palaeoclimatic history of Britain during the Lateglacial is becoming increasingly clearly understood owing to a more thoroughly radiocarbon-dated pollen stratigraphy, especially from highland zone locations (Pennington, 1977; Gray and Lowe, 1977; Lowe and Lowe, 1989). Remarkable clarity, particularly of palaeotemperature, has also been

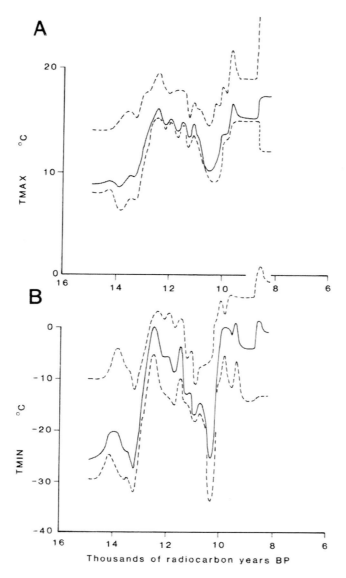

A

B

Thousands of radiocarbon years BP

Figure 2.6: Maximum and minimum values for palaeotemperature in the Lateglacial, derived from coleopteran evidence. Palaeotemperature lies within the limits of the upper and lower lines in each case: the central curve shows the most probable value. (after Atkinson *et al.*, 1987, fig. 2).

gained through analysis of the climatic preferences and tolerances of fossil coleoptera from a similar range of sites (Coope and Brophy, 1972; Coope, 1977; Atkinson *et al.*, 1987). The resulting detailed knowledge of temperature fluctuations for the Lateglacial is unsurpassed for any other prehistoric period. A recent computation of mean annual temperatures for Britain using evidence derived from beetle remains (from Atkinson *et al.*, 1987) is shown in Fig. 2.6.

Wales is fortunate in that both pollen and coleopteran evidence is available and that recent palaeobotanical studies have included a comprehensive series of radiocarbon determinations (Lowe and Lowe, 1989; Walker and Harkness, 1990).

It is now clear that deglaciation had occurred in north Wales by *c.* 14,500 BP and in south Wales by *c.* 14,200 BP (Coope *et al.* 1971; Lowe and Lowe, 1989; Walker and Harkness, 1990). Conditions appear then to be both cold

and dry until *c.* 13,200 BP when basal organic horizons at several British pollen-sampling sites provide dates for significant amelioration just subsequent to the retreat of polar water at *c.* 13,500 BP (Ruddyman and McIntyre 1973, 1981). The earliest organic sedimentation at Llyn Gwernan, Gwynedd, and at Llanilid in the Vale of Glamorgan is dated to 13,200 +120 BP (SRR-1705) and 13,200 +75 (SRR-3455), respectively. Pioneering colonisation by taxa such as *Cyperaceae*, *Rumex* and *Artemisia* at about this time is followed by the appearance of *Juniperus*, dated at Llyn Gwernan to 12,970 +130 BP (SRR-1704). This latter appearance of *Juniperus* has been widely recognised throughout western Britain as a response to a climatic amelioration which coleopteran evidence demonstrates to have peaked at *c.* 12,500 BP (Atkinson *et al.*, 1987). The period from 13,000 to 12,000 BP, when climate would have been as warm as that of the present day, has been defined as the Lateglacial Interstadial by Lowe and Gray (1980). During this time *Juniperus* and *Betula* were common

17

components of the vegetation cover, for instance at Llyn Gwernan, although other taxa such as *Salix* and *Empetrum* were probably also locally present.

At Llyn Gwernan, *Betula* then expands at the expense of *Juniperus* at *c.* 12,120 ±130 BP. Tree cover may have been at its maximum at about this time. The increase of *Betula* pollen, noted at many sites at about 12,200 BP, is, however, accompanied by the occurrence of coleoptera indicative of cooler summers. This change seems to have been synchronous throughout much of Britain (Coope, 1977), and is taken to mark the beginnings of climatic deterioration due to culminate in the Younger Dryas or Loch Lomond Stadial (S. Lowe, 1981). At Llyn Gwernan the Loch Lomond Stadial is defined by an abrupt lithological change from organic lake muds to clay-rich minerogenic sediment, and its onset is dated at 11,160 ±90 BP, in close agreement with the dating of the same event in Scandinavia, Scotland and the Lake District (Mangerud *et al.*, 1974; Gray and Lowe, 1977; Pennington, 1977). Thermophilous pollen-types are again replaced with those of open habitat herbs dominated by *Artemisia*, *Rumex* and *Cyperaceae*. A diversity of arctic-alpine plant species is recorded from many Welsh sites (Moore, 1977), perhaps with stands of shrub species of *Salix* and *Betula* in sheltered and westerly locations. Stunted and sparsely flowering *Juniperus* may have been present, and it has been suggested that *Corylus* may even have found a refuge in the extreme south-west, on the exposed Cardigan plain (Deacon, 1974; Moore, 1977, 1987).

By about *c.* 10,200 BP polar water again extended as far south as south-western Ireland (Ruddyman *et. al.*, 1977) and coleoptera of northern type indicate severe cold. Insect assemblages from Croydon, south London (Peake and Osborne, 1971), and Hawk's Tor in Devon (Coope, 1977) indicate a treeless environment, suggesting that most of Britain, and probably Wales, lay in an open tundra-like zone to the north of birch forests equivalent to those of the present-day *taiga*. At the height of the stadial, there is evidence for the expansion of cirque glaciers in the uplands of north and south Wales (Gray, 1982; Walker, 1982; Robertson, 1988), with the existence elsewhere of large snow patches. Conditions of discontinuous permafrost probably existed, and periglacial processes, particularly solifluction, contributed to a modification of the landscape unequalled at any time since. Such immature and unstable soil conditions may, incidentally, explain the rather slower response of vegetation to interstadial warming, in contrast to the rather more rapid colonization by insects. It might be cautioned here that parameters for palaeoenvironmental reconstruction in Wales throughout the late Devensian and succeeding early Flandrian will show considerable local diversity according to the differing response rates of lithology, flora and fauna to sharp changes in both topography and temperature. The picture so far painted, and indeed much of what is to follow, is of necessity something of a generalization based on limited data.

Estimates for temperature during the Loch Lomond Stadial accordingly vary somewhat as to whether the evidence is derived from coleoptera, pollen or geomorphological indicators. Insect assemblages, perhaps the most reliable of these, imply a minimum winter temperature of about -25° C with a summer value of 9° - 10° C (Atkinson *et. al.*, *op. cit.*). Mean annual temperatures for the stadial shown on Fig. 2.6 are within the range in which many periglacial features are known to form and would agree, for instance, with the development of pingos in west Wales at this time (Watson, 1977).

Botanical records argue for rather warmer temperatures at this time, perhaps not falling below -8° C in winter. For upland Wales (250 - 500 m.), Taylor (1980) has proposed temperatures of -5.5° - -6.0° C in winter (December, January, February) and 4.8° - 9° C in summer (July and August). There is no direct evidence for temperature conditions in lowland west Wales, but temperature lapse-rates for change in altitude (Harrison, 1974) and the oceanic position of the south-west suggest temperatures at, or rather above, the warmest values of these ranges. This might indeed have had to be so had the Cardigan plain supported a late glacial refugium of *Corylus*, a suggestion noted above (but contested by S. Lowe, 1982, and Donald, 1987). The exact degree of severity of the Younger Dryas stadial on the maritime fringe may have been rather greater than pollen records allow, if the arguably more precise dates derived from present day coleopteran tolerances is accepted. Such highly important details will, however, remain imprecise until fresh data from more sites is available. It is at least certain that the cold snap was of short duration, lasting perhaps only some three hundred years.

The Lateglacial/Flandrian transition is marked by the end of the Loch Lomond/Younger Dryas Stadial. This is satisfactorily dated at several sites, including Llyn Gwernan, to *c.* 10,000 BP when *Juniperus* again asserts itself in many pollen profiles.

iii) Lateglacial fauna:
Against the climatic and vegetational background described above, our knowledge of corresponding faunal composition and movement is conspicuously poor, and no more so than in Wales.

Pleistocene vertebrate remains have been found abundantly in many Welsh limestone caves over the last 150 years, and include many of the large mammal species known from English sites (Stuart, 1982). Regrettably, documentation of these finds has been all but non-existent and the bones and teeth of perhaps several Pleistocene episodes are usually co-mingled. In addition, spotted hyaena can be shown to have been present at many locations (although not demonstrably after the Devensian glacial maximum) and will certainly have contributed a faunal residue quite unrelated to any specifically human accumulation.

With such a legacy of disarray left by both carnivores and

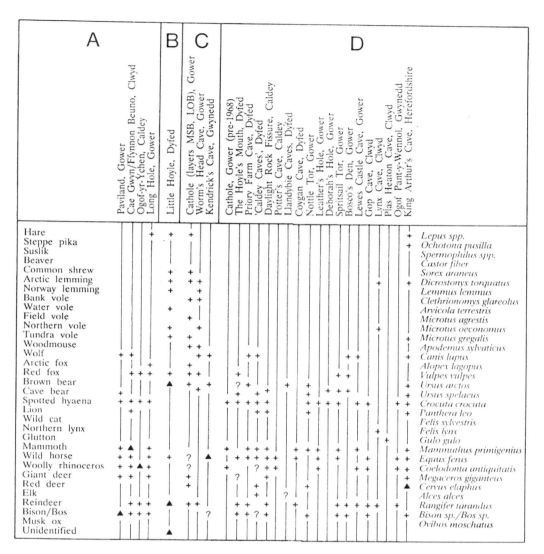

Table 2.4: Records of Devensian mammalian fauna from Welsh caves (including King Arthur's Cave, Herefordshire). List of principle British Devensian fauna compiled from Stuart (1982) and Campbell (1977). For radiocarbon dates see text.

A – Sites with radiocarbon and/or stratigraphic data indicative of the mid-Devensian. Only the species with radiocarbon dates can certainly be attributed to this period.

B - Fauna associated with a pooled radiocarbon date of 18,450 +430 BP (Green, 1986a).

C – Sites with radiocarbon or stratigraphic data, or faunal association (Worm's Head Cave), indicative of the late Devensian.

D – Sites with anattributable faunal remains of probable mid-late Devensian type.

cave hunters of the not so distant past, it is barely possible now to distinguish to which part of the Ice Age the many discoveries of animal species belong. Records for faunal populations during the Lateglacial are particularly unpromising, largely depending as they do on cave assemblages where recorded stratigraphic resolution is at a minimum.

Table (2.4) lists the principal species of the Devensian mammalian fauna recognized from British Devensian find-spots and indicates which of these species have been recorded from Wales. Given the sad lack of detail already noted, such a compilation only hints at the wealth of formerly rich and diverse fossil populations and serves to emphasize the scale of the loss of information suffered in earlier years.

Although it has been suggested that fresh mammal populations would have had to re-immigrate from the Continent at the onset of deglaciation (Stuart, 1982), it is apparent that at least some vertebrates were present in Britain at about the glacial maximum (Table 2.3, above). The return of woolly rhinoceros, lion and spotted hyaena after this time cannot now be discounted given the recent unexpected radiocarbon dates for mammoths:

Condover, Shropshire:

(12,700 ±160 BP, OxA-1021: Hedges *et al.*, 1987)

Pin Hole Cave, Creswell Crags:

(12,460 ±160 BP, OxA-1204: *ibid.*).

Bear and reindeer are also now dated close to the Devensian maximum, from the Little Hoyle, Dyfed (Table 2.3, above) and it therefore seems likely that Wales was not as bereft of fauna at this time as was previously thought.

For the Lateglacial, with which we are now concerned, a solitary radiometric determination is available from Kendrick's Upper Cave in Gwynedd, where a decorated horse mandible is dated to:

10,000 ±200 BP (OxA-111: Gillespie *et al.*, 1985).

No determinations exist, so far, between this date, at the very close of the Devensian, and the series recently obtained from the Little Hoyle Cave.

The fauna recorded from layers LOB and MSB at Cat Hole in Gower, West Glamorgan, whilst undated and probably mixed, suggests only the possibility that reindeer may have been present in the Lateglacial along with fossils identified as bear, arctic fox, red fox, lemmings and other small mammals. Campbell suggests that with these can be included the horse, red deer and giant deer recorded during the earlier investigation of the cave (Campbell, 1977; McBurney, 1959). It must be remembered, however, that this site has produced artefacts of possible 'Gravettian' age, as well as Lateglacial and even Mesolithic types (see below). Hence, little reliability can be placed on any precise association between artefact types and specific animals.

Table 2.5: Lateglacial fauna from Gough's (New) Cave, Cheddar, Somerset.

Species	C14 Date	Lab. No.	Reference
Steppe Pika			
Arctic hare			
Norwegian lemming			
Water vole			
Wolf			
Red fox			
Brown bear			
Arctic fox:	12,400 +110 BP	(OxA-1200)	1
Mammoth:	12,170 +130 BP	(OxA-1890)*	7
Wild horse:	12,470 +160 BP	(OxA-464)*	3
	12,360 +170 BP	(OxA-465)*	3
	12,340 +150 BP	(OxA-589)*	4
	12,370 +150 BP	(OxA-590)*	4
	12,260 +160 BP	(OxA-591)	4
	12,500 +160 BP	(OxA-592)	4
	12,350 +160 BP	(BM-2183R)*	8
	12,250 +160 BP	(BM-2184R)	8
	12,200 +250 BP	(BM-2185R)	8
	12,470 +240 BP	(BM-2186R)	8
	12,300 +200 BP	(BM-2187R)	8
	12,380 +230 BP	(BM-2188R)	8
Red deer:	12,800 +170 BP	(OxA-466)*	3
Wild cattle:	11,900 +140 BP	(OxA-813)	5
Bovid:	12,030 +150 BP	(OxA-588)	4
	12,300 +180 BP	(OxA-1071)*	6
Saiga antelope:	12,380 +160 BP	(OxA-463)	3

References:

1 : Hedges *et al.*, 1988

2 : Burleigh *et al.*, 1985

3 : Gillespie *et al.*, 1985

4 : Gowlett *et al.*, 1986a

5 : Gowlett *et al.*, 1986b

6 : Hedges *et al.*, 1987

7 : Hedges *et al.*, 1989

8 : Bowman *et al.*, 1990

* = determinations on humanly modified bone or ivory

NB: OxA-589, OxA-590 and BM-2183R date the same atlas bone
OxA-591, OxA-592 and BM-2187R date the same metapodial bone

Red fox, lemmings and other rodent species indicative of a late Devensian faunal assemblage have been recovered, along with a few flints and a juvenile human cranium, in a breccia from the Worm's Head Cave, Gower (Davies, 1981, 1986, 1989a; Currant, pers. comm., 1990).

Considering the relatively lowered sea levels of the Lateglacial and the wide ranges of both man and animals at that time it is certainly excusable, when faced by the almost total lack of evidence from Wales, to quote recent evidence for contemporary faunal exploitation in the neighbouring Mendip Hills. The Lateglacial mammal fauna from Gough's (New) Cave in Cheddar Gorge, Somerset has been re-assessed (Currant, 1986) in the light of a new series of radiocarbon dates which suggest that the bone assemblage is chronologically coherent and is coincident with the very considerable evidence for human use of the cave during the period c. 13,000 - 12,000 BP. The faunal list, and associated radiocarbon determinations, is shown in Table 2.5.

Here, steppe pika may belong to the Younger Dryas (being dated to 10,020 +120 BP (OxA-516) at Great Doward Cave in the Wye valley: Gowlett et al., 1986), whilst the reindeer may be of this or earliest Flandrian age. Reindeer from the cave has already been dated to 9,920 ±130 BP (Clutton-Brock and Burleigh, 1983) and further dates are awaited. Beaver may also post-date the Lateglacial. Absent from this assemblage, though, is the so-called giant deer (Megaceros giganteus) which, if the identification is correct, has been shown to have been present at Kent's Cavern at about this time (12,180 ±100; GrN-6204). Unfortunately, this identification cannot now be verified.

With the exception of saiga antelope, which is a rare constituent of south-western English faunas, all but the steppe pika are recorded from Welsh sites and are highly likely to have formed components of the Welsh Lateglacial fauna also. With the exception of the small mammals, such species would have between them provided greatly valued sources of fat, meat, pelts, bone and antler. Cut marks preserved on the bone make it clear that at least arctic hare, wild cattle, red deer, and particularly wild horse were sought and butchered by man. The presence of red deer with wild cattle (and perhaps beaver), would suggest a rather milder and more vegetated environment than is normally associated with Lateglacial hunting. Dated at about 13,000-12,000 BP (NB dates with asterisks in Table 2.5), the cave's occupation falls within the period when the peak thermal conditions of the Lateglacial Interstadial would have allowed expansion to the Mendips, and beyond, of the more temperate faunas and flora detected in the recent analyses. The presence, also, of the more 'open' species such as horse and antelope must indicate the rapidity with which environmental conditions were able to fluctuate, and perhaps also that such conditions could prevail simultaneously at a local or regional scale.

The very major changes in geography and ground cover associated with rapid fluctuations in air and sea

temperatures must have profoundly influenced the character and variety of ecological niches and their incumbent biota. Despite the now clear picture presented at Gough's Cave, and the similar situation that might be expected further west along the dry Bristol Channel and into Wales, it cannot be considered surprising if further variety were encountered in future research. Not only will environmental conditions have varied markedly in both time and space, but so will the nature of the remaining sites' sediment traps and their respective taphonomic histories.

For instance, one member of the British megafauna known to be exploited by man during the Lateglacial is the elk (Alces alces: Lister, 1984). Although contemporary with the Gough's cave assemblage, it is not actually present there and has yet to be satisfactorily recorded from Wales (ibid.). The hunted specimen recovered from Poulton-le-Fylde, Lancashire (Hallam et al, 1973), in association with two fragments of barbed bone points, has now been dated to:

12,400 ±300 (OxA-150; Gillespie et al., 1985).

The environmental implications of this find are discussed by Jacobi et al (1986), who suggest that the dating is fully in agreement with those climatic indicators (see above) which suggest the relatively early onset of woodland conditions attractive to elk in north-western Britain (Pennington and Bonney, 1970, Pennington, 1975 and 1977). This indication of the importance of the milder conditions of the oceanic west country and Wales in the final Palaeolithic introduces a most important theme which will be stressed again when the discussion moves on into the Flandrian.

With respect to birds, fish and marine mammals, Campbell (1977) has summarized the limited British evidence for these, and again, the reliable information from Wales is thin or non-existant. Birds tentatively identified from the Later Upper Palaeolithic (LUP) layers at Cathole are Grouse, Greylag goose and Pipit (Bramwell, 1977). Eagle and black grouse are recorded from early excavations at the North Cave of The Little Hoyle, Dyfed (Rolleston et al., 1879) and 'some fragments of large bird bones' (now identified as Barnacle goose: Table 2.3) are noted amongst more recent finds there (Currant, 1986; Green, 1986b). Bird remains identified by D. Bramwell from an apparently Late Devensian clay at Potter's Cave, on Caldey Island, include large goose, Peregrine or Gyr falcon, Puffin, Manx shearwater, pigeon and duck (van Nédervelde and Davies, 1979-80). Of these, at least the maritime species may be Postglacial, perhaps having been introduced into deeper deposits via nesting burrows. From a more secure Lateglacial context are the avifauna from Gough's Cave which include Whooper swan, Ptarmigan, Willow/Red grouse, Peregrine falcon, Stock dove, Blackbird/Ring Ouzel and Fieldfare (Harrison, 1986): both swan and ptarmigan bones show evidence of direct modification by man.

Especially since the Irish Sea was open at this time (Devoy, 1985), marine mammals, molluscs and both sea and freshwater fish may be expected to have had a role in the later Palaeolithic exploitation in Wales. This is particularly difficult to assess, however, when the sea itself has removed or submerged the sites and situations where such evidence may have existed.

iv) Lateglacial sea-levels:
The reconstruction of Lateglacial sea levels, so critical in an understanding of the movements of man and animals at this time, is particularly difficult owing to the deep submergence of the evidence by the Lateglacial and Holocene transgressions and their sediments. Estimates vary widely, but it would seem probable that at the height of the glacial maximum sea level could have been lowered by as much 120 metres. The rapidity of warming ensured that eustatic rise outstripped isostatic recovery, and in southern Britain sea levels rose swiftly with perhaps only a minor check during the Loch Lomond Stadial. Using many sources, Campbell (1977, p 136) suggests an unimpeded rise from c. 16,000 BP, reaching about -60 metres below OD at the peak of the Loch Lomond Stadial at a little before c. 10,000 BP. More recently, radiocarbon dating of Barbadian coral successions has suggested sea levels of about -100m at c. 13,000 BP, -90m at c. 12,000 BP, -70m at c. 11,000 BP and -60m at 10,000 BP (Fairbanks, 1989, fig. 2).

Previous estimates for local sea level around western Britain at the end of this period may be rather too high in the light of such recent work: Kidson and Heyworth (1973) place it at approximately -36 metres below OD in the Bristol Channel at c. 10,250 BP, although Hawkins (1971) has proposed a lower level of -43 metres for c. 9,950 BP.

Particularly relevant to west Wales is the study of the floor of Cardigan Bay by Dobson et. al (1971 and 1972) who have reported a change of submarine slope at 32.9 - 43.9 metres below sea level. It is suggested that this feature, about 12 metres high, represents the fossil cliff-line of the maximum westward development of the Cardigan plain during the Lateglacial, and futhermore, agrees with the postulated position of a similar feature in the Irish Sea (Burgess, 1953). Dobson et al record a rather sharper change in submarine slope at -27.4 metres, and this may represent a still-stand in the retreat of the coastline during the Loch Lomond Stadial.

The complexities and uncertainties of estimating late Quaternary sea levels in the area of the present Celtic, Irish and Malin Seas have been summarized by Devoy in his review of the evidence for land bridges from the British mainland to Ireland (Devoy, 1985). Such evidence is vital in the formulation of proposals for the immigration of a land-based fauna into Ireland and, with them, Palaeolithic hunters (Woodman, 1986a). The present day insulated and limited Irish fauna is presumed to be a direct consequence of the very early invasion of open water around the island following rapid melting of Midlandian (Devensian) and Irish Sea ice. That an earlier land bridge must have existed is proved by the dating of remains of mammoth and spotted hyena from Castlepook Cave, north Cork, to c. 33 - 34,000 BP. A fresh immigration may have had to take place to re-colonize the island after the subsequent glacial maximum, and the requisite land bridge may only have existed, if at all, as a discontinuous linkage across temporary islands between the north of Ireland and SW Scotland at c. 11,400 - 10,200 ±200 BP (Devoy, op. cit.).

Although parts of the southern continental shelf may have seen phases of brief emergence during the late Devensian, proof of this is lacking, and deep channels reaching as low as >-100 metres below the Celtic Sea would have effectively separated Ireland from areas to the south and east. In the Irish Sea, where routeways across the St. George's Channel, Central Irish Sea and the North Channel have been considered, it would appear that a deep linear trough, at its shallowest, 90 metres below present day sea level, would have precluded any but brief and most inhospitable passage.

Given, then, that any direct linkage between Wales and Ireland is very unlikely to have existed in the Lateglacial, it is nevertheless a fact that large expanses of the continental shelf will have been bared, expanding substantial dry-land territories out across Cardigan Bay and the Bristol Channel.

6. Lateglacial archaeology in Britain

i) The Lateglacial Interstadial
Following the harsh climatic and environmental privations of the Late Devensian glacial maximum, human re-settlement can only be shown to have taken place during the following abrupt climatic amelioration - the Lateglacial Interstadial (c. 13,000 - 12,000 BP). It is from this millennium that evidence for Upper Palaeolithic activity is most abundant in Britain, overlapping in time with the late Magdalenian of northern France and the Hamburgian of northern Germany (Fischer and Tauber, 1986).

The earliest certain British indication of hunters in the Lateglacial is provided by cut-marks on a distal metapodial of a red deer from Gough's (New) Cave:

12,800 ±170 BP (OxA-466: Gillespie et al., 1985),

whilst the only human fossil from this period to have been radiometrically dated is an ulna from Sun Hole, Cheddar:

12,210 ±160 BP (OxA-535: Gowlett et al., 1986a; Burleigh, 1986).

Current research and dating programmes at Gough's (New) Cave, Somerset, Creswell Crags, Derbyshire/Nottingham-shire, Kent's Cavern, Devon, and The Hoyle, in Dyfed, are aimed at refining the evidence for the character and timing of Palaeolithic activity during the interstadial. Other import-ant instances of human exploitation at this time include the wounded elk from Poulton- le-Fylde (above, p. 21), and the

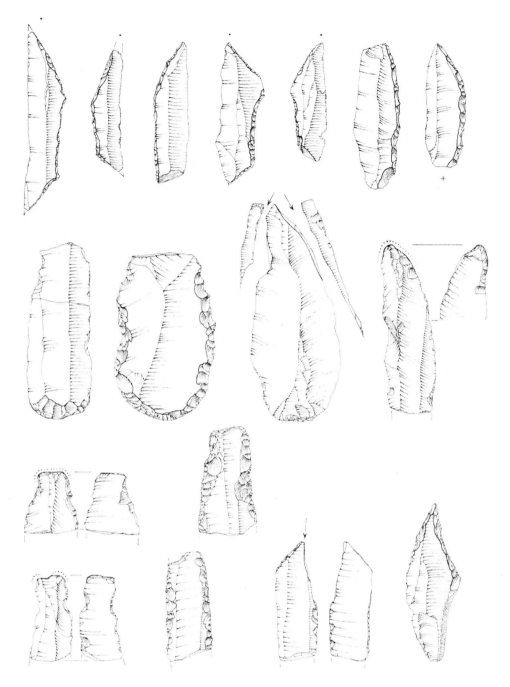

Figure 2.7: Flint artefacts from Gough's (New) Cave, Somerset. Scale – 1:1.35.

large open air site at Hengistbury Head (Mace, 1959; Barton, in press).

The rich lithic assemblage from Gough's (New) Cave (ST 467 539), near the foot of the Cheddar Gorge, provides perhaps the most reliable guide to the nature of the technologies which can be expected to have survived also in Wales at this time. Some 388 classifiable tools remain from an original recovery of about 7,000 pieces of chipped flint and chert. The majority of these tools are believed to belong to the same 'lithic population', ie. to one or more occupations linked within the same time range. Cut marks on the bones of game animals show that at least horse and red deer were butchered at the site during the centuries

between *c.* 12,100 and *c.* 12,800 BP.

A selection of artefacts from the cave is illustrated in Fig. 2.7. Over half of the retouched forms are backed pieces: typical amongst these are bi-truncated 'sideblades' of trapeziform outline ('Cheddar' points, eg Fig 2.7, Nos. 1-2), variants of which may be shouldered (eg Fig. 2.7, No. 3-4). Also present are pieces with a single oblique truncation ('Creswell' points, eg. Fig. 2.7, No. 3), and also points with simple convex backing (eg Fig, 2.7, No. 6-7). There are no 'penknife' points, straight- backed bladelets or tanged points (see below).

Other tools (eg Fig. 2.7, Nos. 8-17) include 52 burins (eg

23

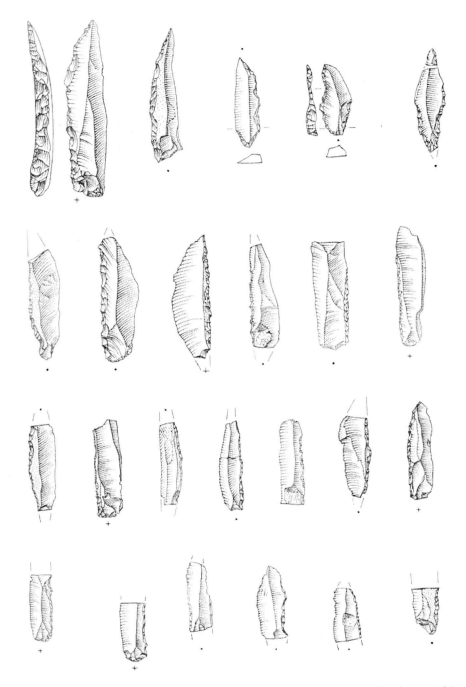

Figure 2.8: Flint artefacts from Seamer Carr (Site K), N Yorks. Scale – 1:1.31.

Nos. 10, 16), mostly on truncations, 44 scrapers usually at the end of blades (eg Nos. 8-9), and 17 piercers (eg No. 17). Deliberate semi-abrupt retouch is a common feature of many tool margins (eg Nos. 9, 13, 15) and is accompanied on some blades by a distal truncation (eg No.13). Several pieces are heavily worn at their extremities (eg Nos. 11, 12, 14), and some of these (eg No. 11) appear to have been used in some kind of drilling or boring activity.

Together, this array of tool types appears closest to the original 'Creswellian' as defined by Garrod (1926, 193-4). Bone and antler tools include two *batons de commandement*, piercers of hare bone, and two bones inscribed with 'notation' marks. Needles seem to have been

cut from 'cores' of swan bone. Amber and sea shell fragments are also present.

The bones from several humans, including a young child, along with the evidence of craft activities and exotic items, might suggest that the cave was more than a simple task or caching site. It is perhaps more probable that it was once part of a more complex system of local sites within an extended annual range (Jacobi, 1986; Currant *et al.*, 1989).

That such a range, along with the same or contemporary groups of hunters, extended westwards across the Bristol Channel lowlands is supported by a small but significant number of sites in south and west Wales (see below).

24

ii) Transition (*c.* 12,000 - 11,000 BP)
In the succeeding millennium of fitful climatic decline (which includes the 'Alleröd' of previous schemes: Mangerud *et al.*, 1974), evidence for an Upper Palaeolithic presence in Britain is extremely limited.

Various indicators all now suggest that climate had already begun to deteriorate from *c.* 12,500 BP. During the transition to full stadial conditions, birch woodland still survived, at least in south Wales (Walker and Harkness, 1990) although contracting in extent as temperatures fell. Despite even more rigorous winters, therefore, it could nevertheless be argued that environmental conditions were tolerable enough to support a continuing human presence, at least in summer. Jacobi has argued (1988) that limestone topography may have been relatively less attractive at this time and that abandonment or loss of lithic equipment may have occurred further afield, and more sparsely, than had been the case earlier in the Interstadial. If this were so, both the sites and their lithic components would be expected to be elusive and uncharacterized. Indeed the British evidence for Late Palaeolithic activity between about 12,000 and 11,000 BP is noticeably sparse: one of two certain instances, however, is provided by the unassociated barbed antler point from Porth-y-Waen, Shropshire (Britnell, 1984; Fig. 2.11) now dated to 11,390 +120 BP (OxA-1946: Bonsall and Smith, 1989). This chance find, isolated though it is, must nevertheless strongly suggest that Wales was exploited to some degree at this time. The second instance of activity at about this time is provided by another antler barbed point, dredged from the Leman and Ower bank in the North Sea (Godwin and Godwin, 1933), now dated to 11,740 +150 BP (OxA-1950: Hedges *et al.*, 1990).

It is to this period that Jacobi (1988) has proposed that lithic technologies that include 'penknife' points and straight-backed blades may belong. The former tools are convex-backed points characterised by additional oblique basal retouch similar to the '*pointes Aziliennes à base retrecie*' (Celerier, 1979). Such points, which are absent at Gough's (New) Cave, are nevertheless a significant component of the lithic collection from the cave site of Mother Grundy's Parlour at Creswell Crags where they are accompanied by short and round scrapers. Trapezoidal and angle-backed points also from the cave may be best explained as the result of mixing with slightly earlier occupation horizons. Significantly, 'Penkife' points occur stratified just below Younger Dryas deposits at Risby Warren, Lincs (May, 1976; Jacobi, 1988), and also at Seamer Carr, North Yorkshire where they are accompanied by short scrapers and backed bladelets (Schadla-Hall, 1987, 52; Cloutman, 1988, 28; Fig. 2.8).

The quality of such surviving evidence relating to any kind of typological patterning cannot, however, allow the resolution necessary for any realistic social or territorial interpretation. Until further data are available to the contrary, the suggested typological changes may perhaps be most economically accounted for in terms of technological evolution alone. If this were so, what evidence is available would suggest that assemblages in which 'penknife' points are the most frequent backed tool may be rather later in date than those dominated by trapeziform and angle-backed blades (Jacobi, 1988).

iii) Final Devensian settlement
No less certain, for England as for Wales, is the character and timing of human activity during the period of sharp climatic deterioration leading up to and during the Loch Lomond/Younger Dryas Stadial (*c.* 11,000 - 10,000 BP).

Radiocarbon dates on individual fossils (Table 2.6) suggest that the cold of the Younger Dryas was not so severe, however, as to deter at least reindeer, wild horse - and man - from entering parts of the British Isles. Two barbed points, of bone and antler respectively, from Sproughton in Suffolk, have recently been dated to *c.* 10,800 BP (Cook and Barton, 1986). From valley deposits of the river Nene near Earls Barton, Northants., a 'Lyngby-axe' of reindeer antler has now been dated to 10,320 ±150 BP (Gowlett *et al.*, 1986b), and horse bones apparently associated with a pointed blade at Flixton Site II are dated to before *c.* 10,400 BP (Moore, 1954; Godwin and Willis, 1959). A flint end-scraper from peat beneath coversands at Messingham, South Humberside, suggests human activity perhaps shortly prior to the most extreme cold of the stadial. The enclosing peat indicates tundra-like surroundings, and has provided a radiocarbon date (perhaps rather too young) of 10,280 ±120 BP (Birm-349: Buckland, 1984).

The ecological relationships between man and animals over this period are debated. It has been suggested that northern and western Britain may have suited reindeer for spring calving and summer browsing (Jacobi, 1982). Lack of any formal linkage between the remains of reindeer and flint artefacts at Ossom's Cave, Staffordshire, reduces certainty in the argument for a springtime reindeer kill here (*pace* Scott, 1986; Jacobi pers. comm.). Scott (*ibid.*) has, nevertheless, suggested that hunters were close to the 'Peak' at other times of the year as well.

In addition, it must remain speculative as to whether or not there is any association between certain finds of 'long blades', as well as the 'Lyngby-axe' mentioned above, and the exploitation of eastern England by hunters, from further afield, using an Ahrensburgian technology in the pursuit and butchery of reindeer and horse. Buckland (1984) envisages peripheral and pioneering hunting forays onto the tundra from more securely based seasonal camps further to the south within Britain. None of these, however, can be linked to any particular lithic assemblage type.

Table 2.6: Radiocarbon dates for individual animal remains and organic artefacts for the period 11,000 - 10,000 BP.

Species/ Artefact	Findspot	Date	Lab No.	Ref.
Wild horse*	Kendrick's Cave	10,000 +200 BP	(OxA-111)	1
Reindeer	Soldier's Hole	10,090 +230 BP	(BM-2249R)	7
Reindeer	Gough's (Old) Cave	10,190 +120 BP	(OxA-1120)	5
'Lyngby-axe'*	Earls Barton	10,320 +150 BP	(OxA-803)	4
Reindeer	Gough's (New) Cave	10,450 +110 BP	(OxA-1461)	6
Wild horse	Robin Hood Cave	10,590 +90 BP	(BM-604)	2
Reindeer	Ossom's Cave	10,600 +140 BP	(OxA-632)	3
Red deer	Elder Bush Cave	10,600 +110 BP	(OxA-811)	4
Antler point*	Sproughton	10,700 +160 BP	(OxA-518)	3
Reindeer	Ossom's Cave	10,789 +160 BP	(OxA-631)	3
Bone point*	Sproughton	10,910 +150 BP	(OxA-517)	3

*indicates human modification

References:
1 : Gillespie *et al.*, 1985
2 : Burleigh *et al.*, 1976
3 : Gowlett *et al.*, 1986a
4 : Gowlett *et al.*, 1986b
5 : Hedges *et al.*, 1987
6 : Hedges *et al.*, 1989
7 : Bowman *et al.*, 1990

7. Lateglacial sites in Wales:

Late Upper Palaeolithic archaeological remains can now be recognized from some 150 find-spots in Britain (Jacobi, pers. comm.; cf *ibid.* 1980b, fig. 4.1). Of these, there are altogether about 16 in Wales restricted mainly to the limestone outcrops to the north and south of the Cambrian mountains (Fig. 2.9). In addition, on the English side of the border, is the important site at King Arthur's Cave, Herefordshire (SO 547 157), and in the same county were found the two backed fragments from separate find-spots near Arrow Court (SO 279 545; Campbell, 1977, fig. 130, 1,2). Table 2.7 lists the all the relevant find-spots, and the following section will deal with each in turn, some more thoroughly than others, as the available data allows.

Table 2.7: Lateglacial find-spots in Wales and Herefordshire.

North Wales:

Lynx Cave	(SJ 1976 5933)
Ogof Tan-y-Bryn	(SH 7994 8159)
Plas-yn-Cefn Cave	(SJ 0202 7053)
Kendrick's (Upper) Cave	(SH 7800 8283)

South Wales:

Paviland Cave	(SS 4372 8588)
Cathole Cave	(SS 5377 9002)
Worm's Head Cave	(SS 3836 8770)
Carn Fach, Rhigos	(SN 944 025)
Gwernvale	(SO 211 192)

Shropshire:

Porth-y-Waen	(SJ 2590 2339)

Herefordshire:

King Arthur's Cave	(SO 547 157)
Arrow Court	(SO 279 545)

West Wales:

Nanna's Cave, Caldey Island	(SS 1458 9698)
Potter's Cave, Caldey Island	(SS 1436 9707)
Ogof-yr-Ychen, Caldey Island	(SS 1468 9691)
'New Cave', Caldey Island	(SS 1470 9688)
Priory Farm Cave	(SM 9789 0184)
Little Hoyle Cave	(SS 1118 9998)
The Hoyle (Hoyle's Mouth)	(SN 1120 0033)

Lynx Cave, Clwyd (SJ 1976 5933)
Excavated by: J. D. Blore, 1962-81, 1981- (Bramwell, 1963; Blore, 1966 and nd; Campbell, 1977; Davies 1989b).
Stratigraphy: seven sediment horizons (A - G) have so far been recognized, contained within a depth of 1.3m. Disturbed layers (A and B) overlie calcareous deposits (C) which include remnants of stalgmite floors. Below these are silt and sand layers (D and E) interpreted as Mesolithic and Lateglacial, respectively. Layers F and G are apparently sterile clays.
Fauna: Dog, badger, reindeer and aurochs have been identified from layer D, and reindeer from layer E. Fauna from other layers could all be Flandrian in age, with the

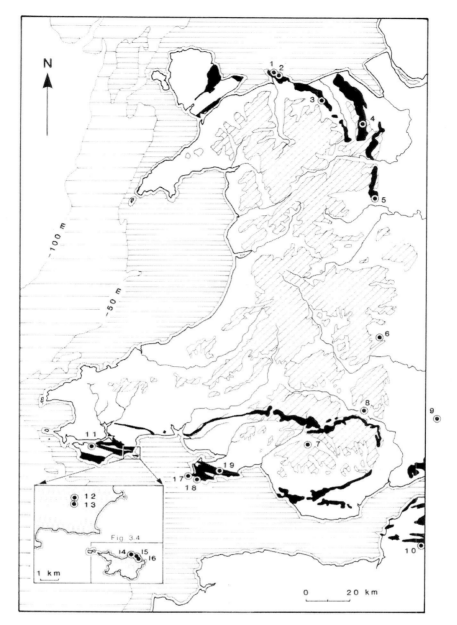

Figure 2.9: Distribution of Lateglacial find-spots in Wales and adjoining areas. 1, Kendrick's (Upper) Cave; 2, Ogof Tan-y-Bryn; 3, Plas-yn-Cefn Cave; 4, Lynx Cave; 5, Porth-y-Waen; 6, Arrow Court; 7, Rhigos; 8, Gwernvale; 9, King Arthur's cave; 10, Gough's (New) Cave; 11, Priory Farm Cave; 12, The Hoyle's Mouth; 13, The Little Hoyle; 14, Potters Cave; 15, Nanna's Cave; 16, Ogof-yr-Ychen; 17, Worm's Head Cave; 18, Paviland; 19, Cathole.

exception of arctic lemming, northern vole and reindeer (layer A). Artefacts: At least 13 flints and one chert artefact have been recovered (some illustrated in Blore, nd). Six pieces are recorded from Layer D and these include two fragments of straight-backed blades of Lateglacial appearance. The remaining pieces are fragmentary debitage, with a retouched flake (Layer A) and a microlith (Layer C). None of these have been seen by the author.

Four bone artefacts seem to be associated with a later prehistoric burial. Romano-British material was also found.

Radiometric dating: none

Problems: the exploration of the cave has been amateur and poorly recorded. No dating has been attempted. Mixing of the cave sediments seems to have been severe, and the lithic

artefacts recovered are largely undiagnostic.

Ogof Tan-y-Bryn, Gwynedd (SH 7994 8159)

Excavated by: D. James and M. Davies, 1975 (Davies, 1975, 29; 1989b).

Stratigraphy: surface litter is underlain by 10-20cms of disturbed brown earth. Below this is an undisturbed stoney yellowish-brown silty clay, of unknown depth, containing flint and bone. Some 2m of cave deposits which originally overlay this sequence appear to have been removed from the front of the cave. No further details are known.

Fauna: 'hacked bone fragments' - unidentified.

Artefacts: several fllints appear to have been found, two of which are reported as 'a fine Creswellian-type blunted back blade..and..a worn leaf-shaped blade' (*ibid.*). The former is a blade, 45mm long, with steep retouch along half the length of one edge.

Radiometric dating: none

Problems: a minimal excavation was 'cursory' and a complete stratigraphic sequence was not observed. Despite the Lateglacial appearance of the retouched blade, there is no other support for a Palaeolithic occupation here.

Plas-yn-Cefn Cave, Clwyd (SJ 0202 7053)

Excavated by: Lloyd and Stanley, 1833 (Dawkins, 1874; Falconer, 1868); H. S. Green, ?1984 (Green, 1986a).

Stratigraphy: Green's excavations have encountered deposits of Middle - Late Pleistocene age overlain by undated fluvial sediments (*ibid.*, Table 9.3, p. 139). No adequate stratigraphic record was made during the previous explorations.

Fauna: hippopotamus and bear are recorded from the lower levels of the cave. The flints (see below) were found 'with' a human cranium, cut red deer antler and Holocene (including domestic) fauna.

Artefacts: 4 flints are recorded (Campbell, 1977), including a retouched blade and a backed point (*ibid.*, fig. 155, 1). Pottery is also recorded.

Radiometric dating: three Uranium-Series determinations pre-date any Devensian occupation of the cave.

Problems: remaining records are insufficient to isolate any late Upper Palaeolithic occupation from both earlier and later events in the cave. The flints have no recorded context, and there is uncertainty as to exactly which cave in the Cefn complex these originally came from.

Kendrick's (Upper) Cave, Gwynedd (SH 7800 8283)

Excavated by: Kendrick, 1879-80; Davies, 1974; Stone and Davies, 1977-8; Davies, 1979.

Main references: Dawkins, 1880; Eskrigge, 1880; Sieveking, 1971; Davies, 1983.

Stratigraphy: Eskrigge describes a basal cave earth or clay of at least 2 - 3 feet (0.6 - 0.9m) overlain by 4 - 6 feet (1.2 - 1.8m) of loosely cemented breccia made up of angular limestone blocks. This was crowned in places by a layer of stalagmite. The 1970s excavations (Davies, 1979, Fig. 1) revealed massive modern disturbance and accumulation. Stalagmite was encountered below this in places, beneath which was a disturbed limestone rubble (itself locally cemented by stalagmite) and cave earth encountered at depths varying from about 0.4 - 1.3m. Towards the base of this latter deposit the cave earth tended to give way to large angular limestone blocks.

Fauna: that from Kendrick's digging include bovid (?bison and wild cow), wild horse, bear, deer, badger, sheep/goat. Davies records wolf (a single canine) and abundant remains of apparently Holocene species: bovid, sheep/goat, roe deer, wild pig, fox, hare/rabbit, bird species, fish, frog and at least 8 species of Mollusca, mostly limpet.

Human remains: the earlier finds 'consist of portions of four skeletons at least - three adults and a child' (Dawkins, 1880, 156). These remains were found near the base of the breccia and were reported (Eskrigge, 1880, 154) 'associated with'

two perforated bear canines, two portions of a horse mandible (one with incised ornament), an abraded oyster shell and 'several boulder stones apparently used as hand hammers'. Some human material which may be attributable to these original finds survives in the Llandudno Public Library and can be attributed to three individuals (Davies, nd).

The more recent excavations recovered 3 metacarpals, a metatarsal, phalange, terminal phalanges, a premolar, patella, verterbra and jaw fragment. These were found variously, in deposits at least partially disturbed, and which also included Holocene fauna (Davies, 1983).

Artefacts: objects of widely differing ages have been found in the cave. Those which may be Lateglacial include the following: the decorated portion of a horse mandible (Plate 2.4), 9 pierced and decorated bovid and deer teeth (Sieveking, 1971, fig. 4) and a pierced and decorated wolf canine (Davies, 1983). The last, partly encrusted with stalagmite, was recovered in 1978 near the base of Trench 4 ('2.3 m below cave datum') in a deposit of angular limestone blocks with a little loose brown cave earth (Davies, 1979). Two pierced and decorated bear canines (Dawkins, 1880, Fig. B) are now lost. Other artefacts reportedly associated with the horse mandible include a utilized oyster shell and hammerstones (Eskrigge, 1880, 154). Although 'a few flint flakes' are mentioned (*ibid.*, 155), none of these survive.

Purported to derive from Kendrick's Cave and now housed at the Llandudno Public Library, are 5 fragmentary metacarpals of sheep/goat or deer, partially stained red and each with a series of engraved marks at right-angles to their long axis (Sieveking, 1971, Fig. 3). These are, however, not mentioned in any contemporary account and their provenance is therefore regarded as not established.

In addition to the wolf canine, the 1970s' excavations recovered later prehistoric pottery, several flints, a utilized oyster shell, a possibly modified pig canine, and a hammerstone. Radiometric date: the decorated horse mandible has been radiocarbon dated to:

10,000 +200 BP (OxA-111: Gillespie *et al.*, 1985).

Problems: the earlier digging was amateur, uncontrolled, and unrecorded. It is unclear in which part of the cave (Upper or Lower) Kendrick's main discoveries were made. Important finds have been lost and much of what remains is muddled. The contents of the cave included deposits of very different ages. Recent excavations have been unable to identify, with certainty, any undisturbed Lateglacial sediments.

Paviland Cave, W. Glamorgan (SS 4372 8588)

Principal excavators: Buckland, 1823; Sollas, 1912 (Buckland, 1824; Sollas, 1913). Plate 2.3.

Stratigraphy: no significant stratification was either observed or recorded.

Fauna: Hyaena, cave bear, mammoth, horse, woolly rhinoceros, reindeer, giant deer and *bos*.

Artefacts: a total of 5,069 stone, bone and ivory artefacts

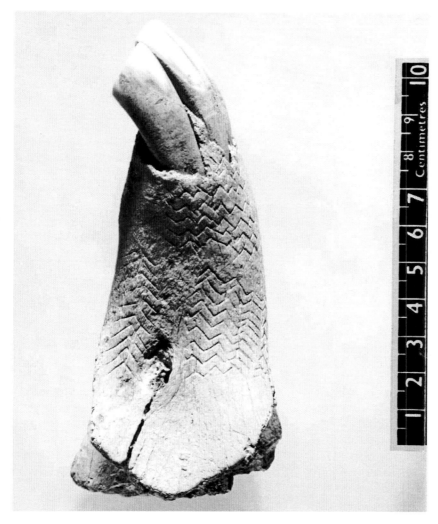

Plate 2.4: Decorated horse mandible from Kendrick's (upper) cave, Gwynedd
(photograph courtesy of the British Museum).

survive in museums. A substantial number of the formal tools and ornaments amongst these are argued to be of earlier Upper Palaeolithic attribution (see above). The lithic inventory does include, however, 23 backed tools (Campbell, 1977, 119), which are of distinctive Lateglacial type. Only a sample of these have been seen by the author, however, and the following table is based on the data presented by Campbell (*ibid.*):

obliquely truncated blades	5
bi-truncated trapeziform blades ('Cheddar' points)	3
angle-backed blades ('Creswell' points)	2
convex-backed blades	4
straight-backed blades	7
convex-backed blades with basal retouch ('Penknife' points)	2

It is not now possible to distinguish which amongst the end-scrapers, burins, awls and miscellaneous debitage once made up the full Lateglacial component at Paviland.
Radiometric dating: there are no determinations of Lateglacial age.
Problems: whilst late Upper Palaeolithic activity at Paviland

seems certain, this is now inseparable from amongst the confusion of remains of both earlier and later events at the cave.

Cathole, W. Glamorgan (SS 5377 9002)
Excavated by: Wood, 1860; McBurney, 1958-9; Campbell, 1968 (Garrod, 1926; McBurney, 1959; Campbell, 1977). Plate 2.2.
Stratigraphy: no record exists of the stratigraphy within the cave. The twentieth century excavations took place in the entrance area and encountered sand overlying bedrock, followed by a complex sequence of thermoclastic and weathered screes (Campbell, 1977, 57, Figs. 15 - 17). *Lithic artefacts* interpreted as of Lateglacial aspect were found within the thermoclastic screes of layers MSB and LOB, at depths between 1.0 and 1.5m below the ground surface. These layers are believed to be contained within the larger sedimentary unit - Layer B - of McBurney (1959) which also contained Flandrian fauna and artefacts.
Flora: pollen analysis was undertaken on samples taken during the 1968 excavation (Campbell, 1977, 102, Fig. 73). The resulting pollen curves were assumed to represent an uninterrupted vegetational sequence from before the glacial

maximum to the present day. The Lateglacial sequence was apparently indicated by substantially lowered tree pollen values. A slight peak in birch pollen in layer UOB was taken to indicate Pollen zone II, therefore suggesting that the underlying screes with presumed Lateglacial occupation (LOB and MSB) belonged to the latter part of pollen zone I. On this understanding, vegetation at this time would have been largely herbaceous with local growth of birch, pine, juniper and willow.

Fauna: species recorded from within the cave in the last century include vole, ?cave lion, wild cat, bear, hyaena, wolf, mammoth, rhinoceros, horse, reindeer, elk, giant deer and red deer.

McBurney (1959) recorded badger, red fox, arctic fox, bear, ?woolly rhinoceros, red deer, roe deer, reindeer, sheep/goat, bovid, lemming and hare. Campbell records (from layers LOB and MSB) field vole, bank vole, arctic lemming, wood mouse, red fox and possibly reindeer. Specimens of bird bone from these layers include ?grouse, ?greylag goose and ?pipit (Bramwell, 1977).

Human remains: two human skulls and some other portions of a skeleton were found near the surface inside the cave.

Artefacts: 130 chipped stone artefacts survive. Wood's digging recovered a 'Cheddar' point from inside the cave (Campbell, 1977, Fig. 133, 1) in addition to the tanged points referred to above. Two end-scrapers and a burin from these early excavations are figured by Garrod (1926, Fig. 9, 4-7).

McBurney's layer B produced one backed tool of Lateglacial appearance (McBurney, 1959, Fig. 1, 1) with a possible bone point and the shank of a bone needle (Green, 1984, Fig.10, g). Campbell's layer LOB and MSB produced only 15 chipped artefacts of which two may be fragments of burins.

Problems: The early digging in the cave, without record, has irreparably damaged a site of great potential. The more recent excavations in the entrance area have encountered a stratigraphy of porous screes in which a downward mixing of artefacts, fauna and pollen has seriously limited the conclusions that can be drawn from these data and their inter- relationships (Jacobi, 1980a, 58). There is no complementary radiometric dating.

Worm's Head Cave, W. Glamorgan (SS 3836 8770)
Excavated by: W. Riches, 1923-4; Davies, 1981, (Davies, 1981; 1986; 1989a).
Stratigraphy: a 'bone layer' overlies bedrock and is itself overlain be a sterile stony clay beneath an upper level of cave earth.
Fauna: bear, wolf, fox, cat, reindeer, bird, ?domestic dog, lemming, arctic lemming, northern vole, bank vole and wood vole (small mammals identified by A. P. Currant).
Human remains: some fragments and a juvenile human cranium.
Artefacts: medial section of large adinole blade and a retouched and utilised flint blade. Also 4 flakes of flint/chert (Davies, 1989a, fig. 7.5)
Problems: lack of adequate documentation.

Carn Fach, Rhigos, Glamorgan (SN 944 025)
Surface find of elongated trapeziform blade, bi-truncated, with additional retouch down the entire longer margin (Green, 1984, Fig. 10, h). National Museum of Wales accession no. 63.25/2.
Problem: an atypical tool-type without association.

Gwernvale, Powys (SO 211 192)
Excavated by: Britnell, 1977-8, (Britnell and Savory, 1984).
Stratigraphy: the supposedly Lateglacial artefacts were recovered from buried soil contexts encountered below a Neolithic long cairn.
Artefacts: amongst a collection of 1,480 classified chipped flint and chert items, seven fragments of backed pieces are distinguished as potentially Lateglacial in age owing to their robust size and deeper surface patina (Healey and Green, 1984, Fig. 46). If this is so, then other tools, such as end-scrapers and burins, also found in the buried soil, may be Lateglacial.
Problems: all the backed pieces are too fragmentary for satisfactory classification. They share the same contexts as artefacts of obvious Mesolithic and later prehistoric attribution and cannot be independently dated.

Porth-y-Waen, Shropshire (SJ 2590 2339)
Artefact: isolated find of a uniserial barbed antler point (Britnell, 1984, 385-6; Fig. 2.11). This was discovered within disturbed material from the excavation of an artificial pond in a narrow valley. Its precise context is unknown.
Radiometric dating: an AMS result on the artefact is as follows:

11,390 +120 BP (OxA-1946)

Problems: lack of context or associations of any kind.

King Arthur's Cave, Herefordshire (SO 054 157)
Excavated by: Anon.; Symonds, 1871; Hewer and Taylor, 1925-7 (Hewer, 1926; Taylor, 1928; Garrod, 1926); ApSimon, 1952 (ApSimon, 1955). Plate 2.5.
Stratigraphy: a complex series of deposits appear to span a period from perhaps the early/mid Devensian to the Flandrian. In the 'Passage' and elsewhere within the cave, deposits have been badly disturbed: the Upper Cave Earth contains a Devensian fauna, as well as Upper Palaeolithic artefacts (including a fragment of a 'leaf-point' (see above). It is uncertain how the more detailed stratigraphy reported from the platform outside should be correlated with the cave earth(s) within. On the platform, some 4 feet (1.4m) of 'rubble' (angular scree) includes, near its surface, a hearth with clear late Mesolithic associations (see Chapter V). Below this were: a 'Yellow Rubble', a 'Second Hearth' and, lowest of all, the so-called 'Mammoth Layer'. This last overlay a red and yellow clay tentatively identified with the Upper Cave Earth inside the cave. It is the 'Yellow Rubble' and 'Second Hearth' which preserve the most useful evidence for Late Upper Palaeolithic occupation(s) at the site.

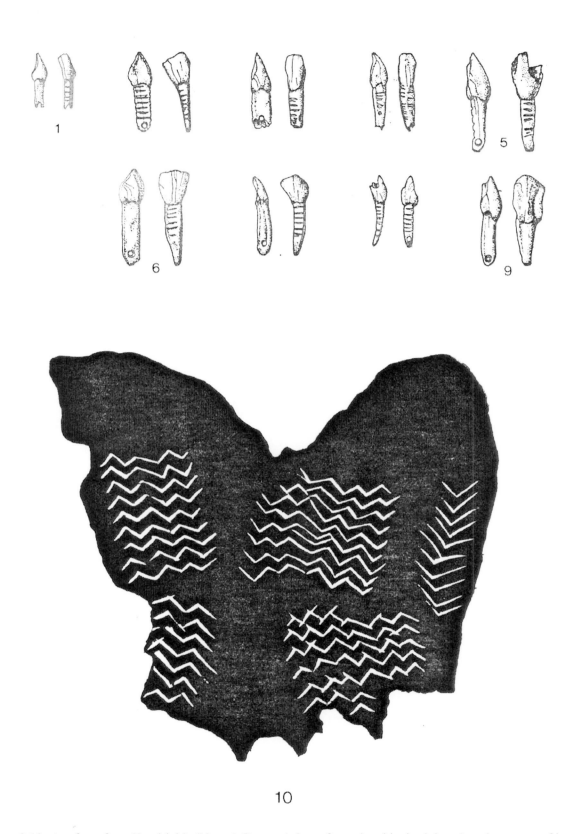

Figure 2.10: Artefacts from Kendrick's (Upper) Cave: - 1-9, perforated and incised deers' teeth; pattern of incised decoration on horse mandible (see also Plate 2.4). Scale – 1:1. After Sieveking (1970).

Figure 2.11: Barbed antler point from Porth-y-Waen, Shropshire. After Britnell (1984).

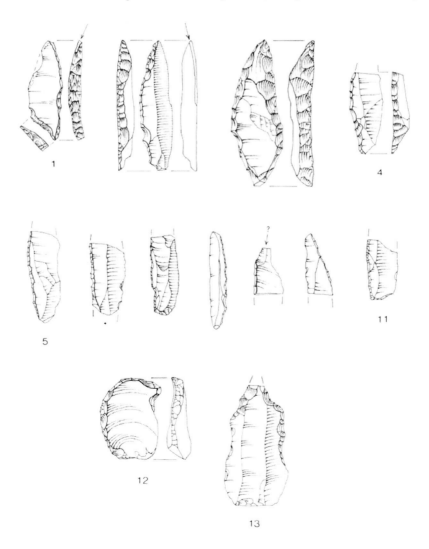

Figure 2.12: Flint artefacts from the "Yellow Rubble" at King Arthur's Cave, Herefordshire. Scale – 1:1.32.

Plate 2.5: King Arthur's cave, Herefordshire.

Table 2.8: Identifiable artefacts from Pleistocene levels at King Arthur's Cave, Herefordshire.

Artefact type	Passage (Upper Cave Earth)	Platform (Yellow Rubble)	Platform (Second Hearth)	Platform (Mammoth Layer)
?leaf-point (fragment)	1			
Bi-trunctaded trapeziform blade ('Cheddar' point)	1			
Angle-backed blade ('Creswell' point)			?1	
Convex-backed blades		1		1*
Convex-backed blade with oblique basal retouch		1		
Straight-backed blade	1	4		
Unclassified backed frags.	6	4	5	?1
Microliths	2	1		
Endscraper (long)			?1	
Endscraper (short)			1	
Scraper (round)		1		
Truncation burin	1			
Dihedral burin			1	
Other ?burin			1	
Piercer	1	1		
Worn piece	1			
Worn piece (?drill)			1	
Utilised/retouched blade				1
Retouched flakes/frags	1	1	3	

Unclassified tools	4	3	2	1
Crested piece			1	
Burin spall		1		
Other ?debitage	1	1		
TOTAL chipped artefacts	20	19	17	4
Utilised pebbles	1		1 +	?1
Bone tool fragments	2			
?Utilised bone fragments			3	
Perforated pig's tooth	1			

*the excavators suggested that this artefact may have derived from the 'Second Hearth'.

Radiometric dating: the following AMS radiocarbon dates are now available on fauna, although none of the samples can be proved to link with human occupation at the cave (Hedges *et al.*, 1989):

Red deer	Yellow Rubble	12,120 +120 BP	(OxA-1562)
Red deer	Second Hearth	12,210 +120 BP	(OxA-1563)
Mammoth	Mammoth Layer	34,850 +1500 BP	(OxA-1564)
Mammoth	Red Clay	38,500 +2300 BP	(OxA-1565)
Mammoth	Red Clay	>39,500	(OxA-1566)

Fauna:
Yellow Rubble: red deer, wild horse, bovid, hare, steppe pika, lemming, vole and hedgehog.
  Second Hearth: red deer, wild horse, bovid, hare and steppe pika (the latter, a tooth, thought to have been derived from the Yellow Rubble). Many bones were believed by the excavators to have been split by man.
Mammoth Layer: deer (sp?), wild horse, rhinoceros, hyena, bovid, mammoth and hare. Bones also believed to have been split by man.

Human remains: 'human bones of little interest' are noted from the 'Old Spoil Heap' and the 'Humus' on the platform.
Artefacts: a few artefacts were recovered by Symonds. Garrod illustrates seven of these (1926, Fig.12), including three scrapers, two backed pieces and a burin, any of which could be of Lateglacial origin.
The 1926-7 excavations recovered 'about 120 retouched tools and 600 other pieces of flint'. Many of these are from mixed contexts or Flandrian levels. The few potentially late Pleistocene artefacts that survive from discrete horizons can be combined with the rather greater number from these layers which are recorded by illustrations in the excavation reports (Hewer, 1926; Taylor, 1928; eg Fig. 2.12). Surviving records suggest that the only clear example of a 'Penknife' point (Fig. 2.12, No. 1) to survive from the site was found in the 'Yellow Rubble'. The following table can be no more than an attempt (limited by an absence of some of the pieces) to tabulate at least a portion of the artefact collection.

Problems: the stratigraphy of the cave interior has been lost, and the age of what remains is uncertain. Artefacts from the Upper Cave Earth, whilst predominantly of Upper Palaeolithic type, are not referable with certainty to any particular sub-division.

The recording of the stratigraphy outside the cave lacks refinement and has not been satisfactorily correlated with that inside the cave. Artefact and bone recovery seems to have been crude, and a certain amount of downward contamination within the rubble layers is possible.
Much of the collection from the 1920s excavations, housed in Bristol, was damaged or destroyed during World War II.

Arrow Court, Herefordshire (SO 279 545)
Two separate find-spots here have each produced the proximal end of a fragmentary flint backed point. (Campbell, 1977, Fig. 130, 1-2). There are no details of context and neither piece can now be precisely classified, one being an angled fragment, the other perhaps part of a 'Penknife' point.

Nanna's Cave, Caldey Island, Dyfed (SS 1458 9698)
Excavated by: Coates Carter and Clarke, 1911; Leach, 1913, 1915; Anon., 1915-49; van Nédervelde, 1949-51, 1973-86. Plate 2.6.
Main references: Leach, 1916; Lacaille and Grimes; 1955; van Nédervelde and Davies, 1977a; Davies 1989b.
Stratigraphy: prior to its first rifling in *c*. 1911, this cave must have contained a highly informative stratigraphy covering much of the time since the last ice age. Its basal deposits seem to have been composed of a yellow silty sand on bedrock, overlain by a red loam capped by stalagmite. Cemented within the latter were traces of a midden composed of cockle, limpet, and oyster shells, charcoal, bone fragments and flint artefacts. Above this were sandy midden deposits of later prehistoric and more recent times.
Fauna: no Pleistocene fauna has been identified from the cave with any certainty. Bone fragments tentatively identified as bovid (Lacaille and Grimes, 1955, 104) were found in the basal yellow silty sand. Pig is also reported

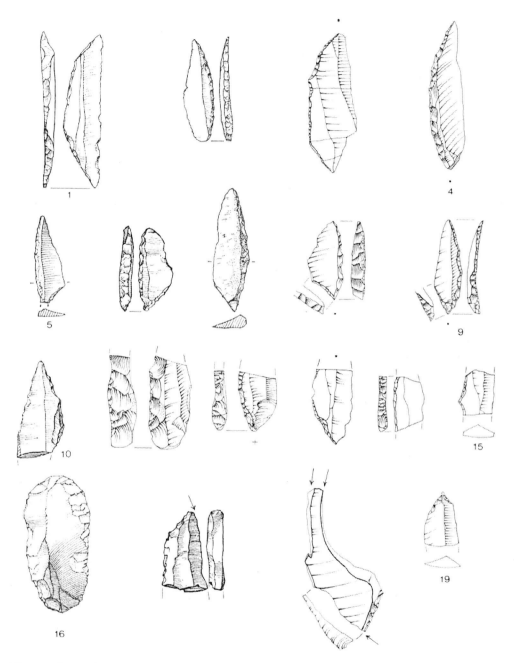

Figure 2.13: Flint artefacts of possible Lateglacial age from Nanna's Cave, Caldey Island, Dyfed: - 1, "Cheddar2 point; 2-4, convex-backed blades; 5-9, "Penknife" points; 10-15, fragments of backed blades; 16, end-scrapers; 17, burin; 18, burin/spall; 19, ?piercer. Scale – 1:1.37.

(*ibid.*) from the 'basal layers'.

Human remains: bones from four humans were found in *c.* 1911, representing parts of three adults and at least one juvenile (Davies, in press). Two groups of bone are encrusted with stalagmite and therefore pre-date its formation in the cave. Occasional further human bones have been found more recently, mostly from the accumulated debris outside the cave.

Artefacts: finds of lithic and other artefacts have been dispersed widely - some 500 flint and stone items survive in various collections, but a true estimate of the full recovery from the cave and its platform cannot now be achieved.

Finds from the basal yellow silty sand, as documented by Lacaille and Grimes (1955, figs. 14-15), are those which most clearly correspond with a potential Lateglacial use of the cave. Also, certain finds from the red loam, by their typology, may date to this time although this latter sediment and the stalagmite may have formed later, during the Holocene. Other potentially Lateglacial tool forms found during recent years, mostly from disturbed contexts outside the cave, can be added to those described in 1955 to form the following table (and see Fig. 2.13).

No organic artefacts resembling known Lateglacial types have been recorded.

Table 2.9: Lithic artefacts of possible Lateglacial age from Nanna's Cave, Caldey, Dyfed.

Artefact type:	Context:				Total:
	Basal silty sand	Red loam	Spoil	Other	
Bi-truncated trapeziform blades ('Cheddar' points)	1				1
Angle-backed blades ('Creswell' points)	1				1
Convex-backed blades	3				3
Convex-backed blades with basal retouch ('Penknife' points)	3		2		5
Fragments of backed pieces	4	6	2		12
End-scraper	1				1
Truncation burins	1	1		1	3
?Piercer		1			1
Retouched flakes	3	3	1		7
Utilised flakes/blades	2	1			3
Microliths (and frags of)	?1	5	3		9
Flakes/blades/frags	9	4			13
Cores	2				2
Crested piece	1				1
Burin spalls	2		1		3
Microburins		2	1		3
TOTAL	34	21	13		68

Radiometric dating: none.

Problems: records of stratigraphy were made at a time when the cave deposits were already badly despoiled and must represent a considerable simplification. Multi-period occupation will also have introduced major disturbance. Subsequent diggings in the cave have been sporadic and totally lacking in any formal record; finds have been lost and dispersed; no radiometric dating has been attempted, although human remains of potential early Flandrian age survive from the stalagmite.

Potter's Cave, Caldey Island, Dyfed (SS 1436 9707)
Excavated by: van Nédervelde, 1950-3; van Nédervelde and Davies, 1973-4, 1976-7 (Lacaille and Grimes, 1955; van Nédervelde and Davies, 1977b; Davies, 1989b).

Stratigraphy: within part of the cave, a 'red/brown loam' may be of early Flandrian age. Elsewhere within the cave, and on the platform outside, so-called 'basal clays' appear to be of Late Pleistocene age later prehistoric occupation deposits were also present.

Fauna: the only Pleistocene fauna to be reported was found on the platform outside the cave and is said to comprise hyaena, wild horse and woolly rhinoceros; bird remains (identified by D. Bramwell) from the basal clays included goose, peregrine or gyr falcon, puffin, Manx shearwater, pigeon and duck (van Nédervelde and Davies, 1979-80; Davies, 1989a)

Human remains: human bones found within the cave, perhaps representing two individuals, may date to the Iron Age (*ibid.*).

Artefacts: only four flint tools, found during the 1970s, appear to be Lateglacial. These are a 'Penknife' point, a straight- backed blade, a convex-backed blade and a broken retouched blade. The last may be a microlith. All these are illustrated in Fig.2.14. In addition, and also quoted as occurring within a Lateglacial brown clay (but not seen by the author), is a bone implement 79mm long with 'a notch or groove, possibly used for rubbing along a thong, and... one end smoothed into a sharp, narrow blade or scraper'.

Radiometric dating: none.

Problems: the site is complex, with ramifying chambers, narrow passages, and two entrances leading on to the steeply sloping remnant of a platform. It is likely to be a multi-period site and the cave has been used for occupation and burial in later prehistory. The resulting complex stratigraphies lack thorough recording and the recent finds, including those of Lateglacial date, await formal and comprehensive publication.

Plate 2.6: Nanna's Cave, Caldey Island, Dyfed.

Ogof-yr-Ychen, Caldey Island, Dyfed (SS 1465 9691)
Excavated by: van Nédervelde and Davies, 1970-84 (van Nédervelde, 1970b, 1972; van Nédervelde, Davies and John, 1973; Jacobi, 1980b; van Nédervelde and Davies, 1986; Davies 1989b). Plate 2.7.

An attempt to summarize the details of this cave is shown in Table 2.10.

Stratigraphy: see Fig. 2.15. The deeper extremities (Chamber 3 and The Pit) of this small but tortuous cave have been reported to contain 'periglacial rubble mixed with yellow silty clay'. Above these, the main chambers (1, 2 and 4) contained a 'red-brown clay' overlain by an 'undisturbed bone layer', itself overlain by disturbed deposits. A rift (the Blowhole) between chamber 1 and the ground surface also contained an 'undisturbed bone layer'.

Fauna: fauna from the cave identified in 1970 (Bateman, 1973) includes the following: hedgehog, mole, hyaena, ?wild cat, wolf, fox, cave bear, brown bear, badger, woolly rhinoceros, wild pig, red deer, roe deer, reindeer, bison and aurochs. Otter may also have been present.

Human remains: bones from three adults were found in various parts of the cave, as well as those from a juvenile of probable Romano-British date.

Artefacts: some 130 flaked flint or stone artefacts have been found in the cave. The provenance of much of the material is unrecorded. The greater number are of unknown age; the presence amongst these of unpatinated flint and scalar flakes and cores (see Chapter V) implies use of the cave late in prehistory, whilst potsherds of Iron Age and perhaps medieval age were also recovered.

Amongst those pieces which have an approximate provenance and context within the cave (Table 2.10) is at least one Lateglacial backed point (Fig. 2.16, No. 1). This was found near the base of Chamber 4. Adinole and chert artefacts (Fig. 2.5) from the Pit have already been discussed above.

Radiometric dating: 22,340 +620 BP (Birm-340: van Nédervelde *et al.*, 1973) on a woolly rhinoceros scapula found in the Pit.

A sample of human skeletal material from the individual found in Chamber 3, apparently associated with early Mesolithic flintwork (see Chapter III), has been submitted by the author for AMS dating.

Problems: Almost the entire contents of the cave were dug out without supervision and within a period of seven months (June - December, 1970). Records are minimal and fauna and artefacts have become dispersed. Finds from the cave indicate a complex multi-period history and it will

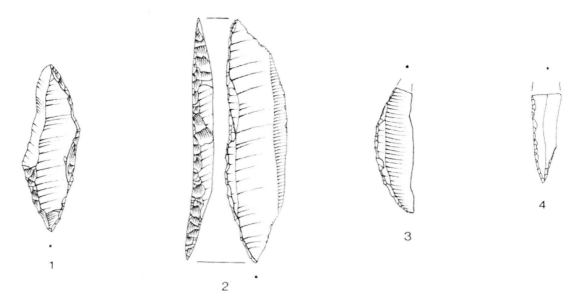

Figure 2.14: Flint artefacts of possible Lateglacial age from Potters Cave, Caldey Island, Dyfed: - 1, "penknife" point; 2, backed blade; 3, convex-backed blade; 4, retouched blade fragment (?microlith). Scale – 1:1.05.

Plate 2.7: Ogof-yr-Ychen, Caldey Island, Dyfed. The figure is standing at one of the cave's entrances, near the opening of The Pit.

	Stratigraphy/ sediments	Fauna	Human remains	Artefacts	'Cultural' presence/dating
'THE BLOWHOLE'	topsoil clay and angular blocks bone layer	deer, sheep/goat	some post-cranial bones from Individual A	1 flint 'blade'	?
CHAMBER 1	soil (in parts) stalagmite (in parts) bone layer red-brown clay	wild cow (ox), bos/bison, badger, fox, fish, small mammals	cranium in roof with some other bones, all from Individual A. Mandible frag from Individual B	4 flint flakes	?
CHAMBER 2	disturbed bone layer undisturbed layer red-brown clay	bos	cranium fragment and other bones from Individual C	3 'geometric' microliths 1 retouched flint blade fragment 1 flint flake 1 utilised stone	Late Mesolithic
CHAMBER 3 'THE ABYSS'	stalagmite periglacial rubble' with yellow silty clay sterile red clay	wild pig – 2 skeletons, red deer, badger, ?otter, fish, wolf	mandible fragment from Individual A. Cranium fragments and other bones from Individual B.	4 'broad blade' microliths 1 piercer 2 flakes all of flint	Early Mesolithic
CHAMBER 4	blown sand (disturbed R-B layer) undisturbed bone layer periglacial rubble with yellow silty clay	deer, sheep/goat, fish, molluscs, fox bos, red deer, roe deer hyaena tooth	some bones from Individual C, and an infant mandible (R-B)	1 flake (R-B layer) 1 retouched flake 1 microlith fragment 1 microlith (bone layer) 1 truncated flake (bone layer) 3 flakes (bone layer) 1 backed fragment (under stalagmite floor) 1 flake (under stalagmite floor) 1 convex-backed blade (red clay) 1 flake fragment (basal silty layer, 20cms from hyaena tooth and near brink of 'The Pit'.	Iron Age Mesolithic Upper Palaeolithic
THE PIT	yellow clay and rubble	hyaena, red deer antler, woolly rhinoceros: 22,350 +620 BP (Birm-340)	none	2 'adinole' flakes 1 chert flake	?EUP/earlier

Table 2.10: an attempted summary of excavation results from Ogof-yr-Ychen, Caldey Island, Dyfed.

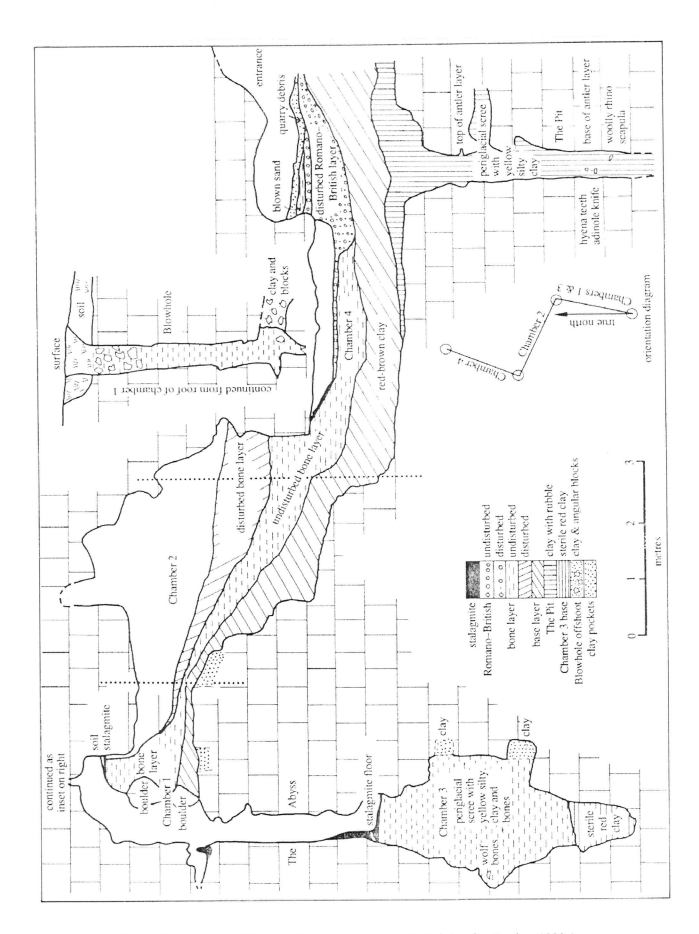

Figure 2.15: section of Ogof-yr-Ychen, Caldey Island, Dyfed. After Davies (1989a).

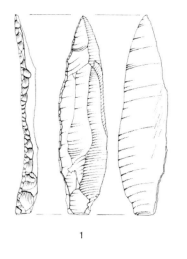
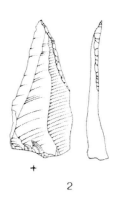

Figure 2.16: Flint artefacts of possible Lateglacial age from Ogof-yr-Ychen (1-2) and "New Cave" (3), Caldey Island, Dyfed. Scale – 1:1.22.

remain uncertain how most of them were introduced into the cave system, an unknown portion of which has been destroyed by quarrying.

New Cave (Ogof-y-Benglog), Caldey Island, Dyfed (SS 1470 9688)
Excavated by: van Nédervelde, 1953, 1969 (van Nédervelde, 1970a; Davies, 1989b)
Stratigraphy: this rock-shelter, as it now remains, may once have been connected with Ogof-yr-Ychen (see above).
The stratigraphy, as observed by van Nédervelde can be summarized (from the surface): blown sand, brown soil containing small limestone rubble fragments and 'midden' material, friable granulated white soil with limpet shells (within the cave only), rubble and clay cemented by stalagmite.
Fauna: some Flandrian species from the surface layers, with 'a few mineralised splinters' from the basal rubble.
Human remains: a human skull and two ribs were found in the midden layer and underlying 'white soil'.
Artefacts: a flint leaf-shaped arrowhead from the midden layer and a fragment of a backed blade (Fig. 2.16, No. 3) from within clay below the compacted rubble. The latter is recorded as lying at a depth of 4.5 feet (1.4m) below the human skull.
Radiometric dating: none

Problems: although the backed blade fragment could well be of Lateglacial age, occurring so deep in the stratigraphy, there is presently no means of confirming this. The 'rock shelter', with the adjacent Ogof-yr-Ychen, is but a remnant of a more extensive cave system, now destroyed by quarrying.

Priory Farm Cave, Dyfed (SM 9789 0184)
Excavated by: A. Hurrell Style and E. E. L. Dixon, 1906-7 (Laws, 1908 ; Grimes, 1933).
Stratigraphy: this is recorded as follows:
 1 - surface earth
 2 - loose clay with rock debris and detritus
 3 - gravel (in the entrance only, and of unknown depth/extent)
 4 - laminated clay (cave interior only)
In addition the remnant of a stalagmite deposit was observed in places, coincident with layer 2.
Fauna: the identified faunal remains are as follows (in stratigraphic order):
 1 - birds, rabbits and small mammals
 2 - bovid, horse and reindeer (from within the cave - ?derived)
 3 - no fauna recorded
 4 - bovid, horse, reindeer, bear, hyaena, wolf and mammoth
Human remains: near the entrance to the inner cave an adult

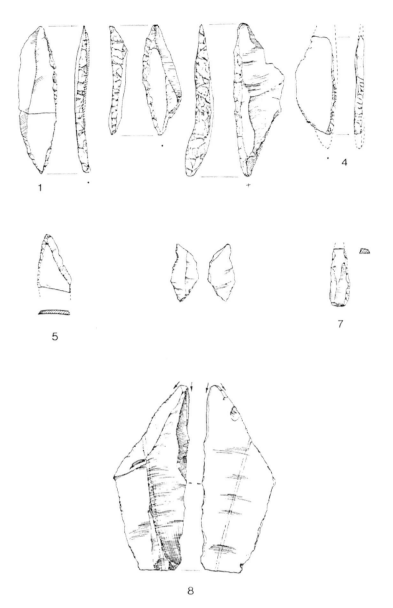

Figure 2.17: Artefacts from Priory Farm Cave, Dyfed. 1-4: "penknife" points; 5-7: backed fragments; 8: burin (chert). Scale – 1:1.45.

human skull and jaw fragment from a juvenile were found in layer 2. The same deposit within the cave produced bones from about three individuals.

Artefacts: a small series of 18 flint and chert artefacts (Fig. 2.17) with 'a small quantity of flakes and spalls of little importance' are recorded from the 'gravel' (layer 3) at the entrance to the cave. Amongst these are four 'Penknife' points, forming a strikingly coherent group, and three fragments of backed blades at least one of which (no. 7) appears to be Mesolithic. The remaining pieces include blades and a burin developed on a pointed flake of Carboniferous chert.

Radiometric dating: none.

Problems: the excavations were never fully recorded and no modern study or re-analysis has been undertaken. The evidence for multi-period occupation belies the apparent simplicity of the stratigraphy and suggests considerable interference amongst the deposits. The apparently

Lateglacial artefacts are without any faunal associations.

Little Hoyle Cave, Longbury Bank, Dyfed (SS 1118 9998) Although most of the deposits from both The Little Hoyle and The Hoyle (see below) were destroyed many years ago (Rolleston *et al.*, 1878; Laws, 1878) more recent excavations at The Little Hoyle (McBurney, 1959) and at The Hoyle's Mouth (Savory, 1973) have provided additional artefacts and information. Yet further excavations by the National Museum of Wales, as part of their 'Palaeolithic Settlement of Wales Research Project', took place at The Little Hoyle in 1984 and at both sites in 1986 (Green, 1986b). Neither site has yet been fully published, and I am grateful to Dr Stephen Green for his co-operation in allowing me to preview some of the assembled data in the following summaries:

Excavated by: Winwood, 1866; Smith, 1870; Power and

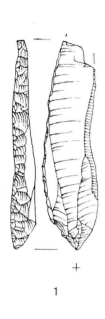

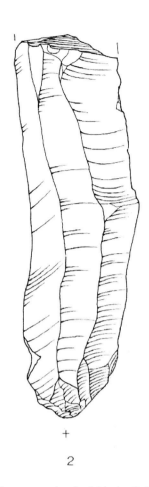

Figure 2.18: Flint artefacts from The little Hoyle Cave, Dyfed; - 1, convex-backed blade; 2, blade. Scale – 1:1.

Laws, 1877; Rolleston, Lane-Fox, Busk, Dawkins, Evans, Hilton-Price, 1878; McBurney, 1958-9, 1963; Green, 1984, 1986.

References: Laws (1879, 1888); Rolleston et al., (1879); McBurney, (1959); Campbell, (1977); Green, (1986b); Rae et al., (1987).

Stratigraphy: platform deposits outside the cave are composed of thermoclastic screes of probable Late Devensian age overlying silts and clays of possible fluvial origin. Within the cave, deposits which include a Devensian fauna are composed of layers of breccia with a silt matrix.

Fauna: excavations in the last century encountered midden deposits with a Holocene fauna. Other finds at this time include mammoth, horse, woolly rhinoceros, bear, red deer, roe deer, eagle and black grouse.

The fauna recovered by McBurney and Green is as follows (from identifications made up until 1984: Currant, 1986b):

Table 2.11: Fauna from The Little Hoyle (1984, 1986).

Platform:

Upper Scree:
    collared lemming, hare
Buff-grey silt:
    reindeer
Silt transition:
    brown bear and ?horse
Stoney silt:
    fox, horse, root vole and cervid
Pink clay:
    bone fragments

North Cave:

Surface:
    bird and frog bones
Green silt with limestone:
    bird bones, ?reindeer,
    collared lemming, Norway
    lemming, water vole,
    narrow-skulled vole,
    shrew and frog
Red sandy silt + limestone:
    brown bear, reindeer,
    fox, collared lemming,
    water vole, narrow-skulled
    vole, hare and fragments
    of large bird bones

Plate 2.8: The Hoyle's Mouth, Dyfed

Human remains: the bones from about 9-11 people were recovered from superficial deposits during 1877-8.

Artefacts: the only diagnostic artefact of Lateglacial appearance is a large convex-backed blade (Fig. 2.18, No. 1) found by McBurney in the Upper Scree near one of the cave entrances. Within the same sediment were 'lumps of charcoal' and the fauna noted above. Other artefacts from the cave, but without reliable stratigraphic provenance, are two flint blades, an adinole scraper and a bone 'bodkin' (Green, 1986b, fig. 28).

Radiometric dating: Uranium Series, radiocarbon and amino-acid racemization determinations are each available for bones of bear and reindeer from the red sandy silt with limestone found within the cave (Rae *et al*., 1987, table 3; and Table 2.3). These results all pre-date any Late-glacial occupation of the cave.

Problems: much of the cave interior was cleared out by earlier excavators. The case for Upper Palaeolithic occupation at the cave rests only on a single artefact and the presence of appropriate prey species, although none of the bone from the latter shows any indication of human interference. The recent excavations have not recovered further diagnostic artefacts and have yet to provide radiometric dating appropriate to the Lateglacial-type backed blade. Further publication is awaited for confirmation of Green's proposal that the Upper Scree and the artefacts from it are of Younger Dryas age (Green, 1986b).

The Hoyle's Mouth, Dyfed (SN 1120 0033)

Only a few minutes walk away from The Little Hoyle is its more prolific and better known neighbour, The Hoyle's Mouth (or The Hoyle). Although its archaeological history is as regrettable as that of all the foregoing cave sites, a relatively substantial artefact collection survives and will be argued here to be of Lateglacial age. The apparent typological integrity of much of the latter, and the promise of continued research by the National Museum of Wales has singled out this particular cave for rather fuller discussion than other Welsh find-spots. Use of the cave in earlier Upper Palaeolithic time has already been noted. The Hoyle's Mouth is a tunnel cave about 40 m. deep and opening northwards to a small platform on a limestone spur directly overlooking the Ritec valley, near Tenby (Plate 2.8). It shares a similar background history to The Little Hoyle and has been the source of numerous finds of fauna and artefacts many of which have been long recognized for their Upper Palaeolithic or 'Creswellian' appearance (Leach, 1918; Garrod, 1926; Savory, 1973).

The nineteenth-century explorers of the site evidently found many of these remains within the inner recesses of the cave (Smith, 1860). Although mammoth has now been shown to have survived the last glacial maximum at least in Derbyshire (Hedges *et. al*., 1988), the presence of woolly rhinoceros and hyaena might suggest that The Hoyle was also open in the early/mid-Devensian. That humans may also have used the cave before the last glacial maximum is

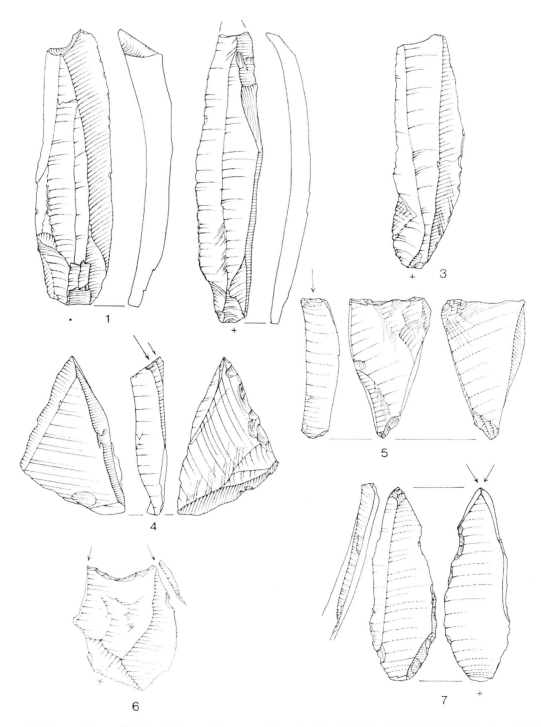

Figure 2.19: Artefacts of "adinole" and other stone from the Hoyle's Mouth, Dyfed: 1-3, blades; 4-7, burins. Scale – 1:1.28.

strongly suggested by recognition of an 'Aurignacian' '*burin busqué*' amongst the Rev. G. N. Smith's collection from The Hoyle and now housed at Tenby Museum (see above). The recent radiocarbon determination on a sample of unidentified animal bone does not have any proven human association:

27,900 ±900 BP (OxA 1024: Hedges *et al.* 1987)

None of the surviving artefactual or faunal material from the site can be related to a satisfactory *in situ* or intact original sediment context. Excavations on the outer platform in 1968 (Savory, 1973) revealed largely mixed deposits containing flint and adinole artefacts probably from spoil which originated within the entrance area and deeper inside the cave. Green's excavations in the entrance in 1986 have recovered further unstratified lithics, again demonstrating the former richness of the site. His investigations suggest that undisturbed basal layers still exist in the entrance and platform areas and may yet provide informative data.

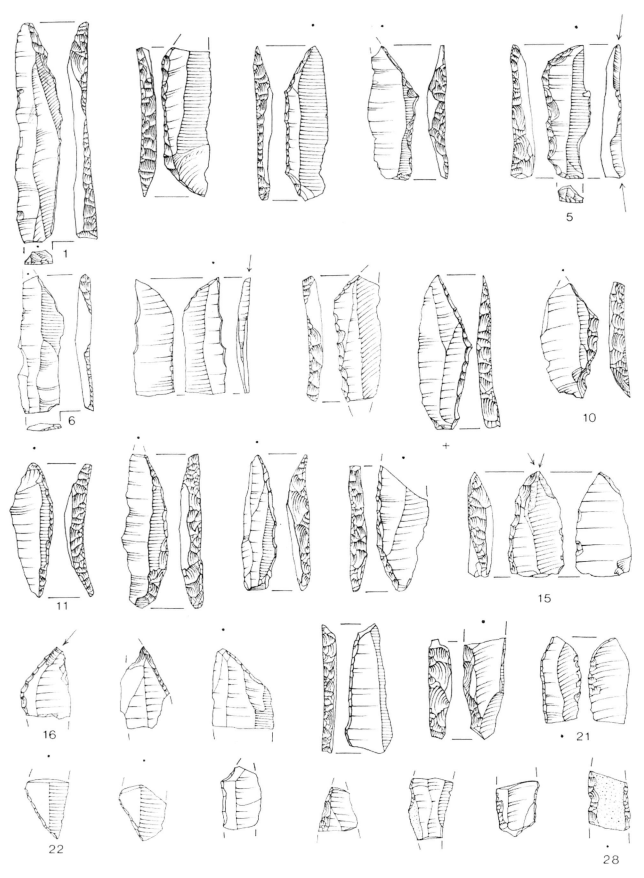

Figure 2.20: Backed blades and fragmentary backed blades from The Hoyle's Mouth, Dyfed: - 1-5, "Cheddar" points; 6, 8, shouldered and truncated blades; 9-10, angle-backed blades; 11-15, convex backed blades; 16-28 unclassifiable fragments. Nos. 5 and 7 have been re-worked as burins. Scale – 1:1.06.

The stone artefacts:

The following collections have been used in assessing the stone artefacts from the cave:

Museum	Excavator	No. of artefacts
Tenby:	G. N. Smith (?and others)	65
	H. N. Savory	134
Cardiff (NMW):	H. S. Green	80
Manchester (M(U)M)):	E. L. Jones	
	W. Boyd Dawkins	60
Bristol (CM):	H. H. Winwood	22

TOTAL: 361

The small collection from Bolton Museum has been excluded as its provenance is uncertain and at least some of the items illustrated by Campbell (1977, Fig.132 nos. 1, 7, 18) can be shown to originate from Kent's Cavern (Jacobi, pers. comm.).

Raw material and condition:

Flint makes up 83% of this collection, and is mostly patinated white. This is particularly true for the blade-like and laminar pieces which were originally of black flint. The smaller unpatinated portion of the group is of an altogether poorer quality flint of beach pebble or 'drift' origin. It varies in colour and, where present, the cortex is consistent with small pebble material.

Of the 60 pieces of flaked stone, apart from flint, 49 are of adinole. This is a metamorphic product of the Cambrian shales of south Wales composed mainly of quartz and albite (Leach, 1918). The flaked surfaces have not undergone any significant physical or chemical modification and show a deep grey-green semi-opaque glassy material with speckly white inclusions. Remnants of the outer surface of the original blocks have a weathered opaque surface penetrating about 2 mm. The morphology of these surfaces and of the primary flakes removed from them suggest that the original raw material was blocky or tabular in shape.

The parent material of 11 of the remaining 12 pieces, previously described as adinole are probably of a different stone. They have a matt surface texture and are opaque dark grey/green in colour. They resemble both the southern Welsh Carboniferous chert and western Welsh extrusive igneous volcanics. Apart from these, there is one piece made of a chalcedonic chert, probably of Cretaceous origin, and not uncommon in local secondary deposits.

The good quality chalk flint, which was apparently the preferred material for most retouched tools, might have been accessible in the Bristol Channel area, although its relative rarity is suggested by the adaptation of broken tools to secondary uses (see below), and by the use of alternative local materials.

Technology:

The largest surviving flakes and blades from the cave are of adinole (Fig. 2.19, Nos. 1-2). Although flawed, it is plain that this material could be worked as dextrously as flint. There are no cores of adinole, and it is possible that these, and other tools of this material, were taken elsewhere. Their absence might of course otherwise result from a bias in the surviving sample of material. It may be significant that no backed implements or scrapers are made of this stone, there being an apparent preference for its use in the manufacture of burins and blades.

Many of the flake and blade fragments of both the main raw material types show features of 'soft' hammer detachment (Ohnuma and Bergman, 1982). There are just four cores, of which the largest is only 4 cms long, of irregular shape with two main platforms, one of which exhibits preparatory faceting and edge-abrasion: it has every appearance of being a worked-out core of the finer quality flint favoured for the manufacture of backed blade blanks. Of the other three cores, one is a fragment and the other two (one on a beach pebble) have more in common with late Mesolithic bladelet cores than with a Lateglacial technology.

The unpatinated and predominantly beach pebble component is characterized by a hard hammer mode, and 3 pieces show clear evidence of scalar core reduction (pièces ecaillées). This latter technology is discussed more fully in chapter V where it suggested that it is typical of post-Mesolithic flintworking. It occurs, along with other evidence of later prehistoric activity, in several of the Dyfed caves.

The retouched tools:

Table 2.12 lists all the recognised tools and tool fragments from the cave. Discounting the 'busked' burin, the microliths and the 'thumbnail' scrapers as irrelevant to the suspected Lateglacial occupation of the cave, we are left with what would appear to be the residue of a formerly numerous and broadly based assemblage in which most of the main contemporary lithic types are represented. There is no significant tool form amongst the very much larger collection at Gough's (New) Cave which is not present at The Hoyle's Mouth. True 'Zinken' and splintered pieces are missing, but all the other forms described by Jacobi (1986, 76- 77) can be identified. It is the close similarity between these two collections which fosters confidence in proposing a broad contemporaneity in the use of the two caves and, by extension, with other sites that also contain this same characteristic suite of stone tools.

The complete and nearly complete backed points (Fig. 2.20) form a clearly defined group made up of angle-backed, trapeziform and convex-backed points, with two shouldered and truncated blades. The outlines of the tools are defined by abrupt retouch which is often bi-directional, indicating the use of an anvil on the thicker portions of some blades. A characteristic noted by Jacobi on some of the Mendip trapeziform ('Cheddar') points is the small protrusion (or gibbosity) at the angle formed by the junction of the lateral retouch and one or both of the oblique transverse truncations. This possibly stylistic feature, distinct at Gough's (New) Cave, can also be seen here (eg Fig. 2.20, Nos. 3-4).

Table 2.12: Composition of the lithic collection from The Hoyle's Mouth, Dyfed.

i) backed blades:

trapeziform blades ('Cheddar' points)	5
angle-backed blades ('Creswell' points)	2
fragments of angle-backed blades	2
obliquely truncated and shouldered blades	2
fragments with oblique truncation	5
convex-backed blades	3
fragments of convex-backed blades	2
obliquely-backed microliths	2
unclassified backed fragments	7

ii) scrapers:

long end-scrapers	5
short end-scrapers	4
broken end-scrapers	7
'thumbnail' scrapers	7

iii) burins:

burins on truncation (1 used as a 'twist drill')	3
angle-burins	2
'burin busqué'	1
?burins	2
(burins on former backed pieces, classed under i)	(2)

iv) other tools:

piercers	3
'twist drills'	3
('twist drill' on burin, classed under iii)	(1)
retouched and truncated pieces	2
retouched pieces	2
retouched/utilized fragments	18
notch at distal end of blade	1

TOTAL of all tools and fragments of tools	90

Notable by their absence at The Hoyle's Mouth are convex-backed blades with an oblique basal truncation - 'penknife' points. That these may be functionally or chronologically separated from assemblages with the other backed tool-types is suggested by their similar absence from the Gough's (New) Cave collection and, in west Wales, their typological isolation at Priory Farm Cave (see above).

The uses of backed blades such as these remains a mystery, although it seems probable that, between them, they fulfilled the function of both knives and projectile armatures in association with hafting devices of wood, bone or antler. The convex-backed points are, if anything, more robust than the other blades, necessitating preparation on an anvil. This is also a feature of their typological counterparts in the French 'Azilian'. Functional analysis of the latter suggests a use as projectile tips (Moss, 1983). Two fragmentary points from The Hoyle's Mouth (Fig. 2.20, Nos. 15-16) exhibit spalling at their tips which, although not diagnostic, might indicate impact damage (Barton and Bergman, 1982; Fischer *et al.*, 1984).

There are 16 end-scrapers, (Fig. 2.21), all of flint, and these may once have been associated with the Lateglacial occupation. Most are broken, but at least four are developed on blades and share, with the shorter examples, a general likeness to items from known Palaeolithic contexts. A semi-abrupt marginal retouch is present on most of the pieces. By analogy with the Mendip material, this marginal modification may be taken as distinguishing these scrapers from early Flandrian artefacts of otherwise similar morphology. One scraper (Fig. 2.21, No. 1), as noted by Garrod (1926), although labelled as coming from The Hoyle's Mouth, is slightly weathered and iron-stained in places. It may therefore be a surface find, as flints are known to have been picked up in the field above and behind the cave.

Burins from the site (eg Fig. 2.19, Nos. 4-7; Fig. 2.20, Nos. 5, 7; Fig. 2.22, Nos. 2-3) show considerably more variety than the other two main tool types described. Two, if not three, raw materials have been used and there is little or no technological or morphological consistency in the group. Most similar to one another are the two pieces, one of which is double-ended, that are interpreted as burins worked on former backed blades (Fig. 2.22, Nos. 2-3). Their narrow burin facets and blade-like proportions are very reminiscent of examples from Gough's (New) Cave (eg. Fig. 2.7, No. 12), and suggest a precise and delicate usage, probably on bone or antler. Our knowledge of the functional roles of burins is so limited, however, that it is not possible to speculate with any real optimism on the contribution of the various implements identified as such at The Hoyle's Mouth. One burin on a truncated flake (Fig. 2.22, No. 1) has clear indications of having been used as piercer - lateral damage to the burin facet and wear showing that the nose of the tool has at one stage has been rotated within the worked material - what Jacobi has nick-named a 'twist-drill'.

Amongst the remaining tools two more 'twist-drills' (Fig. 2.22, Nos. 7, 11) exhibit the same wear and damage as the burin described above. There are three additional piercers. Two flakes and a blade have their distal ends retouched to a narrow prismatic point (Fig. 2.22, Nos. 4-6). Other formal tools that can be recognized amongst the remaining miscellaneous items include a blade and a fragment (Fig. 2.22, Nos. 9, 12) which show extensive semi-abrupt marginal retouch with a distal truncation. There is also the heavily worn proximal end of a broken retouched flake or blade (Fig. 2.22, No. 10).

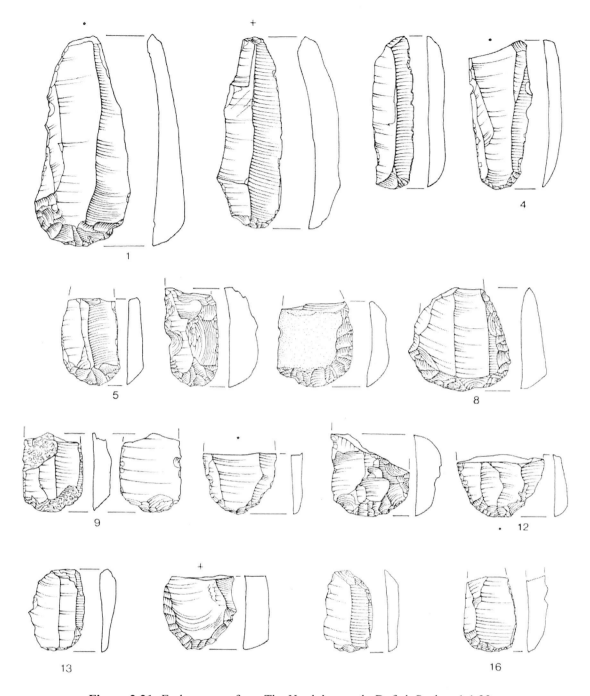

Figure 2.21: End-scrapers from The Hoyle's mouth, Dyfed. Scale – 1:1.23.

On the grounds of surface condition and typology two obliquely-backed microliths and a notched proximal bladelet fragment or miss-hit are believed to be Mesolithic. More recent still are the seven 'thumbnail' scrapers which might be more comfortably associated with later prehistoric activity suggested by the reports of stone and metal 'celts' found in the cave in 1840.

By-products and debitage:

These can be described as follows:

By-products:	miss-hit	1
	'Krukowski' piece	1
	burin-spalls	5
Debitage:	cores	4
	scalar cores/flakes	2
	split pebble	1
	flakes/blades/fragments	267

49

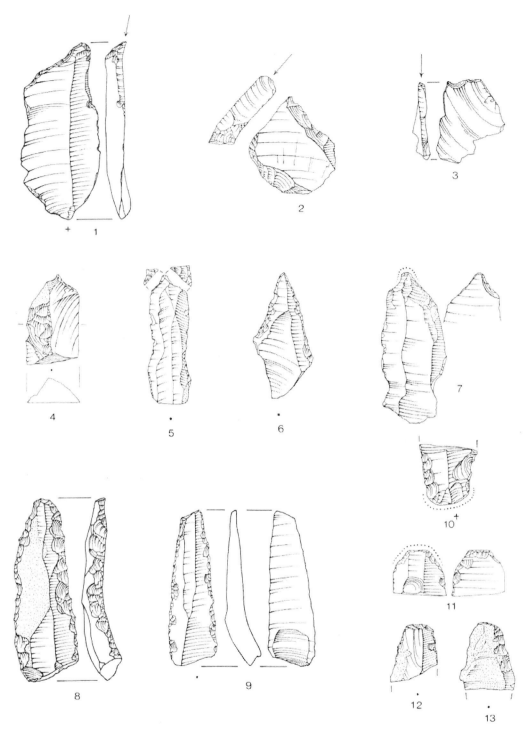

Figure 2.22: Flint artefacts from The Hoyle's mouth, Dyfed: - 1, burin (used as "twisted-drill"); 2-3, atypical burins; 4-6, piercers; 7, 11, "twisted-drills"; 8, retouched blade; 9, 12, retouched; 13, retouched fragment. Scale – 1:1.28.

8. The Late Upper Palaeolithic in Wales - Discussion

Scrutiny of the database outlined in the previous section illustrates only too clearly the shortcomings which any inquiry into Welsh Lateglacial archaeology must come up against. These limitations may be listed as follows:

1. Bias towards cave locations,
2. Inadequate recording of context and association,
3. Incomplete recovery and survival of faunal and artefactual material,
4. Lack of radiometric dating, and
5. Lack of fresh data.

By way of summary, the following table attempts to score the listed find-spots in terms of the 'credibility value' of each of the main categories of evidence. Simplistic though this exercise is, it nevertheless serves to emphasize the very insecure basis currently available for establishing a Lateglacial archaeology for Wales.

Table 2.13: A review of evidence for Late Upper Palaeolithic activity in Wales and adjacent areas.

Find-spot	Artefacts	Stratigraphy	Fauna	Flora	C14 Dating	Summary
Lynx Cave	*	?	*	-	-	*
Ogof Tan-y-Bryn	*	?	-	-	-	*
Plas-yn-Cefn	**	?	*	-	-	**
Kendrick's Cave	***	?	***	-	10,000 BP	***
Paviland Cave	***	?	**	-	-	***
Cathole Cave	***	**	***	*	-	***
Worm's Head Cave	*	?	**	-	-	*
Carn Fach, Rhigos	?	-	-	-	-	?
Gwernvale	*	-	-	-	-	*
Porth-y-Waen	***	-	-	-	11,390 BP	***
King Arthur's Cave	***	***	***	-	-	***
Arrow Court	**	-	-	-	-	**
Nanna's Cave	***	*	-	-	-	***
Potter's Cave	***	?	*	-	-	***
Ogof-yr-Ychen	***	*	**	-	-	***
'New Cave'	*	?	-	-	-	*
Priory Farm Cave	***	*	**	-	-	***
Little Hoyle Cave	**	***	***	***	-	**
Hoyle's Mouth	***	?	**	-	-	***

KEY:
- ? = uncertain
- * = possible
- ** = probable
- *** = certain

The above table underlines the reliance placed on the recognition of apparently distinctive artefact types (backed blades) co-located with a Lateglacial-type fauna. Only in a very few instances do either stratigraphy or radiometric dating contribute any certain confirmation of Late Upper Palaeolithic status. However, re-evaluation of some of this problematic Welsh data can be achieved by extrapolating from recent results of research - particularly AMS dating - from elsewhere in Britain, notably Cheddar and Creswell.

A significant outcome of this latter process has been that the title of 'Creswellian', previously so often applied merely intuitively to single finds or groups of Welsh artefacts, can now be more tightly defined in both technological and temporal terms.

The group of flint and stone artefacts from The Hoyle's Mouth, although small by comparison, accurately reflects the range of 'Creswellian' types represented at Gough's (New) Cave, Cheddar - so much so, indeed, that it becomes a temptation to speculate that the same artesans were responsible for both sets of material. That from The Hoyle's Mouth, albeit probably a fraction of what once existed, is still one of the largest collections available from the British Lateglacial. Having extracted all apparently later prehistoric items and unsatisfactorily classified fragments from the overall total of 361 lithic pieces, one is nevertheless left with a possible total of 52 tools of Late Upper Palaeolithic character - a figure only exceeded by that for the open air site at Hengistbury Head, and at Kent's Cavern, Gough's

(New) Cave, Robin Hood's Cave and Mother Grundy's Parlour. Stone tools in use at The Hoyle include scrapers, piercers, burins, drills, and backed blades.

By analogy with the recent results from Gough's (New) Cave, this material, and elements of it recognized from elsewhere in Wales, can now reasonably be predicted to date approximately to *c.* 12,800 - 12,000 BP. It thus represents the earliest evidence for exploitation of the region following the glacial maximum, and coincides with the relative climatic prosperity at the height of the Lateglacial Interstadial.

Taking the analogy with Cheddar further, one may suggest that horses, red deer and wild cattle were hunted and hares trapped. Even an occasional mammoth, stranded perhaps by the unusually rapid shifts in climatic conditions, may have been sought for its ivory.

Certainly, too little is presently understood of the mosaic of habitats and ecologies that must have swiftly succeeded each other, or co-existed, across Britain at this time. If realistic, the distribution of 'Creswellian' finds (exemplified by 'Cheddar' points: Jacobi, 1980a, fig. 2.13) would suggest that hunters were attracted to the fringes of upland and westerly regions, to refuges conveniently situated with access to a diversity of habitats and raw material sources. Finds of single or small numbers of angle-backed and trapeziform blades in caves suggest the caching of 'insurance gear' (Binford, 1979) or the repair of equipment at 'task sites' near outlying hunting areas, whilst the few larger and more elaborate artefact assemblages; ('passive' or 'seasonal gear') could be taken to imply longer-term craft-based occupation additional to local hunting. The Hoyle's Mouth, with its different types of processing tools as well as evidence for their manufacture, could perhaps be tentatively identified with the latter, whilst The Little Hoyle or Nanna's Cave might represent contemporary tactical use of subsidiary sites.

As will be seen from discussion in later chapters, despite the extensive fieldwork that has been carried out in west Wales over the last 75 years, there are no surface finds of Palaeolithic material from outside the limestone caves and crevices of southern Dyfed. This is probably a simple reflection of the accessibility of cultural debris within caves, rather than any dearth of sites or of hunting activity out in the open. Both Lateglacial and Holocene geomorphological processes, in addition to extensive marine transgression, will have removed most Upper Palaeolithic 'signatures' from the present landscape. The vast accumulations of Mesolithic flintwork found along the present coasts do, however, draw attention to the maritime side of the prehistoric economy, an aspect which for the Late Palaeolithic has been almost entirely eliminated by subsequent sea level rise.

Such a situation seriously limits the potential for establishing satisfactory economic models for the latter period in Wales.

In south Wales, as elsewhere, significant climatic deterioration set in around 12,100 BP (Lowe and Lowe, 1989). Tree and shrub cover - especially birch - was then at its greatest extent but came to be progressively replaced by herb-dominated vegetation at the approach of ever colder stadial conditions. Environmental conditions during this transition need not have been so harsh as to deter a continuing human presence, however, although direct evidence for this in Wales, as for Britain, is very sparse. The chance find, isolated though it is, of the Porth-y-Waen barbed point (11,390 +120 BP: OxA-1946) must nevertheless strongly suggest that Wales was exploited to some degree at this time, and reiterates the point made earlier - that evidence for exploitation of the open landscape, away from caves, is likely to be particularly elusive. The fortuitous location of potentially Late Upper Palaeolithic flints below the cairn at Gwernvale, undated though these are, again points to the probability that open-air activity was indeed significant and remains almost totally invisible to us.

There is, as yet, no direct data from Wales that can indicate the nature of any lithic technology in use during the transition period of c. 12,000 - 11,000 BP. It has already been proposed (above) that such a technology was different from the 'Creswellian', insofar as 'Penknife' points are introduced and appear to replace angle-backed and trapeziform points, whilst scrapers are noticeably shorter

and rounder in shape than earlier end-of-blade types. The nearest site that allows some speculation that this might be true for Wales is King Arthur's Cave in Herefordshire. Here, remains of red deer from the 'Yellow Rubble' and 'Second Hearth' on the platform in front of the cave would appear to date close to c. 12,200 BP (Hedges et al., 1989). However, other fauna apparently from the same units includes open landscape types such as horse, steppe pika and lemming - suggestive, perhaps, of accumulation still later in time. Lithic remains from the uppermost unit - the 'Yellow Rubble' - are of particular interest since angle-backed or trapeziform blades appear to be absent. Instead, there are small straight-backed blades (Taylor, 1928, fig. 6) together with a 'Penknife' point (Fig. 2.12, No. 1), both types which are conspicuously absent from Gough's (New) Cave and The Hoyle's Mouth.

Further west, it may be significant, too, that 'Penknife' points are exclusive of angle-backed and trapeziform blades at Priory Farm Cave and also at Potter's Cave, both locations suitable for caching hunting equipment. Nanna's Cave, by contrast, once contained evidence for lengthy human occupancy, including a wider range of flint tools with backed elements of both 'Penknife' and 'Creswell' type. This rockshelter has a sheltered eastward aspect and sizeable platform commanding extensive views over formerly dry land, and one should not be surprised that it has probably served as a temporary base on many occasions, leaving behind a succession of cultural residues.

During the Younger Dryas itself Wales experienced a climatic regime reminiscent of the rigours of the glacial maximum. Extreme winter temperatures may have descended to -25 C. the timing of this event in south Wales has been shown at Traeth Mawr to fall between dates of 10,620 +100 BP and 9,970 +115 BP (Walker, 1980), giving a duration of some 650 years. At Llanilid, also in south Wales, the equivalent event falls between dates of 11,160 +70 BP and 9,920 +65 BP (Walker and Harkness, 1990), confirming that harsh conditions had already set in by 11,000 BP. For west Wales, the start of the Younger Dryas remains undated, although evidence of annual sediment laminae from basal deposits in a kettle hole at Dolau-duon, Dyfed, suggest a duration of at least 400 years (Donald, 1987).

Exploitation of this stadial environment by Palaeolithic hunters is uncertain for Wales, although the supposition that they did so must be strengthened by rare finds of seemingly contemporary artefacts in eastern England (Table 2.6). Although the composition of the Welsh fauna is unclear at this time, one may argue - as for the glacial maximum (see above) - that if appropriate animals were indeed present, then so may have been their human predators. If this was so, there is still little idea, as yet, of the likely appearance of the lithic components of the latters' tool kits and therefore whether or not these are present amongst artefacts from Welsh sites: claims for the presence of stadial deposits in the archaeological sequence at Cathole (Campbell, 1977) are disputed (Jacobi, 1980a, 57-8) and any contemporary occupation at this cave must remain undemonstrated.

Assuming Britain to have been on the periphery of hunting territories during the coldest parts of the stadial (Buckland, 1984) one is necessarily forced to look to contemporary NW European evidence in any speculation about British flint technology at the time. In particular, attention has been drawn to similarities between Ahrensburgian lithic assemblages (Taute, 1968) and occasional finds in Britain of tanged points, as well as certain 'long-blade assemblages' such as that at Avington VI in the Kennet valley (Barton and Froom, 1986; Barton, in press). The Ahrensburgian-type tanged points are thought to represent arrow tips, perhaps lost in the pursuit of reindeer, whilst the long-blade assemblages with their characteristic 'bruised' blades (*lames machurées*) appear to indicate very task-specific knapping episodes associated perhaps with butchery or antler-working.

Whilst there have been claims for the recognition of Ahrensburgian-type points from as far away as Tiree, off the west coast of Scotland (Morrison and Bonsall, 1989), the 'long-blade' industries seem restricted to lowland eastern and southern England. Neither type has been recognized amongst the Welsh find-spots so far described, although one location might be cited very tentatively as potentially of 'long-blade' association: only five artefacts are involved and these are flakes and blade fragments of volcanic tuff from the clifftop at Parwyd, Aberdaron, Gwynedd (SH 154 244: Davies, 1962). All are of substantial size, and one of the two larger blades has a heavily damaged edge, evidently bruised and crushed through usage (*lame machurée*). Whilst similar artefacts of flint have been argued to date to the very end of the Devensian (Jacobi, 1982, 12) it is also contended that their occurrence may extend into earliest Holocene time (Barton, in press; below, Chapter III). Dating, however, remains insecure.

Wales does however provide one certain instance of terminal Devensian human activity, and this is at Kendrick's (Upper) Cave, on the Great Orme, Llandudno, Clwyd (SH 7800 8283). Here, a horse mandible, decorated with four groups of incised chevron ornament (Plate 2.4), has provided an AMS determination of 10,000 ±200 BP (OxA-111: Gillespie *et. al.*, 1985).

Little information can now be retrieved concerning this find, made in about the 1870s (Sieveking, 1971). It was apparently recovered with a second but undecorated mandible, and these may have been associated with two perforated and decorated bear canines (now lost), and nine similarly modified bovid and deer teeth. Portions of three adult human skeletons and that of a child are also reported (Dawkins, 1880, 156; Eskrigge, 1880, 154), and more recently a perforated and incised wolf tooth has been found in the cave (Davies, 1978, 1983). There would thus seem to be strong circumstantial evidence that the cave may once have formed a Late Palaeolithic burial site.

The dating of this burial coincides precisely with the formal division between the Pleistocene and the Holocene. Basal Holocene organic sediments have now been dated at several Welsh pollen-sampling sites, most of which are synchronous at about 10,000 BP (see Chapter III, Table 3.2). Climatic warming from about this time was so abrupt (Dansgaard *et al.*, 1989) that amelioration may have briefly outpaced the ingress of woodland, thereby encouraging survival into the early Holocene of mammal species such as reindeer and horse (Clutton-Brock and Burleigh, 1983). That wild horse was still a target for hunting at this time is confirmed, for eastern England, by AMS dates on the teeth and a mandible of this species, associated with a scatter of some 700 flints, at Three Ways Wharf, Uxbridge, Middlesex (Lewis, 1989; in press):

10,270 +100 BP (OxA-1778)
10,010 +120 BP (OxA-1902)

Amongst the flints found with the horse (and reindeer) remains at this site were six obliquely backed points of broadly Mesolithic type, but these were apparently in association with a technology more typical of 'long-blade assemblages': a *lame machurée*, opposed-platform cores and blades with facetted butts. No microburins were found.

Finds such as these, and especially those from Kendrick's Cave, must, at the very least, go some way to encouraging the belief that Wales was indeed fully exploited at the end of the Devensian and that, with future fieldwork and research, further evidence for this may be forthcoming.

CHAPTER III

THE EARLY FLANDRIAN (10,000 – *c.* 8,500 BP)

1. Introduction

Between about 10,200 and 10,000 BP a sustained and rapid climatic amelioration withdrew tundra conditions northwards. Throughout Britain and contiguous Europe, the climatic improvement allowed the immigration of an ever more thermophilous flora until a fully temperate environment was established. With the returning woodland came a diverse fauna including red and roe deer, wild cattle, wild pig, and elk.

This chapter looks in more detail at the first two millennia of the Flandrian and for the evidence of an early Mesolithic exploitation of Wales. It will be argued that the latter can be identified by the recognition of a distinctive flint and stone technology.

2. The Late Devensian/Flandrian transition

On the European mainland the transition to full Flandrian temperate conditions is complicated by minor fluctuations in which a cold sub-stage succeeds the initial postglacial warming of *c.* 10,200 BP (Behre, 1967; van der Hammen, 1971). Warmer and more oceanic conditions only returned in the mid pre-Boreal (Zone IV: *sensu* Godwin, 1975) at *c.* 9,800 - 9,600 BP. In Britain, however, warming appears to have been pronounced and rapid, the effects of which were felt even as far north as Scotland by *c.* 10,200 BP (Walker and Lowe, 1980). Soon after *c.* 10,000 BP most parts of the British Isles supported at least some open woodland in which birch was the most common species. Significant pollen frequencies of pine in the south and east of the country, represented an extension of a broad north European zone of birch-pine woodland. Other tree species such as hazel, willow and poplar were not uncommon. Climate was rather continental, anticyclonic, with warming summers contrasting with still cold winters (Lamb *et. al*, 1966).

Sea level, although now rising fast at a rate of some 1.8 cm. per year owing to the addition of large volumes of glacial meltwater, was still very low (Morner, 1969). Recent estimates indicate sea levels rising from about -60m at 10,000 BP (Fairbanks, 1989). Marine incursion was constantly changing the character and outline of coasts, yet vast areas of coastal lowland remained exposed around much of the European sea-board. Ireland was by this time insulated from mainland Scotland, but the southern North Sea was still largely dry south of the latitude of the Humber estuary (Jelgersma, 1961). The Rhine-Meuse, flowed into an enlarging sea basin between East Anglia and Holland connecting to the Atlantic through a narrow channel between the Straits of Dover.

Taken together, climate-induced changes were effecting very considerable geographical and biological disruption to Britain and adjoining Europe. It has already been suggested in the previous chapter that climatic warming at *c.* 10,000 BP may have been so rapid as to outpace the immigration of dense woodland and perhaps therefore to account for the continuing presence into the Holocene of fauna such as horse and reindeer. A related phenomenon may be the postulated extension of Final Devensian human subsistence patterns and their associated lithic technologies into the early centuries of the Holocene (Barton, in press). Evidence that this might be the case rests with the still insecure attribution of certain 'long-blade assemblages' in Britain and abroad to *c.* 10,000 BP, or thereabouts (*ibid.*), and that none of the very different early Mesolithic assemblages (see below) can yet be dated to before *c.* 9,700 BP. Clearly, the ecological reactions to the dramatic climatic shifts of this transitional period are very complex and demand further detailed bio-chronostratigraphic study before the human response to them can be more completely understood.

A further complication, to arise out of recent calibration studies of the radiocarbon record (Becker and Kromer, 1986; in press), suggests that major atmospheric variations in C-14 have resulted in radiocarbon ages remaining constant for several centuries at a time. Such 'plateaux' in the radiocarbon timescale apparently occur at the crucial times of *c.* 10,000 BP and *c.* 9,600 BP and could each last for over 250 years. The implications of such anomalies must represent a serious set-back for the establishment of both archaeological and palaeoenvironmental chronologies for these periods, adding yet further need for caution in the already hazardous interpretation of radiocarbon data. Greater consideration must no doubt now be given to resorting to alternative dating methods, such as thermoluminescence (TL). For the time-being, however, existing timescales provide the only framework for discussion.

3. The early Mesolithic in Britain and Europe

After 10,000 BP, then, and against a background of woodland expansion and extensive land connections with the Low Countries, the first 'Forest Cultures' (Childe, 1931) expanded swiftly and widely over large territories of accessible NW Europe.

Most striking in an examination of the early Mesolithic of NW Europe is its apparent uniformity. Although preservation in the archaeological record is highly variable, there is an unmistakable homogeneity amongst the material remains, especially of flint, on living sites dating from *c.* 9,700 - 8,500 BP. Such typological links exist over most of northern Europe, from Wales to western Poland and from Yorkshire and southern Sweden to Cornwall and the Low Countries (Jacobi, 1976, fig. 4, appendix 1). It has been argued (Clark, 1975; and see above) that this fundamental homogeneity had its origins in the preceding Lateglacial occupation of broad territories of the north European plain.

For Britain and neighbouring Europe the 'techno-complex' (Clarke, 1968, 188) that emerges, from whatever hypothetical source, consists mostly of blade-based lithic assemblages amongst which a consistent feature is the presence of simple microlithic armatures. The earliest of such assemblages have so far been dated to *c.* 9,700 BP and these recur, with only slight modification to their retouched components, throughout the next millennium. The noticeable synchroneity in radiocarbon determinations at about this time might, however, be partly a misleading result of local anomalies in the radiocarbon timescale (see above). This caution accepted, a selection of relevant radiocarbon determinations are listed below:

Table 3.1: Selected radiocarbon dates for British and European early Mesolithic flint assemblages.

Site	Date (BP)	Lab No.	Ref.
Thatcham IV (S. England)	9,760 +120	(OxA-732)	1
Thatcham IV (S. England)	9,490 +110	(OxA-894)	1
Star Carr (N. England)	9,700 +160	(OxA-1176)	2
Star Carr (N. England)	9,500 +120	(OxA-1154)	2
Seamer Carr C (N. England)	9,350 +50	average of 7	unpub.
Seamer Carr K (N. England)	9,575 +80	average of 2	unpub.
Duvensee 8 (Germany)	9,490 +55	average of 5	3
Duvensee 2 (Germany)	9,340 +80	average of 2	3
Duvensee 1 (Germany)	9,150 +80	average of 2	3
Duvensee 6 (Germany)	9,090 +90	average of 2	3
Friesack (Germany)	9,590 (Phase 1)	average of 9*	4
Friesack (Germany)	9,240 (Phase 2)	average of 8*	4
Friesack (Germany)	8,960 (Phase 3)	average of 18*	4
Draved 604 (S. Jutland)	9,390 +120	(K-1466)	5
Draved 604 (S. Jutland)	8,790 +140	(K-1794)	6
Klosterlund (N. Jutland)	8,920 +140	(K-1315)	5

References:
1 : Gowlett *et al.*, 1987
2 : Cloutman and Smith, 1988
3 : Willkomm, 1981
4 : Gramsch and Kloss, 1989
5 : Tauber, 1970
6 : Tauber, 1973

* no combined standard deviation has been quoted by the excavator for the Friesack averages.

The common factors within the lithic artefact assemblages from such sites have been discussed by Jacobi (1976) and Clark (1975). Perhaps the most distinctive is the presence of a range of large and 'broad' (>8mm: for a definition of the term 'broad blade' see Mellars and Radley, 1964) backed bladelets dominated by (non-geometric) obliquely-backed forms, alongside varying proportions of large isosceles, scalene, and bi-truncated trapezoidal pieces. Examples from Duvensee 6 and Seamer Carr are illustrated in Figs. 3.1 and 3.2. Such backed bladelets - or microliths - are usually defined by the deliberate removal and discard of the proximal (bulbar) end of the bladelet. The remaining bladelet fragment may then be modified by further retouch or truncation to any of the shapes mentioned above (Jacobi, 1978, 16). Such microliths are usually accompanied by end-scrapers and burins and sometimes by axes or adzes. Serrated or micro-denticulated blades and narrow steeply trimmed awls (*mèches de forêt*: Clark, 1975, 108, fig. 11),

as well as utilised flakes and blades may occur. Distinctive organic artefacts such as elk antler 'mattocks' (Clark, 1975, map 10) and uniserially barbed points of bone and antler (Verhart, 1988) have also been noted to be a part of this 'techno-complex'.

The richness in preserved organic remains on so many of these European sites (eg Friesack: Gramsch and Kloss, 1989), has allowed a reconstruction of subsistence and technology which in Britain can only be matched at Star Carr, N. Yorkshire (Clark, 1952; 1970). Here, occupation near the water's edge of the former glacial Lake Pickering, appears to have taken place on a seasonal basis on one or more occasions at *c.* 9,500 BP, or later. Abundant flint debris included a range of simple and large microliths with scrapers, burins, *mèches de forêt*, serrated blades and transversely sharpened axes or adzes. Amongst the organic artefacts found with these were parts of some 187 barbed

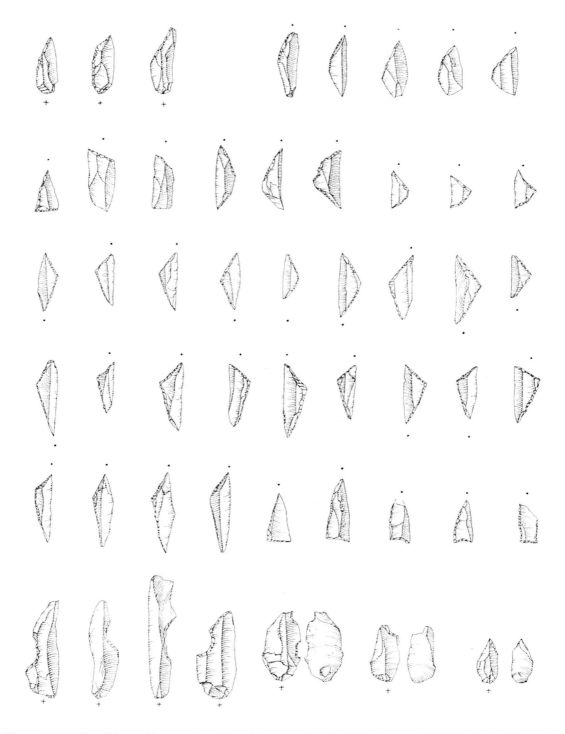

Figure 3.1: Microliths and by-products from Duvensee 6 (after Bokelmann, 1977, fig. 4). Scale – 1:1.2.

antler or bone projectile points, elk antler 'mattocks', 'bodkins', bone scraping tools, rolls of birch bark, and the blade of a wooden paddle. Although no fish remains were recovered, waterfowl were identifiable, as were a variety of woodland mammals. Of the latter, wild cattle, red deer, roe deer, elk and wild pig were certainly prey animals whose contribution to diet could well have been complemented by a wide range of local plant species. Pierced red deer antler masks or head- pieces, amber and tooth pendants, and 27 shale beads are a rare British instance of the preservation of items of adornment and possibly ritual.

Regrettably, the full extent of this site was not fully investigated and all its components may now not be recoverable (although current re-investigation may improve this picture: Mellars, pers. comm.). Re-interpretation of the excavated residues has lead to various commentaries on the nature of the occupation and its apparent seasonal nature (Clark, 1970; Caulfield, 1978; Pitts, 1979; Andreson *et al.*, 1981; Legge and Rowley-Conwy, 1988). Regardless of these differing views it must be conceded that a clear resemblance is shared between residues from Star Carr and those from many other sites, and that this shared similarity

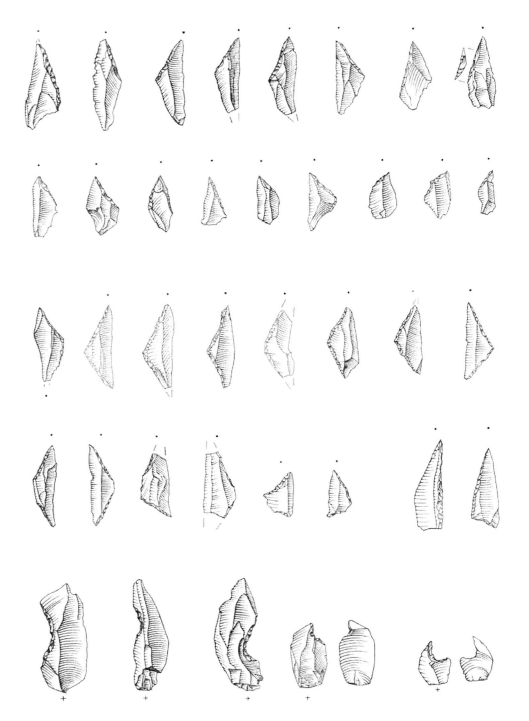

Figure 3.2: Microliths and by-products from Seamer Carr, N Yorks. Scale – 1:1.26.

places Star Carr within the extensive early Mesolithic 'techno-territory' identified widely across NW Europe.

In the following sections attention can now be turned to the specific evidence that links Wales within this same 'techno-territory', dealing first with the environmental background, then establishing a site-based chronology, and finally describing the remaining evidence for other contemporary settlement in Wales.

4. The environment in Wales during the early Mesolithic
The Devensian/Flandrian transition is usually marked in sediment profiles as a distinct change from a minerogenic to a more organic stratigraphy indicative of rapid stabilization of the landscape. At about the same time, or slightly later, pollen diagrams indicate an expansion of juniper in response to climatic amelioration. In Wales these events are dated close to 10,000 BP at many locations, although varying slightly with topography (S. Lowe, 1981; Taylor, 1980). Radiocarbon determinations for this event can be listed as follows:

Table 3.2: Radiocarbon determinations for Devensian/Flandrian transition, or basal Flandrian horizons, from Welsh pollen sites.

Pollen site	Date	Lab No	Ref
Traeth Mawr, Powys	9,970 +115 BP		1
Traeth Mawr, Powys	10,030 +100 BP		1
Snowdonia	9,930 +120 BP		2
Snowdonia	10,030 +100 BP		2
Llyn Gwernan, Gwynedd	10.040 +80 BP	(SRR-1700)	3
Llyn Gwernan, Gwynedd	10,020 +130 BP	(SRR-1702)	3
Llyn Gwernan, Gwynedd	10,400 +130 BP	(OxA-240)*	4
Cledlyn, Dyfed	10,060 +380 BP		5
Cledlyn, Dyfed	10,080 +320 BP		5
Cledlyn, Dyfed	10,170 +220 BP		5
Tregaron, Dyfed	10,200 +200 BP		6
Cilgwyn, Dyfed	10,090 +240 BP	(GU-1328)	7
Hendre Fach, Dyfed	10,145 +195 BP	(GU-1393)	7
Llanilid, Glamorgan	9,920 +65 BP	(SRR-3463)	8

References:
1 : Walker, 1980
2 : Ince, 1983
3 : S. Lowe, 1981
4 : J. Lowe and S. Lowe, 1989
5 : Handa and Moore, 1976
6 : Hibbert and Switsur, 1976
7 : Donald, 1987
8 : Walker and Harkness, 1990

*This date is believed to be *c.* 400 years too early (Lowe and Lowe, 1989).

In west Wales a diverse range of herb species (grasses, sedges and docks) were prevalent at the very beginning of the Flandrian succession, colonising and stabilizing the bare soils of the Younger Dryas landscape. A heathland scenery would have developed, including rich grassland, and giving way subsequently to increasing domination by juniper - an event apparently occurring within a few hundred years, at most, of the first signs of amelioration.

The growth of juniper is usually short-lived, succumbing to the invasion of extensive birch woods, with hazel and local pine, willow and alder stands, for instance at Tregaron, (Hibert and Switsur, 1976), Clarach (Taylor, 1973) and Gwarllyn (Moore, 1972). In western Dyfed, however, the end of the early Flandrian juniper phase cannot be explained by this 'shading out' mechanism, and a reversion to open habitat conditions here may be related to temporary climatic deterioration. Such an event could perhaps correlate with the slight cooling in mean annual temperatures observed in the coleopteran record (Donald, 1987; Atkinson *et al.* 1987). When birch eventually arrived, relatively late here, at or after *c.* 9,400 BP, it had only a limited distribution on the western Dyfed plateau, probably due to exposure (Donald, 1987).

The following expansion of hazel in west Wales has attracted attention, in particular, owing to its early appearance in the pollen profile from Tregaron Bog, dated to *c.* 9,750 BP (Hibbert and Switsur, 1976). Also, at Mynydd Bach, west of Tregaron, hazel starts to rise before the juniper peak. A possible implication of these early occurrences of hazel is that the species had survived the extreme conditions of the Younger Dryas on the exposed lowlands of Cardigan Bay and south-west Wales, and was thus well placed for an early colonisation away from such *refugia* at the earliest climatic opportunity (Moore, 1972, 1987). Both sea and air temperatures are believed to have contributed to a markedly early climatic response in exactly these south-western Welsh coastal lowland zones (Taylor, 1973). Despite this attractive proposal, and its implications for human exploitation, the main expansion of hazel occurs more generally at *c.* 9,000 BP (Smith and Pilcher, 1973). Indeed, dating of this event at Llyn Gwernan, Nant Ffrancon in Wales, Coolteen in SW Ireland and Hawks Tor in Devon falls within the period 9,000 - 9,100 BP, suggesting a marked synchroneity in the south-western region (S. Lowe, 1981; Donald, 1987).

From about this time, therefore (equivalent to pollen Zone V (*sensu* Godwin, 1975)), hazel, with birch, expanded to dominate an increasing range of woodland species. Considerable local variety is indicated in the contemporary landscape: for instance there is some evidence for the expansion of ericaceous species on the Prescellies (Donald,

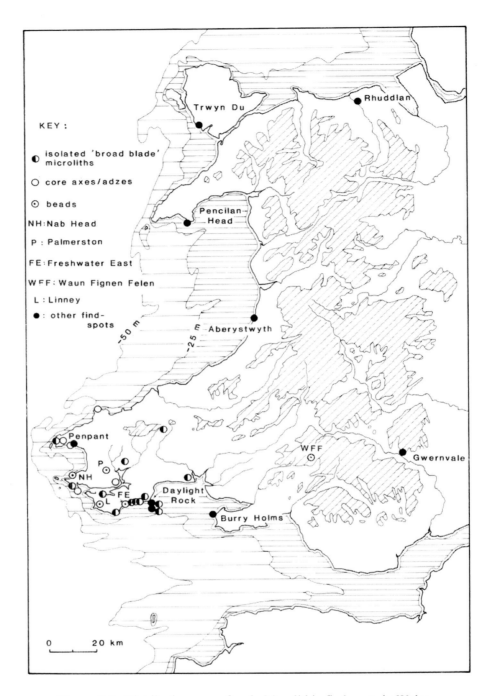

KEY:

◑ isolated 'broad blade' microliths

○ core axes/adzes

⊙ beads

NH: Nab Head

P : Palmerston

FE: Freshwater East

WFF: Waun Fignen Felen

L : Linney

● : other find-spots

Figure 3.3: Distribution map of early Mesolithic find-spots in Wales.

1987). Elsewhere oak and elm were present although not yet significant. With Zone VIa hazel reached its maximum throughout Wales and in the lowlands birch declined in favour of oak, elm and pine, with pine and birch predominating on higher ground. In Zone VIb hazel and birch both declined, with hazel surviving in the understory and pine in the uplands. In Zone VIc alder and lime arrived, particularly near the coast (Taylor, 1980). In western Dyfed, mixed alder-oak-elm forest became established in sheltered valley locations although elm may not have been able to compete in the more exposed areas (Donald, 1987).

As noted in the discussion of environmental change during the Lateglacial in Chapter II, any transformation in

vegetation over the Welsh landscape is likely to have been very variable at local and regional scales owing to relatively small-scale changes in factors such as elevation, soil type and aspect: abrupt changes in environment are still a distinctive feature there today.

Despite the influence of local conditions, however, the major component of change was climate. The successive phases of climatic warming during the pre-Boreal and Boreal were dominated by a continental type of regime with relatively low precipitation, low humidity, with a somewhat pronounced seasonal contrast between hard winters and short but warm summers. The Welsh uplands were relatively late to respond to warming trends, imposing a

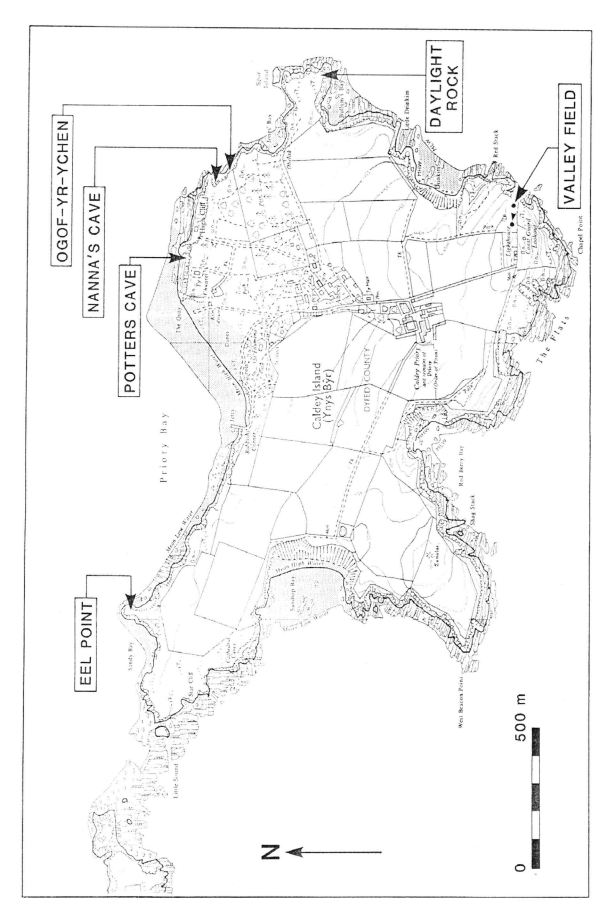

Figure 3.4: Map of Caldey Island, Dyfed, showing the location of caves and surface find-spots.

Plate 3.1: Aerial view of Caldey Point and Daylight Rock (arrowed), Caldey Island, Dyfed (see Fig. 3.7, p. 66).

strong contrast to the swifter climatic response of the maritime Atlantic fringe.

It was at this latter coastal fringe that sea level at this time was rising at a rate approximately in step with climatic improvement (Fairbridge, 1961; Fairbanks, 1989) - rapidly throughout the early part of the post-glacial, only decelerating at about the 'climatic optimum' of *c.* 6,000 BP (West, 1977). British west coasts have provided a considerable body of sea level sensitive deposits, radiocarbon dates for which have allowed the plotting of several curves for eustatic sea level rise (Hawkins, 1971; Kidson and Heyworth, 1973, 1977; Tooley, 1974). Although the detail of such curves may not be in exact agreement due to a number of complex factors (Kidson and Heyworth, 1982), the general trend and depth ranges are clear enough. Estimates of sea level at the opening of the Flandrian are not available for our area (Tooley, 1978) yet a general curve developed for Britain suggests a level of about -37 m. at *c.* 10,000 BP (Godwin *et al.*, 1958). This is in rough agreement with a depth of -34 m. at *c.* 9,500 BP (Ters, 1973), although doubt has been expressed on the accuracy of the data leading to such estimates (Devoy, 1982, 1983). However, from depths such as these (or even considerably deeper: Fairbanks, 1989) levels may have risen at a rate of about 20 mm./year (Hawkins; 1971, but see comments in Tooley, 1978, 176). Despite this rapid rise, substantial areas of the Bristol Channel lowlands and Cardigan Bay would have remained dry at the time of the

first Mesolithic human activity there (see Fig. 3.3). The coasts of western Dyfed, between Fishguard and Tenby, off which submarine contours shelve fairly abruptly, would have seen only a modest extension of their present outline. Milford Haven and much of St. Brides Bay would have been dry, and Caldey, Skomer and Ramsey Islands would have been connected with the mainland.

The advancing sea would raise the local water table, creating a margin of swamp and carr in areas of formerly well-drained woodland. In many circumstances peat might then develop until overtaken by increasing salinity and finally inundation. Marine transgression is likely to have been somewhat uneven and marked by sudden incursions as natural barriers were breached during storms and tidal surges (Kidson and Heyworth, 1973).

5. The chronology of the early Mesolithic in Wales

i) Introduction

Until very recently the chronology for the appearance of characteristic early Mesolithic stone tool assemblages in Wales was dependant on a small series of radiocarbon dates from three sites in the north of the country - Trwyn Du on Anglesey (White, 1978), and Rhuddlan sites E and M, in Clwyd (Jacobi, 1980b). These dates, listed in Table 3.3, are all clearly significantly later than might be predicted from datings obtained elsewhere in Britain and Europe (see Table 3.1). In each case, too, there are grounds for believing them to be in error or, at least, to be unrepresentative of the earliest Mesolithic settlement of Wales: all five determinations are on aggregates of charcoal or carbonized nutshells from locations with significant evidence for late- as well as post-Mesolithic usage. Rather than attempt to explain the appearance of an early Mesolithic in Wales a millennium or so *later* than at its English counterparts, it has been an aim of the research reported upon here to obtain additional and, hopefully, more secure dating evidence from other sites.

The opportunity to attempt this was provided by the author's excavations at two well-known find-spots of early Mesolithic material in south-west Wales: Daylight Rock on Caldey Island and The Nab Head, near St. Brides, both in Dyfed. Of the two sites the integrity of the lithic collection at Daylight Rock determines that it should be described in the next section. The following sections will detail other find-spots from west, south and north Wales (Fig. 3.3). A full account of The Nab Head (Site I) will then follow in Chapter IV.

Table 3.3: 'Early' Mesolithic radiocarbon dates from north Wales.

Trwyn Du, Anglesey:	8460 ±150 BP	(Q 1385)
	8590 ± 90 B	(HAR 1194)
	7980 ±140 B	(HAR 1193)
Rhuddlan, Clwyd, Site E:	8739 ±86 BP	(BM 691)
Rhuddlan, Clwyd, Site M:	8528 ±73 BP	(BM 822)

ii) Daylight Rock, Caldey Island, Dyfed (SS 1495 9663):
Caldey is a small irregularly-shaped island lying about a kilometre off-shore to the south of Tenby (Fig. 3.4). Its geological trends of Carboniferous limestone and Devonian Old Red Sandstone clearly identify it as an eastward extension of the adjacent mainland landscape from which it is now separated by Caldey Sound. The limestone occupies the northern part of the island, extending for about two kilometres east to west. At its eastward limit, extending out into Carmarthen Bay, is Caldey Point from which projects a small promontory of steeply pitched rock pierced from side to side by a small cave: Daylight Rock.

The Daylight Rock promontory is an almost bare limestone ridge aligned east-west (Plate 3.1). To its south the rock descends to the outer margins of a small sandy inlet (Bullum's Bay), whilst to the north the ridge falls away abruptly down to a small gulley and then on, northwards, to the rocky outline of Caldey Point. The northern edge of the ridge is therefore defined by a small inland cliff at the foot of which is a sheltered area of irregularly sloping turf, boulders and bare rock. It was here, whilst digging out the contents of a small cave, that Brother James van Nédervelde, of the Cistercian Community on Caldey, was encouraged by A. D. Lacaille to extend his exploration on to the adjacent slope where he then encountered large quantities of flints. During 1951 and 1952 the entire area at the foot of the cliff was dug over in the search for further artefacts until 'digging ceased eventually to produce any'. The results of this work were summarized by Lacaille and W. F. Grimes in their survey of the early prehistory of Caldey (Lacaille and Grimes, 1955).

The lithic artefacts (1951-2):
Few pieces now survive from this original exploration when about 7,454 flint and flaked stone artefacts were reported to have been recovered. The great majority of these apparently came from two fairly discrete concentrations at the foot of the cliff (*ibid.*, fig. 20). This and the quantities of cores and debitage suggested that '...the place, however, besides being a factory, was also the occupation site of food-gatherers as is, of course, demonstrated by the numerous burnt flints, charcoal and other domestic refuse found all over the excavated area...' (*ibid.*, 137).

Although there may be some doubt as to the contemporaneity of the organic remains with the lithic industry (Jacobi, 1980b, 184), the latter is of importance for its apparent integrity and absence of any obvious signs of cultural mixing. However, only the identifiable tools amongst the lithic artefacts were retained by the excavators - the majority of the collection now being lost. The composition of the surviving material, housed at the National Museum of Wales, is tabulated below in Table 3.4, and a selection are illustrated in Fig. 3.5.

Table 3.4: Artefacts from Daylight Rock, Caldey.

microliths:	
obliquely-backed points	27
isosceles triangles	2
large scalene triangles	9
fragment of triangle	1
bi-truncated pieces of trapezoidal outline	5
bi-truncated piece of rhombic outline	1
?convex-backed piece	1
unclassified fragments	8
other tools:	
scrapers	48
burins	11
truncated pieces	8
nosed piece	1
notched pieces	9
mèches de forêt	15
?axe/adze	1
retouched pieces	14
utilized pieces	2
others	2
by-products:	
axe/adze-sharpening flakes	10
TOTAL	**175**

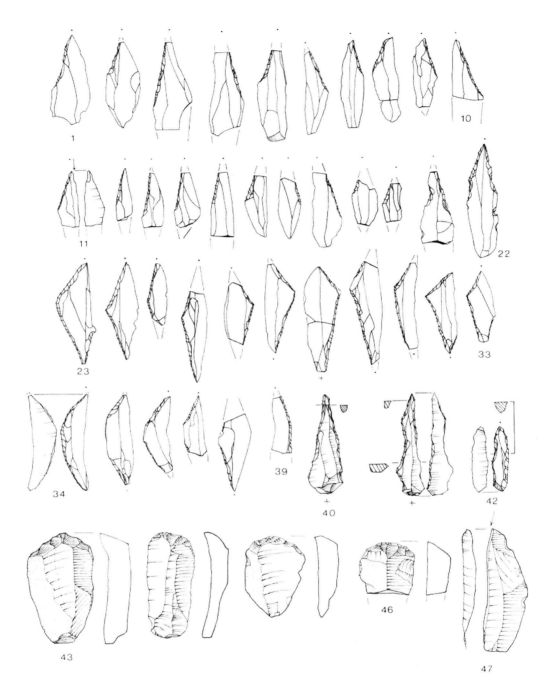

Figure 3.5: Flint artefacts from Daylight Rock, Caldey Island, Dyfed (1951-2): - 1-39, Microliths; 40-42, *mèches de forêt*; end-scrapers; 47, burin. Scale – 1:1.39.

Most characteristic amongst the microliths are large and simple obliquely-backed points, accounting for 59% of classifiable pieces. The remaining microliths are geometric in shape, dominated by large scalene triangles (22%). Convex, trapezoidal and rhombic shapes are present (15%) but greatly outnumbered by the others.

End-scrapers are the commonest of the formal tools (31%), followed by microliths (29%). Next in numerical significance (10%) are steeply trimmed bladelets interpreted as awls or drill-bits (*mèches de forêt*: Jacobi, 1980b, 154). The relatively high representation of the latter is a significant characteristic of the collection, shared with only

a few early assemblages elsewhere (see below, and Chapter IV). Other tools include burins (7%) and yet smaller numbers of truncated, notched, nosed, retouched and utilized pieces none of which have important diagnostic value.

By-products that survive in the collection comprise 10 axe/adze sharpening flakes - representative of a further significant addition to the tool inventory characteristic of early Mesolithic assemblages. Notably, several of the sharpening flakes are composed of non-flint material of igneous origin, in all probability reflecting the unavailability of flint of the requisite size for the manufacture of

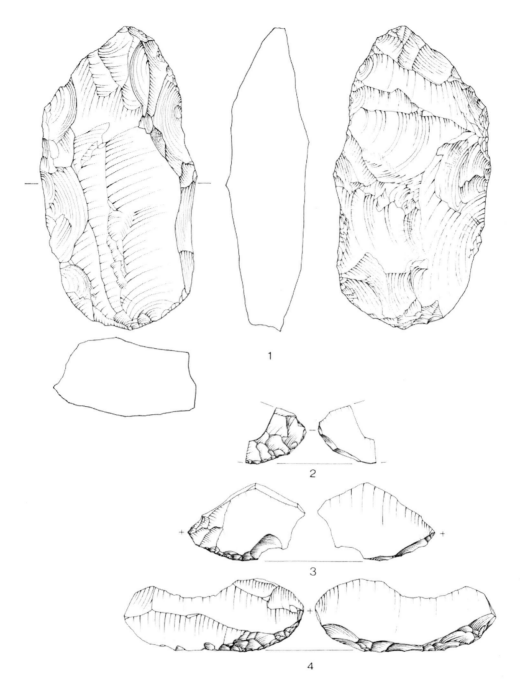

Figure 3.6: Axe/adze and sharpening flakes, all of igneous stone, from Daylight Rock, Caldey Island. Scale – 1:1.35.

large core tools. Although one non-flint core tool from this collection might be a worked- down axe/adze (Lacaille and Grimes, 1955, fig. 22, no. 22), this tool-type is better represented by a more recent find at the site of an axe/adze, also of igneous stone, by Brother James (Fig. 3.6). The latter was recovered from the spoil of the earlier excavation and is included amongst a further 113 artefacts found by Brother James in 1969 from both the spoil and an 'undisturbed layer' on the northern edge of the previous excavation (van Nédervelde, 1970a).

Parallels:
The range of tools thus represented at Daylight Rock appears to show significant similarity to that identified earlier in this chapter as broadly distinctive of a NW European early Mesolithic 'techno-complex'.

Within Britain, parallelism with early Mesolithic tool inventories becomes even more pronounced. The microlithic component at Daylight Rock, for instance, is dominated by simple obliquely-backed points but also includes large geometric shapes, especially triangles, a characteristic form shared also amongst microlith groups in both southern and northern England. Of the latter, Star Carr (Clark, 1954, fig. 35) and Flixton I (Moore, 1950, fig. 4), both situated in the Vale of Pickering, North Yorkshire, provide exact parallels. Very close by, at Seamer Carr (Sites C and K), recent excavations have recovered further

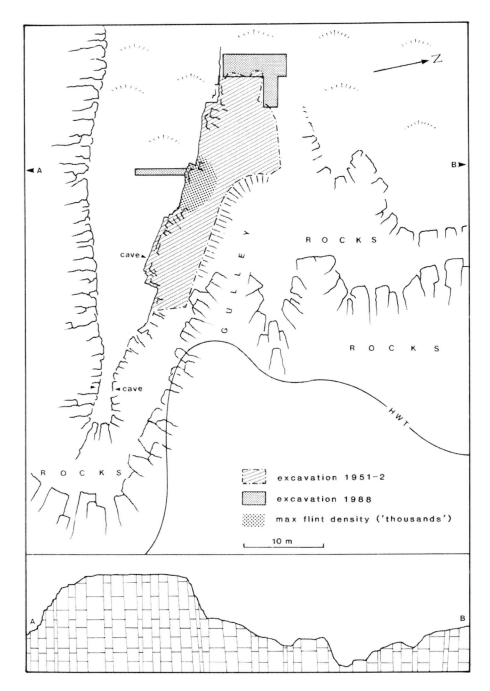

Figure 3.7: Location of excavations at Daylight Rock, Caldey Island.

comparable microlith groups (Fig. 3.2). Radiocarbon dates for the latter focus at *c.* 9,575 BP (Site K) and *c.* 9,350 BP (Site C) suggesting a use broadly contemporaneous with that of Star Carr (see Table 3.1).

Southern English find-spots with comparable microlithic elements include Thatcham II and Broxbourne 104 (Jacobi, 1980b, 149). Only Broxbourne provides a direct radiocarbon date (on bones of bovid and cervid), and this is 9,350 +120 BP (Q-3033: Jacobi, pers. comm.). An indication of the age of the Thatcham II material is provided by approximately contemporaneous horizons at Thatcham IV. Here, a worked antler artefact and a burnt elk antler have given dates at *c.* 9,600 BP (Gowlett *et al.*, 1987; and

see Table 3.1). Similar datings have also been obtained on samples of (non-artefactual) wood from the same horizon at the adjacent Thatcham V (Churchill, 1962), an internally consistent group of 5 determinations providing a weighted mean of 9,644 +74 BP.

In addition to a distinct range of microlith types, the sites mentioned above, as well as others, share with Daylight Rock the specific combination of short end-scrapers, burins, *mèches de forêt* and axe/adze sharpening flakes. Altogether, therefore, such strong lithic analogies lead to the reasonable prediction that the equivalent assemblage-type from Daylight Rock is likely to be of similar age, ie that occupation(s) at the site will have taken place at

Plate 3.2; Excavation at Daylight Rock, Caldey Island, Dyfed (1988). The figure at the top right indicates the position of the second trench, from which AMS samples were obtained.

sometime between *c.* 9,000 - 9,700 BP. Renewed excavation at Daylight Rock was therefore undertaken in September 1988 with the specific intention of testing this proposal.

Daylight Rock 1988:
Despite the wholesale removal of apparently all the cultural remains from the site in the 1950s, it nevertheless remained a possibility that *in situ* artefacts and organic material might be preserved beyond the limits of the earlier trench. The most appropriate location for such a search lay up-slope and to the north and west of the old trench, the approximate edges of which were still just visible (see Fig. 3.7). A T-

shaped area of 32 square metres was therefore opened here and excavated by hand to bedrock in 50 cm quadrants.

The earlier excavators reported a simple stratigraphy (Lacaille and Grimes, 1955, 133):

3) Grass-grown dark vegetable mould containing some stony elements.
2) Reddish loam, charged with angular blocks of limestone of all sizes derived from the fall of the cliff.
1) Greyish-yellow sandy silt, compact and practically stoneless.

Limestone rock.
The cultural material was reported to be confined to layer (2).

Results from the new trench were disappointing: topsoil cover was mostly extremely thin and was everywhere disturbed, lying in most places directly on bedrock (Plate 3.2). Intervening subsoil deposits (equivalent to the 'yellowish silty sand') were preserved only in the deeper bedrock depressions and were confirmed to be unproductive of organic remains or artefacts. The 'reddish loam' was only encountered in the eastward (down-slope) extension of the trench and was also almost entirely sterile. Such results showed that the earlier work had indeed probably encompassed the full extent of the artefact scatter.

A modest number of chipped stone artefacts were recovered, however, albeit almost entirely from topsoil - along with quantities of recent animal bones, modern detritus and a human tooth (most probably modern: S. Mays pers. comm.). Of the 84 lithic items found (see Table 3.5), there were 7 cores, an obliquely-backed point, a *mèche de forêt* and a serrated flake (Figure 3.8, Nos. 2, 17 and 18). None of these pieces are in any way inconsistent with an early Mesolithic typology and, with the exception of the serrated flake, are all represented amongst the earlier material. The latter flake has extremely fine and deliberate serrations (Fig. 3.8, No. 18) and is therefore fully in keeping with the micro-denticulates recognised amongst other early assemblages (see below). An absence of micro-denticulates from the earlier Daylight Rock collection may be due a failure to recognize them - such pieces now being presumed lost along with most of the debitage.

Two cores and a flake had each at one time evidently been burnt, giving rise to the slim possibility (given the shallow and disturbed nature of their context) that a TL dating might be possible. Subsequent measurement by Dr Joan Huxtable (Research Laboratory for Archaeology and the History of Art, Oxford University) resulted in dates considerably later than anticipated:

OxTL-263 : 7,700 BP (error margin: 1,200 years)
OxTL-263 : 6,700 BP (error margin: 1,000 years)
OxTL-263 : 7,900 BP (error margin: 1,200 years)

These dates, indicating a late Mesolithic age (see Chapter V), are very unlikely to be compatible with their associated lithic industry. Sources of error that could lead to such anomalies include the heating of the flints at some considerably later date than their manufacture. Also, their lack of primary context can be expected to result in misleading TL values.

Faced with a lack of suitable material for radiocarbon dating, and in anticipation of difficulties with TL, it was decided - as a last resort - to examine the top of the Daylight Rock headland, that is, above the position at the foot of the small cliff where the densest finds had been made in the 1950s (Plate 3.2). This decision followed from speculation that the early Mesolithic occupation could well have taken place on top of the headland as well as in the lee of the cliff below, or even that the original finds may have fallen or been discarded from above. Although there was scarcely any soil under the thin and discontinuous turf cover on the headland plateau, it was hoped that early deposits might still survive within solution fissures penetrating the limestone.

A trench of 1 x 5m, aligned at right-angles to the cliff-edge (see Fig. 3.7), was excavated. Once the remaining topsoil had been removed, excavation was taken down into the several narrow solution pockets and fissures, the deepest of which were filled with a stiff red clay containing abundant artefacts. One fissure in particular, only some 20 cms wide and excavated to a depth of 75 cms over a length of 1.5m, produced 956 flaked items with fragments of charcoal and charred hazel nutshell. The total lithic recovery (see Table 3.5) from the trench was 1,515, albeit including the very smallest items. Unfortunately, none of the larger pieces of flint were burnt, denying the opportunity for TL dating in more satisfactory conditions than had prevailed in the other trench. The charred nutshells, although only a few very small fragments, were ideal for AMS radiocarbon dating, however.

The lithic artefacts (1988):
The lithic artefacts from the upper trench are listed in Table 3.5 and the diagnostic pieces are illustrated in Fig. 3.8. Most of this collection (97%) is of flint, deeply patinated an opaque dirty white by its alkaline environment. 51 pieces are of igneous stone resembling rhyolite.

The only formal tool-type to be recovered was the microlith, the classifiable examples of which comprise two obliquely-backed points and three large scalene triangles. Two fragmentary microliths are unclassifiable, but would appear to belong to the same 'broad blade' category. Identifiable products of microlith manufacture include 7 micro-burins and a mis-hit. No item from the collection is therefore inconsistent with an early Mesolithic attribution, and this suggestion is further strengthened by the presence also of the fragment of a ?rhyolite axe/adze sharpening flake.

Dating:
The collection from this upper area, therefore, has all the appearance of being typologically discrete and in all its parts identical to the material recovered previously from below the cliff. No cultural material of obviously later date was identified and the apparent sealing of the lithic material (associated with hazel nutshells) in a red clay lent confidence to the potential for dating the industry. Three fragments of charred nutshell were therefore submitted to the Oxford AMS Unit with the following results:

9,040 +90 BP (OxA-2245)
9,030 +80 BP (OxA-2246)
8,850 +80 BP (OxA-2247)

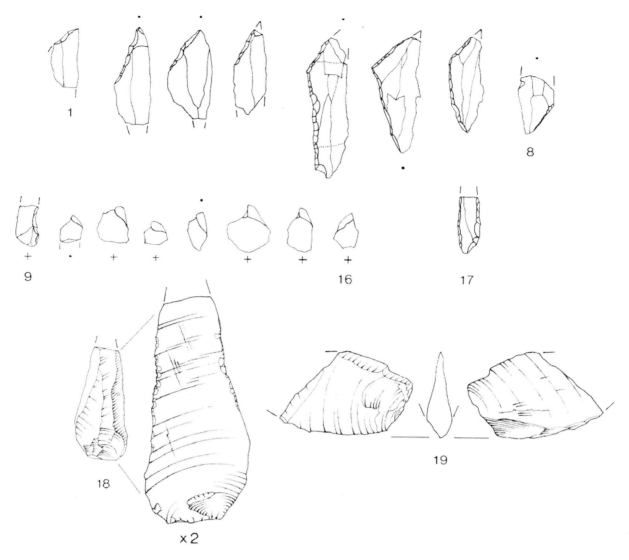

Figure 3.8: Artefacts recovered from Daylight Rock in 1988: - 1-8, Microliths; 9-16, microburins; 17, *mèches de forêt*; 18, microdenticulate; 19, axe/adze sharpening flake. Scale – 1:1.

Discussion:

This small group of new determinations is at once impressive for its internal consistency, suggesting an average date of *c.* 9,000 BP for the associated artefacts. Clearly, though, some caution is necessary in emphasising such consistency when the possibility exists that this might simply result from inadvertently dating fragments of the same nutshell (OxA-2245 and OxA-2246?). A further proviso - common to the dating of any very small items - is that these might have somehow been physically introduced into their containing deposit at some date later than its initial formation. In this case, however, there is no clear evidence that either factor has influenced the outcome, and these cautions (whilst noted) may be set aside and the archaeological significance of the results considered.

The dates obtained are all earlier than those from north Wales (Table 3.3) although the latest of the three (8.850 +80 BP) comes close to the determination from Rhuddlan E (8,739 +86 BP), and is within about 400 years of datings for Rhuddlan M and Trwyn Du. A final date, from Trwyn Du

(7,980 +140) is significantly later and has been argued to be erroneous (White, 1978, 28).

The central dating of *c.* 9,000 BP, therefore, when compared with these other dates and those for equivalent lithic collections in England (eg Myers, 1989, fig. 9.1), falls towards the later end of an early Mesolithic continuum. The typological arguments, above, would have suggested an earlier dating by some 500 years, in line with that for Star Carr, Seamer Carr or Thatcham. Instead, the dates fall closer to the series from Oakhanger VII (Phase 2) in Hampshire, centred also at *c.* 9,000 BP. This dating depends, however, on bulked samples. Also, the associated lithic material, whilst clearly of early Mesolithic character (Jacobi, 1978), is distinct from that of the foregoing sites in that different proportions of microlith shapes are represented: convex-backed points share a relatively higher proportion of the microlith assemblage, at the expense of obliquely-backed points, and large triangular shapes (especially scalene triangles) are almost absent.

Table 3.5: Artefacts from Daylight Rock, Caldey (1988).

	Upper Trench	Lower Trench
Tools:		
microliths:		
obliquely-backed points	3	1
large scalene triangles	3	0
fragments	2	1
mèches de foret	0	1
micro-denticulate	0	1
retouched flake frags	3	0
?utlised flakes	2	?1
By-products:		
microburins	7	0
miss-hits	1	0
axe-sharpening flakes	1	?1
Debitage:		
cores	0	7
core rejuvenation flakes	1	2
flakes and fragments	1492	69
TOTAL flaked items	**1515**	**84**
igneous pieces	51	4

iii) The Nab Head (Site I)

Although this site will be dealt with in detail in the following chapter, radiocarbon dates recently obtained from it should be noted here in order to complete the above discussion of Welsh early Mesolithic chronology.

The following AMS dates are the result of determinations made on charred hazel nutshell fragments from near the base of a soil profile containing elements of a lithic assemblage identical to that from Daylight Rock:

> 9,210 +80 BP (OxA-1495: Hedges *et al.*, 1989)
> 9,110 +80 BP (OxA-1496: Hedges *et al.*, 1989)

Both these determinations overlap with the two earlier dates from Daylight Rock, so supporting the dating of this assemblage-type to *c.* 9,000 BP, or very slightly earlier (Fig. 3.9). The Nab Head dates draw the earliest evidence so far obtained for a Welsh Mesolithic technology slightly nearer its inception in England. There is still a potential shortfall of up to 500 years between these events, however: dating of additional Welsh sites will thus be necessary before any apparent delay in the appearance of this 'Forest'-adapted technology can be assumed for Wales.

6. Early Mesolithic find-spots in west Wales:
Having described Daylight Rock in the previous section, and setting aside a fuller account of The Nab Head until the next chapter, it now remains to mention several other find-spots, also in west Wales, of lithic material possessing early Mesolithic attributes.

Fig. 3.3 shows the location of all documented early Mesolithic find-spots in Wales. Within Dyfed, whilst such finds are rather more numerous than elsewhere in the Principality, the quality of the evidence is nevertheless poor - either because of inadequate recording of early excavations or through the inherent limitations of surface recoveries. There are, for instance, several further find-spots on Caldey Island suggesting that Daylight Rock was not in isolation:

Ogof-yr-Ychen, Caldey Island, Dyfed (SS 1468 9690):
This cave has already been described in Chapter II where it became apparent that residues from several episodes widely separate in time had become incorporated into its filling (see Table 2.10). Amongst such human and artefactual remains, those from the deep vertical rift, Chamber 3, stand out as of potential significance here.

The lowermost part of this chamber was apparently filled with a mixture of cave earth and boulders and was partially sealed by a capping of stalagmite (Fig. 2.15). About 80 cms below this, 'in a clay layer' were found large pieces of a human skull. Parts of long-bones were also discovered and could belong to the same 'Individual B' (van Nédervelde and Davies, 1986). Two mandible fragments were recovered, one of which was observed to join with a third such fragment from 6.5m above in 'The Blowhole', a fissure once open to the surface. The two joining mandible fragments have been attributed to 'Individual B' (*ibid.*, 9), although there would still seem to be the possibility that this jaw could instead have belonged with the incomplete skeleton ('Individual A'), for which there is no record of a mandible, found lodged head-down in 'The Blowhole', above Chamber 3. Alternatively, but less probably, 'Individual B' may itself have been lodged in 'The Blowhole' before falling into Chamber 3, leaving part of its jaw behind.

Of the several flints found in Chamber 3, 8 survive and are illustrated in Fig. 3.10, Nos. 1-8. There are 4 microliths of which one - a convex-backed point (No. 4) - was reportedly found at the same level as the human bones of 'Individual B' (not 'A', as labelling with the find suggests). The remaining microliths comprise two obliquely-backed points and a large isosceles triangle. The other flints include a bladelet seemingly once used as an awl or piercer, and three flakes.

None of these flints would necessarily be out of place if found amongst lithic material at Daylight Rock, only some 450m to the south-east, thus introducing the possibility that the deposits in Chamber 3 could be of early Mesolithic derivation. Fauna from the chamber filling is clearly Postglacial in age and would be consistent with such an interpretation: 'just below the place of skull (B), two big canines appeared, then a broken jaw with a tusk attached ... soon there was a near complete skeleton of a wild boar ... further on it was the turn of a "baby boar" ... then the skull

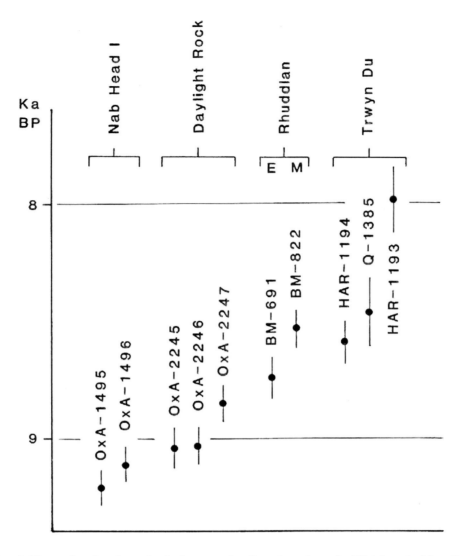

Figure 3.9: Graph illustrating the chronological range of radiocarbon dates for Welsh early Mesolithic find-spots.

of an otter with some fish bones nearby.' (van Nédervelde, 1970b, 11). The skull of a wolf was found deeper in the deposit, about a metre below skull 'B'. Fragments of charcoal had been found throughout.

In order to test the possibility that 'Individual B' might be contemporary with the early Mesolithic flints, and perhaps even represent a deliberate burial of this age, a sample from one of the two joining jaw fragments attributed to this skeleton has been submitted for AMS dating. The fragment concerned is that which was found near the skull (B) sealed in clay 80 cms below the layer of stalagmite. As explained above, however, it joins with another fragment from higher in the cave, allowing of the alternative interpretation that the jaw may in fact belong with 'Individual A'. The latter is itself a candidate for a Mesolithic inhumation, being partly cemented by stalagmite and therefore perhaps pre-dating the 'Atlantic' climatic optimum (c. 7,000 BP) when the development of flowstone may have been most active (Evans, 1975). Also, the excavators noted that the opening

of 'The Blowhole' to the ground surface had apparently been deliberately blocked with rocks (van Nédervelde, 1970b, 12 - 13).

Some confidence that burial might be involved is strengthened by the recent demonstration of several instances where human bone material from caves has been dated to the Mesolithic.

Most of these dates for apparent burials fall within the chronological range for the Welsh early Mesolithic as defined above: the sepulchral use of caves at this time seems certain, therefore, and it would come as no real surprise if Ogof-yr-Ychen were to produce yet further evidence for this practice.

Apart from within Chamber 3, 'broad blade' microliths have also been found elsewhere in Ogof-yr-Ychen, for instance in Chamber 4, but little further information is available on these (Fig. 3.10, Nos. 9-17).

Table 3.6: Radiocarbon dates for human bone of Mesolithic age from caves in Britain.

Cave	Date	Lab No.	Ref.
Aveline's Hole, Mendip	9,100 +100 BP	(OxA-799)	1
Aveline's Hole, Mendip	9,114 +110 BP	(BM-471)	2
Aveline's Hole, Mendip	9,090 +110 BP	(Q-1458)	3
Aveline's Hole, Mendip	8,860 +100 BP	(OxA-800)	1
Aveline's Hole, Mendip	8,740 +100 BP	(OxA-1070)	4
Gough's (New) Cave, Mendip	9,100 +100 BP	(OxA-814)	1
Gough's (New) Cave, Mendip	9,080 +150 BP	(BM-525)	2
Kent's Cavern, Devon	8,070 +90 BP	(OxA-1786)	5
Badger Hole, Mendip	9,360 +100 BP	(OxA-1459)	5
Paviland, Gower	7,190 +80 BP	(OxA-681)	6

References:
1 : Gowlett *et al.*, 1986a
2 : Barker *et al.*, 1971
3 : Tratman, 1977
4 : Hedges *et al.*, 1987
5 : Hedges *et al.*, 1989
6 : Gowlett and Hedges, 1986

Nanna's Cave, Caldey island, Dyfed (SS 1458 9698)
Lithic finds traceable to Nanna's Cave include several microliths (Table 2.9), of which four or five (Figure 3.10, Nos. 18-22) correspond with their equivalents at Daylight Rock and may be of the same age: however, no further useful information is now likely to be obtained on these or other possibly related artefacts from the cave. Particularly interesting, however, in the context of Mesolithic burial discussed above, is the occurrence of human skeletal material at Nanna's Cave. Amongst other bones recovered from here in *c.* 1911 (Leach, 1916) were those, representative of two individuals, made distinct by their encrustation with stalagmite and midden material. Traces of the latter ('a hard stalagmite crowded with shells': *ibid.*, 163) were ascertained by Leach to occur below later prehistoric material and above the basal yellow silty sand now believed to be of Lateglacial age (see Chapter II). That these might also be the remains of Mesolithic inhumations seems a strong possibility, therefore, although the presence of sea shells suggests that they may belong later rather than earlier within this period (see Chapter V).

Potter's Cave, Caldey Island, Dyfed (SS 1436 9707)
An early Mesolithic attribution for lithic and faunal material reported from a basal deposit ('reddish-brown loam': Lacaille and Grimes, 1955) has been very tentatively proposed by Jacobi (1980b, 183). No diagnostic microliths were found, however, although the fauna - including dog - is certainly Postglacial. More recent explorations at the cave have recovered at least one undiagnostic microlith fragment, as well as Lateglacial artefacts (see Chapter II).

Eel Point, Caldey Island, Dyfed (SS 1305 9727)
Excavations of fissures near the summit of Eel Point have taken place in 1969, 1979 and in 1986. This work has resulted in the finding of a small collection of at least 9 flints which include three broken microliths and a retouched blade (Fig. 3.10, Nos. 23-26). These were apparently found 50 cms below the surface and above clay deposits containing a Pleistocene fauna (van Nédervelde, 1970a; van Nédervelde and Davies, 1987; Davies, 1989a). On typological grounds the microliths could be early Mesolithic.

Valley Field, Caldey Island, Dyfed (SS 1443 9595) (SS 1450 9594)
Two find-spots are reported here, to the east of the lighthouse near the south-eastern extremity of the island (Lacaille and Grimes, 1961). Both are apparently prolific surface scatters of lithic material from which samples have been collected casually over the years by Brother James. Most of this material is debitage but the following tools can be recognized, most of which are illustrated in Fig. 3.11:

Table 3.7: Diagnostic artefacts from Valley Field, Caldey Island.

obliquely backed points	2
fragments of ?obliquely-backed points	4
bi-truncated piece of trapezoidal outline	1
unclassified microlith fragment	1
retouched blade fragment	1
mèches de forêt	4
?micro-denticulate	1
end-scrapers	3
burins	2

(Sources: Jacobi (unpublished: material in NMW); Lacaille and Grimes, 1961; collections on Caldey).

A second group of 5 microliths and 5 *mèches de forêt* (Fig. 3.11) might also be provenanced to Valley Field although

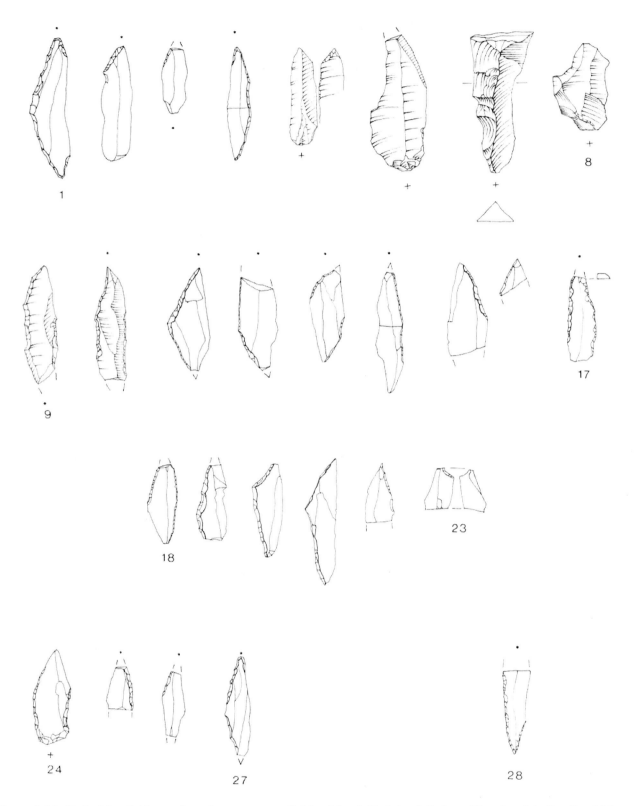

Figure 3.10: Early Mesolithic artefacts from caves on Caldey Island, Dyfed: - 1-8, from Chamber 3 in Ogof-yr-Ychen; 9, Chamber 2; 10-15, Chamber 4; 16-17, unstratified. 18-22, from Nanna's Cave; 23-26, from Eel point; 27, from Potters Cave. Scale – 1:1.12.

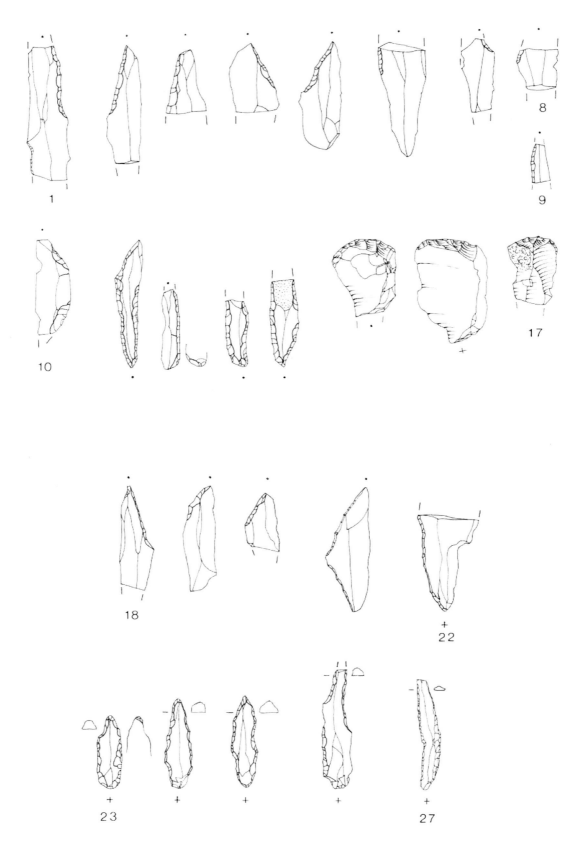

Figure 3.11: Flint artefacts from Valley Field, Caldey Island: - 1-10, Microliths; 11-14, *mèches de forêt*; 15-17, end-scrapers. Nos. 18-27 are from either Valley Field or (less probably) Daylight Rock: see text. Scale – 1:1.06.

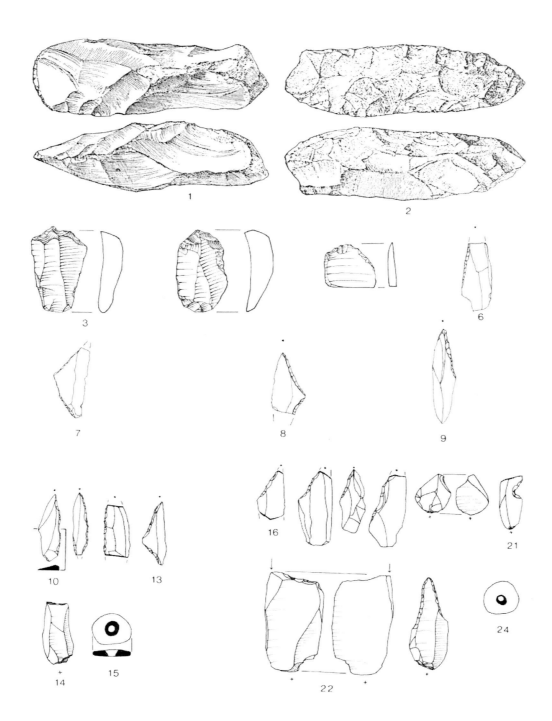

Figure 3.12: Examples of casual finds of early Mesolithic artefacts from mainland Dyfed: - 1-2 tranchet axe/adzes from Pencaer and Benton; 3-6, from Wiston; 7, from Coygan Camp; 8, from Glyn-y-Fran; 9, from Wogan cave; 10-15, from Linney Burrows; 16-24, from Freshwater East. (10-24 after Jacobi, 1980b). Scale – Nos. 1-2 at 1:2.7, remainder at 1:1.35.

they are labelled 'probably from Daylight Rock open working floor 1970' by Brother James. That there is potential for confusing the two locations must emphasize the identical nature of their respective artefacts.

Additionally, a collection of 703 pieces of debitage certainly from Valley Field was examined by the author and classified as follows:

Table 3.8: Debitage from Valley Field, Caldey Island

primary flakes	67
secondary flakes	473
igneous/chert flakes or fragments	20
burnt flakes/fragments	103
blade cores	20
scalar core	1
flaked flint pebbles	8
core-rejuvenation flakes	3

burin spall	1
?utilized piece/sharpening flake	1
?broken axe/adze blade	1
polished axe fragment (igneous)	1
unclassified retouched pieces	3
retouched fragment	1
TOTAL	**703**
igneous/chert	3%
burnt pieces	15%

Disregarding the ambiguously labelled group of retouched pieces, one is left with a collection of lithic material nearly identical to that from Daylight Rock. Only the scalar core and polished axe fragment stand apart as minor intrusive elements. More significantly, common factors include the predominant presence of 'broad blade' microliths, convex scrapers, *mèches de forêt* and burins. Similar non-flint raw materials were in use on both sites and one could risk the further surmise that axe/adzes were also once present at both.

Valley Field would thus seem to represent an important addition to early Mesolithic surface sites in this part of Wales. Although two artefact scatters are known in the field, none of the surviving lithic material can be re-allocated to one or the other, and fresh fieldwalking has not been possible for lack of recent ploughing. The author has, however, been able to re-locate the easternmost scatter with a small test trench of 1.0m x 1.5m at SS 1450 9594. 20 pieces of flint debitage were recovered from the ploughsoil, but included no diagnostic items. Further fieldwork in the area might well be re-paid, therefore, and is in prospect for a future research programme.

Having considered find-spots on Caldey, it is now useful to look at their equivalents on the mainland of Dyfed (see Fig. 3.3). Of the 20 or so locations involved many are of small groups of lithic items, or even isolated artefacts which, for lack of adequate contextual information, do not warrant detailed individual discussion and are therefore limited to

Table 3.9: Finds of isolated or small groups of artefacts of possible early Mesolithic age from Dyfed (excluding Caldey).

Find-spot	NGR	Artefacts	Ref.
The Hoyle's Mouth	SN 1120 0033	microlith, fragments	1
Priory Farm Cave	SM 9789 0184	?microlith fragments	2
Swanlake (A8)	SS 043 982	microlith, + various	3
Swanlake (C12)	SS 033 981	microlith, + various	3
Brownslade Burrows (C17)	SR 895 980	microlith, + various	3
Manorbier (C8)	SS 065 976	microlith, + various	3
St Govan's Head	SR 975 927	microlith, + various	4
Wiston	SN025 168	microlith frags/scrapers	1
Clyn-y-Fran, Llanfyrnach	SN 1856 3077	microlith	1
'Castell Pocha' Pencaer	SM 910 400	tranchet axe/adze	5
St Davids	?SM 75 25	tranchet axe/adze	6
Porth-y-Rhaw, Solva	SM 786 244	tranchet axe/adze	5
Brunt Farm	SM 810 040	tranchet axe/adze	7
Benton	SN 005 068	tranchet axe/adze	5
Coygan Camp	SN 284 092	microlith	8

References:
1 : this thesis., Fig. 3.12
2 : Grimes, 1933, fig. 5, nos. 13, 14, 16
3 : Leach, 1913, fig. 10
4 : Wymer, 1977
5 : Grimes, 1951, fig. 7, no. 1, 2
6 : Jacobi, 1980b, 146
7 : Wainwright, 1963, fig. 9, no. 4
8 : Wainwright, 1967, fig. 47, no. 2

basic itemization in Table 3.9. Selected pieces are illustrated in Fig. 3.12. Also to receive only brief notice here is the collection from Aberystwyth (Thomas and Dudlyke, 1925; collection: NMW). Whilst this is accepted as probably possessing an early Mesolithic component, it combines material from two discrete excavation areas now incapable of separation. (Jacobi, 1980b, 139). Remaining to be described, therfore, are four find-spots: Palmerston Farm,

Freshwater East, Linney, and Penpant.

Palmerston Farm (SM 9369 1439):

This thin scatter of flint and stone artefacts is located on a gentle valley slope 8 km. east of the present St. Brides coast and 10 km. north of the sea at Milford Haven, the western branch of which reaches its tidal limit only about 2 km.

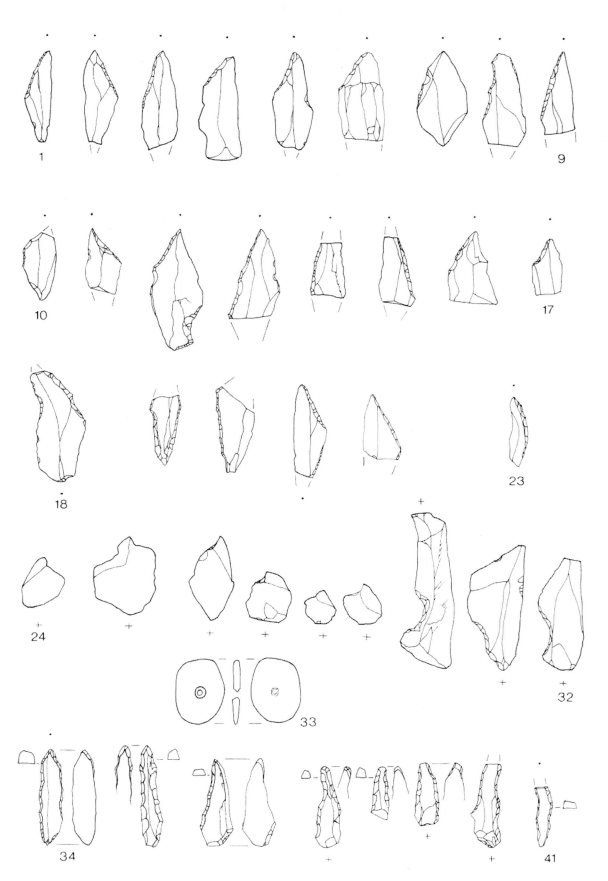

Figure 3.13: Artefacts from Palmerston farm, Dyfed: - 1-23, Microliths; 24-29, micro-burins; 30-32, notched blades; 33, stone bead; 34-41, *mèches de forêt*. Scale – 1:1.0.3.

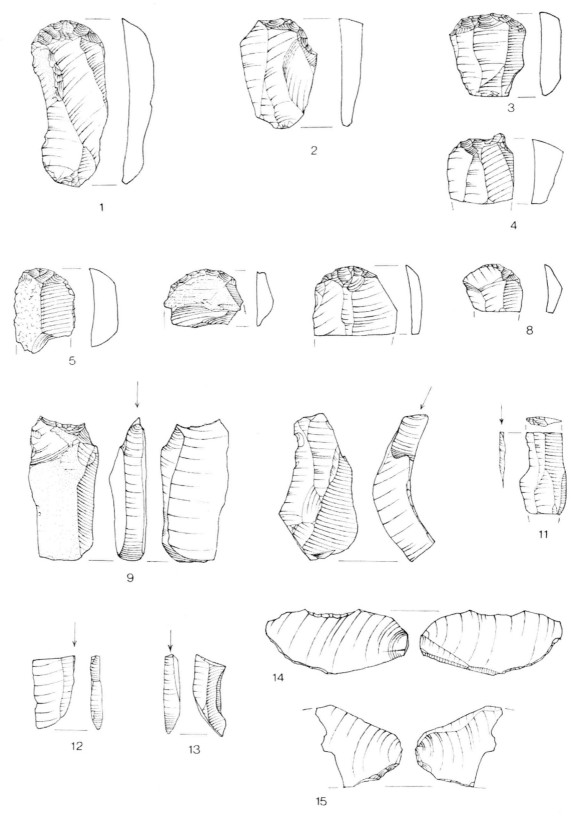

Figure 3.14: Artefacts from Palmerston Farm, Dyfed: - 1-8, scrapers; 9-13, burins; 14, 15, axe/adze sharpening flakes.
Scale – 1:1.06.

from Palmerston Farm. The find-spot was identified by Miss Joan Rees of Haverfordwest in a ploughed field (Rees, 1973) and it is mainly the contents of her collection, picked up casually over several years, which are summarized

below.

In addition, the author prompted the Dyfed Archaeological Trust to undertake a gridded collection over the field

(Stenger and Williams, 1980). Although few diagnostic artefacts were found, 280 pieces were recovered from a total of 2,375 sq m., and these allowed the scatter to be accurately mapped. Its main density (with a maximum of 2 artefacts/sq m) covers about 500 sq m., although finds were made even more diffusely over a still wider area.

Table 3.10 lists the artefacts from this find-spot and a selection are illustrated in Figs. 3.13 and 3.14. Excepting a relatively small number of post-Mesolithic forms, the retouched component of this collection possesses all the attributes argued as early Mesolithic. Raw materials are mostly of pebble flint (97.6%), some of which may have been collected from beach shingle. The remainder are of igneous and an unidentified chert-like stone. The latter is a finely mottled semi-opaque blue-grey material. A micro-burin and *mèche de forêt* are made from it, as is a single end-scraper from The Nab Head Site I and three flakes from Valley Field, Caldey.

Debitage and waste from the site are not especially distinctive, although the cores, with an average 'height' of 39 mm, share a range of sizes in common with other suspected early Mesolithic sites (for a fuller definition and discussion of core 'height', see below).

Amongst the microliths, only a small convex-backed piece (Fig. 3.13, No. 23) is without a close parallel amongst find-spots already discussed. The other classifiable microliths and fragments could all be from the obliquely-backed and triangular classes already noted from Daylight Rock. The platformed blade cores and the relatively numerous micro-burins, mostly of a size proportional to the microliths, imply that the latter were produced on the site.

End-scrapers, burins and *mèches de forêt* all match material from sites shown to date early in the Flandrian. Axes or adzes are absent but are represented by sharpening flakes of flint. A final possible indicator of early date, is the find of a small perforated shale disc, interpreted as a bead. The significance of this discovery will be discussed below.

Freshwater East (SS 023 981):
Re-location of this find-spot (designated A5 by its finder, A. L. Leach: 1913, 396 - 400) does not now seem possible. Investigation of the area indicated suggests that the artefacts (now in Tenby Museum) may have come from an eroding cliff-section at the eastern end of Freshwater East beach. Although occasional flints can still be found here, none has proved diagnostic.

In addition to a single perforated shale bead, similar to that from Palmerston Farm, the artefacts from Site A5 include 4 fragmentary obliquely-backed points, 2 end-scrapers, a burin, *mèche de forêt*, micro-burin and miss-hit (Wainwright, 1963, fig. 5 nos. 11, 26; Jacobi, 1980b, fig. 4.5; see Fig. 3.12).

Linney Burrows (SR 894 974):
Four microliths and a stone bead are amongst the author's collection of mostly later prehistoric artefacts from an extensive surface at Linney exposed by deflation. The microliths include a lanceolate, a straight-backed piece and a bi-truncated trapezoidal piece. Perhaps only the latter can be compared with early Mesolithic types: the group is, however, at best only loosely defined (see Fig. 3.12).

Table 3.10: Artefacts from Palmerston Farm.

i) Tools:

microliths:	
obliquely-backed points	10
incomplete obliquely-backed points	6
isosceles triangles	2
incomplete isosceles triangle	1
convex-backed bladelet	1
unclassified fragments	11
convex-ended scrapers	12
burins	6
denticulate	1
notched pieces	8
mèches de forêt	8
truncated pieces	2
retouched flakes	56
utilized flakes	26

ii) By-products:

micro-burins	21
micro-intermediates	3
miss-hits	6
?axe/adze-sharpening flakes	2

iii) Debitage:

cores	71
core fragments	1
core rejuvenation flakes	13
flakes, blades, frags./waste	3667

iv) ?Post-Mesolithic

'thumbnail' scrapers	6
hollow-based arrowhead	1
?plano-convex knife	1
pieces with scalar retouch	3
scalar cores/frags	2
TOTAL	**3947**

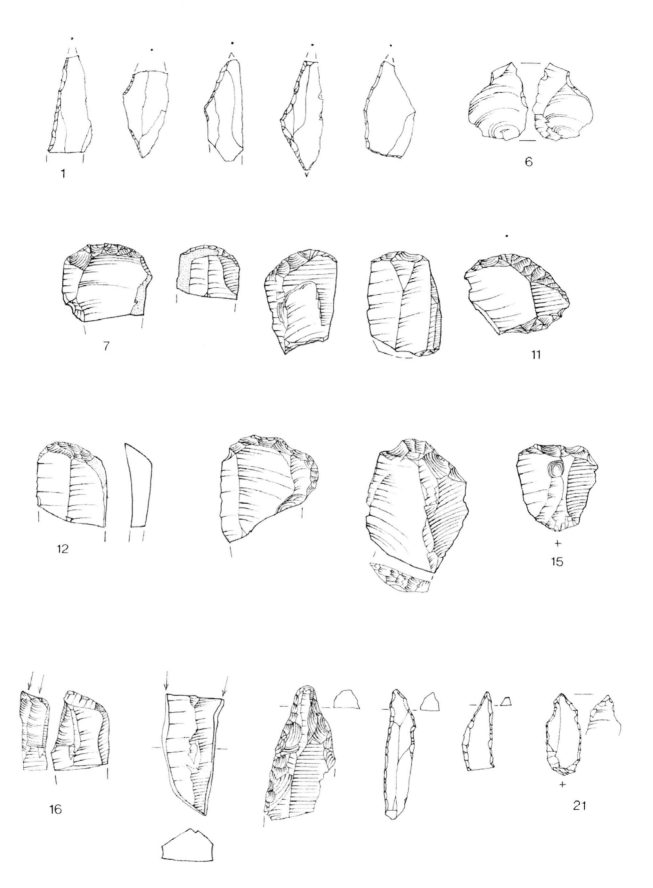

Figure 3.15: Artefacts from Penpant, Solva, Dyfed: - 1-5, Microliths; 6, microburin; 7-15, scrapers; 16-17, burins; 18-21, *mèches de forêt*. Scale – 1:1.

Table 3.11: Artefacts from Penpant, Solva.

i) Tools:

microliths:

obliquely-backed piece	1
large scalene triangle	1
other 'broad blade' pieces and frags	3
'narrow blade' microliths	10
unclassified fragments	6
convex-ended scrapers	13
denticulates and large convex scrapers	21
burins	3
'nosed' pieces	6
'becs'	3
mèches de forêt	3
truncated pieces	8
core tool (and frags	3
utilized pieces	8
retouched pieces	11
other	5

ii) By-products:

micro-burins	3
?burin spalls	2
?axe/adze-thinning flakes	3

iii) Debitage:

cores	145
core fragments	78
core rejuvenation flakes	18
partially worked and unworked flint pebbles	46
flakes, blades, blade frags	2774

iv) Post-Mesolithic:

arrowheads	3
'thumbnail' scrapers	18
scalar cores	4

TOTAL flaked pieces	**3199**

(of these, 8% are of igneous rock and Cretaceous chert)

v) Pebble tools:

hammerstones	2
bevelled pebbles	6

Penpant (SM 7869 2502):
Aside from isolated finds of transversely sharpened axes/adzes (Fig. 3.3; Table 3.9), there are two further surface collections of material, both of which were found as a result of fieldwalking by the author. At Penpant, near Solva on the southern side of the St. Davids peninsula, an area of about 5,000 sq. m. has produced over 3,000 artefacts of chipped flint and stone. Many of these can be diagnosed as more recent than the early Mesolithic and are more probably late Mesolithic (see Chapter VII) whilst others are clearly of still later date. There are, however, several apparently early artefact types. The collection is summarized on Table 3.11 and relevant artefacts are illustrated in Figs. 3.15 and 3.16.

Compared to the collection from Daylight Rock, which has been argued to be certainly of early Mesolithic date, and with that from Palmerston Farm, basic elements in the lithic inventories can be seen to be shared, as follows:

Table 3.12: Artefact-types from Daylight Rock, Caldey, common to surface collections at Palmerston Farm, and Penpant.

	Daylight Rock	Palmerston	Penpant
'broad blade' microliths:	x	x	x
convex-ended scrapers:	x	x	x
mèches de forêt:	x	x	x
long cores (av. >35mm):	x	x	x
axes/adzes/sh. flakes:	x	x	x

Although such a listing ignores the divergent elements from each site's lithic range, it nevertheless signifies that distinct early Mesolithic components can be recognized amongst multi-period surface collections (see Chapter VII). One such component is the core axe/adze, tentatively represented at Penpant by the core tool illustrated in Fig. 3.16. This latter is similar to examples from The Nab Head Site I (Fig. 4.12, 4.13) and is of interest as transversely sharpened axes/adzes are also recorded not far from Penpant, at Porth-y-Rhaw (SM 786 244) (Grimes, 1955, 14), and at St. Davids, 3 km. to the west (Jacobi, 1980b, 146). Other single finds of tools (see Table 3.9, Fig. 3.3) with transversely sharpened blades have been made at Pencaer on Strumble Head, at Benton on the Milford Haven estuary (Grimes, 1955, fig. 7) and at Brunt Farm, Dale (Wainwright, 1963, fig. 9, no. 4). The *tranchet* axe recorded by Wainwright from Freshwater West (*ibid* fig. 9, no 5) is not certainly of this type.

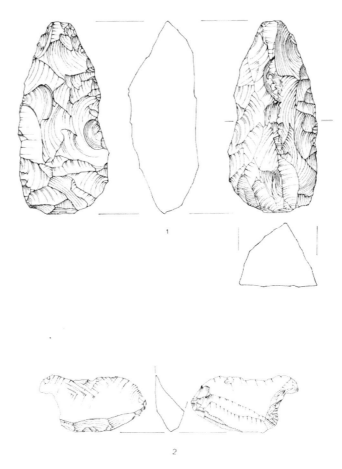

Figure 3.16: Artefacts from Penpant, Solva, Dyfed: - 1, flint core tool; 2, axe/adze sharpening flake. Scale – 1:1.63.

Plate 3.3: The site of the Mesolithic finds on Burry Holms W. Glamorgan.

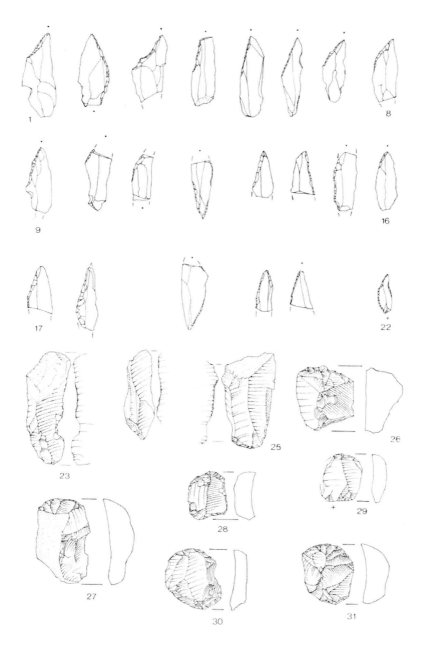

Figure 3.17: artefacts from Burry Holms, W Glam: - 1-21, "broad-blade" Microliths; 22, "narrow-blade" microlith; 23-25, microdenticulates; 26-31, end-scrapers. Scale 1:1.54.

7. Early Mesolithic find-spots in South Wales:

Outside Dyfed, distinctive artefacts would appear to identify Burry Holms and Cathole Cave, both in Gower (West Glamorgan) and the upland sites of Gwernvale and Waun Fignen Felen (Powys) as possessing an early component.

Burry Holms (SS 401 925):
Discovered in 1919 by H. E. David and T. *c.* Lethbridge on the edge of a small island on the north-west tip of the Gower peninsula (Plate 3.3), this find-spot consisted of a scatter of flints, with some bone fragments, visible in the cliff edge at a depth of about 30 cm (H. E. David, 1923-4, 29 - 30). The retouched tools, predominantly broad forms of microlith together with end-scrapers, are illustrated in Fig. 3.17. In addition, there are two blades and a flake, parts of the edges of which show fine serration, or micro-

denticulation (Fig. 3.17, Nos. 23 - 25).

Bone fragments, probably from the island, and housed at the National Museum of Wales are mostly unidentifiable, but include two fragments believed to be of pig bone and one possibly of roe deer (Stanton, 1984, 43).

Also from Burry Holms (T. *c.* Lethbridge collection at Cambridge (AEM)) is a worked pebble akin but not identical to late Mesolithic bevelled examples. If classed amongst the latter (rather than as a whetstone), this, with at least one later Mesolithic microlith (Fig. 3.17: No. 22) may indicate more recent admixture, possibly from another localization close at hand (H. E. David, ms; Wymer, 1977).

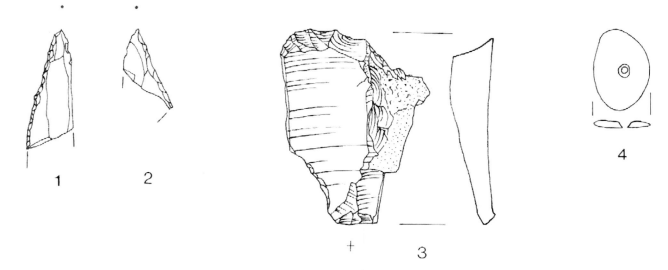

Figure 3.18: Artefacts from Site 6, Waun Fignen Felen, Glam. Scale – 1.27:1.

Cathole (SS 5377 9002):

The 152 artefacts from this cave, also on the Gower peninsula, have been used in the literature to argue for both Early and Late Upper Palaeolithic occupations (see chapter II). They also include pieces of likely Mesolithic age. There are two micro- burins, and amongst the fragmentary backed material are two pieces of early Mesolithic type - an obliquely-backed point and a convex backed piece (McBurney, 1959, fig. 1, nos. 9, 2; Campbell, 1977, fig. 131, nos 2, 3). Other fragments of backed bladelets are probably late Mesolithic. An end-scraper and two scraper fragments could be either Palaeolithic or Mesolithic. Campbell (1977) records an apparently contemporary pollen assemblage of Zone IV - VI type dominated by birch, hazel and pine. Fauna from the same units includes the field vole, wood mouse, and birds such as goose and grouse.

Gwernvale (SN 211 192):

Amongst a mixed lithic assemblage of 1480 pieces recovered from the buried soil beneath this Neolithic long cairn are perhaps 4 obliquely-backed microliths (Healey and Green, 1984, fig. 47, nos 29, 31-33). There are several other fragments which may have been derived from 'broad blade' microliths but, like the supposed Lateglacial fragments, are unclassifiable.

Waun Fignen Felen (SN 824 184):

This is another cluster of find-spots in the southern Welsh uplands, lying on the limestone escarpment some 50 km. north of Swansea. Blanket bog overlies a small late Devensian lake basin which, with its immediate surroundings, has been the subject of recent intensive palaeoenvironmental research (Smith and Cloutman, 1988). Small concentrations of lithic material have also been investigated (Berridge, 1981), and a full report on these is in preparation (Berridge, forthcoming). Of nine sites investigated by excavation and/or walking, six produced lithic remains, none of which have been directly dated (information supplied by P. Berridge):

Site 1: 12 late Mesolithic scalene micro-triangles found during walking. Excavation at the find-spot located nothing further (area 2.5 x 5 m).

Site 2: walking and excavation recovered 52 flints - a late Mesolithic microlith from the surface, and 2 obliquely-backed points and a large scalene triangle from the excavation area of 5 x 5 m.

Site 6: walking and excavation recovered a total of 104 artefacts, the majority of which seem to have derived from a single beach pebble (with re-fitting pieces). These occurred in an area of deep peat (excavation area: 2 x 3 m). The artefacts include an obliquely-backed point and part of a large triangular microlith. With these was found a perforated shale bead. They are illustrated, with a convex scraper, in Figure 3.18.

Site 7: walking and excavation resulted in the finding of 181 flint and chert artefacts originating from the base of the peat (excavation area: 5 x 4.5 m). These and a single microlith from the general area suggest an early Mesolithic presence.

Site 8: excavation of about 30 sq m here has recovered 590 artefacts, 97% of which are of Cretaceous chert. All the 12 microliths are early forms (10 of chert), and there are 5 scrapers, 1 awl and 2 retouched pieces. Some re-fitting has been possible, although there are no cores.

Site 9: 10 scalene micro-triangles recovered from an erosion gulley.

A further 162 pieces have been recovered from general walking of which 131 roughly relate to seven concentrations.

8. Early Mesolithic find-spots in north Wales:

Moving to north Wales the most significant finds of

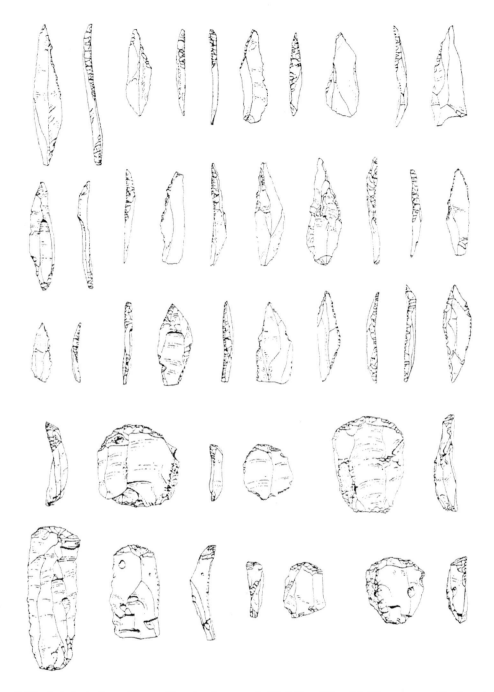

Figure 3.19: Artefacts from Trwyn Du, Anglesey: - 1-15, Microliths; 16-22, scrapers. Scale – 1:1.29.

relevance to the present discussion are at Trwyn Du (Aberffraw) on Anglesey and from Rhuddlan (Sites E and M), Clwyd, both of which are excavation sites and which produced the radiocarbon datings referred to earlier in the chapter.

Additional find-spots, but for which equivalent detail is unavailable, include that at Pencilan Head (SH 295 233) on the Lleyn peninsula (Gwynedd) where a small surface collection includes flakes, blades, blade cores and 4 fragmentary microliths of 'broad blade' appearance (Wainwright, 1963, 123 and fig 15, 1 - 6; Jacobi, 1980b, 139). 'A few microliths of non-geometric type' (*ibid.*) are also noted amongst debitage collected from the cliff-top at

Pared Llechymenin (SH 147 246) near Aberdaron, Gwynedd (Maltby, Oakley and Howarth, 1938; Wainwright, 1963, 123). Two cores from Porth Ruffydd, Anglesey (SH 216 800), have been compared with examples from Trwyn Du and have therefore been claimed to be early Mesolithic (Kelley, 1982). Other find-spots of small groups of potentially early material include Ogof Pant-y-Wennol (SH 8081 8160: Davies, 1989b, fig. 8.4, a-f), and the Aled valley, Clwyd, where surface finds of 'non-geometric' type have been reported (White, 1978, 28).

Trwyn Du, Anglesey (SH 352 679)
Here, a large collection of chipped flint and stone artefacts has been excavated from an old land surface, partially

overlain by an early Bronze Age cairn, on a rocky headland overlooking the mouth of the River Ffraw (Aberffraw: Houlder, 1957; White, 1978). Excavations in 1974 (White, 1978) resulted in the recovery of 5,605 artefacts classified by the excavator as follows:

Table 3.13: Artefacts from Trwyn Du (1974)

blunted points	123
triangles	7
tanged points	8
scrapers	87
axes	2
miscellaneous tools	75
flake waste	4,300
lump waste	238
cores	84
core trimmings	365
stone rubbers	7

A selection of these artefacts is shown in Figure 3.19. What is immediately apparent from this and Table 3.13 is the predominance amongst the diagnostic tools of simple obliquely-backed points. Large triangular microliths are also represented, but are few in number, whilst the so-called 'tanged points' - an unlikely constituent of any British Postglacial assemblage - could as well be re-classified amongst the other more conventional categories represented.

Significantly, the 'broad blade' microliths are accompanied by many end-scrapers (White, 1978, fig. 16) and two chipped stone transversely-sharpened axes/adzes, one of Carboniferous chert and the other of volcanic tuff (*ibid*, fig. 12). Apparently, however, there are no *mèches de forêt* or burins. The stone 'rubbers' (*ibid.*, fig. 19) are unmodified elongate pebbles, a not uncommon, but unexplained, feature of some early Mesolithic lithic collections, for instance from Star Carr and Oakhanger.

The collection from Trwyn Du, then, shows some similarity to that from Daylight Rock. Radiocarbon dating of hazel nutshell samples from a pit and a natural hollow (F16 and F13), both penetrating the gritty natural clay, gave the results listed in Table 3.3. Given greater credibility by the excavator were the two dates from the hollow: 8640 +150 BP (Q-1385) and 8,590 +90 BP (HAR-1194). Both these are, however, rather late in comparison both to Daylight Rock and other 'early' sites (see above), and, indeed, as will be seen in the next chapter, they overlap significantly with datings for strikingly different assemblages of 'narrow blade' type. These dates are suspect in that they are based on bulked samples, possibly containing nutshell fragments of varying ages. Such samples could presumably include material deriving from later use of the site, as evidenced by the find of a flake of polished stone axe of Group XXI on the same ancient ground surface as the Mesolithic scatter (Houlder, 1957).

Whilst typological considerations would therefore surely place this find-spot amongst others of early Mesolithic age, the exact timing of its occupation has yet to be satisfactorily identified.

Rhuddlan, Clwyd,

Site M (SJ 020 770)
Site E (SJ 020 770)

Excavations at Rhuddlan, Clwyd, in the 1970s recovered 13,330 pieces of struck flint and chert (Berridge, pers. comm.), mostly divided between the adjacent sites E (63%) and M (20%). Nearly 84% of these are made from Carboniferous (Gronant) chert. Table 3.14 below lists the principal artefact categories identified amongst the lithic material from Mesolithic (as opposed to later) contexts (data derived from ms supplied by P. Berridge).

Apart from the markedly 'early' character of the microliths in this assemblage (see Jacobi, 1980b, figs. 4.8, 4.12), the large number of end-scrapers, complemented by axe/adze-sharpening flakes, and at least three *mèches de forêt* support this attribution. As at Trwyn Du, it would appear that there are no burins which, if a genuine absence, might imply the exclusion of certain types of craft activity at these locations.

It is of interest that micro-denticulates are present at Rhuddlan but only from within disturbed contexts. As these contexts also contained much residual early Mesolithic flintwork, it could be suggested that these tools are to be associated with the latter, and in doing so to provide a further link to both English and other Welsh early assemblages. Micro-denticulates do, however, occur later in prehistory (Smith, 1965), and have also been been associated with late Mesolithic flintwork at Hendre, Rhuddlan (Healey and Manley, 1982). A small number of late Mesolithic narrow-blade microliths have been recognized from disturbed contexts on the Rhuddlan sites as well as an elongate 'bevelled pebble' and surface flaked arrowheads. With such later prehistoric and historic activity present, it would not be surprising that bulked radiocarbon samples, even from apparently 'secure' Mesolithic contexts, were to result in potentially misleading determinations (Table 3.3).

Table 3.14: Artefacts from Mesolithic contexts at Rhuddlan.

i) Tools:
    microliths:

obliquely-backed		62
convex-backed		13
isosceles		5
scalene	1	
others/unclass		20

    scrapers:

end-scrapers	41
double-ended	8
others/broken	21

awls (incl. *mèches de forêt*)	8
notched pieces	3
fabricator	1
ground-edged pieces	7
micro-denticulates (?intrusive)	8
utilzed/retouched	115

ii) By-products:

micro-burins	6
miss-hits	7
notched bladelets	1
axe/adze-sharpening flakes	5

iii) Debitage:
    cores:

single platform	78
double platform	54
other	4

core rejuvenation flakes	211
flakes, blades, blade frags.	6699

That the chronology for Rhuddlan requires further investigation is made all the more important by the recovery of six engraved pebbles, so far unique within Britain. Five of these were broken in antiquity but subsequent to decoration with narrow incised lines. These were almost certainly engraved with flint, chert or quartz. The sixth stone (S6), from an early medieval soil on Site T is entire and carries a complete 'motif' or composition of superimposed lines. Of the remaining pebbles (S1 - S5), only S2 was recovered *in situ* in a Mesolithic context, within a shallow hollow (M90) on site M also containing 'early' items of flint and chert and from which the radiocarbon date of 8528 ±73 BP (BM 822) was derived. S2 and the flints found with it are illustrated in Fig. 3.20. The other engraved pebbles are shown in Figure 3.21.

9. Summary

The acceleration of climatic warming at *c.* 10,000 BP appears to have been so rapid that the details of the changes that took place at this time are scarcely detectable in conventional stratigraphies. The resulting ecological transitions are yet to be adequately understood, but one may speculate that there was considerable biogeographic instability. The human response to this, when Postglacial conditions may have followed periglacial ones within the span of a single generation cannot yet be gauged. There seems to be growing evidence, however, that open environments persisted into the earliest Postglacial and, with them, the fauna and perhaps even the hunting practices of the Lateglacial. That such a scenario may be relevant in Wales is implied by evidence from pollen-sampling sites, and by the engraved horse mandible from Kendrick's Cave.

A forested landscape was quickly established, however, and a proliferation in evidence for human activity within it marks the conventional beginning of the Mesolithic.

In Wales, a suite of chipped flint and stone tool forms, including 'broad blade' microliths, end-scrapers, burins, *mèches de forêt* and axe/adzes, has been identified from several find- spots. Although the organic component of this technology is so far unknown, the range of lithic tools have clear analogues further afield in England and continental Europe, thus indicating that Wales belongs within a widespread 'techno-territory'. Radiocarbon dating of this technology suggests its emergence at *c.* 9,700 BP although acceptance of any apparent synchroneity at about this time must await independent dating.

Taken as typical of the early Mesolithic technology in Wales is the lithic collection from Daylight Rock on Caldey Island, Dyfed, a find-spot from which recently obtained AMS radiocarbon dates indicate use at *c.* 9,000 BP. This estimate is rather earlier than that obtained by conventional radiocarbon methods for early Mesolithic find-spots in north Wales, but is nevertheless still significantly later than its typological equivalents in England, such as Thatcham and Star Carr. Further determinations from other Welsh sites will therefore be necessary before an earliest Mesolithic exploitation can be identified, or before the proposal for its delayed appearance in Wales can be confidently upheld. Although early Mesolithic find-spots are abundant in Britain and new finds are filling out this distribution, it remains true that relatively few of these, and none with any satisfactory radiocarbon dating, come from the Marches or adjoining areas of the Midlands (Saville, 1981), thereby imposing a probably false impression of isolation to the Welsh occurrences. Lack of fieldwork and the obscuring of early Mesolithic sites by later deposits may partly account for this.

However, having now examined something of the currently known environmental, technological and chronological parameters of the early Mesolithic settlement of Wales, the next chapter goes on to examine evidence from one site in particular - The Nab Head I.

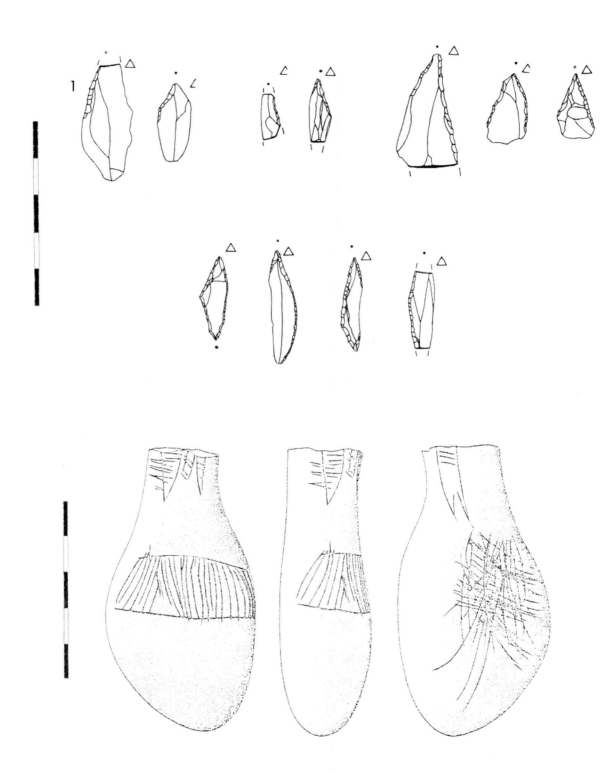

Figure 3.20: Microliths and engraved pebble from feature M90 at Rhuddlam, Site M. (drawing of pebble courtesy of P. Berridge). Scale in cms.

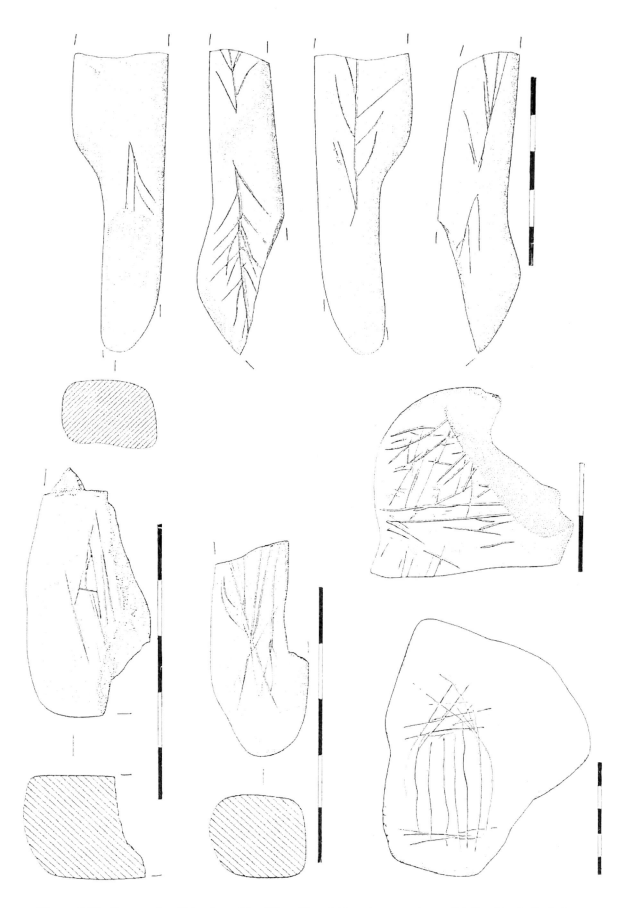

Figure 3.21: Engraved pebbles from Rhuddlan, Clwyd (drawings courtesy of P. Berridge). Scale in cms.

Plate 4.1: Aerial view of The Nab Head, Dyfed: sites I and II are arrowed.

1. Introduction:

The Nab Head is one of the more prominent of the many small headlands along the irregular perimeter of the Skomer peninsula which divides St. Brides Bay to the north from Milford Haven to the south. The headland thus lies almost at the farthest south- western extremity of Wales, forming a small northward-facing promontory of Old Red Sandstone which extends seawards from the Devonian coastline on the southern edge of St. Brides Bay.

The Nab itself is about 100m long and some 40 m. across at its widest point (see Plate 4.1). It is surrounded on all sides by cliffs which are at their most abrupt and tallest along its western edge. The surface of the headland, here at about 20 m OD, then slopes away to a more rocky and subdued eastern cliff edge, and in doing so forms the eastern flank of a former small valley now partially eroded by the sea. Both this small valley and the headland itself owe their shape to the selective coastal erosion of fault zones on either side of the promontory. The headland narrows at its junction with the mainland at a point called 'The Neck', and it is here that further faulting is concentrating an erosion which will

eventually isolate the headland entirely. Severe periglacial activity in the Lateglacial exploited this weakened area which became choked with frost- shattered and involuted rock debris which in turn was overlaid by solifluction deposits. Modern gulley erosion is now eating into both this and the overlying postglacial soil in which quantities of Mesolithic flints are being exposed. This is The Nab Head Site I.

2. History

The area of 'The Neck', and indeed much of the western side of The Nab Head, has been stripped bare of soil and turf in the teeth of the westerly Atlantic weather. Flints are known to have been observed towards the end of the last century when Edward Laws noted 'an actual stratification of worked flint chips and flakes.....covered by about three feet of soil on the very edge of the cliff...' (Laws, 1880, 241; 1888, 17). From that time, if not earlier, until the present day, flints have continued to be exposed and have been collected in their thousands by any number of antiquarians and curiosity hunters (Leach, 1933, 229).

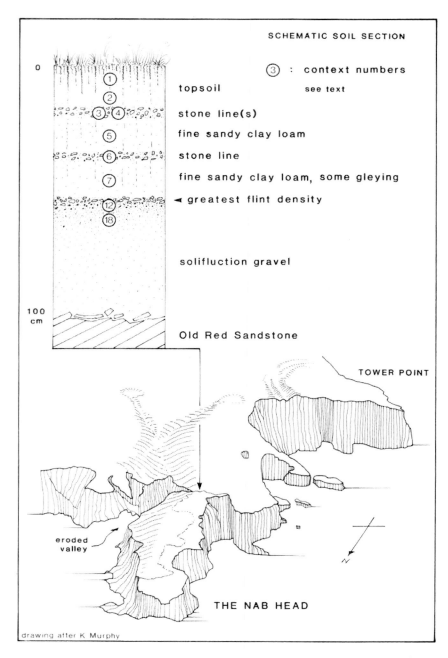

Figure 4.1: The Nab Head Site I. Soil section at the area of "The Neck".

Colonel F. W. Lambton of Brownslade collected stone tools and beads from a 'factory' at the The Nab Head at much the same time as Laws made his visits. Subsequently Lord Kensington, with his eldest brother, dug profitably at the site in about 1885-7, whilst in 1909 Professor O. T. Jones, then working with the Geological Survey, found many more flints. Further digging took place in 1925, this time by the Reverend J. P. Gordon-Williams who made well over 3000 finds (Gordon-Williams, 1925, 1926). Whilst not leaving any detailed excavation records he noted no stratification but instead that the flints lay scattered throughout the soil, the weightier material 'checked by a layer of stiff clayey grit which overlies the live rock at a depth which varies according to contours from one foot to three feet' (Gordon-Williams, 1926, 88). The next investigations to be recorded at the site were two perfunctory trial trenches excavated by

G. J. Wainwright to the north and east of the eroded area and which revealed few flints and no stratification (Wainwright, 1969, 1970). In view of later discoveries it might be worth quoting this excavator's comments at the time:

'On account of the depredations by private collectors and the erosion of turf from the promontary, a rescue excavation was undertaken at this mesolithic occupation site in order to establish the extent of the chipping floor and to collect any flints which still survived in the eroded areas. *From these investigations it may be concluded that the site has been destroyed by the agencies noted above.*' (Wainwright, 1969, 13: my emphasis).

It is largely the finds of Lord Kensington (Leach, 1933) and Gordon-Williams (1926), divided between the Tenby Museum, The Pembrokeshire Museums and the National Museum of Wales, that have given rise to the principal publications within which The Nab Head has been assessed (Clark, 1932; Wainwright, 1963; Jacobi, 1980b).

In the most recent of these appraisals Jacobi (1980b) proposed that many of the lithic artefacts are of early Mesolithic age, closely resembling those from Star Carr, N. Yorkshire, whilst others from the same site are of 'narrow blade' type (*sensu* Buckley, 1924; Radley and Mellars, 1964) and hence of later Mesolithic date. Although it is true that such an interpretation ignores the possibility that the assemblage may instead represent a single discrete episode, there has yet to be a satisfactory demonstration that 'broad' (early Mesolithic) and 'narrow blade' assemblages have ever been so combined. Reports of lithic assemblages which combine both suites of artefacts, (eg at Farnham: Clark and Rankine, 1939), have yet to be shown not to result from natural processes by which formerly separate groups of material have become mixed together (Newell, 1981). The 'Horsham' assemblages of southern England, as re-defined by recent research and excavation (Jacobi, 1978; 1981) are suggested to be intermediate only in chronological terms between early and late Mesolithic: their lithic components are markedly different from those assemblages at both extremes of the Mesolithic and also from those found at The Nab Head.

Whilst it may be plausible to accept Jacobi's (1980b) proposal that The Nab Head assemblage is an amalgam of material deposited by occupants of the site at widely different times, this nevertheless required testing. Work on the headland subsequent to Jacobi's paper, has provided an opportunity to do just this, and has not only amplified his interpretation but, more importantly, assisted further in the explanation of other sites in the Welsh Mesolithic record.

Examination by the author of the eroded ground and cliff sections at 'The Neck' in 1978 confirmed earlier reports from R. Kennedy and R. Jacobi that cultural material was still present in some quantity at the site (Kennedy, 1977). It appeared also that, in all probability, recently undisturbed deposits still existed and were immediately threatened by both cliff erosion and souvenir hunters. These circumstances suggested that a last opportunity might exist to excavate at the site in order to rescue a fresh and representative sample of artefacts, to fully examine their depositional context, and perhaps even to date them - thereby providing the chance to assess Jacobi's assertions in the light of a new and more reliable database. Initial proposals along these lines were submitted to the Dyfed Archaeological Trust who agreed to conduct trial excavations. Some ten days of excavation then took place in 1979 under the co-directorship of the author and D. Benson and, after promising results, were then followed by more extensive work in 1980 .

3. Soils and stratigraphy:

From earlier accounts, there seems to be some confusion as to whether or not there is any stratigraphy to be seen at the site. The most accurate observations were in fact those of Gordon- Williams, quoted above, who noted flints throughout the soil but with a concentration of the weightier material accumulating at the surface of a 'stiff clayey grit'. It was this latter accumulation which accounts for Laws' 'actual stratification of worked flint chips and flakes'.

A detailed examination of the soil profile shows that there are several clearly identifiable soil layers or horizons which give a resemblance to actual stratigraphy, although their formation is probably the result of a complex combination of soil processes, with phases of accumulation, sorting, and erosion. The layers are, therefore, only stratigraphic in a limited sense, and their relationship to the spread of cultural material through the profile is discussed below. The nature of the soils at The Nab Head and their genesis is at present under study by Dr. S. Limbrey.

A generalized soil profile from 'The Neck' area (Site I) is shown in Fig. 4.1 The narrowest part of 'The Neck', in which the bedrock is faulted across the axis of the headland, is filled with cryoturbated stony debris overlain by a thick and dense solifluction deposit of stony grit in a matrix of sand and clay. Such solifluction deposits are a common feature in west Wales (locally described as 'rab') and here form the subsoil (contexts 11, 12 and 18) upon which a post-glacial soil developed. The top 5 cm. of the solifluction deposit has apparently at one time undergone a degree of sorting and consists of a stony fine sandy clay-loam (context 12) in which small stones are rather more densely packed than underneath. A sharp boundary divides this from the overlying soil which is typically 40 - 50 cm. thick. It consists mostly of a fine sandy clay-loam containing two distinct thin (2 cm) stone lines (contexts 4 and 6) forming sharp and even boundaries within the soil itself. A further stone line (context 2) may be present just below the root mat. The intervening stone- free layers (contexts 7, 5, and 3) are at present assumed to be the result of at least two separate phases of soil accumulation, perhaps resulting from local human activity, after which sorting processes have led to downward movement of heavier material and the formation of the stone lines. It is significant that the upper stone line (4) can be shown to post-date the counterscarp bank of the Iron Age promontory fort at Tower Point, some 200 m. from Site I. This suggests that much of the local soil profile could be of later prehistoric origin, and therefore that contemporary (ie Iron Age) cultivation could perhaps have contributed to its formation.

An alternative interpretation of the stone lines is that they may have been brought about by periodically intense phases of sub- aerial erosion of the active cliff face.

The probability that the upper layers of the soil at Site I are at least later prehistoric in age implies that the history of the Mesolithic occupation at the site is confined to a thin and

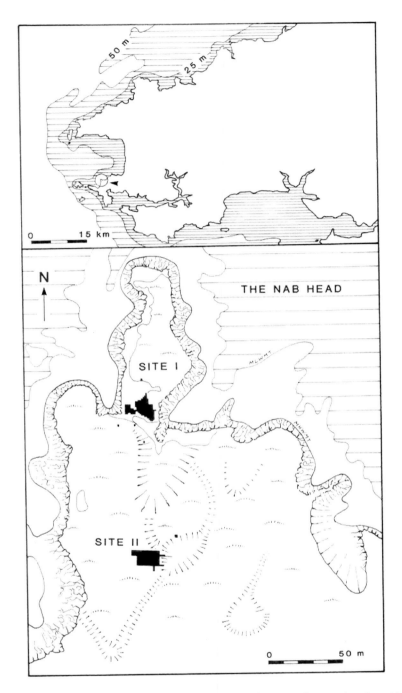

Figure 4.2: The Nab Head. Location of excavation trenches at sites I and II.

worm-sorted horizon, perhaps truncated, which originally lay immediately above the subsoil. The potential for stratigraphic resolution of separate Mesolithic occupations in these circumstances therefore seems remote, barring the presence of sealed features. However, an analysis of the lithic material and its distribution through the soil profile does support the fundamental proposal that two different episodes are represented at the site, albeit blurred by the vertical movement. This will be more fully discussed below (p. 99). At the moment it is enough to say that artefacts were found throughout the soil profile, but that by far the majority were concentrated near the base of context 7. Some pieces were found up to 30 cm. into the solifluction deposit, indicating occasional disturbance at least to that depth. In

the almost total absence of present-day earthworm activity, downward movement within the remaining soil profile is aided by the presence of a polygonal pattern of cracks, separating the slightly gleyed peds of context 7, which open in dry weather by up to about 4-5 cm. at the soil surface.

4. Excavation strategy:

After a preliminary topographic survey of the headland, the excavation strategy in 1979 was to quadrant the exposed area at 'The Neck', excavating in 1 m. grid squares. Soil was removed by context and sieved through 6 and 3 mm. sieves using high-pressure industrial sprays. Over 12,000 flints were recovered, but largely from what were then identified as disturbed contexts. However, examination of a

Plate 4.2: The Nab Head Site I under excavation (1980)

few square metres of undisturbed soil still protected under the turf revealed considerable densities of flint. It was plainly this latter area, to the east of the exposed and disturbed surface of 'The Neck', that warranted wider coverage, and this was achieved in the following year.

In all, a total of 186 square metres were completely or partially excavated and about 30 tons of sediment were wet sieved. Because of the extreme hardness of the soil under dry conditions, trowelling by hand in the conventional way was both difficult and damaging. The soil was therefore usually excavated using the point of the trowel, and bagged by metre square and context (soil horizon). It was not feasible to process all the soil removed in this way, and therefore only sample transects 1 m. wide and spaced at 1m intervals across the site were totally sieved. Contexts 7 and 12, containing most of the flint, were sieved throughout, however, with the result that the overall artefact distribution plots do not appear noticeably biased by this sampling strategy.

Sieving allowed for the recovery of most of the smaller fraction of lithic debris and tools - that is, the components which are noticeably absent from previous collections from the site. Despite the high water pressures used (1,500 - 2,000 psi), artefacts were not broken, and robust charcoal and hazel nut fragments were also retrievable. Most of the shale beads were recovered in this way.

Artefacts located during trowelling were bagged on site. The necessity of bulk sieving made initial attempts at 3-dimensional recording of artefacts of limited value, and this was abandoned in favour of recording by grid square and context alone. Sections through the deposits were drawn and levelled at 2 m. intervals across the site. The site grid system is labelled on Figure 4.12.

1 x 1 m. test pits were excavated at various locations to north and south of the main trenches in order to examine the soil profile and the extent of the lithic scatter.

5. Excavation results - summary:
It was soon established that the bare soil exposed at 'The Neck' had been extensively turned over and contained a complete mixture of those horizons present in an undisturbed form under the turf. In spite of this, artefact densities here were pronounced, reaching a maximum of 854 pieces per grid square (A9). The larger items had plainly been removed, and it seems certain that this was once the richest part of the site and was no doubt the first to attract the attentions of antiquarians. At the base of the disturbed soil were features that may have been Mesolithic although their fillings were of mixed material and there can be no certainty that they are not of relatively recent origin. Two of the features were irregular oval depressions, measuring 0.9 x 0.65 m. and 0.85 x 0.55 m. respectively. A third was a shallow gulley 0.35 - 0.40 m. wide and 0.15 m. deep running in a straight line for about 2.5 m.

139 square metres of apparently undisturbed sediment were excavated, mostly in 1980, from that part of the site concealed beneath turf to the north of the eastern gulley (Plate 4.2). No features were seen over this area and the sequence of soil layers was maintained throughout, overlying a mostly even but sloping surface of bedrock and solifluction deposits. Considerable densities of artefacts were found, however, concentrated at the base of the soil profile. As anticipated, the greatest number of lithic remains

Figure 4.3: The Nab Head site I, distribution of flaked flint and stone. 4 artefacts/dot. A: total distribution; B: distribution from "undisturbed" contexts.

were found nearest to the disturbed part of 'The Neck', and here as many as 866 chipped artefacts were found per grid square (K7). These densities fell away gradually in all directions (see Fig. 4.3), although a limit to the scatter was not located, and certainly a part of this eastern edge of the site must be assumed to have been truncated by the cliff.

Single square metre test holes were excavated to the north of the denuded area of 'The Neck' (L30) and also to the south and south-east of the main trench (M-13, G-1, square omega), and in each case, flints were located. Significant concentrations of 184 and 285 in G-1 and square omega, respectively, suggest that the lithic scatter extends in undisturbed soil for a considerable distance to the south of the eroded Neck. Charcoal (*Quercus, Prunus, Leguminosae*, and *Corylus*) was abundant, weighing in all over 18 gm., in square omega.

Charcoal was otherwise found sparsely across the site, as

were fragments of charred hazelnut shells. A relative concentration of charcoal was detected near the eastern limit of the main trench centred on grid square R7 which contained a maximium of 7.1 gm/sq.m., and covering an area of some 12 square metres. Wood species represented in this concentration include *Pomoideae, Prunus, Quercus, Salix/Populus, Alnus,* and possibly *Corylus.*

Slightly acid soil Ph values ensured that no other organic remains were found. Pollen is also preserved only scarcely, if at all, and samples from the site recently investigated for their pollen content at University College, Lampeter were unproductive (M. Lewis pers. comm.). Measurements of phosphate concentration were made across the site, but with the exception of a small number of isolated high readings from the disturbed Neck area, values were minimal and uninformative.

Lithic remains were, therefore, by far the most abundant and informative indicators of the nature of this site, and these are discussed in detail below.

6. The flint and flaked stone artefacts:

i) Raw materials:
With a varied solid geology and having also been traversed by at least one ice front, west Wales has a wide range of erratic material of both local and regional origin accumulated on its beaches. There seems little doubt that it was the contemporary early Flandrian beach shingle which provided flakeable raw materials for the inhabitants at The Nab Head.

Of the lithic sample from Site I some 98.8% is of pebble flint presumably introduced onto the contemporary beaches through the erosion of terrestrial glacial deposits, or through the on-shore accumulation of Pleistocene sediments from the Bristol Channel, or Celtic and Irish Seas. As is to be expected from such a random catchment, several colours and textures of flint are represented - as they are on the beaches today. Shades of opaque grey and pale flint with mottling tend to predominate, with rarer translucent black, grey and yellow pieces. The degree of subsequent patination is also extremely variable. The surfaces of most artefacts types are either unchanged or patinated in degrees up to a dense opaque white. A noticeable feature of the flint assemblage, however, is that patination is more pronounced amongst those artefacts interpreted as later in the occupation sequence. Such a reversal of the usual correlation of increasing patination with age may perhaps eventually be explained in terms of a change in raw material sources or were this not the case, perhaps of evolving soil conditions on the headland. A consideration here, is the possible influence of shellfish middens later in the Mesolithic which, if they once existed on the site, might have provided the calcareous conditions responsible for the observed differential patination.

Apart from flint, there are several types of fine- textured extrusive igneous rock types - tuffs and rhyolites particularly - which fracture conchoidally and may be flaked in much the same way as flint. Most of the 488 non-flint artefacts from Site I are of such material, the primary sources of which are among the many outcrops of Ordovician volcanics now exposed both in north Pembrokeshire and, nearer by, on Skomer Island and the Wooltack peninsula. In view of the variety of the Pembrokeshire volcanics and the confusion arising from drift-derived secondary sources, specific petrological identification of this flaked material is unlikely to have any significant archaeological bearing (R. Sanderson, pers. comm.). Such raw material can be expected to have been collected from beaches along with flint cobbles, the main attraction being its larger size and suitability for manufacturing tools such as axes/adzes for which the flint pebbles were rarely bulky enough (see below).

Finally, amongst the flaked tools and debris found on Site I are small quantities of Cretaceous Greensand chert. This is another component of local beach shingle and, as with the other stone and flint types, its presence on the site reflects nothing more than the opportunistic gathering of workable raw material.

ii) The debitage:
Altogether, 39,863 items of flaked flint and stone were recovered from the excavated area. The distribution is illustrated on Fig. 4.3. This large total reflects the exacting recovery rate of the sieving system: approximately 58% are pieces 10 mm. or less in size.

Of this material, 98% is composed of the debitage resulting from the reduction of pebbles, up to about 200 gm. in weight, to the range of retouched tools to be described below. A fuller analysis of the bulk of this material is to be prepared in advance of the publication of the recent excavations. Comment here will be confined to the cores alone in the hope that they may demonstrate the apparent mixture of Mesolithic occupation remains on the site rather better than the mass of otherwise somewhat indeterminate waste pieces.

There are 155 blade and bladelet cores, and these are typically single- or double-platformed. Their size-range is shown on Fig. 4.4. The histograms here illustrate the variation in core 'height' (taken as the distance between the core's apex and the centre of the opposing platform) from several sites chosen from Cornwall and west Wales. To a certain extent the size of cores within a discrete assemblage will be an index of the character of the tools and debitage struck from them. At The Nab Head Site I the range of sizes accommodates both large and small cores at either extreme of the average of 35 mm. (standard deviation: ±9.9). When compared to the sizes of cores from other sites, such as Daylight Rock or The Nab Head Site II, this particular range is noticeably more extended than for assemblages assumed to be of either early or late Mesolithic, respectively (Johnson and David, 1982, 80-84).

This fundamental difference in size throughout the core reduction sequence and its products, between early and later Mesolithic flintworking, is a crucial factor in many British lithic assemblages. It is noticeable that the larger 'broad blade' microliths appear to rely on minimal modification to the outline of the original blade blank, whilst smaller and later microlith shapes are usually defined by elaborate retouch (Myers, 1989a). Such changes in the technology of hunting equipment (if not a function of the changing availability of raw material) were perhaps a response to the constraints of altered hunting strategies necessitated by changing environmental conditions (Myers, 1989a, 1989b). However, explanations - if they are to be found - will have to define variability in function more closely and place it alongside stylistic change within an evolving social as well as physical background.

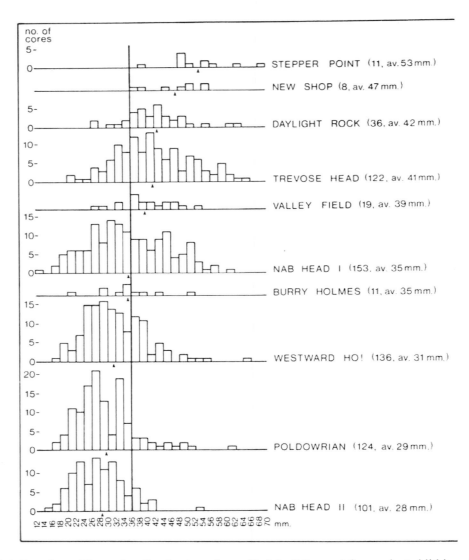

Figure 4.4: Bar charts illustrating distribution of core "heights" (in mm) from selected lithic collections.

iii) The retouched tools and their by-products:

The composition of the lithic assemblage from the site is shown in Table 4.1, below. The following major categories of tool were recognized: 'broad' and 'narrow blade' microliths, end-scrapers, burins, *mèches de forêt*, denticulates, and a single core axe or adze. By-products include axe/adze sharpening and thinning flakes, burin spalls, and micro-burins.

In the preceding chapter, a close parallel was drawn between certain Welsh lithic collections (eg Daylight Rock, Caldey) and those excavated from dated early Mesolithic sites in northern and southern England. Exactly the same tool types are present amongst those from The Nab Head (Table 4.1; Figs. 4.5, 4.7-4.11). Here, however, there is a suspected late Mesolithic component represented mainly by 'narrow blade' microliths and denticulates. Each category of artefact needs to be considered separately. The theme of the present chapter remains with the early Mesolithic, however, and the later period will be fully introduced subsequently.

Microliths:

The 143 classifiable microliths and microlith fragments (defined after the scheme illustrated by Jacobi: 1978, 16) are divisible in terms of shape and size into two main groups approximating to the 'Broad' and 'Narrow' forms originally identified by Buckley amongst assemblages on the Pennines (Buckley, 1924). Representative examples from Site I are illustrated in Fig. 4.5, Nos. 1-43 and 44-80, respectively.

The most notable feature of the 'broad blade' microliths is the relatively large number of scalene triangles - forming 27% of this group (eg Fig. 4.5, Nos. 23-43). Equivalent large triangular forms are not common in British Mesolithic assemblages, but where they do occur as more than just isolated examples they are to be associated with an early Mesolithic date. Examples of sites demonstrating this association are Star Carr (Clark, 1954) and Flixton (Moore, 1950), both in North Yorkshire and fairly confidently dated to *c.* 9,500 BP, or slightly later (see Table 3.1).

Table 4.1: Artefacts from The Nab Head Site I

i) Tools:

microliths:

obliquely-backed pieces	21
large scalene triangles	20
isosceles triangles	3
frags of triangular-shaped pieces	10
large convex-backed pieces	3
other 'broad blade' microlith frags	33
scalene micro-triangles	27
other 'narrow blade' microliths	26
frags of 'narrow blade' microliths	57
unclassified microliths/frags	13

scrapers:

end-scrapers	100
double-ended scrapers	6
other scrapers	8

denticulates	15
burins	26
mèches de forêt/frags	44
axe/adze	1
truncated pieces	6
nosed piece	1
notched pieces	8
retouched/utilized pieces	145
others	51

ii) By-products:

micro-burins	69
miss-hits	12
micro-intermediates	3
burin spalls	21
axe/adze sharpening/thinning flakes	31

iii) Debitage:

cores	155
flakes, blade fragments	38,948

TOTAL flaked flint and stone	**39,863**

Underlying Zone VIa peat and, therefore, arguably of about the same age is the assemblage from Broxbourne 104, Hertfordshire, which also includes large scalene triangles (Jacobi, 1980b, 154; and above).

Obliquely-backed points (Fig. 4.5, Nos. 1-17), forming 23% of the broad-blade group, are an invariable component of early Mesolithic assemblages. Further parallels can also be found between items in some of these assemblages and the rarer large isosceles triangles and convex-backed points at The Nab Head. Absent from The Nab Head, though, are examples of the bi- truncated pieces of rhombic or trapezoidal outline and all forms of basally retouched points.

If the majority of microliths from Site I can be argued to be early Mesolithic, there remain 53 others (and 57 fragments) which possess features of shape and size, only known from part-way through the Mesolithic, and which indicate equally clearly that they derive from later re-use of the site. These are so-called 'geometrics' or 'narrow blade' microliths (classes 5-9: Jacobi, 1978, 16) which are typically small and slim and include a diversity of outlines.

Most distinctive are 'micro-triangles' with a scalene (and sometimes isosceles) outline (Fig. 4.5, Nos. 44-60). These account for 51% of the 53 classifiable 'narrow blade' microliths. The remaining 26 pieces mostly have convex or lanceolate outlines, although varying somewhat in both size and the extent of their retouched perimeter (Fig. 4.5, Nos. 61-80). The earliest dating for assemblages from mainland Britain that contain microliths such as these appears to be *c.* 8,700 BP, from sites in northern England (Mellars, 1976a). Recent radiocarbon results from Prestatyn (Clwyd: see Chapter V) indicate that late microlith types also occur at about this time in Wales. They then occur throughout Britain until the beginning of the Neolithic. In addition to the narrow triangles, there is a single example of the very distinctive 'micro-*petit-tranchet*' (class 5c: Fig. 4.5, No. 73) from The Nab Head, a microlith-type for which there is some evidence, again from the northern England, of a relatively late appearance in the Mesolithic (Radley, 1970).

The many microliths from Site I, because of their clear typological polarity, provide an opportunity to test the proposal that there may be a stratigraphic separation between items attributed to 'broad' and 'narrow blade' technologies at The Nab Head. Figure 4.6 illustrates the relative proportions of the two microlith groupings for each soil layer, thereby giving an impression of the relative frequency of the two types vertically through the soil profile. It is apparent from this diagram that, although both types of microlith are found throughout most of the profile, there is, nevertheless, a clear trend in which 'broad blade' pieces form a greater proportion of the microliths as depth increases. Reciprocally, 'narrow blade' pieces are more common nearer the surface. Significantly, no late Mesolithic microliths were recovered from the base of the profile (context 18).

If the suggestion of a succession of occupations at the site is strengthened by these data, however, it is also clear that mixing of their components has taken place.

Scrapers:
Including all recognizable fragments, there are 114 scrapers from Site I characterized by convex retouch (Fig. 4.7) Of these, 100 are, or appear to have been, worked on the ends of flakes or blades and a further six are double-ended scrapers. Such scrapers, often with neat inclined and radially directed retouch at the distal ends of blades or long flakes are characteristic of a majority of early Mesolithic assemblages and also have very close parallels from Lateglacial contexts.

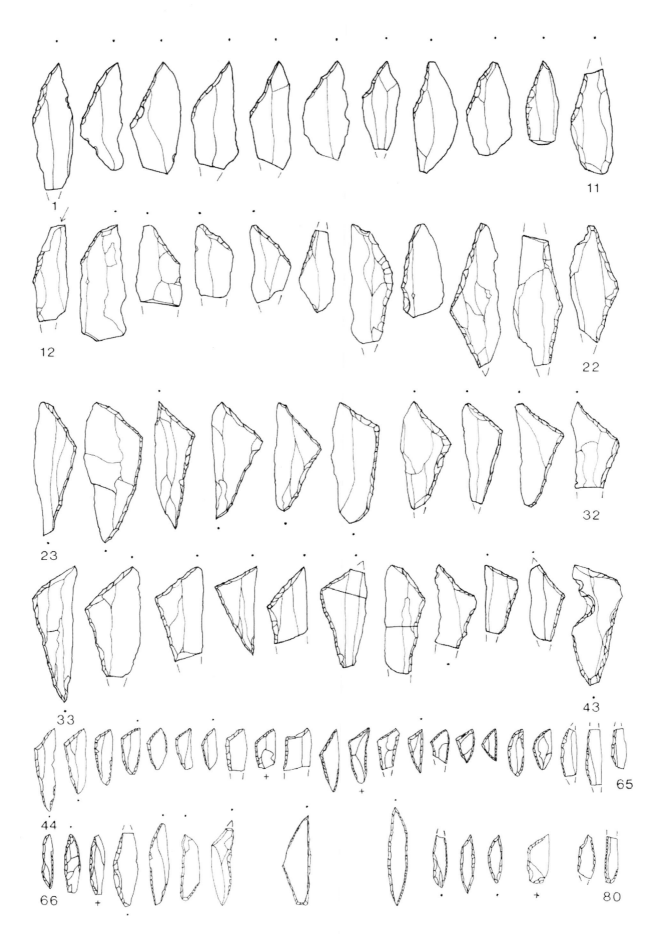

Figure 4.5: The Nab Head Site I. Microliths. Scale – 1:1.

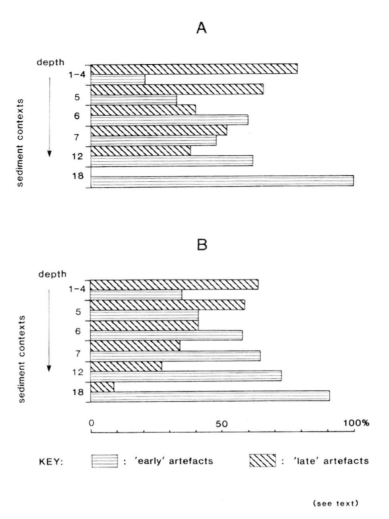

A

B

KEY: ▭ : 'early' artefacts ▨ : 'late' artefacts

(see text)

Figure 4.6: Bar-charts illustrating the percentage representation of "early" and "late" artefact types by depth (sediment context). A: microliths; B: other artefacts (see text)

Also interpreted here as components of the early Mesolithic technology are scrapers with steep convex retouch around much of the perimeter of six flakes, lending them a disc- or 'horse-shoe' shaped outline (eg Fig. 4.7, Nos. 12-13). As these occurred low in the soil profile amongst mostly earlier lithic types (see above), their close similarity to later prehistoric forms is probably coincidental - and indicates the fallibility of any rigid chronological labelling of this and other scraper types.

Denticulates:
These artefacts will be encountered in the following chapters where their association with later Mesolithic collections will be more fully explored. At Site I, however, there are 15 examples of flakes, usually thick primary flakes, which have been coarsely retouched or 'denticulated' around their distal edges.

Mèches de forêt:
There are 44 examples of *mèches de forêt* or 'drill-bits' amongst the excavated assemblage, and attention has also been drawn both to their occurrence at Daylight Rock and to their restricted early chronological appearance on sites in

both England and Scandinavia (Clark, 1975, 108, fig. 11). Here, the 35 substantially complete specimens (see Fig. 4.8, Nos. 1-24) are usually blades or bladelets narrowed by abrupt bi-lateral modification to a rod-like, or awl-shaped, outline with a near cylindrical section at their distal ends. Their tips are frequently somewhat rounded, as if by abrasion, and a rotational movement during use is indicated both by this and the presence of invasive micro-scaling damage to the ventral surface.

An equivalent representation of drill-bits at Site I (7% of the tools) is shared at both Daylight Rock (10%) and Star Carr (12%). However, the drill-bits from Star Carr and nearby Flixton tend to be rather larger than those from The Nab Head, (Clark, 1954, fig. 39; Moore, 1950, fig. 2).

Burins:
Only 26 burins (Fig. 4.9) have been identified. Three are burins on prepared truncation and the remainder burins on breaks or unretouched truncations.

The role of burins in the British Mesolithic is not well understood, despite their plentiful occurrence in

101

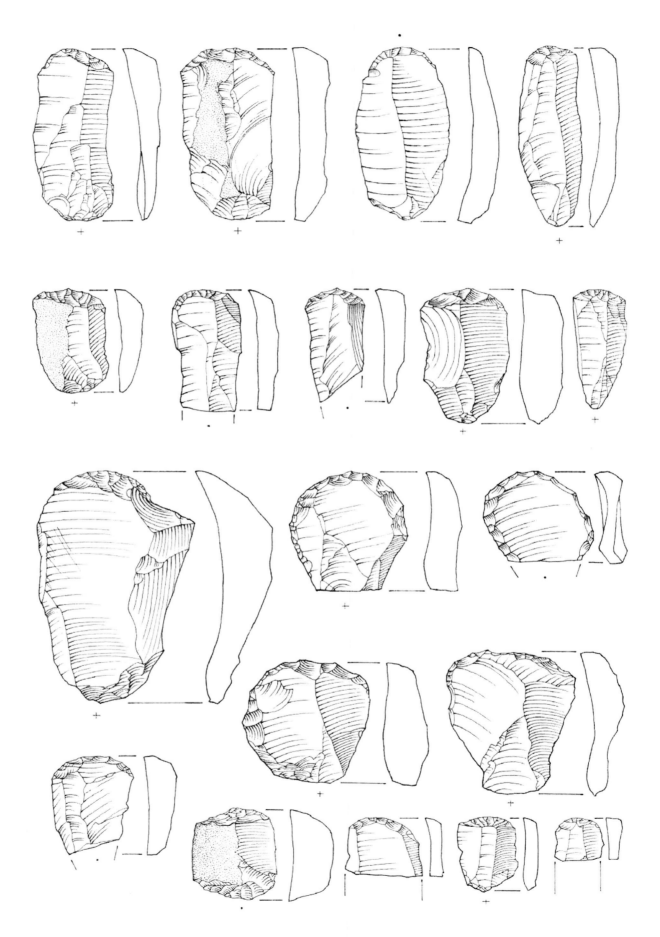

Figure 4.7: The Nab Head Site I. Scrappers. Scale – 1:1.

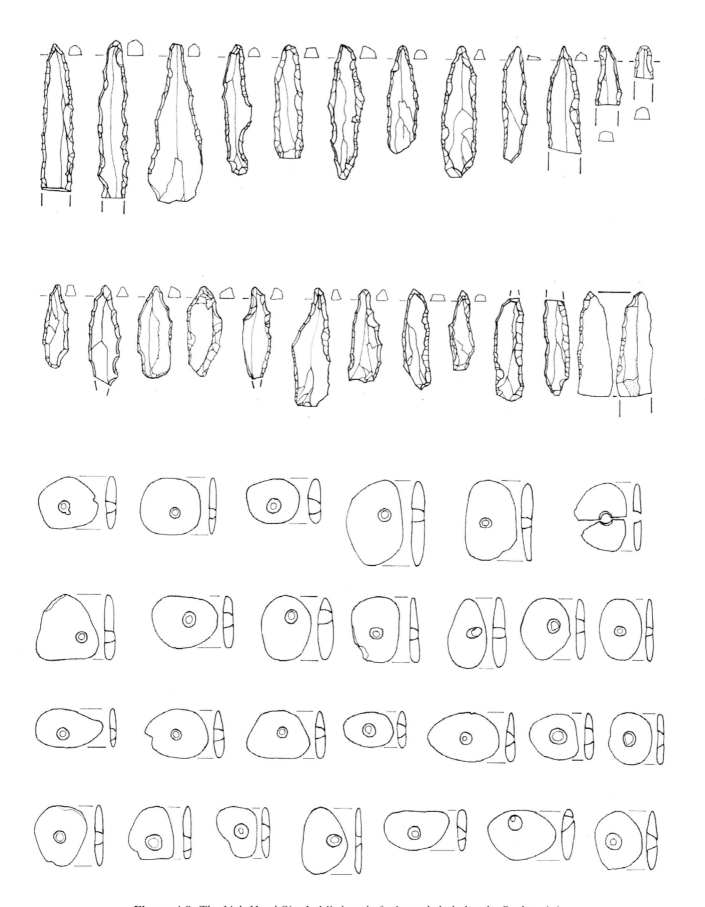

Figure 4.8: The Nab Head Site I. *Mèches de forêts* and shale beads. Scale – 1:1.

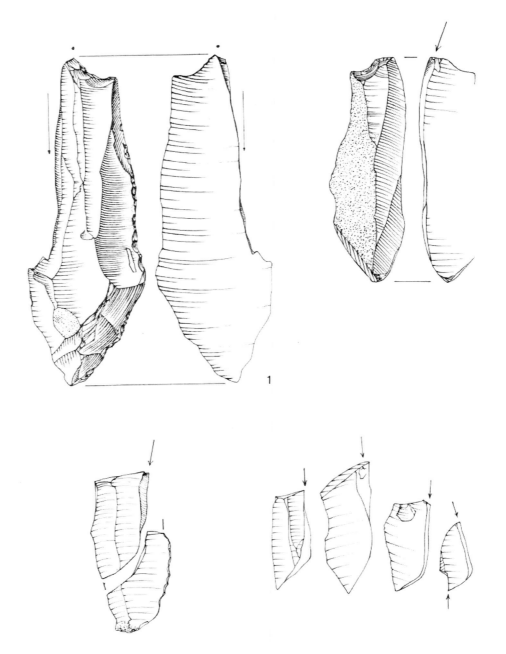

Figure 4.9: The Nab Head site I. Burins. No. 1 is from the Tenby Museum collection (drawing courtesy of R.Jacobi), the remainder from the recent excavations. Scale -1:1.26.

assemblages of various dates. Only at Star Carr, where they are the most numerous tool form, can they be convincingly associated with the working of bone and antler (Clark, 1954; Dumont, 1983). In some cases the burin blow may rather be an aid to hafting or an alternative to the 'blunting' of retouch (Moss, 1987).

As burins can be numerous on late Mesolithic sites (see Chapter VI), and as they occur throughout the profile at The Nab Head Site I, it remains unknown whether they belong to one or both of the suggested occupation phases at this site. Turning to the closest local analogy to an unmixed early Mesolithic assemblage - Daylight Rock - we can note eleven burins and therefore suggest that at least some of those from The Nab Head might be their contemporaries.

Axe/adze:

One example of a transversely sharpened axe or adze was recovered during the excavation (Fig. 4.10, No. 1), and is in keeping with the general appearance of the four others found by Gordon- Williams some sixty years ago (Fig. 4.11). It was these early finds, together with those of the shale beads and figurine, which originally drew attention to The Nab Head at a national level, in Grahame Clark's synthesis of 1932. Ever since, the presence of transversely sharpened axes or adzes has been recognized locally as an indicator of early Mesolithic activity and in 1963 Wainwright noted that The Nab Head was the only Welsh site with microliths that demonstrated a 'Maglemosian influence' (Wainwright, 1963, 126).

The recent example is only roughly worked, with a poorly developed blade, and in section is sub-rectangular or trapezoidal. It has been flaked from a fine-grained recrystallised rhyolitic tuff (C. Houlder, pers. comm.) which in this case has not responded well to knapping.

Other tools:
In addition to the tool forms already discussed are truncated pieces (6), notched pieces (8) and a single 'nosed' piece. There are also 145 pieces with retouch or clear signs of utilization, yet which have otherwise to remain unclassified.

By-products:
By-products of tool manufacture and maintainance include micro-burins and 'related' pieces (84), burin spalls (21) and axe- or adze-sharpening and thinning flakes (31: eg Fig. 4.10, Nos. 2-5).

Their presence here is a clear confirmation, if any were needed, that their corresponding tools were made and re-sharpened on the site. The variation in micro-burin breadth indicates an equivalence with both early and late Mesolithic microliths. Of 68 micro-burins, 61 are proximal ends of bladelets amongst which there has been a clear preference for notching on the right lateral edge (72%). This bias is matched in the microlith sample: for instance, 81% of the obliquely-backed points have been truncated from the same side, and point to the right. If all microlith types are included, this proportion falls to about 63%. In terms of shape, when oriented with shorter sides uppermost (as in Fig. 4.5), 92% of the scalene micro-triangles point to the right, whilst 65% of the large scalene triangles point the other way. Such preferences, particularly amongst the smaller scalene triangles and the obliquely-backed points, may relate either to the handedness of the knapper, or to the functional positioning of the microliths in predominantly uniserial or bi-serial composite tools.

Amongst the 29 certain axe- or adze-sharpening flakes, 16 are of non-flint material, such as rhyolite, demonstrating a specific selection of such raw material for this particular tool-type. There are no other tools made of anything but flint. Judging by the flaking and large size of some of the sharpening flakes (see Fig. 4.10, Nos. 4-5), it seems probable that their parent tools were at one time both large and carefully finished, in contrast to the five somewhat diminutive and worked-down examples which are actually known from the site. Sharpening flakes are also numerous in earlier collections from The Nab Head and a possible explanation of their preponderance over the number of actual axes or adzes recovered may be that the latter were used away from the site, returning only to be re-sharpened. An equivalent possibility is that these tools were produced at the site but were then exchanged elsewhere. That axes or adzes were in use 'off-site' is indicated by instances of isolated finds of these tools in the landscape, for instance at Benton (see Fig. 3.3 for the distribution of such finds).

iv) Other worked stone:
In addition to flaked flint and stone, former collections of artefacts from The Nab Head, as well as the assemblage currently under consideration, contain other very important items of worked and worn stone. These may be divided into worked shale items and pebble tools and it is the presence of the first of these, in the form of hundreds of shale beads and a carved 'amulet' which has so often singled the site out for comment.

Shale beads:
At the time of writing some 692 beads are known to have been found at The Nab Head. Of these, 64 complete or partial beads were recovered during the recent excavations. A selection of these is illustrated in Fig.4.8. With one exception, of Old Red Sandstone, all are made of small discs of water-smoothed blue- grey shale, identical to specimens that can now be collected from the beach at St. Brides Haven only a kilometre along the coast to the east. The discs are usually oval in shape with occasional rounded sub-angular perimeters, and are typically some 2 - 3 mm thick. With few exceptions they are perforated by a central hole, U-shaped in section, and drilled from only one face.

Many of these finds were made in disturbed contexts. Those recovered from undisturbed sediments, however, came from either context 7, or below in the top of the underlying solifluction deposit (contexts 12 and 18). Diagnostic retouched items from the latter are exclusively early Mesolithic in type. On this evidence it seems a strong probability that they belong with the characteristically early Mesolithic flintwork also encountered in these lowest levels of the site (see Fig. 4.6). Within these levels there is a noticeable concentration in an area of some 6 square metres (L7, M7, N7, L6, M6 and N6) where 27 beads or bead fragments were found. This concentration contrasts with the otherwise sporadic distribution of beads across the site (see Fig. 4.12) and lies slightly to the south of the focus of the associated lithic scatter. No features were noted in this area and analysis of phosphate values at 20 cm intervals across the surface of the solifluction deposit showed no anomalous levels that could be taken to be indicative of the former presence of burials.

The presence of partially drilled beads and bead 'blanks' (or unworked discs of shale) clearly indicate that the site was a production centre. This impression is confirmed by the many flint drill-bits whose rounded tips fit neatly within the bead perforations. Replicas of such drill-bits have been used to produce identical beads of local shale. Two people can make about 100 beads in an hour using a bow- or pump-drill, although without such mechanical assistance the process is much slower and more laborious. Given the facility with which they can be made, and the quantities of potential drill-bits discarded at the site (a total of at least 75), it would not be surprising if the extant sample of beads from The Nab Head were in fact only a small fraction of a potentially prodigious quantity of such items. So much of the site has been lost to erosion and careless excavation that

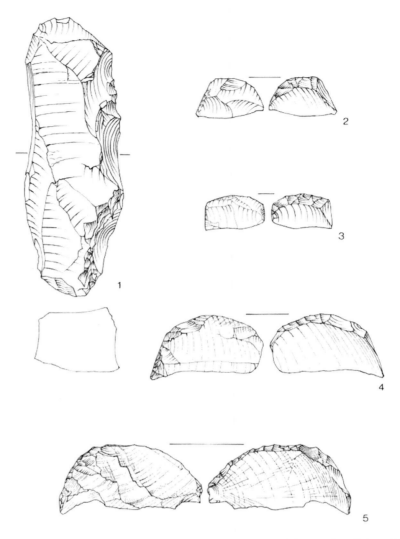

Figure 4.10: The Nab Head site I. Transversely sharpened axe/adze, and sharpening flakes (1979-1980 excavations). 1,4 and 5 are of igneous rocks; 2 and 3 are of flint. Scale – 1:1.55

this may very well have been the case, although we can now never be sure. Certainly, very many beads must have been lost, and they continue to erode occasionally from exposed soil and sections at the Neck.

There are many uses for beads, but here it is possible only to speculate. They are unlikely to have had any practical role and were most probably of aesthetic, 'psychic' (*sensu* Clark, 1975) or status value. In all probability they may have been worn about the person as adornment for both the living and the dead - although there is no supporting evidence for burials at the site. They may be strung in several ways, not least edge-to-edge, forming elaborate designs incorporated into garments, hair, or extraneous decoration to personal items, tools, weapons or cult objects. So many drill-bits at the site hint that shale may not have been the only material so treated - soil conditions have not favoured the preservation of shell, bone, antler, fossil or walrus ivory, teeth, leather or wood, all of which could be decorated or pierced using the same basic instrument. The surface condition of the flint drill-bits has so far precluded microwear study. In his examination of examples of such

tools from both Star Carr and Mount Sandel (N. Ireland), Dumont has suggested that they were used on bone, wood, hide, and unidentified materials. Potential hafting traces were found on two of the Mount Sandel tools, and for most instances of use-wear, a boring and rotary motion was indicated (Dumont, 1983, 1985).

Decorated objects are all but absent from the early Mesolithic record of Britain, and it is unlikely that these were made with awls or drill-bits. Apart from the engraved pebbles from Rhuddlan there are only the examples of incised chevron ornament on a deer antler tine from Romsey, Hants (but only doubtfully Mesolithic: Jacobi, pers. comm.), and a perforated ox-bone 'pick' head from the Thames (Smith, 1934; Sieveking, 1971). In contrast to incised or engraved decoration, pit ornament is a common feature amongst the richer series of contemporary artefacts known from southern Scandinavia and the north European plain (Clark, 1975). The technique of delineating designs by a series of drilled pits has its origins in the Palaeolithic (Marshack, 1972), especially in eastern Europe and Russia. Within the Boreal of the west Baltic area Clark (ibid,

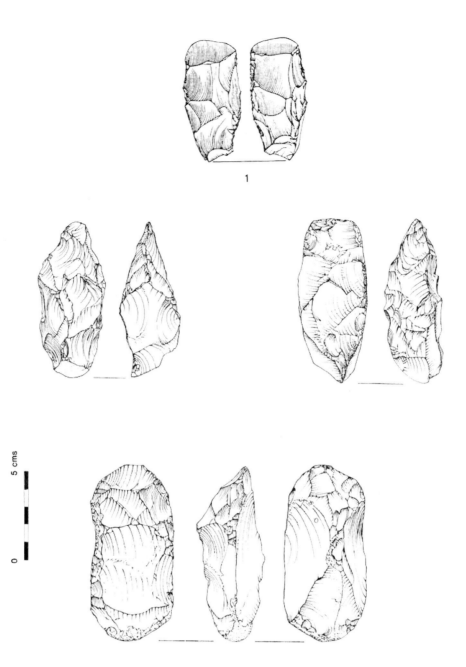

Figure 4.11: Transversely sharpened axes/adzes from The Nab Head
(museum collections: drawing of no. 1 courtesy of R.Jacobi).

Appendix D) lists 86 decorated items 18 (21%) of which have motifs defined by pits (*Bohrornament*). Drilling, of course, has many more essentially practical roles and at The Nab Head it must be admitted that the piercing of shale beads may therefore be only one of several potential functions for the drill-bits. It is significant that no stone beads were found at Daylight Rock (van Nédervelde, pers. comm.) where drills are an important element of the toolkit (10% of all tools and fragments).

The very substantial number of beads recorded from The Nab Head, however, sets the site apart from its apparent contemporaries both in Britain and further afield (Newell, forthcoming). British sites on which similar beads occur can be briefly listed:

Star Carr, N. Yorks, (Clark, 1954): 27 beads of Lias shale, mostly found clustered in two distinct groups. The excavator pointed out that these 'find their closest affinities with those found ..... on Nab Head' (ibid. 190).

Staple Crag, Co Durham, (Coggins *et al.*, 1989: fig. 3, no. 35) a ?shale bead, sub-oval in shape, 50 mm. long and centrally pierced from one face. This was a surface find on a small river terrace from which early ('broad blade') microliths have also been recovered.

Manton Warren,S. Humberside, Area 5: a bead of grey-brown shale measuring 17 x 14 x 3.75 mm, found in a sand blow-out (Jacobi, pers. comm.). Microliths from the same location include both early ('broad blade') and late

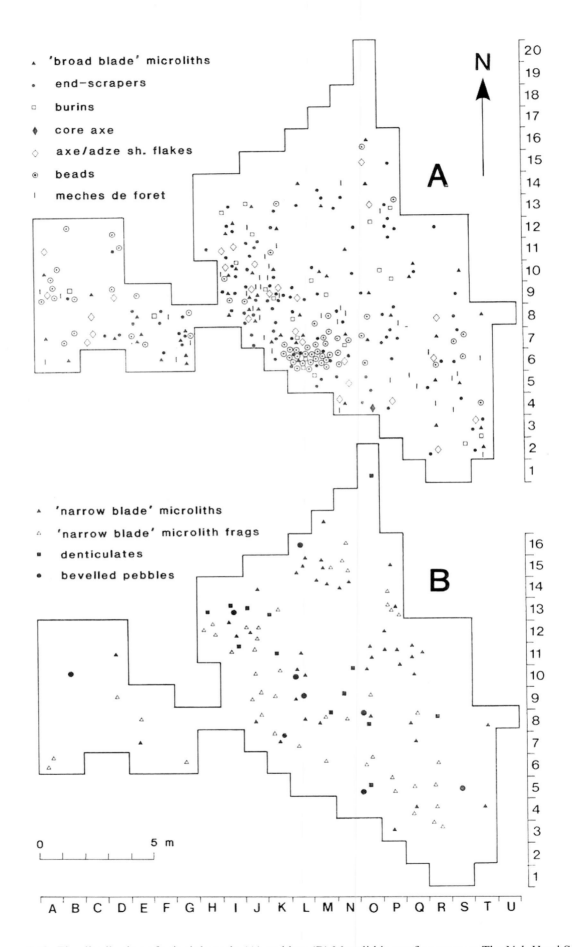

Figure 4.12: The distribution of principle early (A) and late (B) Mesolithic artefact types at The Nab Head Site I.

Mesolithic shapes. Some of the 'broad blade' microliths are identical in terms of size and outline to specimens from Star Carr.

Rushy Brow, Anglezarke Moor, Lancs.: 4 bead fragments of unidentified stone found within sediment samples collected from a site with 'broad-blade' microliths, interpreted as a short-term shelter (C. Howard, pers. comm.). The microliths are, again, indistinguishable in terms of size and outline from those at Star Carr.

Thatcham, Site VI, Berks.: a fragment of a small perforated oval pebble (13 x 10 x 3 mm) of ?chalky material found with early Mesolithic artefacts including microliths (Jacobi, pers. comm.).

Waun Fignen Felen, Site 6, W. Glam.: a ?shale bead, closely similar to those from The Nab Head, excavated with probable early Mesolithic artefacts (Fig. 3.18, No. 4; and Berridge, 1981).

Freshwater East, Dyfed: a shale bead like those from The Nab Head, found eroding from a coastal section along with flints of an early Mesolithic aspect (Leach, 1913; Jacobi, 1980b, fig. 4.5).

Linney Burrows, Dyfed: a surface find of a bead of unidentified stone, only loosely associated with flints from the same area which include both microliths and later prehistoric pieces (Fig. 3.12).

Palmerston Farm, Dyfed: a surface find of a ?shale bead (Fig. 3.13, No. 33) which, with a substantial assemblage of chipped flint and stone artefacts (Figs. 3.13, 3.14) clearly resembles material from The Nab Head.

In sum, this listing is strongly suggestive of the association of such stone beads with presumed early Mesolithic flintwork. There are no instances where such beads can be demonstrated to be associated only with later Mesolithic ('narrow blade') material.

As the mèches de forêt from Star Carr are mostly too large to have drilled the beads from that site, it is only at The Nab Head that one could suggest that beads were actually being manufactured. The presence of individual beads on the four remaining Welsh sites may imply that these objects, in addition to a possible ornamental role, also played a part in a system of exchange. Alternatively, it is possible that the mobility of human groups at this time was great enough to account for one or more such groups leaving similar material traces at different and sometimes widely separated locations.

In either case, it could follow that such beads were invested with a symbolic value in addition to that of simple adornment. In this context it might be worth repeating the comments offered by Swanton (1946, p. 481) and more recently cited by Yerkes (1983) in his discussion of shell beads in early Mississippian societies, where it is argued that these could be made instantly available as a medium of exchange whilst at the same time serving as a 'visible witness to the standing and credit of the wearer'. Without the full material context for The Nab Head beads it is not now possible to guess whether they served as a primitive 'currency', that is having token rather than practical value (Sahlins, 1972, 227), or more probably whether they held a less structured role as part of prestige items expressive of social relationships. If this were so, these beads might hold a genuine cultural significance, even going so far as to indicate an ethnic identity: 'we can thus look at the Mesolithic ornaments as insignia of group membership and as the signs of the internal ordering and structure of Mesolithic societies' (Newell, et al., in press). For Wales and the rest of Britain, this proposition awaits substantiation and yet remains a most important element in any discussion that must inevitably seek explanations for observed relationships between, for instance, west Wales and northern England. The author has initiated XRF analyses of shale beads from different sites in the (admittedly remote) hope of distinguishing common sources.

Other objects of shale:
One object in particular must stand out in any treatment of the artefacts from the site, and this is the 'phallus', 'amulet' or 'figurine' found by the Rev. J. P. Gordon-Williams in about 1925 (Gordon-Williams, 1925, 1926) and illustrated here in Fig. 4.13 and Plate 4.3.

The circumstances of discovery are as follows. During his digging in the area of the Neck, Gordon-Williams removed two residual 'islands' of turf and soil, under one of which he found the 'phallus' and at least 9 beads. He was of the impression that this was an associated group of which the beads had formed part of a necklace. 'It [the phallus] lay on live rock with nine beads, almost in contact with a "scoop". I think it safe to say it marks the centre of dispersion of the necklet. It was encrusted with a grey-brown soapy substance, which I washed off before its character became evident.'

The 'phallus' appears to be carved out of a shale similar to that of the beads. It is now a very dark grey in colour with a texture and appearance not unlike graphite, presumably owing to persistent handling, not least since its discovery. The finder's reference to a coating of 'soapy substance' is particularly curious and both the longevity of the site and its soil conditions belie his suggestion that the object retained an original deposit of fat or clay in which it had been stored in a bag alongside the 'necklace'. [It might be stated here, for the record, that it was W. F. Grimes's opinion (pers. comm.) that Gordon-Williams's scruples may not have allayed a temptation to invent such an important discovery. Professor Grimes knew the clergyman well but this suggestion is based only on a personal assessment of his character, rather than on any specific indications or intimations of forgery. A motive might be found in the intense rivalry between local amateur collectors at this time].

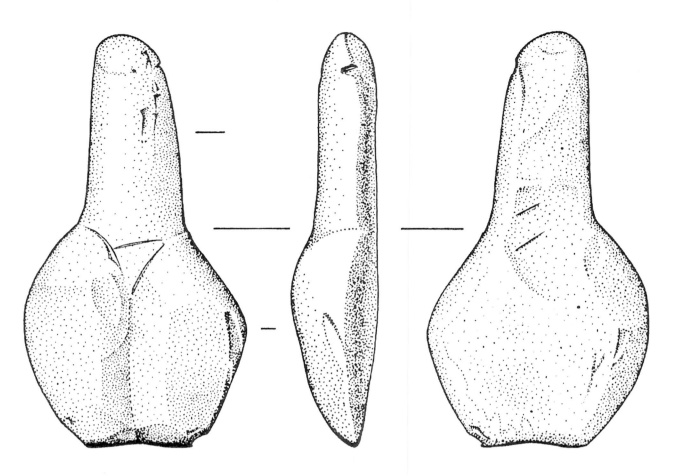

Figure 4.13: The Nab Head. The carved "amulet", "figurine" or "phallus" (see also Plate 4.3). Scale – 2.6:1

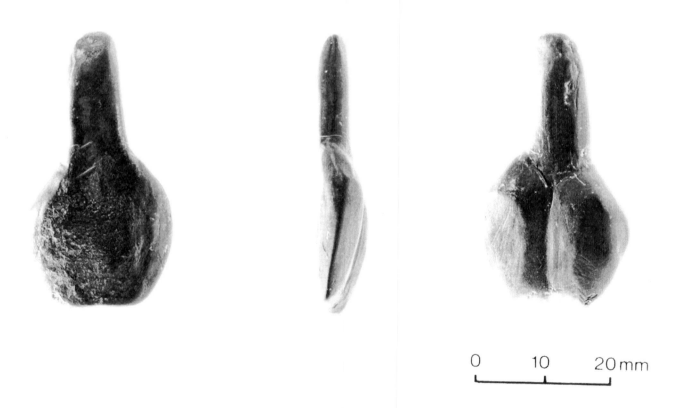

Plate 4.3: The Nab Head "figurine"

110

Microscopic examination shows some slight modern damage and extensive but faint signs of the original sculpting: narrow incised grooves define the Y-shaped central area, whilst the 'testes' appear to have been modelled by abrasion, leaving a faceted surface with very faint directional striations overlain in places by more random scratches. The 'shaft' has striations parallel to its axis, but this, like most of the dorsal surface, is much muted and smoothed by soft attrition or polishing. The ventral surface is flat and seems to be largely unmodified.

Whether or not there are any grounds to be sceptical of Gordon-Williams's enthusiasm for 'The Duck-head' as he preferred to call it in polite company, it is worth quoting the comments of the Abbé Breuil to whom the artefact was soon sent for expert opinion. The Abbé was later (1953) to publish a short note on this 'remarkable Palaeolithic trinket', but in the meantime replied in a long letter to the finder:

'[it] interests me greatly. I have checked my impressions by showing [it] to several others. Some say a phallus with exaggerated testes; some say a female steatopygic figurine. These were my own conclusions. Most likely both are right, mixed up in a sort of plastic play on words. The stem must be a human member with a very slight incision differentiating the glans; but the way in which the double spread out scrotum is treated is evidence of the will to bring to mind the hips and thighs and the lower belly of a woman.'

What is at first glance clearly a phallic representation can therefore, with a little conceptual licence, become a symbol of the two sexes very subtly blended into a single bisexual object. Such stylization and economy of expression, but limited to one sex or the other and particularly associated with the 'Venuses', is common in Upper Palaeolithic figurines from throughout Europe (Leroi-Gourhan, 1968). Examples of intentional bisexual representations, however, are unusual in the European Palaeolithic. Breuil (ibid.) compared The Nab Head piece with a figure from Trasimeno (Italy) and another from Weinburg, Mauern (Germany), but neither parallel is very satisfactory (Delporte, 1979: figs. 64 and 79).

In support of the feminine aspect of the Welsh piece is its profile (Plate 4.3, middle), which is reminiscent of the stylized engravings of women found at several western European late Magdalenian sites such as Lalinde, France, or Gonnersdorf, Germany. Although stylized anthropomorphic figures engraved or drilled on to bone or antler occur within the early Flandrian (Clark, 1975, fig. 35), figurines 'in the round' do not re-appear until the early Neolithic cultures of parts of the eastern Mediterranean. The Nab Head specimen would seem to be entirely isolated from any meaningful comparative studies.

In conclusion, therefore, despite the attraction of Breuil's 'plastic play on words', it is perhaps more realsitic to view The Nab Head object as simply a phallus, perhaps an amulet, without any convenient parallel. If genuine, its association seems most likely to be with the beads, also of shale, found with it and which have been attributed, with much of the flintwork, to the early Mesolithic use of the site. For a discussion of the 'scoop', see below and Chapter V.

Other shale items from the site deserve brief mention. For instance, Gordon-Williams illustrates a rounded sliver of shale with a groove apparently incised into its broader end, parallel to the long axis (Gordon-Williams, 1926, plate 3). Oriented vertically with the groove at the bottom, Jacobi has proposed that this piece might be interpreted as a stylized Venus figurine (1980b, 159). Its surface is unfortunately too much weathered even to be sure if it has in fact been artificially modified (Plate 4.4).

The recent excavations recovered several additional pieces of shale and other stone, mostly fragmentary, and in all cases waterworn. Although presumably introduced onto the site by man, and occasionally bearing traces of interference, they otherwise have few or no distinguishing features allying them with any definable artefact of either Mesolithic occupation. To a certain extent it was a disappointment that the recent work at Site I failed to produce good evidence for carved shale in support of earlier finds.

Also of unknown derivation is a naturally rounded, sub-angular, cobble, recovered from the topsoil, on part of the surface of which are three incised lines arranged rather in the manner of an Ordnance Survey bench-mark (see Plate 4.5). This resembles more the 'dart' signs of Palaeolithic art, rather than those thought to signify vulvas which are more usually distinguished as closed triangles (A. Sieveking, pers. comm.). Further comment is clearly unjustified, for lack of precise contextual evidence.

Bevelled pebbles:
These artefacts - the 'scoops' of earlier commentators - will receive fuller attention in the following chapter. It must be noted here, however, that they have been a common find at Site I throughout its history and 10 examples were found during the 1979-80 excavations. There is no evidence at all from independently researched sites that this tool-type can be associated with early Mesolithic activity. Rather they seem to be exclusively associated with later Mesolithic coastal sites (Jacobi, 1980b, 188 - 189), and are interpreted here as supporting evidence for such a presence at some time after at least c. 8,500 BP. They are assumed to have been associated with the geometric ('narrow blade') microliths and denticulates already noted.

Stone 'rings' and pecked axe/adze:
Finds in Tenby Museum provenanced to The Nab Head, and therefore arguably from Site I, include two stone rings and a pecked stone axe or adze-head. These objects are discussed and illustrated in Chapter VI where it will be suggested that, along with the bevelled pebbles, they too were discarded by the late Mesolithic inhabitants of the site.

```
0        10        20 mm
```

Plate 4.4: ?Modified stone from The Nab Head

```
0   10  20  30  40  50 mm
```

Plate 4.5: Engraved stone from The Nab Head Site I.

7. Chronology:

The foregoing description of Site I and the artefacts from it could be interpreted as supporting Jacobi's earlier proposal, based on extant museum collections, that at least two main Mesolithic occupations, perhaps divided by some considerable time, succeeded each other at The Nab Head. The evidence for this depends upon the typological characteristics of selected stone artefacts and ornaments which, by analogy with dated and chronologically discrete assemblages elsewhere, allow a broad division of the occupation residues into an 'early' and a 'late' Mesolithic grouping.

The occurrence of charcoal and charred hazel nutshell fragments on the site raised the possibility that radiocarbon analysis might be able to provide an estimate of the absolute ages involved. Unfortunately, as such organic fragments were found throughout the soil profile, and in view of the evidence for downward movement within the latter (see above), such potential was limited. However, the availability of AMS did at least provide the opportunity of dating individual items of charred material, thus at least overcoming the hazards of using samples bulked up with many separate items of, no doubt, differing ages.

Given that dating of the 'narrow blade' component of occupation at The Nab Head was to be attempted at Site II (see Chapter VI), it was decided to try and date only the supposed earlier phase at Site I. This decision was supported also by the increased likelihood that charred material of this period should be confined to the base of the soil profile, and perhaps at a depth great enough to significantly reduce the risk of contamination from above.

As previously observed, 'broad blade' microliths were proportionately more numerous than later types near the base of the soil profile. The same pattern is detectable amongst the larger artefact types ascribed to each phase, although it should be cautioned that the latter distributions might be biased by the heavier 'early' material gravitating downwards preferentially to the lighter and 'later' material. The earliest occupation on the site may reasonably be assumed to have taken place on a thin soil developed on top of the solifluction gravel (contexts 12 and 18), leading to a concentration of artefacts just above the latter, in context 7. Both artefacts and charred matter had become incorporated into the upper levels of the solifluction deposit itself (context 12), whilst a few items penetrated deeper still (context 18).

As the artefactual content of the solifluction deposit was almost totally confined to 'early' types it was felt that samples from this level would be the most appropriate for dating. Accordingly, two fragments of charred hazel nutshell from context 12, just below concentrations of largely 'early' artefacts (in grid squares J9 and L6), were selected and submitted for AMS dating. Although three complete and four fragmentary 'narrow blade' microliths, as well as three denticulates, were recovered from context 12, this horizon and the two grid squares sampled were instead dominated by 'early' lithic types. Grid square L6, for instance, contained no less than 12 shale beads, 8 of which were from context 12 or below. Confirmation of the early dating of these and their associated flint and stone tools was provided by the following determinations:

J9   9,210 +80 BP (OxA-1495: Hedges *et al.*, 1989)
L6   9,110 +80 BP (OxA-1496: Hedges *et al.*, 1989)

These dates have already been incorporated into discussion of the Welsh early Mesolthic chronology initiated in the last chapter. One can repeat here that they fall within the later part of a spectrum of British early Mesolithic dates, and are very closely comparable to, if marginally earlier than, determinations for the equivalent lithic range at Daylight Rock on Caldey (Fig. 3.9): The Nab Head therefore now provides the earliest evidence so far available for the occupation of Wales following the Lateglacial.

8. Discussion

The economic setting of sites such as The Nab Head Site I, in the total absence of directly relevant data, must also remain speculative. A detailed knowledge of the available biota is missing, as are any informative organic remains.

Equally problematic is the eustatic rise in sea level which has overtaken the contemporary coastal zone (Fig. 3.3, 4.2). During the first two millennia of the Flandrian, the pace of the marine transgression was rapid following the onset of climatic warming. If The Nab Head and Daylight Rock were indeed inhabited at c.9,000 BP, then contemporary sea levels might have been as low as -40m (Fairbanks, 1989). More conservatively, estimates based on correlated sea level data from western Britain suggest a height of about 25m below OD (Heyworth and Kidson, 1983). Taking the latter estimate as a minimum , the sites under discussion would then have been approximately 6 and 10 km., respectively, from the coast. Assuming, therefore, that territories at a 10 km radius around these two sites will have been largely dry land, and using the parameters applied to Star Carr (Clark, 1972), Jacobi has calculated the potential annual meat weight which may have been available. The resulting figures for the principal Welsh sites are as follows:

Table 4.2: potential daily kill of red deer, expressed as meat weight (60% of deadweight), from territories below 200 ft and within a 10 km radius of the principal Welsh early Mesolithic sites, and Star Carr. Calculations based on 1 deer/100 acres, and a 1:6 cull. (Data from Jacobi, 1980b, 163).

The Nab Head	21.5 kg
Daylight Rock	21.0 kg
Rhuddlan	26.0 kg
Trwyn Du	26.0 kg
Burry Holms	31.0 kg
Aberystwth	22.7 kg
Star Carr	21.7 kg

These figures would suggest that all the Welsh sites could have been as well supplied with deer meat as Star Carr may have been, and could, by further assumption (following Clark, 1972), have fed four families of about six persons each. As these figures do not include contributions from other animals, or vegetable foods, and do not account for any annual variations in their availablity, they must be considered simplistic. Nevertheless, it does seem a reasonable conclusion that these sites were well placed for dry land subsistence needs.

The only indication from The Nab Head that the coast played any economic role is the evident use of beach pebbles as lithic raw material. Flint, chert, flakeable volcanic stone, and possibly also the shale bead blanks, can be expected to have been collected during visits to the coast for other purposes (Binford, 1979). The small valley on the side of which the site lies would have provided convenient access to a proto-St. Brides Bay only a short distance (about 6 km.) to the north-east. The occupants of the site could thus easily have taken advantage of the full range of potential resources from both terrestrial and marine environments and, indeed, that early Mesolithic mobility was extensive can be judged by the dispersed find-spots of apparently closely related lithic remains.

Early Mesolithic flint and stone artefacts have been recovered from an existing area of some 200 sq m. The focus of this scatter would seem to have been situated at 'The Neck', and may have extended over much of the area now stripped of soil by erosion and previous excavation. That many of Gordon-Williams's finds may have come from north of the recent excavations is suggested by the presence of grassed-over spoil heaps there. Because of truncation by the cliffs, no very clear estimate of site size is possible. It would seem, though, that this exceeded the area originally identified at Daylight Rock, at 110 sq m., and may have once approached the size of the main lithic spread at Palmerston Farm - 500 sq. m. The figure for Daylight Rock might be considered a minimum owing to the constraints of the local topography and the recent discovery of lithic remains on top of the headland (see Chapter III). Parts of this site too may also have been lost to the sea.

At the simplest level there seem to be two extremes in terms of the size and content of lithic scatters. Smaller ones seem to be more frequently encountered at higher altitudes, and are interpreted as short-lived special-purpose sites with a correspondingly limited range of lithic tool types (Mellars, 1976b). Larger sites, however, are seen to imply longer-term residence with a broader and less specialized range of activities. Crude calculations of the constituent numbers of occupying groups (Naroll, 1962; Wiessner, 1974) suggest that these may have been in the region of about 24 people.

Apart from its relatively large size, and in the absence of organic remains and structural features, the lithic components at The Nab Head provide the only indication of function. The lithic composition of the assemblage gives it a 'balanced' character (Mellars, 1976b): the three major 'early' tool components are end-scrapers (18%), 'broad blade' microliths (14%) and *mèches de forêt* (7%). The majority of the remainder of the inventory are unclassified retouched and utilized pieces, and tools such as narrow-blade microliths and denticulates which are believed to be intrusive.

The large number of scrapers, and perhaps some of the burins, are indicative of the processing of organic materials such as hides, bone and antler, and carry the implication that such activities were of a domestic, 'base-camp', nature. The procurement of game is suggested by the presence of microliths, although the function of these flints as hunting armatures has yet to be proven in this country.

The importance and relatively long duration of the occupation at the site is perhaps most strongly hinted at by the evidence for manufacture of axes/adzes and, of course, beads. It has been argued that axes/adzes were made here for use elsewhere, and it could be suggested that the accumulation of several types of lithic raw materials might also be seen as an index of duration of use of the site.

The manufacture of beads is a rare specialized activity for which the site can be singled out. The speculation that these held special value as tokens of status, perhaps even passing into an exchange system, suggests that The Nab Head might even have been prominent within in any regional site hierarchy. The extremely tentative suspicion of the former presence of human burials would, if they were ever found, considerably help to consolidate such theory building.

Finally, the seasonal implications of any of the cultural residues found at the site cannot be considered convincing: the inferred hide-working may, imply an autumn inhabitation; hazel nuts might suggest the same, although they could represent stored resources for use at other times of the year. Lowland sites of 'base-camp' status were once thought to have been a winter phenomenon, and yet even where organic preservation is exceptional, as at Star Carr, this proposition has had to be revised to accommodate evidence for occupation at other times of the year (Rowley-Conwy, 1987; Legge and Rowley-Conwy, 1988).

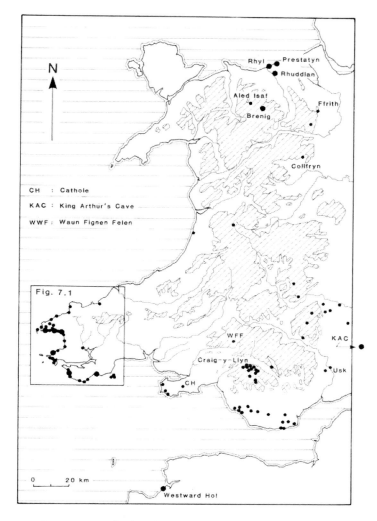

Figure 5.1: Principal late Mesolithic find-spots in Wales.

1. Introduction

The definition of a late or later Mesolithic in Britain has its origin in the recognition of distinct lithic assemblages which date no earlier than *c.* 8800 BP. In particular, after this time there is a marked change in the composition of the microlithic component: the limited range of relatively 'broad' and large early microlith shapes being succeeded by a suite of more various and smaller 'narrow blade' or 'geometric' types. Especially common amongst the latter are narrow elongated scalene triangles, straight- and convex-backed bladelets, lanceolates, and less commonly, four-sided and 'micro-*petit-tranchet*' forms, amongst others. The non-microlithic tool-kit that accompanies such items is variable but is perhaps less distinguished from its predecessors in that scrapers and burins feature in both. Core axes/adzes seem to disappear in some areas, such as northern England, but continue to be found in late contexts in parts of southern England. Micro-denticulates and

mèches de forêt appear to be absent from micro-triangle assemblages. Alongside such changes in the tool inventory, some parts of the country also saw a change in the types of raw material exploited (Pitts and Jacobi, 1979).

In Wales, amongst the 296 recorded Mesolithic find-spots (Wymer, 1977; Jacobi, 1980b), there are many more with 'narrow blade' material than with only earlier lithic types. The former collections are mainly characterized by the presence of scalene micro-triangles, 'rods', and various points of lanceolate outline. These are associated on many sites with burins, denticulates, notched, nosed and truncated pieces, and choppers. A recurring feature in the lithic inventory of coastally located sites is the presence of pebble tools, usually elongated beach pebbles with bevelled ends.

The distribution of the 'narrow blade' find-spots in Wales (see Fig. 5.1) is biased by the constraints of surface cover and concentrated local collecting, with the consequent clustering of sites on the coasts of south and west Wales and in the Glamorgan uplands. Outside these areas, only Prestatyn (Clark, 1938, 1939), Brenig (Jacobi, 1980b) and Rhuddlan (Manley and Healey, 1982) have received any detailed treatment. With the exception of recent work at The Nab Head, systematic exploration or documentation of other sites has been minimal.

This chapter will first of all assess the chronological framework for the Welsh late Mesolithic, using available radiocarbon determinations both from Wales and further afield in Britain. Discussion can then turn to vegetational, geographical and faunal changes during this time before detailing certain individual instances of late Mesolithic activity in Wales. A full discussion of recent research at The Nab Head Site II, and the results of other relevant fieldwork in west Wales will follow in Chapters VI and VII, respectively.

2. Chronology

i) Introduction

The radiocarbon record applicable to late Mesolithic technologies in Britain (eg Mellars, 1976a; Myers, 1989b) is still very far from comprehensive and has yet to take full advantage of the potential offered by AMS dating. This situation is largely the result of archaeological circumstance, whereby remarkably few 'narrow blade' find-spots have produced datable organic artefacts or infallible stratified contexts. 'Sites' are usually identified only from scatters of lithic material, often at the surface or at shallow depth, consequently with little or no stratigraphic integrity. Most of the radiocarbon dates obtained so far are from aggregated samples of charcoal or nutshells and consequently have to be treated as potentially misleading.

The dating evidence from Wales is especially poor (Jacobi, 1980b) and it has been one of the aims of this research, if possible, to provide an improved chronology for the Welsh late Mesolithic. In reviewing the Welsh archaeological record for 'narrow blade' lithic technologies, only one find-spot - at Prestatyn in north Wales - appeared to avoid the difficulties referred to above and to have the potential for providing contextually secure material suitable for AMS dating. Samples were therefore submitted by the author, leading to important new determinations which are discussed below, alongside a description of the archaeological material from Prestatyn. This new evidence can then be followed by an account of other relevant radiocarbon determinations for Wales.

ii) Prestatyn, Clwyd (SJ 060 820)

During 1926, Mr F. Gilbert Smith, a local architect and surveyor as well as enthusiastic antiquarian, made several archaeological discoveries during the building of a housing estate at Bryn Newydd, Prestatyn. Amongst these, and unconnected with other finds of later date, was a small group of chipped flint and chert items as well as artefacts of

bone, antler and seashell. These finds came from the bottom of an excavation made to receive the foundations of a man-hole for a sewer - an area of only about six foot square (3.3 sq m). The section recorded by Gilbert Smith (ms at BM) shows that the archaeological material came from a thin layer of black soil (5 cms) overlain by clean white tufa (56 cms) and topsoil (33 cms). Below the archaeological horizon was a 25 cm layer of sand and clay overlying angular stones (30.5 cms) resting on basal boulder clay. The find-spot is interpreted as the top of a small eminence within a tufa-filled depression in the boulder clay (Smith, 1926; Clark, 1938, 1939).

The artefact collection was published by Clark (ibid.) who emphasized the secure nature of the context, stating: 'the workshop material was thus sealed and provides us with that rare phenomenon in Welsh archaeology, a well insulated mesolithic industry' (ibid., 330). This comment would still seem to be valid today, over 50 years later, and the artefacts and associated organic remains warrant due consideration.

The lithic assemblage, then, is composed mostly of chipped black and grey chert and some flints, and amounts to a total of 141 items (excluding plain primary flakes). These can be classified as follows (after Clark, 1938, 330):

Table 5.1: Lithic artefacts from Prestatyn

microliths (with fragments)	65
scrapers	15
obliquely truncated flake	1
notched flakes	2
flakes with retouch	11
micro-burins	5
miss-hits	5
cores	26
core-rejuvenation flakes	11

The classifiable microliths and a selection of the retouched tools are illustrated in Fig. 5.2. The microlith assemblage is dominated by narrow scalene triangular forms (29), there being fewer small obliquely-backed bladelets (9), straight-backed bladelets (3), and an isosceles micro-triangle. The remainder are unclassifiable fragments. Alongside the microliths the most conspicuous tools are retouched flakes and convex scrapers.

The organic component of the collection includes a perforated oyster shell disc, a pointed bone object (ibid., fig. 1, 64 and 65), and an unworked deer antler tine. With these and the flint and chert tools were found about a dozen pieces of red ochre and 'large numbers of fragments of hazel-nut shells, clearly broken by human agency' (Smith, quoted by Clark, 1939, 201). Fortunately much of this material, including a number of nutshell fragments, was preserved by Gilbert Smith and is now housed at the British Museum. Two nutshell fragments were released for AMS dating, with the following results:

8,700 +100 BP	(OxA-2268)	unpublished
8,730 +90 BP	(OxA-2269)	unpublished

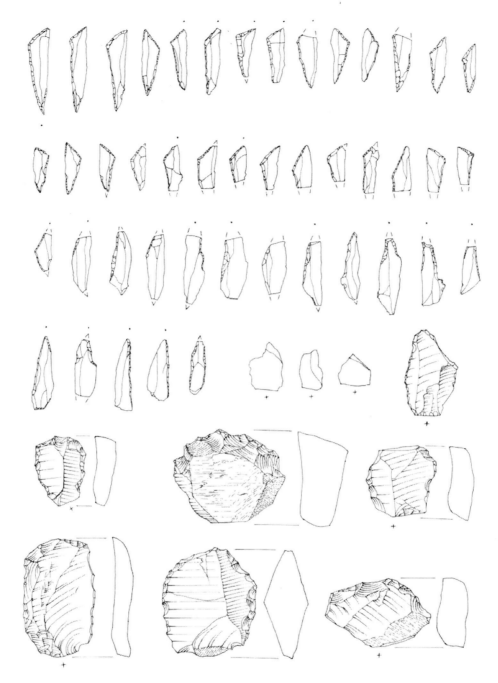

Figure 5.2: Flint and chert artefacts from Prestatyn, Clwyd. Scale – 1:1.33

iii) Discussion

That these two samples are identical in age increases the confidence expressed above in the integrity of the archaeological deposit at Prestatyn. Further, the immediate interest of the dates is that they would appear to place the associated 'narrow blade' lithic assemblage very early in the chronological sequence so far established for both British and adjacent continental late Mesolithic technologies.

At Duvensee, in Germany, for instance, the latest date obtained for an early Mesolithic microlith assemblage (living-site 6) is 8,840 +110 BP (Kl-1112; Willkomm, 1985), whilst an assemblage of narrow scalene triangles and obliquely backed bladelets (Bokelmann, 1985, fig. 2) very similar to those from Prestatyn is recorded from living-site 13 and dated to *c.* 8,670 BP (Willkomm, 1985). For Britain, the only relevant determination to precede those from Prestatyn is that for Filpoke Beacon, County Durham, of 8,760 +140 BP (Q-1474: Jacobi, 1976. fig. 6).

Other 'narrow blade' find-spots in northern England have produced relatively early dates (Mellars, 1976a) leading to the impression that such technologies may have first appeared in this area. Within Britain, then, the determinations from Prestatyn would seem to introduce the possibility of a slightly different, or at least enlarged, focus for the earliest appearance of 'narrow blade' technologies, shifting attention south-westward from northern England. At present, however, the persisting lack of adequate data from a much wider range of find-spots does not allow sufficient spatial or temporal resolution for reconstruction of the transition from 'earlier' to 'later' technologies. Whilst apparently of a similar age, the Prestatyn microliths differ in composition from those of both Filpoke Beacon and its contemporaries in the Low Countries such as Aardhorst Vessem III and (somewhat later) Rotsterhaule (see Jacobi, 1976, figs, 6, 8 and 9). Also, there are significant differences between all these and assemblages with scalene micro- triangles which are already present in Ulster by this time (Woodman, 1978a).

Immediately apparent, too, is that the Prestatyn 'narrow blade' material would seem to *pre*-date that of 'broad blade' type at Trwyn Du and Rhuddlan M, and is nearly identical in age to that from Rhuddlan E (see Table 3.3). The doubts expressed above concerning the reliability of these other datings from north Wales (Chapter III) would thus seem to be emphasized by the Prestatyn results. With these reservations in mind, it is nevertheless of interest to note that simple obliquely backed points are common to all these collections, although at Prestatyn they are subsidiary to narrow scalene triangles. The latter are typologically very distinctive, with only two sides entirely retouched, and additional retouch on the third edge being limited only to the 'tail' of the piece in several instances - a feature also observable on some 'broad blade' scalene triangles (eg Fig. 4.5, Nos. 33, 36; Fig. 3.5, No. 19). One may wonder, perhaps, whether such a feature might thus be inherited from earlier microlith styles and might form just one part of a morphological continuum spanning the transition between early and 'later' microlith groups. Certainly, the size of obliquely backed points has been shown to diminish with time (Pitts and Jacobi, 1979), and one could speculate that an evolution in both size and style of retouch amongst scalene triangles may also be detectable. The 'narrow' triangles from Prestatyn are, in these terms, both simpler and larger than other 'narrow blade' microlith assemblages of later date which contain both smaller and more various microlith shapes. With their significant representation of obliquely backed points, the Prestatyn microliths might thus be argued to conform to some kind of technological development sequential with earlier forms. Such theoretical links are less obvious amongst the non-microlithic component of the tool-kits, although it could be significant that end-scrapers are common to both the Prestatyn and early Mesolithic artefact groups.

Such attempts to see typological links spanning 'early' to 'late' Mesolithic technologies may well be unfounded, however, and do not - as yet - take into account important additional factors such as the influence of changing raw materials, or the needs of different hunting strategies (Myers, 1989a,b). More significant, too, may be the differences between the two groupings, rather than any similarities: core-axe/adzes and *mèches de forêt* are apparently absent from later assemblages, although at Prestatyn it is important to remember that only a very small area was investigated and the resulting collection probably unrepresentative of the whole. Clearly, more sites, larger artefact assemblages, and closer dating are required to begin to explain this transition properly.

Despite the absence of such much-needed data it seems unlikely that there is any evidence from Wales for the intermediate assemblage type, recognized in south-eastern England, in which 'broad blade' isosceles triangles and obliquely-backed points are combined with hollow-based, or 'Horsham', points. On the limited evidence so far available, the chronological position of the latter seems to lie between the local earliest and latest lithic assemblages - innovated from Continental sources from perhaps *c.* 8,800 - 9,000 BP (Jacobi, pers. comm.). None of the Welsh material so far discussed would appear to fall into this latter category, and the evidence from north Wales might favour local rather than intrusive development at this time.

Whatever the character of change at this apparent interface, and regardless of the mechanisms of transition, instances of 'narrow blade' activity rapidly become widespread following their innovation at *c.* 8,800 BP. At *c.* 8,500 BP geometric microliths characterize artefact groups from find-spots as far apart as Broomhill in central southern England (O'Malley and Jacobi, 1978) and Kinloch, Rhum, in the Scottish Hebrides (Wickham-Jones, 1989, 1990).

iv) Other late Mesolithic dates from Wales

Splash Point, Rhyl, Clwyd (SJ 0200 8250):
Not far from Prestatyn, the unstratified find of a laterally perforated red deer antler beam 'mattock' from the foreshore at Rhyl (Morris, 1923; Smith, 1989) has recently provided the following AMS radiocarbon date:

6,560 ±80 BP (OxA-1009: Hedges *et. al.*, 1988)

It is one of many finds of artefacts from 'estuarine clays' and peat beds, mostly of post-Mesolithic date, exposed on the foreshores of north Wales (eg Morris, *ibid.*; Smith, 1925; Glenn, 1926, 1930; Neaverson, 1936). The implement is perforated above the trez tine and has been truncated to form a blade parallel to the shaft-hole. The blade is badly damaged but smoothing by apparent use is visible (Smith, 1989, fig. 5c)

Shaft-hole antler implements are widespread in parts of northern Europe, and in Britain the earliest recorded are those of elk antler, from Star Carr (Clark, 1954). Red deer antler examples appear in late Mesolithic contexts, but have now been dated from all periods up to and including the Iron Age (Hedges *et al.*, 1987). The Rhyl specimen (Type D: Smith, 1989) has technological similarities to the large group, of mixed chronology, known from the Thames area (Lacaille, 1961), but is noticeably different to those from Scottish Obanian and Danish late Ertebölle contexts. This

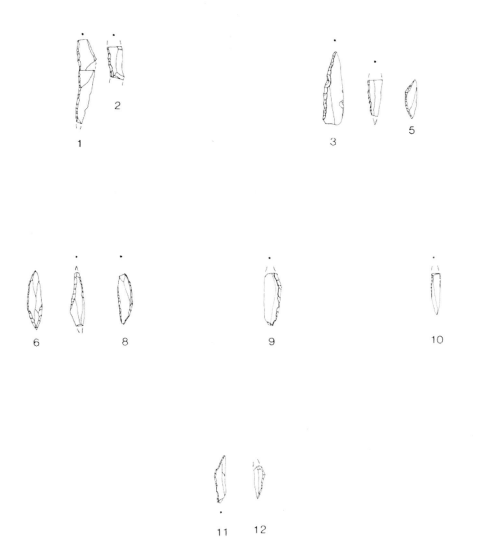

Figure 5.3: Isolated finds of "narrow-blade" microliths from Dyfed:- 1-2, from the foreshore at Lydstep; 3-5, from Nanna's Cave, Caldey Island; 6-8, from Ogof-yr-Ychen, Caldey Island; 9, from foreshore at Abermawr; 10, from Ogof Carreg-Hir; 11-12, from Stackpole Warren. Scale – 1:1.22.

last group, in which the perforation is made through the stump of the trez tine, would appear to date to the very end of the Mesolithic.

The Rhyl implement therefore stands alone as the only directly dated late Mesolithic artefact from Wales. Without any associated cultural material, however, its value beyond that of a chronological marker is limited.

Brenig 53, Clwyd (SH 983 572):
This site remains largely unpublished (Musson, 1975; Allen, 1975), yet was until recently the only source of radiocarbon dates for the late Mesolithic in Wales:

7190 ±100 BP
7300 ±100 BP

These two determinations are on charcoal from within a pit below a Bronze Age barrow. This feature also contained worked flint, amongst which the only culturally diagnostic piece was a small scalene triangle. However, although there is no proven association, it seems possible that both

flintwork and charcoal may be contemporary with a larger scatter of lithic material from below the same barrow. This latter includes small scalene triangles and no pieces that are specifically of any earlier derivation (Jacobi, 1980b, 174).

Lydstep, Dyfed (SS 094 985)
The foreshore at Lydstep conceals one of the many outcrops of 'submerged forest' that occur so frequently below high water mark along British Atlantic coasts. The complete skeleton of a pig was found there during a temporary exposure of the 'forest bed' in 1916 (Leach, 1918). In the woody peat directly above the neck vertebrae were two small backed bladelets (Fig. 5.3). Although no lesions are detectable on the surviving skeletal material (S. Payne pers. comm.), it nevertheless seems justifiable to regard the group as representative of a hunting loss at a time when projectiles equipped with 'narrow blade' armatures were in use (Jacobi, 1980b, 175). A recent AMS radiocarbon date for the skeleton is as follows:

5,300 +100 BP   (OxA-1412: Hedges *et al.*, 1989)

This dating is of considerable interest on account of its coincidence with earliest Neolithic determinations at Ballynagilly in Ulster (ApSimon, 1976b) and at Llandegai, Gwynedd (Houlder, 1968). The date does, however, just precede that for the earliest local formal Neolithic activity so far recognized - that provided by an isolated pit containing pottery, charcoal, struck flint, as well as cattle and sheep bone fragments, at Coygan Camp, Dyfed (Wainwright, 1967): 5,000 +95 BP (NPL-132: Callow and Hassall, 1968).

The implications of these datings are more fully discussed below (Chapter VII). For the time being, however, the Lydstep determination would seem to provide a reasonable estimate for terminal Mesolithic activity in S W Wales.

It is unfortunate that the artefactual record for the latest stages of the Mesolithic remain obscure. The backed bladelets from Lydstep are unhelpful in determining what other microlith forms may have been used at about this time. For instance, there can be no confirmation from Wales that, as has been argued for England and the continental mainland, four-sided and transverse forms of projectile point might have succeeded assemblages in which straight-backed bladelets or micro-triangles were dominant (Radley, 1970; Jacobi, 1976; Clark, 1980).

v) Summary

The few certain instances of late Mesolithic activity that have been dated with any confidence, suggest that Wales was exploited by 'narrow blade' communities from c. 8,800 BP - c. 5,300 BP. Detailed characterization of the evolution of artefact technologies in use between these extremes cannot at present be attempted. Datings from Brenig, Splash Point and The Nab Head Site II (see Chapter VI) point to a continuous exploitation throughout this period.

3. The environmental background

The developing woodland succession of the Postglacial reached its peak of dense mixed deciduous woodland during the Atlantic, Zone VIIa, phase (sensu Godwin, 1975). The rapid rise in sea level from as low as -15.2 m. OD in the early Mesolithic to about -4.64 m. OD at c. 7,000 BP (Tooley, 1978), with the isolation of the British Isles at c. 7800 BP, led to a climate of increasing oceanicity. Wetter and windier conditions, in combination with warmer summers and milder winters, induced exceptional growth of mixed alder-oak woods with elm, and occasional lime and ash, replacing the birch and pine of the preceding Boreal. Stable, brown earth soils developed below the woodland, and the high moisture balance in this encouraged colonization by alder. Birch, hazel, and pine survived as secondary species, however, where local conditions allowed them to compete favourably with the taller trees (Taylor, 1980, 116). Hazel had earlier spread rapidly from western refugia and had dominated the vegetation at upland sites, at least in the Brecon Beacons and the Black Mountains of south Wales (Walker, 1982; Smith and Cloutman, 1988). The presence of both hazel and other light-demanding under-storey species such as holly and ivy, indicates that although the succeeding mixed forest may have been dense it was unlikely to have been impenetrable.

As in the pre-Boreal and Boreal periods, however, there was considerable local diversity in the response of vegetation to the varying constraints of topography and geography. The western 'maritime fringe' experienced exceptionally mild winters, although temperature lapse rates with altitude ensured a significant contrast with adjacent uplands. The wooded landscape of oak-alder-hazel forest was nevertheless very extensive here, although on the most exposed areas only hazel scrub may have survived, leaving oak and alder confined to sheltered valley locations (Donald, 1987).

Wood peats exposed at inter-tidal locations around south and west Wales indicate the prevalence of a uniform alder-carr vegetation in less exposed coastal and estuarine areas (Lewis, forthcoming). The initial spread of alder was probably concentrated along coastal zones, and occurred at various times in Wales from as early as c. 8,700 BP in the north (Chambers and Price, 1985). In south-west Wales alder carr was already established at Abermawr Bog (SM 883 345) by 7,640 +150 BP (OxA-1411: Hedges et al., 1989), although at other locations on the Dyfed coast equivalent wood peats are dated closer to c. 6,000 BP.

Much of the Bristol Channel and Cardigan Bay areas were probably flooded by c. 8,800 BP when sea level was at about -22 m (Heyworth and Kidson, 1982, fig. 2). Sea level continued to rise throughout the succeeding late Mesolithic period, reaching about -2 m at c. 6,000 BP (ibid.). In many lowland coastal areas a rising water table kept pace with sea level, encouraging the upward development of peats supporting woodland carr. Inundation of these woodlands appears to have been spasmodic, dependent on the breaching of off-shore barriers during storm surges and/or exceptional tides (Kidson and Heyworth, 1982; Lewis, forthcoming).

Inland, in upland areas, an imbalance in water loss led to the initiation of ombrogenous peats as early as c. 7600 BP in the uplands of south Wales, although it has been argued by Smith (Smith, 1984; Smith and Cloutman, 1988) that after an initial climatic change at the end of the Boreal period, both the spread of alder and the initiation of upland peats may have been encouraged by environmental damage by man.

4. Fauna

The main components of the terrestrial fauna inhabiting the largely forested conditions of the late Mesolithic had already become well established in the earlier Boreal and pre-Boreal. Only the elk seems to have disappeared, there being no dated remains more recent than those from Star Carr, Flixton and Thatcham (Lister, 1984). Otherwise, prey species include red and roe deer, wild pig and wild cattle. All these have been identified on at least some British late Mesolithic occupation sites, although there is rather less evidence for predator species and the smaller mammals.

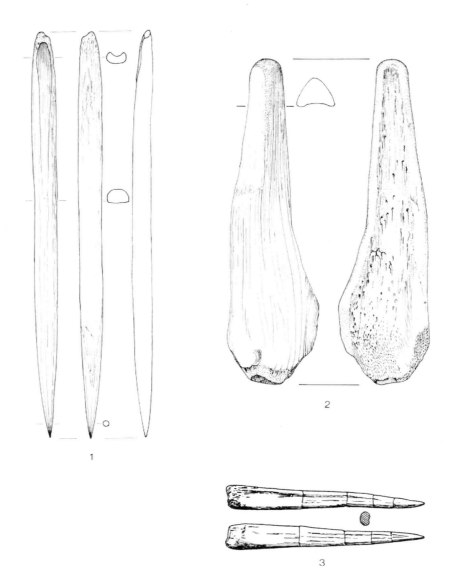

Figure 5.4: Late Mesolithic artefacts of bone: - 1, from the Severn levels; 2, from Frainslake; 3, from Prestatyn. Scale 1:1.57.

Otter and brown bear have been identified in Atlantic age contexts (Grigson, 1981), and it may also be assumed that wolf, beaver, pine marten, badger, hedgehog, mole, common shrew and the watervole were common throughout the post-glacial (*ibid.*).

Marine mammals recorded from Scottish midden sites, and which may have frequented other parts of the British coast, include Common and Grey seal, rorqual and dolphin. Scottish sites such as those on Oronsay and at Morton Tayport also provide evidence for an abundance of fish species: saithe, cod, haddock, turbot, salmonid and sturgeon have been identified (Mellars, 1987; Coles, 1971). At Morton some 40 species of shellfish were recognized, and also crab. Molluscs frequently encountered on some late Mesolithic sites are limpets, cockles, mussels and oysters. Freshwater fish such as pike and perch may have been confined to the river systems draining into the southern North Sea (Wheeler, 1977), whilst salmonids and eels were probably present throughout the country.

Birds are also well represented on northern sites and coastal species are most frequent, including the great northern diver and the great auk (Lacaille, 1954). Guillemot was most common amongst eleven bird species identified at Morton. Wildfowl and woodland birds will have been abundant nearly everywhere.

With such faunal diversity, it is a disappointment that evidence for it, and its exploitation by man, is so limited in Wales. Although it may be a safe probability to assume the presence of many elements within the faunal range pieced together from diverse locations elsewhere in Britain, such instances from Wales are all but missing. Those that there are come from either submerged peat deposits or from a small number of stratified cave sites. Perhaps the most convincing evidence for the association of man and fauna from Wales is the find of the pig skeleton and microliths at Lydstep (see above).

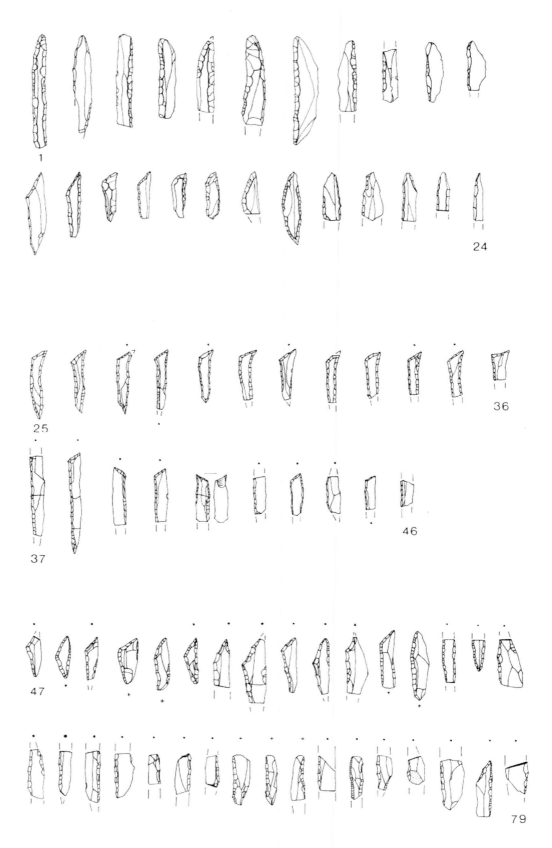

Figure 5.5: "Narrow-blade" microliths from inland find-spots:- 1-24, from the "First hearth" at King Arthur's Cave, Herefordshire (after Taylor, 1927); 25-46, from Waun Fignen Felen, Glam (25-36 from site 1; 37-46 from site 9); 47-79 from find-spots near Craig-y-Llyn. (47-79 after Jacobi, 1980b). Scale - 1:1.1.

Less satisfactory is the find, also from the submerged peat, at Frainslake, Dyfed, by Gordon-Williams of a bone 'implement' (see Fig. 5.4) which has been identified as the heavily rolled proximal fragment of the radius from a juvenile bovid (Jacobi, 1980b, 175). Wear at its distal end may be artificial but this is not certain. The find was made from site D (Gordon-Williams, 1926) along with flint-knapping debris and at least three bevelled pebbles. Although no specifically diagnostic flints survive from here, none of these finds would be inconsistent with a late Mesolithic attribution.

At Potter's Cave on Caldey, Dyfed, a fauna including aurochs, pig, fox, wild deer (unspecified) and dog have been identified (Lacaille and Grimes, 1955). Whilst these were apparently associated with unretouched blades and cores of Mesolithic character (Jacobi, 1980b) it cannot be certain to which part of this period they belong. Much the same comment could be made for the occurences of faunal and artefact remains at Nanna's Cave and Ogof-yr-Ychen, also on Caldey (see Chapters II and III).

On the mainland, at Ogof Carreg Hir (SR 9428 9387: Davies, 1978a; 1989a), a late Mesolithic microlith (Fig 5.3, No. 10) was recovered from 'midden' deposits, possibly of mixed ages, which also included remains of red and roe deer, fox, wolf, bear, and bird bones.

For a slightly wider picture of contemporary fauna, it is necessary to look beyond the Welsh border to King Arthur's Cave, Herefordshire, and the inter-tidal site at Westward Ho!, Devon. At the former, where late Mesolithic flints (Fig. 5.5, Nos. 1-24) were associated with the so-called 'First Hearth' (Taylor, 1927), were red deer, wild pig, horse, wild cattle, beaver, wild cat or marten and hedgehog. Reindeer was encountered at the base of the layer, and it may be speculated that both this and horse may be intrusive from Lateglacial contexts. The microliths from the 'First Hearth' (Taylor, 1927, fig. 4) are predominantly narrow rod-like pieces (16), many of which are fragmentary, with some small scalene triangles (5) and convex-backed pieces (2). There are also about 6 obliquely-backed points: an exact assessment of the lithic finds from this feature is not now possible.

At Westward Ho! where late Mesolithic 'midden' deposits have occasionally been exposed by tides and currents since at least the last century, bones of red, and roe deer, wild cattle and pig are recorded (Churchill, 1963). Analysis of fresh samples from the midden (Balaam et. al, 1987) adds frog, slow worm and a small species of inshore fish to this list, whilst the presence of *Mytilus* and *Scrobicularia* molluscs can be added to the *O. edulis* shells of earlier reports.

Recent work at Westward Ho! has allowed a more accurate assessment of the local environment at the time of midden accumulation than has hitherto been possible. The much eroded remnants of the 'Forest Beds' were accurately

located and surveyed for the first time and a series of new radiocarbon dates obtained (Balaam *et al.*, 1987, Table 1, fig. 6). It may be appropriate to summarize these results here:

The Mesolithic deposits lie near the present lowest limit of spring tides and consist of fragmented shell, humified organic matter, charcoal, bones and flint artefacts - all within a mainly silt matrix. This accumulation, interpreted as an anthropogenic deposit, is underlain by 'blue clay' of possible estuarine origin and is succeeded by wood peat. The earliest dating that may be of archaeological significance is of 8,180 +150 BP (HAR-5643) on charcoal from a gulley feature (also containing worked but undiagnostic flint) cut into the underlying sediments. This pre- dates the midden by at least a millennium, however, as samples of charcoal and bone from the latter fall between *c.* 6,955 +140 BP (Q-1211) and 6,100 +200 BP (HAR-5632). The wood peat started to develop at or shortly after this time.

Lithic remains totalling 1,167 pieces were recovered during the recent survey, not only from the midden but also from small outlying remnants of peat and clay. Worked on small cobbles of beach-derived flint (and some chert), this material is mostly debitage and tiny fragments recovered from fine environmental sieving. Out-numbering all tools were the by-products of microlith manufacture: micro-burins, miss-hits and micro- intermediates. Taken with the 25 small bladelet cores, this would seem to indicate a pre-occupation with making or re-tooling hunting or fishing equipment at the site. Only three classifiable microliths were found, however, and combine with the twelve from earlier collections to form a small series of 'narrow blade' forms typical of south-western assemblages (Jacobi, 1979). A minority of other tools (2% of the total collection) include five scrapers, although burins and heavier tools such as picks, choppers and bevelled pebbles are absent.

Biological data suggests that the rather specialized activity that appears to be represented by these lithic remains, with their associated food debris, took place within a fairly dense fen carr. This was a mixed oak woodland with some grasses and sedges, amongst which there are likely to have been pools of standing water. Willow, birch and ivy become more frequent in the higher levels of the midden, but there is little evidence for human influence on the vegetation. Using data presented by Heyworth and Kidson (1982) it can be estimated that sea level at this time was below at least -7 m OD, and although the shore may have been nearby during the occupation there is no evidence that the site was at the strandline. However, early reports of finds from the beach (Inkerman Rogers, 1908; E. H. Rogers, 1946) could be taken to suggest that the Mesolithic deposits were at one time both more extensive and perhaps of varying composition. Nevertheless, even if important remains are now irrecoverable, this site, supplemented by that at Blashenwell in Dorset (Preece, 1980) provides the only securely associated environmental evidence for late Mesolithic activity anywhere in southern England.

At both Westward Ho! and King Arthur's Cave, the association of faunal remains and Mesolithic occupation residues can be considered amply demonstrated. With the possible exception of the Lydstep pig, such clear associations are so far missing for Wales. Of potential significance, however, is a recent find from the foreshore on Horton beach, Gower. Here, at approximately 2 m. OD, several undiagnostic flint flakes and broken bladelets were recovered with fragmentary remains of red deer, small mammal bones, insects, charcoal and wood (M. Davies 1985). Further sampling of this site is needed, if conditions allow, before its real significance can be assessed.

Given the comparatively very poor evidence from Wales, it seems legitimate to mention some of the many examples of apparently archaeologically unassociated finds of large mammal bones from coastal areas of Wales. For instance, wild cattle are recorded from Borth (Taylor, 1973), Amroth, Wiseman's Bridge and at Whitesands Bay, all in Dyfed, and are also recorded from the Alexandra Dock, Newport (Matheson, 1932), Rhossili, Rumney, and the Gwent Levels (Green, 1989; Noddle, 1989). Inland, but also without any archaeological association are fragments of wild cattle bone from Foel Fawr cave, Llandovery, Dyfed, three dates for which centre at c. 7,200 BP (BM-1809, BM-1810, BM-1903; Burleigh et al., 1982). Finds of red deer are as frequent as for wild cattle, and include examples from Newport, Whitesands Bay, and Frainslake in Dyfed, and Cardiff, Swansea and Horton Beach in Glamorgan. Other species are rarer: brown bear from Whitesands Bay, Dyfed (Hicks, 1887) and wolf from Newport Docks (Matheson, 1932). Many such finds are casual and probably go unrecorded - a comprehensive listing would no doubt considerably extend the distribution of such findspots along most of the Welsh coast.

Despite this apparent abundance of faunal material, it would be a mistake to assume that even the majority is actually of Mesolithic age. Recent radiocarbon dates obtained on bones of wild cattle from Whitesands Bay, Dyfed and Runmey on the Severn Levels indicate Neolithic and Bronze Age derivation:

Whitesands Bay   4,540 +70 BP (CAR-1183: Lewis, forth-
                                                coming)
Rumney   4,060 +70 BP (CAR-851: Green, 1989)

5. Other late Mesolithic find-spots in Wales:

i) North Wales;
Hendre, Rhuddlan, Clwyd (SJ 027 781):
A group of 1182 artefacts of a composition, morphology and raw material very similar to that from Prestatyn was recovered from disturbed contexts during rescue excavations here (Manley and Healey, 1982). Mesolithic material, identified by the presence of microliths, was recovered from two trenches 50 m. apart, perhaps suggesting a considerable spread of activity. Flints were

also recovered from other trenches, but none of these are certainly Mesolithic.

The microliths (21 identifiable) are all of narrow-blade type, again with a predominance of small scalene triangles (10). Other types include small obliquely-backed points (2), straight (4) and convex-backed (5) bladelets. As at Prestatyn, the non-microlithic component has retouched flakes (11) and convex scrapers (7), but at Rhuddlan also includes serrated flakes or 'micro-denticulates' (5).

There is no dating evidence for this apparently late Mesolithic activity at Rhuddlan and caution must obviously be required in an area where both earlier and later human settlement has been concentrated. For instance, 'micro-denticulates' are not known from late Mesolithic find-spots elsewhere, but are to be found in many earlier assemblages. Indeed, they are present at the nearby early Mesolithic sites at Rhuddlan (Chapter III).

Aled Isaf Reservoir, Clwyd (SJ 2915 3595):
Few details of this find-spot, found in 1974, are known to the author. Excavation and surface collection there has, however, apparently revealed hearths, stakeholes and other features as well as several thousand flints. The latter include 'worked Mesolithic barbs', as well as scrapers, burins, debitage and cores (Jenkins, 1990). Charcoal apparently 'associated with the flints' (*ibid.*) has given a radiocarbon date of 5,810 +150 BP (*ibid.*, no lab. reference). A date from well above this horizon has given a date of 4,010 +120 BP (*ibid.*, no lab. reference). Although late Mesolithic activity might therefore be represented here, this remains very ill-defined, pending the availability of further details.

The remaining evidence for late Mesolithic settlement in north Wales is limited to small quantities of unstratified material in which occasional microliths have been recognized (Wainwright, 1963). Some of the microliths from Gop Cave, Clwyd, may be late Mesolithic (eg Grimes, 1951, fig. 4, no. 2), as may those recorded by Davies (1989b) at other caves such as Ogof Pant-y-Wennol (Clwyd) and Lloches-yr-Afr (Gwynedd). In addition, a small group of microliths, also largely unstratified, has recently been reported from below the Iron Age settlement at Collfryn, Powys (Britnell, 1989, fig. 36). None of these groups, including small excavated samples from the Roman sites of Ffrith, Clwyd, and, to the south, Usk, in Monmouthshire, can add significantly to the present discussion (Jacobi, 1980b, 169).

ii) South Wales:
Craig-y-Llyn area (SN 91 03):
Before turning to west Wales, attention should be drawn to over forty find-spots at which late Mesolithic activity has been recognized on the Glamorgan uplands. These have recently been discussed by Stanton (1985). These find-spots are located on the upland interfluves drained by the south Wales Valleys and are mostly at heights exceeding 1,500 feet (500 m.). They were found during fieldwork and

limited excavation during the 1960s and 70s (Savory, 1960-2; Stanton, 1985), and illustrate the dramatic effect on distribution plots that may result from intensive local fieldwork.

The sites have been arbitrarily exposed by erosion and the works of the Forestry Commission. In most cases they are represented by small concentrations of knapping debris, not necessarily in situ, and composed of several raw materials. 'Narrow blade' microliths are the most common component, with occasional scrapers. No dating of any kind is so far available, however, and although hearth features and charcoal have occasionally been noted, there is no evidence that these may not belong to the later prehistoric activity also recognized for the area. The most complete series of lithic finds is from the Craig-y-Llyn region, and here, as amongst the material from many of the other sites, there is an apparent mixture of both 'broad' and 'narrow blade' forms of microlith (Jacobi, 1980b, fig. 4.23). Confirmation that this is evidence of an equivalent amalgamation of both early and late Mesolithic activity on these uplands is not assisted by a generally poor level of provenancing and will depend on the further discovery of chronologically discrete localizations from which reliable radiocarbon samples can be collected.

Waun Fignen Felen, W. Glamorgan (SN 824 184):
The nine find-spots from this upland area have already been noted in Chapter III. 'Sites' 1 and 9 are of particular relevance here, however, in that they are the find-spots of two small groups of scalene micro-triangles (12 and 10 microliths, respectively: see Fig. 5.5, Nos. 25-46). That these are isolated from any other flint or chert artefacts or debitage suggests that they could very well represent the loss of composite projectile points. If so, then they would join the few other instances, particularly from upland sites in northern England, where isolated groups of 'narrow blade' microliths have been so interpreted (Rozoy, 1978, fig. 265; Myers, 1987, 1989a,b). It has been suggested that these microliths represent a technological refinement, in stone, of the barbs of bone and antler points, these latter being more laborious to make, repair or re-cycle (Mellars, 1976b; Myers, 1989a,b).

These finds from the uplands of south Wales clearly bring to mind those reported from areas of the Cleveland Hills and the Pennines of northern England above 1,000 feet (350 m.) (Radley, 1970; Radley et. al., 1974) where clusters of flintwork, especially microliths, are abundant. Both early and late Mesolithic sites are known from these latter areas, and have been interpreted as temporary seasonal hunting locations (Clark, 1970; Mellars, 1976; Jacobi, 1978). It can perhaps be predicted that exploitation of the Welsh uplands was of a similar nature and may also have been as spatially and chronologically widespread.

Other sites in south Wales:
Hints of further upland Mesolithic activity are given by isolated finds from the Two Tumps Barrow on the Kerry Hills (Daniels, 1927) and at Pant Sychbant (Burke, 1966), both in Powys. Also in Powys is the Neolithic long-cairn at Gwernvale below which were found 28 (mostly fragmentary) 'narrow blade' microliths mixed amongst a lithic confusion of several prehistoric derivations. Because of this, little confidence can be placed in the date of 6,895 +80 BP (CAR-118) from a hearth 'possibly associated with later Mesolithic flintwork at the site' (Britnell, 1979).

Within Glamorgan are several further find-spots from lowland locations (Stanton, 1985, fig. 12a), yet none of these are distinguished by useful contextual or chronological data. Small microliths from Merthyr Mawr and Ogmore closely resemble those from Craig-y-Llyn, but the improbable association of the latter with later Neolithic pottery implies that their original context is lost. Fragmentary 'narrow blade' microliths have also been recovered from the upper layers at Cathole, Gower (Campbell, 1977).

With an increased awareness of the potential of waterlogged inter-tidal deposits, it is perhaps in circumstances such as those at present under investigation on the Severn Levels, Gwent, that hold promise for an improvement on this very scanty dry land record. The discovery of a bone point (Fig. 5.4, No.1) and even the impression of human feet in a blue silt lying below peat (the base of which has been dated to 6,260 +80 BP (unpublished: Hammond, 1988)), is an early indication of the delicate and detailed remains at risk here (PAST, 1988).

iii) West Wales:
The description of the later Mesolithic in west Wales, as for the rest of Wales, is hampered for want of chronologically discrete and stratified archaeological find-spots. The exploration of caves, sand dunes, beaches, cliff paths and ploughed fields by generations of flint-hunters has resulted in a substantial array of material of very variable interpretative potential. As indicated above, it is perhaps those find-spots in foreshore locations which hold particular significance.

It was Leach (1913, 396 - 400) who originally pointed out that landward soil deposits (palaeosols) containing artefacts were in places continuous with the blue clays (minerogenic sediments) underlying foreshore peats (Wainwright, 1963, 107). Recent studies of both sediment types from several coastal locations suggest that they may be derived from similar parent materials, although the mode of deposition (by freshwater or marine processes) has yet to be established (Lewis, forthcoming). The sometimes complex stratigraphic records for such sites may result in part from the effects of both changes in sea level and coastal geomorphology (see above).

Present data, however, would certainly seem to support the probability that artefacts from the minerogenic sediments below and at the interface with the submerged peats are probably of late Mesolithic age. Attention has already been

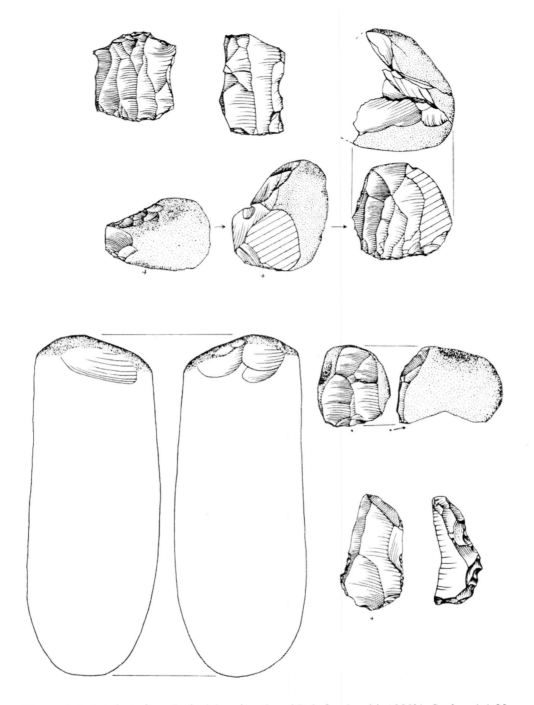

Figure 5.6: Artefacts from Frainslake, sites C and D 9after Jacobi, 1980b). Scale – 1:1.22.

drawn to the discovery of the pig skeleton apparently in association with flint armatures found within the wood peat at Lydstep (above), and apparently of terminal Mesolithic or earliest Neolithic age. To this can be added small groups of worked flint from Abermawr and Newport on the north Dyfed coast, and Amroth, Frainslake, and Freshwater West, to the south (Wainwright, 1963, and references therein).

Abermawr, Dyfed (SM 881 345):
A small group of flints including bladelet cores and one lanceolate-shaped microlith (Fig. 5.3, No. 9) is recorded from the interface between the blue 'clay' and overlying

peat on the foreshore here (J. G. Evans, and M. Lewis, pers. comm.). The overlying intertidal peat is undated but pollen analysis indicates an alder carr vegetation with hazel and oak (Lewis, forthcoming). There is some slight evidence for anthropogenic activity (an increase in hazel pollen recorded at a single sampling level) near the base of the peat (*ibid.*).

Landward of the beach, coring has revealed a depth of over 8 m of mid-late Flandrian sediments (Lewis, forthcoming). The lowermost peat here is also derived from an alder carr and is considered to be the equivalent of the foreshore sequence. The base of the inland peat profile is dated to

7,640 +150 BP (OxA-1411), whilst possible anthropogenic disturbance of the local valley-side vegetation is noted rather higher in the profile, dating to *c.* 5,520 +150 BP (OxA-1377).

Flints have occasionally been found in palaeosols within the Abermawr valley (Dunn, 1968; Lewis, forthcoming) but these are undiagnostic and the recent palaeoenvironmental work suggests their derivation from different periods (Lewis, *ibid.*).

Newport, Dyfed (SN 063 395):
Very similar lithic material to that from Abermawr, again including a 'narrow blade' microlith, is recorded along with charcoal from immediately below a deposit of peat lying on rubble 'head' at Traeth Mawr Bridge, to the north of Newport (SN 063 395: Thomas, 1923; Rees, 1973). Recent palaeoenvironmental work (Lewis, *ibid.*) has failed to identify a date or context for these finds, however.

Amroth, Dyfed (SS 170 070):
Leach (1913) recorded two localizations in foreshore exposures revealed by stream erosion. In both cases (sites B2 and B3), flints were found in blue 'clay' underlying peat. No microliths were found but none of the few artefacts from either localization would be incompatible with Mesolithic flintworking. Three flakes from site B2 are conjoinable.

Frainslake, Dyfed (SR 889 977):
Both Leach (1918) and Gordon-Williams (1926) recorded finds from intertidal deposits here, and in the latter case these offer a tantalizing glimpse of an evidently richly preserved area of prehistoric activity. There were two flint scatters, C and D, the former of which revealed 'a windscreen of gorse, birch, hazel and alder ... set in peat ...[with]... on the north side of this shelter which ran in a gentle curve for 4.5 yards ... an area bearing much charcoal, flint chip ... a large rabattu point ... etc.'. On site D was found the bone 'implement' referred to already (Fig. 5.4, No. 2).

None of the 56 flaked artefacts which survive from these two sites are specifically diagnostic, yet the presence of bladelet cores (7), to one of which re-join two flakes, is consistent with late Mesolithic workmanship, as might the 'rabattu point'. There is no evidence for the use of a scalar core technique (see below), and the presence of bevelled pebbles from both localizations is also indicative of late Mesolithic activity. A selection of artefacts from these scatters is illustrated in Fig. 5.6.

Freshwater West, Dyfed (SM 886 000):
Cultural debris has also been observed on the foreshore at Freshwater West, a beach adjacent and to the north of Frainslake (Leach, 1913, 1918; Wainwright, 1963). Flints were noted both from the peat and the 'clay' below, and samples of the peat were attributed to pollen Zone VIIa (Lambert, 1963), and provided a radiocarbon date of 5,960

±120 BP (Q-530: Godwin and Willis, 1964). The broken flint implement found on the surface of the blue 'clay' (Wainwright, 1963, fig. 9, 5) with several flakes is not considered diagnostic (pace Wainwright, *ibid.*).

Recent palaeoenvironmental work (Lewis, *ibid.*) somewhat inland from these sites, at Castlemartin Corse (SR 897 977) has identified a woodland pollen assemblage tentatively thought to be equivalent to that recognized on the foreshore (Lambert, 1963). However, the former peat growth began at *c.* 4,140 +70 BP (CAR-1143), a date substantially later than that obtained from the foreshore (Q-530). Lewis explains this disparity as a result of diachronous peat development, extending landwards with time as the rising sea level and that of the local water table matched each other. Such a diachroneity would suggest that (despite many dates for intertidal peats falling near to *c.* 6,000 BP: Jacobi, 1980b, 174) no single chronological horizon is represented either within the peat or at its interface with the underlying 'clays'. Certainly, finds from within these peats can now be shown to be of widely differing ages (see above), whilst finds from the underlying peat/mineral interface, where sedimentation was interrupted for an unknown interval, remain largely undated.

iv) Other find-spots in west Wales:
Complementing the small number of flint scatters so far described that lie on or near the foreshore are a very much larger number of late Mesolithic finds from caves and land surfaces in west Wales. Amongst the former are microliths from Caldey (Ogof-yr-Ychen and Nanna's Cave), Ogof Carreg-Hir and The Wogan Cavern (Fig 5.3) for all of which contextual information is either very poor or missing altogether.

The additional recoveries from surface sites are the work of several collectors, and have been described in varying detail in as many publications (for instance, Cantrill, 1915; Leach, 1913; Grimes, 1932, 1935, 1951; Gordon-Williams, 1926; Bosanquet, 1923; Wainwright, 1963; de Quincey, 1969; Wymer, 1977). Material from these collections is widely dispersed, and much has no doubt been lost. The many pitfalls of drawing satisfactory conclusions from such collections are well known, the most obvious being related to insecure provenancing, collectors' biases and chronological mixture. Even on excavated sites, 'narrow blade' material is residual (Benson *et al.*, 1990). Given such limitations, all that has been attempted here, by way of accounting for these find-spots, is the compilation of the distribution map (Fig. 7.1) in Chapter VII. Flint scatters contributing to this late Mesolithic activity are included on the basis of corroborative data provided by the author's independent fieldwork and, more importantly, from the results of his excavations at The Nab Head Site II (see Chapters VI and VII).

6. Local post-Mesolithic technologies

At Freshwater West, but from the Burrows well above high water mark, is a group of 7,700 flints excavated by

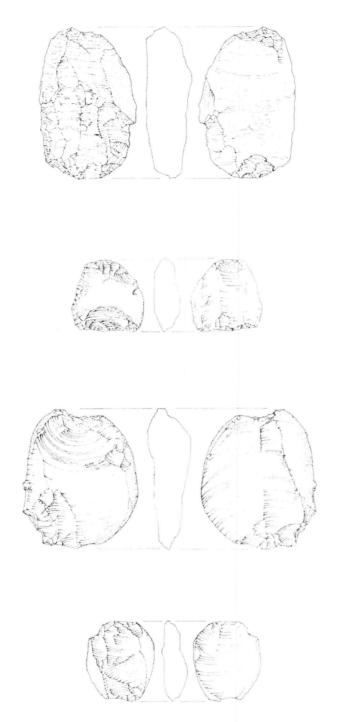

Figure 5.7: *Pièces écaillées* from Stackpole Warren, Dyfed. Scale – 1:1.14.

Wainwright (1959). A re-examination of this assemblage confirmed the presence of many cores, or splintered flakes and nuclei (*pièces ecaillées*). With perhaps few exceptions, the entirety of the assemblage is composed of the products of a very different strategy of core reduction to that usually associated with Mesolithic flintwork.

The term 'scalar piece' may be given to both the cores and the flakes produced from them. Instead of the formal development of a striking platform on a beach cobble, followed by the removal of bladelets, the scalar technique involves the reduction of the cobble through bi-polar

percussion between an anvil and a hammerstone. This action results in the removal of splinters of flint which have various shapes ranging from thin scalar or squamous pieces to more prismatic bi-concave or banana-shaped pieces. There are no platforms and often the flakes show shatter marks and conchoidal rings at both ends. The residual nuclei, or cores, are often wedge shaped, rather than prismatic, and typically show the bruising and splintering of percussion at both ends (Fig 5.7). More often than not, after the initial splitting of a pebble, the consequent larger split pieces and secondary flakes are themselves subjected to bi-polar scaling.

This method of breaking up flint and stone cobbles is perhaps a great deal more common than is usually admitted in the literature. It has seen use in widely differing cultural and chronological contexts and in Europe is known from Swedish, Finnish and Norwegian sites of Mesolithic to Neolithic age (Broadbent, 1979). In Norway, splintered pieces are considered to be time diagnostic of the late Mesolithic (B. Skar, pers. comm.) and are characteristic of middle Mesolthic sites in Sweden (Welinder, 1977). In western Britain, as in Norway, where raw material is poor, the technique has been seen as a direct response to this deficiency. This could certainly be argued to be the case on sites from western Scotland (Mellars, 1987; Wickham-Jones, 1984; 1990), north-west England (Bonsall, 1980), Wales (Jacobi, 1980b) and Cornwall (Johnson and David, 1982). Along this entire western seaboard, flint is only readily available as small beach pebbles and splintering these may on occasions have been the preferred method of core reduction. A pratical acquaintance with the technique indicates that the method of producing flakes is considerably more predictable than would at first appear. With controlled and carefully directed percussion desired flakes can be removed somewhat as they can from a platformed bladelet core (Wickham-Jones, pers. comm.).

Aside from core reduction alone, there is uncertainty whether the products of this technique were themselves used as tools. The residual nuclei, so often wedge-shaped and heavily worn at their edges, have been considered to be wedges, chisels or retouching tools (Broadbent, 1979). The primary and secondary flakes are often suitable as supports for convex edge-retouch and the broad and thinner flakes could occasionally serve as blanks for pressure-flaked tools. Where assemblages using this technique have been encountered, such as on Oronsay (Mellars, 1987) and Constantine Island, Cornwall (Norman, 1977), and here at Freshwater West, formal tool-types are restricted to scrapers, denticulates, chopping tools and casually retouched flakes.

At Freshwater West there is a striking absence of microliths - a feature which is hardly surprising in view of the lack of bladelet cores. Apart from the single barbed and tanged arrowhead, the retouched flake (perhaps a hollow-based arrowhead, but incorrectly diagnosed as a 'Horsham point': Wainwright, 1959, fig. 4, 20), and the 'burins' (now recognized to be the inadvertent products of the splintering technique), the predominant tool-type at the site is the convex scraper. In every respect these scrapers are indistinguishable from those commonly associated with early Bronze Age flintwork - especially the 'button' or 'thumbnail' types (class A(ii) - short end- scrapers: Clark, 1960). Recent excavations at Stackpole Warren, on the coast south of Milford Haven, have demonstrated the association of neat convex scrapers with this technology in the filling of an early Bronze Age hut feature which has been radiocarbon dated to c 3345 ±70 BP (CAR 100: David, in Benson et. al., 1990). A scalar core from Drigg on the Cumbrian coast is associated with radiocarbon dates of

3780 ±55 BP (UB 905) and 4135 ±55 BP (UB-906: Pearson, 1979; Cherry, 1982). At Freshwater West, the post-Mesolithic dating of the flint assemblage under discussion seems certain owing to the presence of a scaled piece worked on a flake from a polished flint axe (Jacobi, 1980b, 178).

On the evidence above, it seems highly probable that a technology which makes use of scalar cores is to be associated with Neolithic - Bronze Age flintworking. This suggestion is supported in west Wales also by the contrasting patination encountered in some collections which appear to be of mixed ages. Thus there is a repeated tendency for the scalar pieces to be less patinated that the microlithic component, and in some cases differential patination clearly demonstrates the use of splintering on former Mesolithic flakes (see Plate 7.3). It yet remains, however, to demonstrate satisfactorily whether or not the use of this technology is of cultural or chronological significance, or whether it is nothing more than a response to deficiencies in raw material. In contrast to the later prehistoric dating suggested above, the preferential use the technique on bloodstone raw material at Kinloch, Rhum, is regarded as a late Mesolithic activity (Wickham-Jones, 1990). It may be significant, too, that a single *pièce ecaillée* has recently been found 6 cm below the base of foreshore peat at Lydstep which began growth at c. 6,150 +120 BP (OxA-1378: Hedges *et al*, 1989; Lewis, forthcoming).

6. Summary:

Although the number of Mesolithic find-spots in Wales that can be assigned with reasonable confidence to a time after c. 8,800 BP is very much greater than for earlier periods, their contextual and chronological setting is still only poorly understood.

The lithic components of such find-spots are distinguished by a bladelet core technology with small ('narrow blade') microliths. In contrast to earlier accounts, find-spots in upland Wales have been noted as potentially 'prolific' but, with their lack of processing tools, may relate specifically to small-scale hunting episodes. Hunting also undoubtedly took place nearer the present coast, but these lowland artefact scatters appear characterized by larger and more diverse lithic assemblages (see Chapter VII).

Having now set the scene in general terms as far as it is possible, the following two chapters can now enlarge upon the exploration of the late Mesolithic archaeological record for west Wales, and its implications, in the light of recent excavation and fieldwork.

1. Introduction

Site II at The Nab Head was originally located whilst excavation was in progress at Site I in 1980. Several flints were found in a small soil test pit situated about half way between the cliff top at Site I and the promontory fort at Tower Point. Expansion of this shovel pit into a trench measuring 1 x 3 m. revealed a moderately dense scatter of patinated flint artefacts and debitage which included small bladelet cores and narrow scalene triangular microliths. This material, apparently lacking the characteristics of early Mesolithic flintworking, such as were now familiar from Site I, was instead closely in keeping with the predicted appearance of a late Mesolithic industry.

As discussed in Chapter IV, there is clear circumstantial evidence to suggest that the accumulated lithic residues at Site I are in fact the product of separate early and late Mesolithic phases of activity. The attraction of the new finds was therefore their apparent homogeneity - providing an opportunity to examine a sample of late Mesolithic material in isolation. In turn, this might allow a much sounder understanding of the mixture of evidence from Site I. The new site appeared also to have escaped modern cultivation and disturbance, and not to have been truncated by cliff erosion. There was thus a chance to examine the nature of late Mesolithic activity which, although known to be abundant along these coasts, had until now only been recognized from ploughed and eroding surfaces and from very occasional glimpses between spring tides. The extent of flint scatters in ploughed fields indicate that where such sites are identifiable they may cover a substantial area. Indeed the presence of late Mesolithic flints at Site I and also in the fields adjacent to Tower Point suggests the possibility of widespread activity at this time over most of the headland area.

With the discovery of further Mesolithic activity at The Nab Head, the two sites were therefore designated I and II, and excavation continued at the latter, directed by the writer, during short seasons in 1981, 1982 and 1986. Lack of any significant threat to the site meant that sponsorship had to be sought through small research grants, while the Dyfed Archaeological Trust continued to provide invaluable practical assistance.

2. Local topography and soils:

The Nab Head is strictly the 'nose' forming the extremity of an altogether broader headland of naturally vegetated clifftop. This latter area, covering about a hectare, slopes gently down to The Nab and is traversed by two streamlets that have their origin at springheads in the adjacent field, and which converge near the cliff top (see Fig. 4.2 and Plate 4.1). In their course over the headland, these streamlets encounter small secondary springs and boggy patches which intervene between subdued knolls of Old Red Sandstone bedrock and areas of more level ground. The whole gives the impression of an unkempt and uneven clifftop plateau descending down towards to the cliff-edge on three sides, the landward and southern side being delimited by a field-wall. The vegetation is mostly a coarse springy and hummocky turf interspersed between growths of bracken, brambles and heather. At one point, near the western cliff-edge, the roof of a marine cave opening at the foot of the cliff has collapsed, leaving a gaping hole.

Soils exposed here and along the circumference of the headland, as well in the excavations themselves, vary in depth and complexity. The deepest profiles, in excess of 40 cm. occur over depressions in the bedrock and at the base of slopes and are at their most complex at Site I (see chapter IV). One or more stone lines are visible in the cliff edges and extend away from these, inland, for at least 10 metres. These are visible, for instance, in the cave collapse, and are assumed to be post- Mesolithic. At site II itself, some 50 m. from the nearest cliff edge, there are no stone lines, and the soil profile is a simple succession of dense turf-mat overlying an A horizon of sandy clay loam resting directly on bedrock. The depth of topsoil varies according to the prominence of bedrock: the latter is close to the surface at the eastern edge of the excavation but shelves away westwards, leaving a shallow topsoil of only some 10 cm. at the eastern edge of the excavation area deepening westwards to a depth of 35 cm. at its other end. The topography of the underlying Old Red Sandstone is guided by faulting. Lateglacial periglacial activity has exploited areas of structural weakness and has infilled these with a solifluction grit comprising the C horizon in the deeper parts of the excavation. Post-glacial stream activity has also followed lines of weakness and in places has deposited clay, now gleyed.

The archaeological horizon - that is, where the flint and stone artefacts had evidently accumulated - was within a 10 cm. deep zone at the base of the topsoil, at its junction with either the bedrock or with solifluction deposits. Both artefacts and natural residual stones seemed to have found their level here as a result of mechanical and biological soil processes - no vertical stratigraphy was apparent.

3. Excavation strategy:

As a preliminary to excavation, a magnetometer survey was undertaken over the site and revealed complex anomalies. These are interpreted as relating both to archaeological features and to variations in bedrock and overlying natural deposits.

Plate 6.1: The Nab Head Site II excavation (1986).

After removal of turf and topsoil to a depth just above the main artefact concentration, a 1 m. grid was laid out centred about and in alignment with the original exploratory trench. The excavation then followed the procedures already used so effectively on Site I. Soil from each 1 m. unit was removed by hand and was sieved to recover the smaller lithic items and charcoal not already bagged and recorded on site. Initial attempts to plot the location of each artefact were abandoned because of the profusion of finds and the necessity for sieving. All pebble tools, though, as well as the larger unmodified stones were plotted, as were all subsoil features.

As the artefacts appeared to belong to a worm-sorted layer with no specific stratigraphic integrity, the archaeological horizon was initially excavated en bloc with no recourse to spits - levels being taken at its surface and base. In 1986, however, this worm-sorted layer was removed in 5 cm. spits to test whether any stratigraphic separation might be detectable. Also, during 1982 and 1986, the excavated grid units were reduced to 0.5 m. squares to improve the resolution of the resulting distributional data.

During the first two seasons, soil samples were taken from the artefact-rich layer, at 70 cm intervals across the excavation grid, to test for magnetic susceptibility and phosphate concentrations.

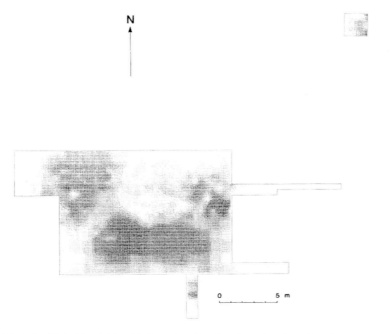

Figure 6.1: The Nab Head Site II. Density distribution plot for all flaked artefacts.

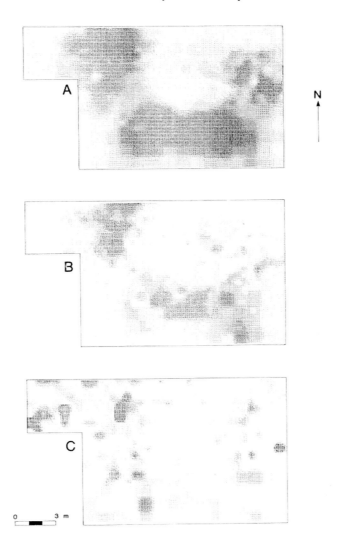

Figure 6.2: The Nab Head Site II. Density distribution plots for all flaked artefacts (A), burnt flint (B) and charcoal, by weight (C).

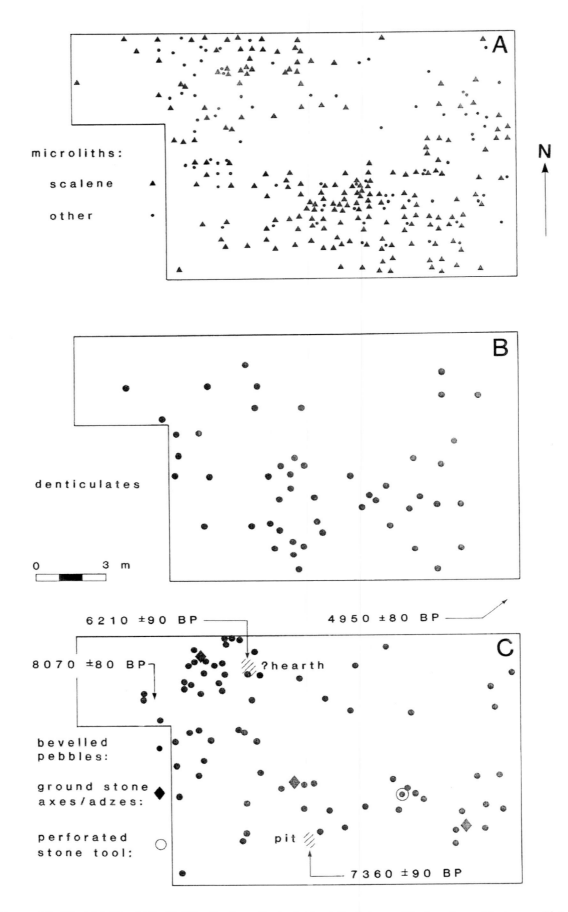

Figure 6.3: The Nab Head Site II. Distribution of principal artefacts types. The location of features which have provided radiocarbon dates are also indicated.

4. Excavation results - summary

A total of 195 square metres of the site have now been excavated, and about 28 tons of soil wet-sieved. Altogether, 31,797 pieces of chipped flint and stone have been recovered along with many bevelled pebbles, three ground stone axe- or adze heads, and a perforated 'macehead'. Few features were located.

Separate to the main excavation area, a 2 x 2 m. test trench sited on the top of a small knoll some 14 m. to the north-east of the main trench located a further concentration of late Mesolithic flintwork and bevelled pebbles. A sample of oak charcoal from this trench produced the following unexpected AMS date:

4,950 ±80 BP (OxA-1498: Hedges *et al.*, 1989)

The site chronology will be discussed in a later section (see below).

The distribution of artefacts is illustrated in Figs. 6.1 and 6.3. In the absence of satisfactory evidence for structures and habitation features, it is this pattern of lithic debris and discarded tools upon which speculation about activities at the site must depend. The composition of the flint and stone artefacts from the excavations is shown in Table 6.1, and a more detailed description of these will follow below.

Flint and struck stone debris was encountered across the site, but in markedly different densities. No significant vertical separation was noted. Examination of Fig. 6.1 shows clearly that the excavation trench encompasses three main aggregations of flint debris which surround a central area of greatly reduced density. Fig. 6.2 compares the pattern of burnt flint, charcoal and total flint across the excavation.

Burnt flint, in particular seems to emphasize an 'edge' between the main clusters and the central area of lower density. Individual components of the lithic assemblage, such as microliths, denticulates and bevelled pebbles also generally respect this central area (see Fig. 6.3), although it is not otherwise defined by bedrock, subsoil or features dug into these. That the surrounding clusters of lithic debitage and tools are discrete from each other is suggested by the conjoining of 33 elements of a single core-reduction sequence from the north- western concentration (see Fig. 6.4 and Plate 6.2). The latter is one of the few examples of the use of a non-flint raw material, rhyolite, allowing the distribution of its component parts to be clearly distinguished from amongst an otherwise undifferentiated mass of patinated flint.

Excepting the distribution of flint and stone artefacts, features are mostly restricted to an apparently patternless scatter of small holes penetrating either the bedrock or the solifluction gravel. Some of these may be stake holes, but positive evidence for this is lacking. More certainly artificial is a small and shallow pit or scoop, measuring 40 x 30 cm.

and 15 cm. deep. Its surface was distinguished by tightly packed angular stones below which was a filling of burnt soil. Heating was indicated by an enhanced magnetic susceptibility, and dispersed throughout was a thin scattering of charcoal. This feature might, therefore, represent a small hearth or hearth sweepings. Charcoal fragments from its fill have produced an AMS radiocarbon date of:

7360 ±90 BP (OxA-860)

Charcoal and burnt soil was also concentrated at a point within the north-western flint scatter although, in this case, there was no associated subsoil feature. Attention had been drawn to this spot by detection of a clear magnetic anomaly responding to the burnt soil. As the density of burnt flint was also greater than usual at this point there has to be a strong probability that a hearth or fire was once present. Charcoal from this 'feature' was of mixed types, including *Quercus, Prunus, Corylus, Pomoideae, Leguminosae*. An AMS determination on a charcoal sample from this concentration gave the following result:

6,210 ±90 BP (OxA-861: Gowlett *et al.*, 1987)

A second item of charcoal (*Quercus*) from about 4.5 m to the SW gave a date of:

8,070 ±80 BP (OxA-1497: Hedges *et al.*, 1989)

These dates are discussed at the end of the chapter.

Stones occur throughout the site and with the one exception of their concentration in the uppermost filling of the shallow pit mentioned above, do not appear to show any clearly recognizable preferential distribution. Apart from artefacts made from beach pebbles, all the stones are angular fragments of a coarse quartzite which outcrops locally in narrow bands within the Old Red Sandstone. Its extreme durability ensures its persistence as a residual component at the base of local soils.

Other features at the site include a partially preserved and very shallow gulley of uncertain origin. On the western edge of the excavation a depression containing a spring and streamlet was sectioned in two places and found to contain gleyed clay up to a metre or more in thickness. Although artefacts, such as cores and a bevelled pebble were found within this material, pollen analysis through the deposit indicates that the clay is likely to be post-Mesolithic (M. Lewis pers. comm.) and, therefore, that the contained artefacts are probably in a secondary depositional context. Further excavation is required to explore other suspected deep features detected by the magnetometer, which may have archaeological potential.

5. The flaked flint and stone tools

i) Raw materials:
These consist almost exclusively of flint, the immediate origin of which would have been local beach shingle.

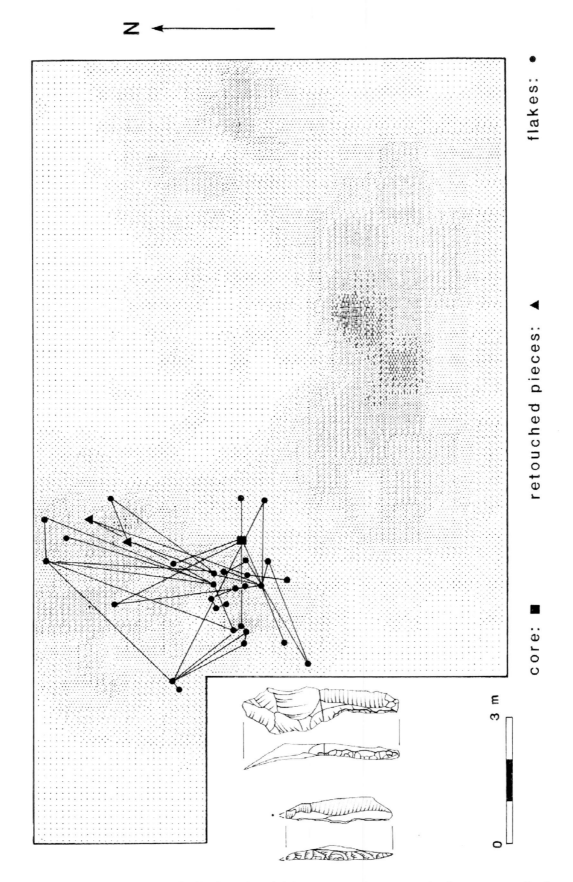

Figure 6.4: The Nab Head Site II. Distribution of conjoining elements in a core reduction sequence. Background flint density is also indicated. The two retouched pieces from the sequence are illustrated alongside (at scale – 1.1:1).

Plate 6.2: Reconstruction bladelet core of igneous stone from The Nab Head Site II.

Unused cobbles from the site are rounded and the rind on all cortical pieces is characteristic of that on beach pebbles. Most of the flint debitage and tools are heavily patinated, but recent breaks and unpatinated pieces indicate an original colouring of grey, black and honey-brown.

Apart from an overwhelming dominance of flint, occasional cobbles of other materials were sometimes knapped. There are rare flakes of Cretaceous Greensand chert (0.1% of the assemblage) and two cores of igneous material (0.3% of the assemblage), one of which has provided the pattern of conjoining elements referred to above. Such raw material is not uncommon on the present-day beaches, derived from local exposures, and may be expected to have been collected as an acceptable alternative to flint.

The raw material in use here is thus closely similar to that noted at Site I where beach pebble flint also forms the dominant constituent, with small proportions of chert and igneous material (1.2% of the total lithic sample). At Site I, however, there is a rather greater range in size and type of raw material. Possible explanations for this can be sought in the early Mesolithic presence there, in which larger flint microliths were required, and core axes/adzes were manufactured of suitable large cobbles, often of igneous origin. Also, at a time of more lowered sea level, a greater choice of rock types may have been accessible.

ii) The debitage:

As for Site I, comment here will be limited to a brief consideration of the cores as indicators of the general nature of the debitage. All stages of core reduction are abundantly represented on the site, from unworked cobbles (20) to those with preliminary primary removals (88), to the residual cores themselves (337). By far the larger part of the flaked assemblage (95%) is composed of the resulting flakes, bladelets and fragments.

The cores are usually extremely small, a measured sample of 101 pieces having an average 'height' of 28 mm., thereby placing the assemblage at the lower extreme of Mesolithic sites for which measurements have been recorded (see Fig. 7.2). The cores normally have a single platform, although double- and multi-platformed examples are not uncommon. In many cases frustration at working such small pebbles is evident from the pattern of irregular multi-directional removals, stepped 'hinge fractures' and 'overhangs'. Neatly worked pyramidal or prismatic cores are exceptional and formal core rejuvenation flakes rare. Knapping seems to have been altogether rather casual as raw material, if poor, was at least plentiful.

iii) Retouched forms:

Microliths:

There are 313 classifiable microliths, substantially outnumbering any other tool type found on the site. Rather more fragments were recovered although these cannot be classified in any detail. The typological composition of the microlith collection is as follows:

Table 6.1: Microlith composition at The Nab Head Site II

	No.	% of classified microliths
obliquely-backed points	18	5.8
other 'broad blade' forms	5	1.6
complete narrow scalene triangles	89	28.4
fragments of narrow scalene triangles	118	37.7
convex-backed pieces	38	12.1
straight-backed pieces	16	5.1
lanceolate pieces	19	6.1
four-sided forms	3	0.95
'points'	4	1.3
'points' concave basal retouch	3	0.95
TOTAL classified microliths	313	100.00
unclassified microliths	5	
unclassified microlith fragmgents	319	
TOTAL microliths and fragments	637	

A representative range of the microlith types is illustrated in Fig. 6.5. Immediately apparent from this and Table 6.2 above is not only that the microlith assemblage is large, but that it demonstrates a striking homogeneity in which a limited range of 'narrow blade' forms predominate.

Narrow scalene triangles (eg Fig. 6.5, Nos.25-137) clearly outnumber all other shapes and it is likely that their contribution would be greater if only their presence from amongst the hundreds of fragments could be accounted for. Although the scalene shape is so common, there is nevertheless a certain variation in the overall size and position of retouch. Modification to all three sides is a frequent attribute (66% of scalene triangles) in which the microlith is all but rod-shaped with an oblique termination to produce a scalene outline. Where these latter pieces are preserved entire, their broader termination can support an almost needle-like point. Other scalene triangles may be retouched on only two edges and have an outline more nearly isosceles.

After scalene triangles, most numerous are convex-backed pieces. These are quite distinct from the former in that an angular outline has been deliberately avoided. The convex-backed outline is itself similar to that present on the lanceolate microliths, except that the latter have additional retouch defining a point at one or other end of the bladelet. Straight-backed bladelets, retouched along one edge and without a point are also present in small numbers although their status as finished or complete items may be in doubt. One such bladelet has been re-fitted within the rhyolite core flaking sequence, along with a mis-snapped notched bladelet, or 'miss-hit'. Both of these were probably discarded, whilst other bladelets (now missing from the sequence) may have been successfully converted into microliths.

Finally, amongst the 'narrow blade' microliths, are rare examples of pieces with retouch on four sides, or with concave basal retouch, or shaped to define 'points' (eg Fig. 6.5, Nos. 165- 168). These cannot be further classified.

Contrasting with this range of 'narrow blade' microliths are a relatively small number (18) of obliquely-backed pieces (eg Fig. 6.5, Nos. 1-17). Other 'broad blade' forms include two fragmentary large scalene triangles (Fig. 6.5, Nos. 23-24), an isosceles triangle (Fig. 6.5, No. 22), and a broken bi-truncated piece of rhombic outline (Fig. 6.5, No. 21). All these, amounting to 7.3% of the classifiable microliths, together with two fragments of large microliths, could be assigned to an earlier Mesolithic technology of the type recognized at Site I. Given the proximity of Site I it would, perhaps, not be surprising to find a 'background noise' of earlier artefacts nearby. A possible *mèche de forêt* and some of the scrapers might also be early Mesolithic although their similarity to equivalent tools at Site I is not fully convincing. Neither is there any clear stratigraphic or spatial relationship with the remainder of the assemblage to support or refute any separate status for these 'broad blade' microliths.

Obliquely-backed pieces (although often rather smaller than their early Mesolithic counterparts) are, however, a recognized but minor constituent of Horsham-type and some other later Mesolithic lithic assemblages (Pitts and Jacobi, 1978). They are, for instance, a significant part (22%) of the classifiable microliths at Prestatyn (see above). It is possible, therefore, that those from Site II are actually genuine components of an otherwise 'narrow blade' technology, and it is notable that there are no other lithic types from Site II which are certainly indicative of early Mesolithic activity. The significance of these 'broad blade' microliths from Site II, therefore, remains unknown.

Although only by-products, it is appropriate to mention micro- burins and related pieces here. There are 79 micro-burins and 56 related pieces such as miss-hits, rejects and micro- intermediates. Whilst there are, therefore, four times

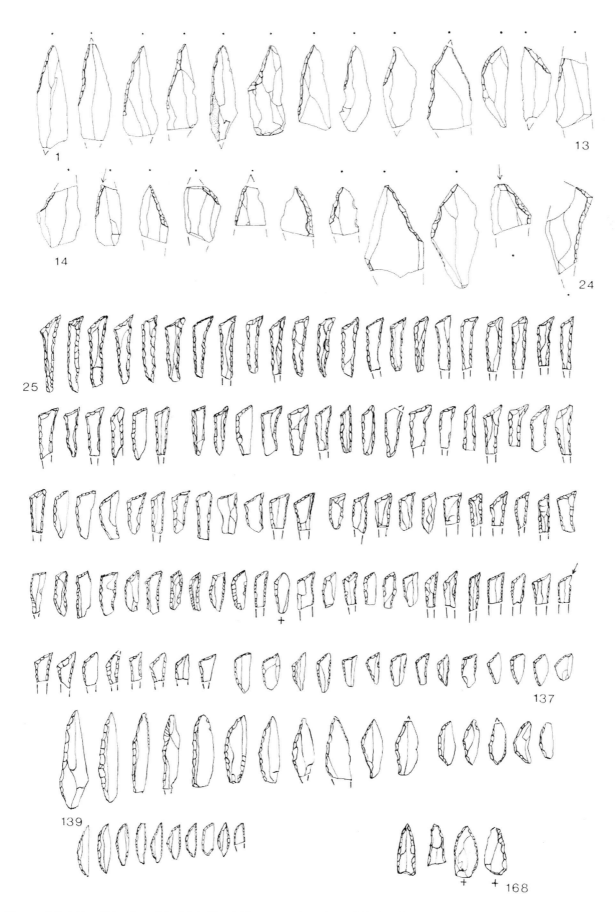

Figure 6.5: Microliths from The Nab Head Site II: - 1-24, "broad-blade" forms; 25-137, scalene micro-triangles; 138-168, other "narrow-blade" forms. Scale – 1:1.07.

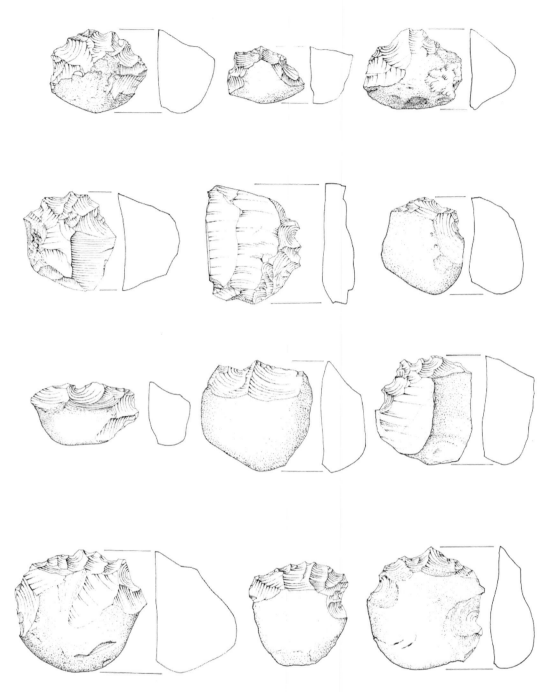

Figure 6.6: Artefacts from The Nab Site II: - denticulates. Scale – 1:1.27.

as many finished microliths as micro-burins, there is little more to add other than the obvious observation that microliths were clearly being manufactured on the spot, and that this manufacture may well not have always made use of the notching technique. All the bulbar micro-burins (44) display right-hand notches, consistent with the rightward points of the great majority of the microliths - a characteristic typical of these tools at many late Mesolithic sites.

Denticulates:
After microliths, the most numerous tool type is the denticulate: there are 50 of these, forming 11% of the tool assemblage. This tool type has already been encountered in small numbers amongst the large mixed assemblage on Site I. Here at Site II such denticulates are more convincingly associated with both 'narrow blade' microliths and bevelled pebbles.

Denticulates are made on large primary or secondary flakes, often D-shaped in cross-section, and can be identified by steep and coarse retouch around a part of their perimeter, lending them a notched or denticulated outline (Fig. 6.6) An alternative term for these might be 'denticulated scrapers', although their function is not yet understood and their form is often intermediate between scraper and bladelet core.

Scrapers:
There are 22 convex-edged scrapers (Fig. 6, Nos. 1-13) in the assemblage. The smoother outline of their working edges defines them apart from denticulates. They are different also, however, from the majority of scrapers encountered on Site I, in that their retouch is neither so neat nor so regularly applied to the ends of blades and short flakes. There are no double-ended scrapers.

Retouched pieces:
Slightly more numerous than scrapers are 25 varied flakes which appear to share no common outline but support steep retouch along part of their edges (Fig. 6.8, Nos. 16-27). They therefore resemble the series of retouched flakes from Prestatyn (see Chapter V), but are otherwise undistinctive.

Other retouched tools:
The categories so far described account for about 93% of the classified tools. The remainder of the tool assemblage is composed of small numbers of 'becs', truncated pieces (Fig. 6.8, Nos. 1-6, 8-13), 'nosed' and notched pieces (Fig. 6.7, Nos. 14-19; Fig. 6.8, Nos. 14-15), a single possible *mèche de forêt* (Fig. 6.8, No. 7) and a bi- facially flaked pebble or 'chopping tool' (Fig. 6.9, No. 3). Fig. 6.9 No. 4 is a large flaked segment of a flint pebble the edge of which bears severe wear and polish from use. 'Becs' (Fig. 6.8, Nos. 8-13) are flakes or blades on which a point, often curved in outline, has been developed by bi-lateral retouch. Also in this category are fortuitously pointed flakes or blades which bear traces of retouch or utilization at their tips. Not classified are 76 pieces with edge-damage or casual retouch suggestive of 'utilization'. There are no burins.

Table 6.2: flint and stone artefacts from The Nab Head Site II

i)   Tools:

microliths:		
'broad blade'		23
'narrow blade'		290
unclassified microliths		5
unclassified microlith fragments		319
denticulates		50
scrapers		22
becs		7
truncated pieces		12
nosed pieces		7
notched pieces		5
?mèche de forêt		1
bi-facially flaked pebble or 'chopping-tool'		1
retouched pieces		25
utilized pieces		76
other piece		1

ii) By -products:

micro-burins	79
micro-intermediates	9
miss-hits	23
other microlith by-products	24

iii) Debitage:

cores	337
core fragments	58
flaked flint pebbles	88
unflaked flint pebbles	20
flakes, blades, fragments	30, 315
TOTAL flaked flint and stone	31, 797
(Cretaceous chert	33)
(igneous rock	92)

iv) Pebble tools:

bevelled pebbles	55
unmodified elongated pebbles	16
fragments of elongated pebbles	20
ground stone axes	3
ground and perforated disc	1
?hammerstones	3

iv) The pebble tools

The pebble tools from The Nab Head, because of their numerical importance both here and amongst many other lithic collections up and down the western coasts of Britain, are treated in some detail below.

Bevelled pebbles:
Quite as distinctive a component of Welsh late Mesolithic tool kits as small scalene triangles and denticulates are bevelled pebbles. Fifty-five of these were found scattered across The Nab Head Site II and there were fragments of perhaps many more. Examples are illustrated in Figs. 6.10 and 6.11. In each case the tool is made from an elongate and usually flattish water-worn pebble probably originating, like the flint, from nearby beaches. In well-preserved examples there is usually a pronounced bevelled edge on either side of one or sometimes both ends. Very often, it is clear that the end of the tool has also been flaked by percussion and then abraded or bevelled. Sometimes there is evidence for pecking or percussion on the flanks of the stone, and in one case the end and part of the lateral margin has a distinct polish through use.

Although bevelling and flaking are characteristic of these pebbles there is considerable variety in both their shape and size and the degree of bevelling or abrasion. There are, for instance, 16 elongate pebbles which seem entirely unmodified, whilst others have a scarcely detectable bevelling. Some are symmetrical and flattened in section, others are irregular and prismatic. Lengths can vary by up to 200 mm., within the range 100 - 300 mm.

Bevelled pebbles - the 'limpet scoops' or 'limpet hammers' of former literature - have been the subject of much

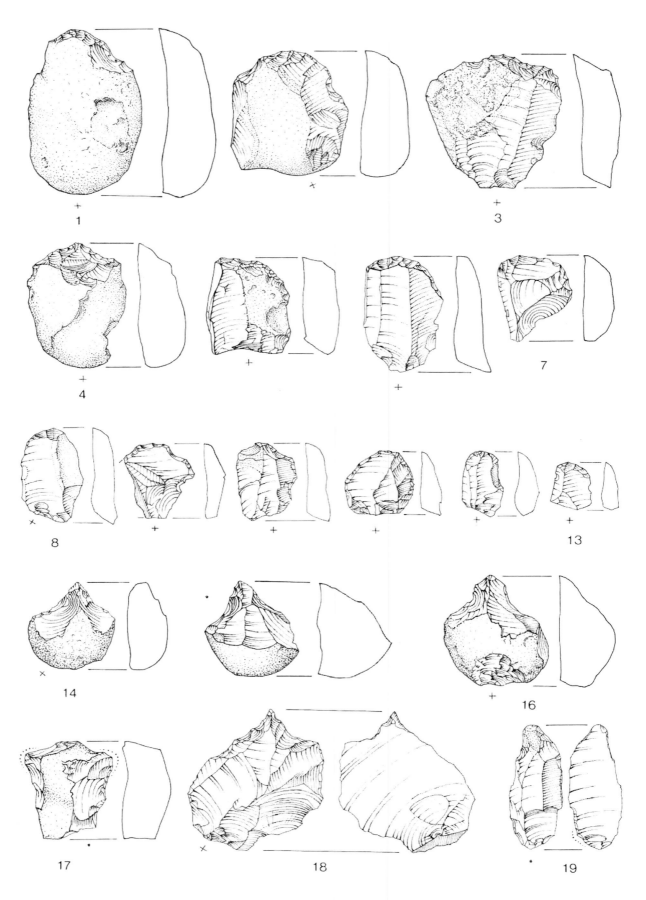

Figure 6.7: Artefacts from The Nab Head Site II: - 1-13, scrapers; 14-17, "nosed" pieces; 18-19, Scale – 1:1.

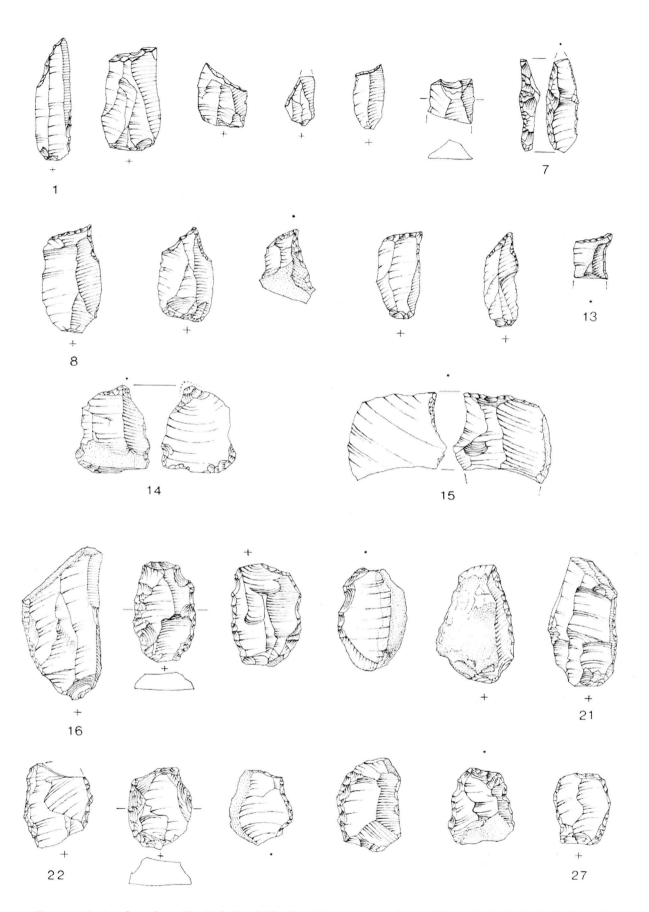

Figure 6.8: Artefacts from The Nab Head Site II: - 1-6, truncated pieces; 7, ?*mèche de forêt*; 8-13, "becs";
14-15 ?"becs"/worn pieces; 16-27, steeply retouched flakes. Scale – 1:1.

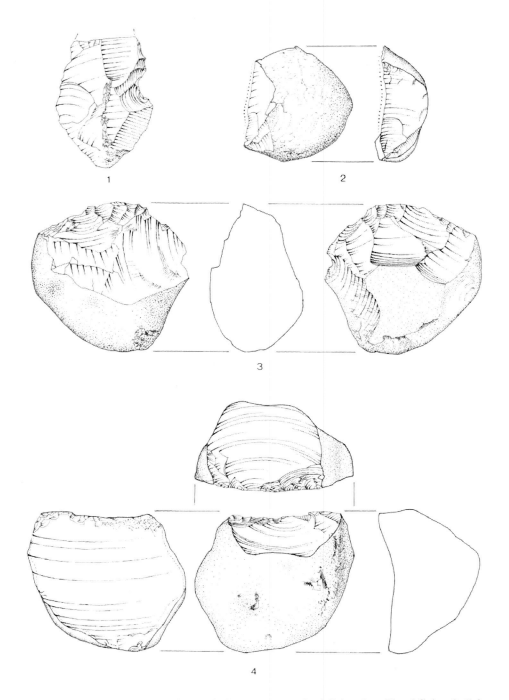

Figure 6.9: Artefacts from The Nab Head Site II: - 1, notched flake; 2, utilized flake; 3, "chopper"; 4, heavily utilized flake. Scale – 1:1.31.

discussion ever since their recognition in the 'Obanian' caves and middens of western Scotland (Grieve, 1885; Anderson, 1895, 1898; Bishop, 1914; Cantrill, 1915; Breuil, 1922; Gordon-Williams, 1926; Movius, 1942; Lacaille, 1954; Clark, 1955; Jacobi, 1980b; Reynolds 1983; Mellars, 1987; Roberts, 1987). It is not intended to re-state the debate in detail here since attempts to resolve the function of these enigmatic tools are no further advanced than they were at the outset, almost a hundred years ago. Experimentation has, however, thrown doubt on their association with limpets or other shellfish and instead a possible role in hide-working is favoured by some recent writers (Jacobi, 1980b;

Smith, 1982; Johnson and David, 1982). Others have proposed a function associated with percussion (Breuil, 1922; Wickham-Jones, 1984; Roberts, 1987).

There is one factor in particular, however, which links the many find-spots upon which bevelled pebbles have been found. They are, without exception, coastal or near-coastal and, more particularly, widely spread along the Atlantic seaboard. Jacobi (1980b, fig. 4.30) has mapped their occurrences on the coasts of Wales and the south-western peninsula whilst bevelled pebbles are also recorded from Ireland (Movius, 1942; Woodman 1978a) and the Isle of

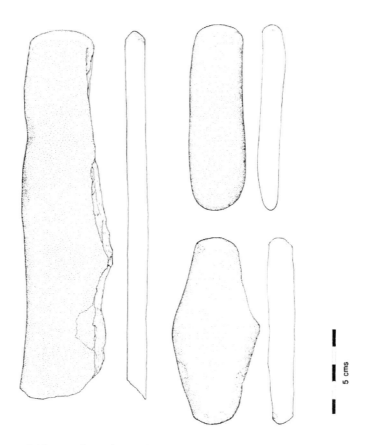

Figure 6.10: Artefacts from The Nab Head Site II: - bevelled pebbles.

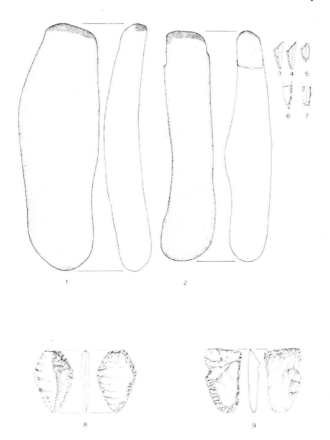

Figure 6.11: Artefacts from The Nab Head Site II: - 1-7, from subsidiary 2x2m test square NE of main trench, found with charcoal dating to 4,950 +80 BP; 8, leaf arrowhead; 9, chisel arrowhead. Scale – 1:1.2.

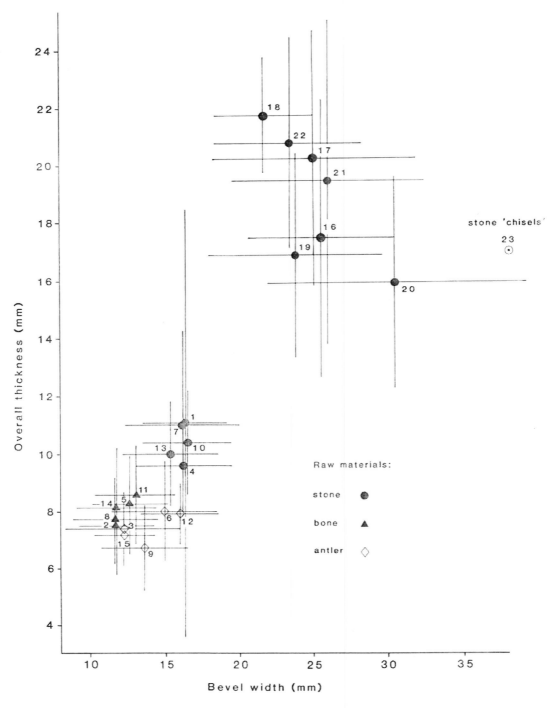

Figure 6.12: Plot of average values (with standard deviations) of thickness and bevel-width for samples of bevelled tools of different raw materials from selected British sites. Also plotted are the values for a sample of Australian stone "chisels".

Man (Woodman, 1978b). The author has examined many examples from as far south as Alderney in the Channel Islands and they are known, of course, in their thousands far to the north on the Scottish west coast (Lacaille, 1954; Mellars, 1987). In view of the association with seal skin working sometimes suggested (Movius, 1942; Jacobi, 1980b), it is perhaps significant that similar bevelled tools are not reported from the Scandinavian littoral - unless some other tool form supplied this function there.

The flint and flaked stone artefacts which appear associated with these bevelled pebbles are usually those which, as at The Nab Head, can be attributed to the late Mesolithic - for example, 'narrow blade' microliths and/or denticulates. It would seem, though, from the evidence of dated 'Obanian' sites on Oronsay, in the Inner Hebrides, that bevelled tools are also to be associated with terminal Mesolthic scalar core technologies in which microliths are absent (Mellars, 1987).

Despite their wide geographical spread along the Atlantic margin, and the common factor of bevelling, there is very considerable variation in the morphology of these tools. Both the width and shape of the bevelled end(s) vary, as do the pebbles on which they are worked. Most of those from west Wales are somewhat less 'shapely' than those on 'Obanian' and some Cornish sites where they can be small, neat and symmetrical (Lacaille, 1954, fig. 88,94; Smith, 1982, fig. 15, no 77). The slimness of some of the latter is reminiscent of early Bronze Age 'finger-stones', but the impression is belied by the mis-shapen and casual nature of many others. Raw material is also variable, with bone and red deer antler bevelled artefacts precisely analogous to their stone counterparts recorded from the calcareous 'Obanian' deposits.

The relationship between size and raw material of bevelled tools from a range of British sites is shown in Fig. 6.12. From this, it is clear that tools of all three raw materials (stone, bone and antler) from the 'Obanian' middens are distinguished by their overall smallness and relatively narrow bevelled ends (Reynolds, 1983). Within this group, the stone bevelled pebbles are predominantly larger than their bone and antler counterparts, yet none approach the dimensions of the bevelled pebbles from Cornish and Welsh sites and Alderney. Such variation may in part be explained by the selection imposed by geology upon the availability of suitable pebble-blanks. However, as small stone pebbles could be argued to have been more or less equally available to 'Obanian' and Welsh Mesolithic groups, but unused by the latter, some genuine functional or cultural difference would appear to have existed in the use of these tools as between the two areas.

As some 33% of the bevelled implements from midden sites on Oronsay are of bone or antler (Reynolds, 1983), it must remain speculative whether tools of these materials were also used on the more southerly find-spots, where soil conditions are acidic, or even on sites located inland. In south-west Wales a clear example of a bevelled tool made of bone is recorded from Nanna's Cave, Caldey (Lacaille and Grimes, 1955, fig. 17), and it is just possible that the suspected bone implement from Frainslake (Fig. 5.4) also belongs in this same general category. Interestingly, the dimensions of the Nanna's Cave specimen place it within the Scottish group.

If the multifarious shapes and sizes imply a whole range of different functions for these tools, then it is possible that at least one such function, if not the only one, might have been the treatment of seal pelts. Dried or cured skins require tanning, one means of which is by the rubbing in of fats or grease, and this could have been successfully achieved using a suitably prepared pebble. Impregnation with grease may also be necessary if vegetable tanning or smoking has been used. Once tanned, the skin must usually be worked over to enhance its softness and flexibility. Once again, bevelled pebbles would provide suitable tools. This 'currying' of leather in more recent times (Salaman, 1986) involves a range of processes and implements most of which could be achieved with the use of various pebble or bone artefacts during the Mesolithic.

Despite the attractiveness of such an interpretation, one should also consider the possibility that at least some bevelled pebbles (not bone or antler) could have been used as wood-working tools. In his account of Australian stone hatchets, Dickson (1981) describes a class of Aboriginal pebble tool which, by experimentation, he has interpreted as hand-held wood-working chisels, used in conjunction with a wooden hammer. These 'plain stone chisels' are precisely analogous to many British bevelled pebbles (ibid, plate XIII). All are made on natural pebbles of comparable dimensions, and the Australian examples appear similarly blunt, with bevel angles of 75° - 80°. For comparison, average measurements of a sample of Aboriginal chisels are plotted on Fig. 6.12 (as data on bevel width is unavailable, overall tool width has been used, producing a rather larger value in this dimension than is actually the case: *ibid.* Table 3). Damage to experimentally used chisels, followed by re-grinding, produced features identical to those seen on both the British and Aboriginal examples (ibid. plate XIV).

A final consideration of functional roles for bevelled pebbles returns to the original speculation that they may have been used for the gathering of shellfish (Grieve, 1885). Rather than being used by hand, as has been supposed, they would have been more effective if hafted and used to adze limpets from rocks. If so, then the necessity of curating hafted equipment might explain the otherwise rather enigmatic presence of the 'limpet-hammers' up on the clifftops away from the shoreline. Experimentation to examine breakage and wear patterns would be needed to support this argument, and it must be admitted that the bone and antler tools cannot be so explained. Again, the damage to limpet shells, at least from the Oronsay middens, is not consistent with cropping by the use of stone adzes.

A use as 'scoops' for removing the animal from its shell

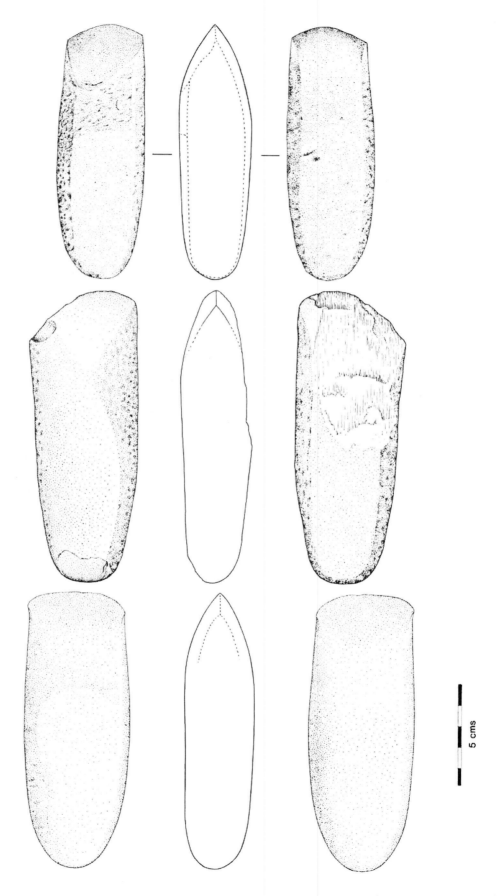

Figure 6.13: Artefacts from the Nab Head Site II. Ground stone axe/adze heads.

5 cms

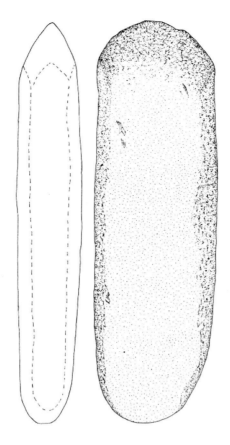

Figure 6.14: Pecked stone axe/adze from The Nab Head (specimen from Tenby Museum). Scale – 1:1.6.

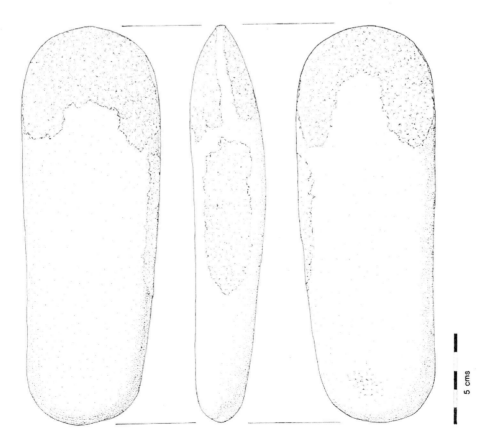

5 cms

Figure 6.15: Pecked stone artefact from Scalby Moor, near Dale, Dyfed.

does not appear a realistic function for the Welsh tools, although the bevels on the Scottish examples may have been small enough for such a purpose.

To avoid indefinite speculation on these matters of function, one will have to await the discovery and evaluation of sites in which the organic component is preserved. Only then, perhaps, may one go on to speculate further on the possible status of these enigmatic tools as cultural markers, independent of function. For the time being, however, it is fairest to acknowledge that they may simply have served many purposes, and that individual implements may even have had several uses.

Ground stone tools:
Whilst quantities of bevelled pebbles are a not uncommon feature of our coastal find-spots, The Nab Head Site II is distinguished by the additional presence of altogether more finished and elaborately modified ground stone tools. These are pecked and ground stone axes or adzes, of which three have been recovered (Fig. 6.13), and a single perforated and ground stone disc (Fig. 6.19, No. 1).

Pecked and ground stone axes/adzes:
The find-spots of each of these three artefacts are shown on a distribution plot (Fig. 6.3c). In each case the object was lying on or near to the sub-surface and was in close association with the pebble and flint industry already described. Axe No.1 was found in contact with, and underlying, two bevelled pebbles - a strong suggestion that the group was in contemporary use and had perhaps been 'cached'.

No precise analogues for such axes have yet been recovered from any excavated British prehistoric context. Most striking about their appearance is their similarity, one to another. All three have a clearly defined symmetrical working-edge ground from both faces. The blade is gently curved, flaring to give a very slight but distinctive 'flange' at either side. The 'trunk' is approximately cylindrical in outline, tapering to a rounded butt. In section it is oval with the faces of the tool locally ground or polished flat. The flanks and much of the overall surface of both axes 1 and 3 are pecked, and it may be assumed that no 2 also owes its finished shape to a deliberate and thorough modification of its entire surface.

Thin-sections of nos. 2 and 3 identify their raw material as deriving from medium-grained basic igneous rock, (C. Houlder, pers. comm.) belonging to outcrops in west Wales, erratics from which will have become incorporated in the local drift geology, and subsequently into beach shingle. No. 1, the most recent find, has not yet been petrologically identified but appears to be of a similar rock-type. The most plausible explanation for the manufacture of these objects is that they were judiciously selected from beach shingle as suitably shaped, dense and workable pebble blanks, which were then pecked and ground into their pre-determined shape. A stray find of an unfinished axe from Brunt Farm,

nearby, supports this suggestion (see below). The selection of appropriately shaped blanks followed by a minimal surface modification seems also to have been the procedure followed in the manufacture of some maceheads (see below) and, later in prehistory, stone axe-hammers (Fenton, 1984). This method of selection and manufacture can again be seen as an economic and effective response to the lack of suitable flint in the area. Pecked and ground stone axes may also have had some functional superiority over any flaked counterparts.

The other lithic associations from the site would seem to place these axes securely within the later Mesolithic. Their technological characteristics differ both from those of the bevelled pebbles and the 'finer' Neolithic axes to which they bear only some resemblance. With the latter in mind, a preliminary search through records for all finds of Welsh axes indicates that perhaps a handful have significant similarities to those from The Nab Head Site II. Some of these are illustrated in Figs. 6.14 - 6.18, and those of special relevance are described below:

1) The Nab Head: This pecked sandstone axe was amongst a small group of artefacts collected 'from a spot near The Nab Head' by Lord Kensington and his brother in about 1885-7 and presented to Tenby Museum in 1932 (Leach, 1933). Preserved with it are two stone discs (to be described below), shale beads and some flaked flint and stone tools. The presence of beads and what appear to be early Mesolithic flints in this collection strongly suggests that these finds may come from 'The Neck' (Site I) which was known at this time to be 'an important factory' (Laws, 1888, 17). It is particularly fitting that this axe (Fig. 6.14), with its pecked surface and slightly splayed edge should have been found at The Nab Head and, if indeed from Site I, its associations could now be argued as most likely to be with the late Mesolithic lithic material identified at that site.

2) Scalby Moor, near Dale: a partially pecked large axe-shaped sandstone pebble in Tenby Museum (Acc. No. 2022; Fig. 6.15). This specimen is clearly the beginnings of an axe-like implement which remains unfinished and without any other distinguishing characteristics. It does, however, convincingly demonstrate that naturally-shaped pebbles were used for at least some axe-manufacture, and that pecking was the initial shaping procedure.

3) Caron-uwch-clawdd, near Strata Florida, Dyfed: a pecked, ground and polished axe of quartz-dolerite, perhaps originating from northern Pembrokeshire (Shotton, 1972). It is now in the National Museum of Wales (Acc. No. 47.164/201; Fig. 6.16). This dark-green coloured axe has all the features of The Nab Head axes but it is larger and has a 'slicker' polished finish. Its shape and section correspond well with the Mesolithic examples as do the splayed blade and the clear evidence for shaping by pecking. Both faces are, however, rounded rather than flattened. If of north Pembrokeshire origin, its presence some 80 km. further north must be due to human transfer rather than any natural agency.

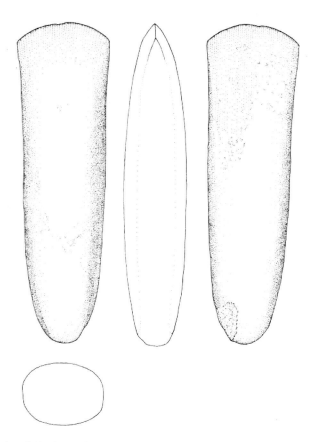

Figure 6.16: Pecked and polished axe from Carn-uwch-clawdd, near Strata Florida, Dyfed. Scale – 1:1.88.

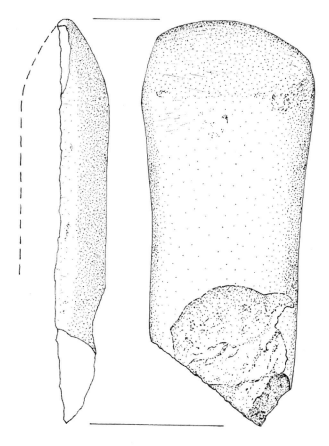

Figure 6.17: Fragment of a possible stone axe from Stackpole Warren, Dyfed. Scale – 1:1.02.

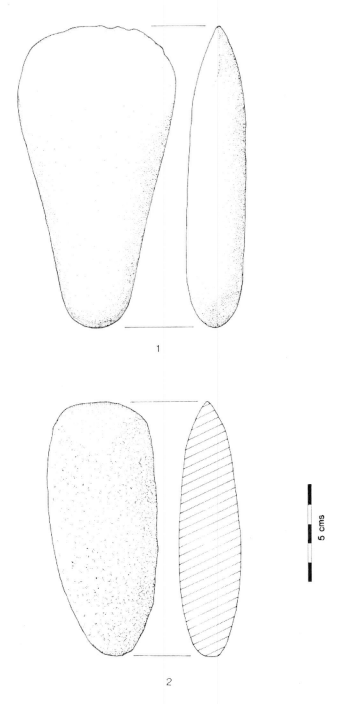

1

2

Figure 6.18: Stone axes, both from Brunt Farm, near Dale, Dyfed.

4) Stackpole Warren, Dyfed: this specimen was excavated from a buried soil in an area (Site A) of intense later prehistoric activity (Benson *et al.*, 1990). Finds from the buried soil were mixed, therefore, including both 'narrow blade' microliths (ibid., fig. 39, 1-2) and Bronze Age scrapers and arrow-heads.

All that remains of the axe (Fig. 6.17) is part of an elongate and slightly spatulate pebble the broader end of which has been ground down to a shallow-angled bevel. There are signs that the bevelling was accompanied by pecking although the remaining surface is unaltered. Unfortunately,

the tool has one end broken and has also cleaved down its long axis.

5) Brunt Farm, near Dale, Dyfed: two axes from this area are preserved in Tenby Museum (Acc. nos. 1983 2021 and 1983 2020). The first (Fig. 6.18, No. 1) is a naturally-shaped spatulate pebble the broader end of which is axe-like in profile although there are no clear traces of manufacture. The second (Figure 6.18, No. 2) more nearly represents the shape of Neolithic examples and has a smoothed working edge. Its remaining surface is pecked all over.

Whilst these surface finds of axes are suggestive, none are associated with Mesolithic artefact types (with the probable exception of no. 1, from The Nab Head itself). It will be a future concern, now that at least some pecked and ground implements are known certainly to be associated with a purely Mesolithic technology, to trace further examples and explore their associations.

Outside mainland Britain, an immediate comparison is prompted by the 'literally thousands' of stone axes attributed to the Late Mesolithic of north-eastern Ireland, especially amongst the complex of sites in the Bann valley, north of Lough Neagh (Woodman, 1978, 108-114; 1987, 144). Although few of these axes, mostly of mudstone, shale and schist, are actually from sealed Mesolithic contexts, they occur throughout the Newferry 3 sequence, dating from c. 8,200 to c. 5,500 BP. Here, small schist axes are found in the earlier levels, whilst larger baked mudstone tools are common from Zone 4 (6215 ±100 BP UB-490). Stone axes which may be rather earlier than those from Newferry are known from later contexts at the Early Mesolithic sites of Mount Sandel (upper: Woodman, 1985) and at Lough Boora (Ryan, 1978).

None of these Irish axes is exactly like those from Site II at The Nab Head (Woodman, pers. comm.). Although they are mostly made from pebbles, as are those from Wales, they do not exhibit the same controlled overall surface modification. The Irish examples are for the most part sharpened pebbles which retain much of their natural surface and, despite a very wide morphological range, do not show any preference for the splayed edges which are such a deliberate and distinctive feature of The Nab Head pieces. Another possibly significant difference may be the apparently inland distribution of most Irish axes compared to the coastal find-spots of the only known Welsh specimens. It can be conjectured, however, that the latter distribution is biased by a lack of fieldwork in the interior of Wales, and perhaps by the mis-identification of Mesolithic axes as of Neolithic date. There are no records, to the author's knowledge, of comparable axes from Scotland.

Mainland Britain is perhaps rather exceptional in not having clear evidence for the use of stone axes in the Mesolithic. The Danish 'stump-butted' pecked and ground stone axes of the late Mesolithic Kongemose (Vedbaek) phase (Petersen, 1984) are like those from Wales but without the 'flanges', as are the stone axes of the succeeding mid-late Ertebölle phases. Pecked stone axes feature earlier than this and were already in use in later Boreal times at Agerod I in southern Sweden (Althin, 1954) and also feature consistently in the Mesolithic of central Sweden and coastal Bohuslän (Welinder, 1977). Pecked and ground 'core adzes', many of which are closely reminiscent of The Nab Head implements, are present on coastal Norwegian sites from the beginning of the Middle Mesolithic at c. 9,000 BP (Gjessing, 1920; Olsen and Alsaker, 1984; Nygaard, 1987).

Clark (1975) has suggested that the adoption of stone axes on the flint-rich Danish late Mesolithic sites is due to cultural contact with the more stone-dependant cultures of the Scandinavian shield. By the time of the 'semi-sedentary' Ertebölle phase, stone axe technology could also have been introduced through exchange from the Neolithic settlers already established in Germany to the south.

There are at least two observations to make on the apparent absence or, at least rarity, of stone axes from most of the British Mesolithic. Over much of lowland England the more suitable flint raw material was abundant, therefore removing the necessity for a use of less tractable stone. Secondly, within the later Mesolithic the evidence for axe manufacture would in any case appear to be confined to southern England and then only to a limited number of sites. There are, however, few excavations to qualify this generalization: late Mesolithic axes were in use at Broomhill, Hants (O'Malley and Jacobi, 1978), Hermitage Rocks (Jacobi and Tebbutt, 1981), Wawcott IV (Froom, 1972) and Culverwell (Palmer, 1977).

The near-absence of axes or adzes from the highland and coastal zones cannot be satisfactorily explained by, for instance, submergence of sites, and one is left instead with a range of core-tools which appear only to have local significance. Examples of the diversity apparent amongst these are provided by chert 'picks' from Portland and other southern English coastal find- spots (Palmer, 1977), and large bi-facial chopping-tools of Greensand chert from Cornwall (Smith, 1982, and forthcoming). Although the functions of these various artefacts are unknown they join a suite of late Mesolithic 'heavy-duty' tools now supplemented by stone axes from The Nab Head, and bevelled pebbles of many shapes and sizes from this and very many other locations up and down the coast.

Just as bevelled pebbles may possibly have had a function associated with the processing of hides (see above) one may also speculate whether axes may not also have had a part to play. Amongst the lithic remains at The Nab Head and many other such sites, there is scarcely a suitable tool present for the very important task of removing subcutaneous tissue from the inner surface of pelts and skins. Whilst this has been the traditional role cast for flint scrapers, and would certainly appear to be the case in many instances (Dumont, 1987), the scrapers, denticulates and retouched flakes on Welsh and other late Mesolithic sites seem inadequate, or at least inefficient, for the job of de-fleshing and scraping large mammal skins. Perhaps circumstances at The Nab Head have not allowed the preservation of relevant bone or antler tools (eg antler 'mattocks'). Equally, there is no evidence for the expedient use of mollusc shells such as the valves of Pecten on Oronsay (Lacaille, 1954), or Cardium, at Téviec and Hoëdic (M. and S. J. Péquart, 1954), for such jobs.

Like the deer antler 'blubber mattocks' of the Scottish carse clay (Clark, 1952), the stone axes from The Nab Head may have had a function in dismemberment, jointing, and

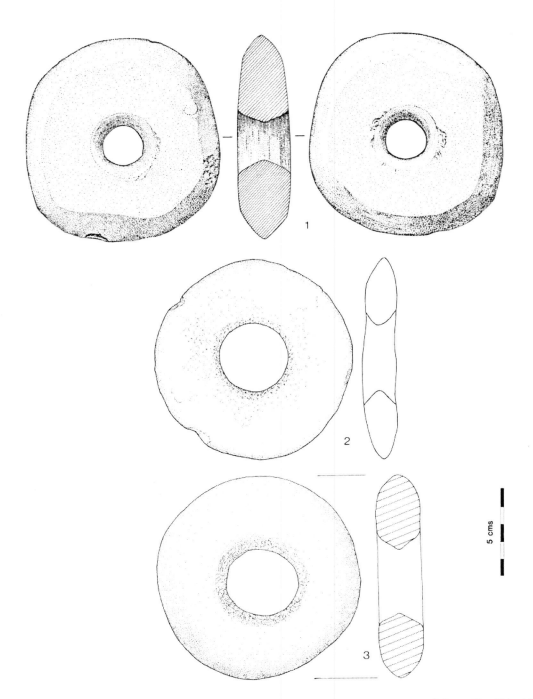

Figure 6.19: Three perforated stone discs from The Nab Head. No.1 was recovered from Site II in 1981. Nos. 2 and 3 are from Kensington collection in Tenby Museum.

5 cms

smashing bones, but also perhaps for the more delicate job of paring away unwanted tissue from fresh skins. They could have been used as adzes, hafted, or held in the hand and worked plane-like over a level surface. The latter action might account for the flat polished faces on all three axes, if these were not otherwise explained as a facility for hafting. The 'flanged' edges of the axe blade, deliberately developed by concentrated pecking on the flanks to either side of the blade, would help prevent the snagging of the tool in the skin. In the absence of better organic preservation, and without experimental and use-wear analysis, any such suggestions may be little more than fancy. They should perhaps have rather less precedence over the more practical

probability that these tools were in fact chisels (Dickson 1981) or axes for wood-working.

Perforated stone disc:
Another find from the excavation at The Nab Head which setsSite II apart from other British late Mesolithic assemblages is that of a perforated and ground stone disc (Fig. 6.19, No. 1). It was found in a position slightly above bedrock amongst one of the densest flint concentrations so far encountered on the site (see Figs. 6.1 and 6.3). It is made of extremely fine-grained altered igneous rock (C. Houlder, pers. comm.) which has weathered to a light green-brown colour. As with the axes and other non-flint raw material

154

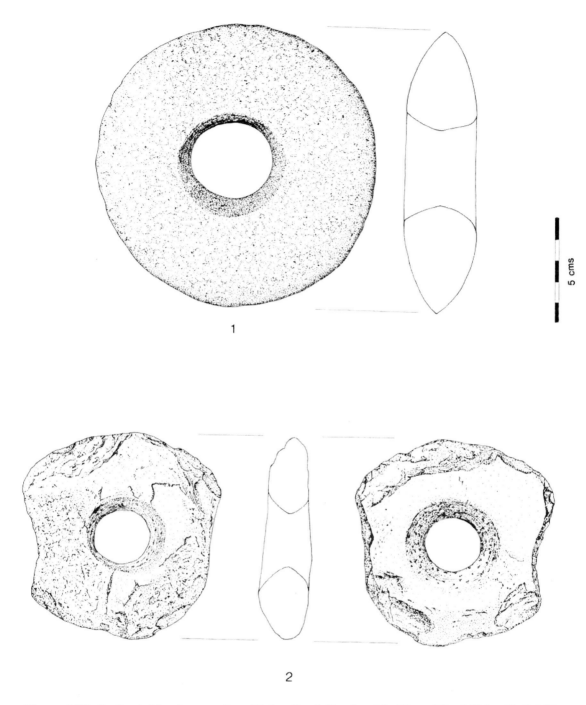

Figure 6.20: Perforated implements from Bigby, South Humberside (1), and Porthllisky, Dyfed (2).

at the site, this rock type would have been available on local beaches.

The stone has a centrally pecked hour-glass perforation (diameter: 22 mm.), and its entire and nearly circular perimeter (diameter: 118 mm. by 109 mm.) has been ground to an edge, from both faces, presenting an angled 'blade' of between 70° and 90°. Both faces are smooth and probably consist of a natural pebble surface, whilst the edges clearly preserve the traces of a concentric grinding. The implement is scarcely damaged and has no obvious signs of functionally related use-wear.

Parallels for this tool, if such it is, are quite as difficult to find as for the stone axes already discussed. Just as the latter were conveniently paralleled by an earlier find of a pecked stone axe from The Nab Head, attention is again drawn to the Tenby Museum collections from the headland in which there are two further perforated stone implements (Leach, 1933, fig 1; Fig. 6.19, Nos. 2 and 3). Both of these are rather more weathered than the excavated example and there are variations in details of shape between all three. The museum examples might better be described as stone 'rings', so large are the central hour-glass holes (both with an identical diameter of about 40 mm.), and whilst one is doughnut-like in section the other is lenticular with an angled edge more akin to the excavated piece. Being part of the Kensington family's collection, neither item, nor the accompanying sandstone axe, is precisely provenanced.

In searching for parallels to these implements from Britain, one has first of all to discount almost all (98%) of the 975 or so 'shaft-hole adzes' and 'pebble hammers' so far recorded from the country (Roe, 1979). The majority of these perforated stone tools, mostly made from pebbles, are quite unlike those from The Nab Head. They share a considerable range of shapes and raw materials and what little contextual evidence there is places their occurrence, in one form or another, anywhere between the early Mesolithic (Mellars and Rheinhardt, 1978) and the early- middle Bronze Age (Roe, *op. cit.*).

The sharpened edges of two of the Welsh specimens give them a passing resemblance to some of the shaft-hole adzes although these are only very rarely circular in shape, such as that from Kenilworth in the West Midlands, illustrated in Roe (1979, fig. 13, Wa 12/h). This example, and others, are made from stone of petrological groups XV and XVIII and may therefore date to the early Bronze Age along with the battle-axes also of these materials. There are perhaps only about 20 comparable implements from Britain, none with fully satisfactory associations (Roe, n.d.). One of the latter, in particular, a surface find from Bigby (South Humberside: Scunthorpe Museum), is very like the excavated Nab Head specimen and is illustrated here for comparison (Fig. 6.20, No. 1). Illustrated alongside the latter is a stray surface find from Porthllisky Farm (SM 7348 2370) on the St. Davids peninsula, north-west Dyfed. Although not found amongst the late Mesolithic flint scatters from this area (see Chapter VII), and evidently much damaged, this object might once have shared a strong similarity to those from The Nab Head.

Suggesting a function for The Nab Head Site II perforated implement is no less problematical than for the other stone tools. Of significance is its sharpened edge and the absence of signs of heavy use-wear. The ethnographic record suggests that such objects were used in some recent primitive societies as weapons, and such an explanation cannot necessarily be excluded in this case. Although the links between weaponry, ritual and social values are more commonly associated with later prehistoric communities (Clarke *et al.*, 1985), it would be premature, in our greater ignorance of Mesolithic society, to assume that complex social interaction - including fighting - was not taking place at this earlier time. It is curious, however, that neither the stone macehead nor the axeheads were found in exclusive circumstances suggestive of status, for instance in pits or graves. Instead, they were each found apparently casually associated amongst the ordinary lithic clutter about the site.

If not an object of ritual or prestige value (literally a 'mace-head'), or a fighting-mace, then the function of the perforated stone was no doubt much more prosaic. Its axe- or adze-like perimeter must have had a distinguishing functional role, but one that would have precluded hammering or heavy-duty work. The considerable investment in painstaking manufacture would suggest that it was used neither for such menial tasks as a weight for a net or digging stick, nor even as a fly-wheel for a pump or bow drill for which the perforation has, in any case, too great a diameter. Use as a spindle whorl for rope-making also seems an unlikely suggestion. Could it rather have been part of the hide- working processes speculated upon above for the bevelled pebbles and axes? If such a tool were hafted or even held in the hand, it might have been suitable for de-fleshing or currying.

Such speculation is of course somewhat empty in the absence of satisfactory supporting evidence.

Other pebble tools:
Requiring less comment are the remaining pebbles and pebble fragments on Site II. There are 16 un-modified elongated pebbles which may be either undeveloped bevelled pebbles or, in one or two cases, blanks for the manufacture of axes. Pebbles showing no outward signs of use are not an unusual feature on Mesolithic find-spots of all periods.

There are 20 fragments of elongated pebbles some of which were broken in antiquity and may or may not have been bevelled when entire. Such fragments suggest that pebbles were in use on the site or were returned to the site in broken hafted implements.

There are 3 ovoid pebbles which show slight traces of battering and which may be assumed to be hammerstones used, in all probability, for knapping. Most of the flaked debitage from the site has been hard hammer-struck.

6. The Nab Head Site II - summary and chronological considerations:
The recent excavations on both sites at The Nab Head have recovered substantial lithic assemblages. That from Site II is in keeping with expectations for flint and stone-working attributed elsewhere to late Mesolithic subsistence activity. By implication, the directly comparable suite of lithic forms from Site I, is also attributed to a later phase of activity on the headland.

The distribution of occupation residues so far uncovered at Site II is one of interconnecting foci of flint-working debris and tools within which are many pebble implements. All the artefacts are at a common level on, or above, the bedrock. Apart from an ill-defined hearth and a shallow pit, sub-soil features are scarce and so far uninformative.

Two tool-types stand out in characterizing this and other local artefact assemblages: 'narrow blade' microliths, most of which are scalene triangles, and bevelled pebbles. These are accompanied by much smaller numbers of denticulates, scrapers, truncated pieces, retouched and utilized flakes. Three ground stone axes and a perforated stone implement complete the inventory.

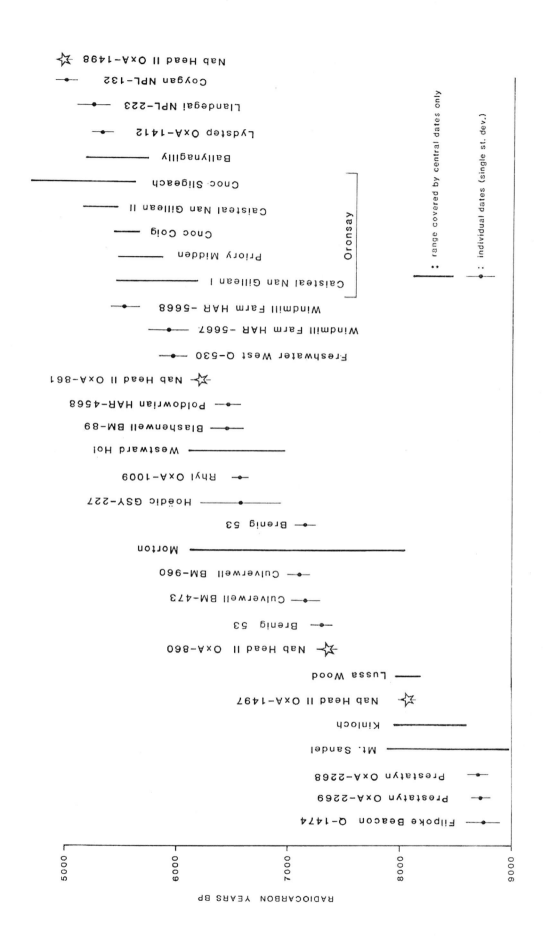

Figure 6.21: Radiocarbon date chart for selected Mesolithic and Neolithic sites.

Chronology:

How might such an artefact assemblage fit within the chronological evidence so far obtained for other 'narrow blade' material from Britain and Wales, as outlined in the previous chapter?

The AMS radiocarbon dates from the site are summarized below (and see Fig. 6.21):

4,950 ±80BP (OxA-1498)   charcoal from NE scatter
6,210 ±90 BP (OxA-861)   charcoal from 'hearth' area
7,360 ±90 BP (OxA-860)   charcoal from shallow pit
8,070 ±80 BP (OxA-1497)   charcoal from SW of 'hearth'

These determinations are on individual items of charcoal, and therefore should not present the sort of interpretational problems involved with 'average' dates on bulked charcoal samples. At The Nab Head, however, soil profiles are relatively thin, and allowance must nevertheless be made for the mobility of individual charcoal fragments of different ages, and that these have accumulated at the same horizon as the lithic industry. The introduction of charcoal from different sources at or near the site must, indeed, explain the very wide chronological spread of dates obtained.

Post-Mesolithic activity on the site cannot now be discounted. Amongst the lithic finds are a patinated leaf-shaped arrowhead and an unpatinated chisel-ended arrowhead (Fig. 6.11). An Iron Age presence is indicated by the recovery of two blue glass beads. Occasional pieces of slag and clinker have been noted and a single much corroded fragment of iron. Items such as these could have been introduced amongst the Mesolithic material either through previous cultivation on the site or as the result of natural downward movement in a shallow soil profile. The tendency for substantial desiccation cracks to open up in the The Nab Head soils during dry weather has already been noted (Chapter IV).

Despite these latter indicators, it has already been stated that the lithic assemblage appears to be homogenous and to belong, if not to a single event, then to repetitive occupations over a relatively brief timespan - perhaps of a few generations. Now that the AMS dates indicate activity over at least three thousand years, such an impression has to be carefully re-considered.

Of the four dates available, only the most recent, OxA-1498, could be argued to be inconsistent with the accompanying 'narrow blade' lithic types. Contrary to this supposition, however, is the fact that, at two standard deviations, this determination overlaps with the earlier date obtained for the Lydstep pig skeleton (5,300 ±100 BP: OxA-1412), above which lay two backed bladelets (see Chapter V). Such an overlap, even if at something of a statistical extreme, at least opens the possibility that the more recent of the two determinations could represent a very late but nevertheless realistic dating for a 'narrow blade' technology at The Nab Head.

More significant, perhaps, is that OxA-1498 (4,950 ±80 BP) is nearly identical to that (5,000 ±95 BP) obtained on partly charred hazel nutshells from a pit containing pottery and domestic fauna at Coygan Camp, 50 km to the east of The Nab Head. Elsewhere in Britain, many instances of early Neolithic activity could be cited which pre-date both the above determinations (eg Zvelebil and Rowley-Conwy, 1986, fig. 3; Williams, 1989, fig. 1). Surviving cultural material accompanying such Neolithic activity is quite different to that considered to be Mesolithic and includes plain pottery ware, polished axes and leaf-shaped arrowheads. Burial in communal tombs and the construction of earthwork enclosures also feature at this time.

There is no evidence for either Neolithic occupation sites or sepulchral monuments near The Nab Head, and the only artefact from the site itself that might be in keeping with OxA-1498 is the leaf-shaped arrowhead referred to above (Fig. 6.11). The latter is a conveniently shaped flake with minimal surface retouch. A slightly reduced patination on the retouched area suggests the possibility that an older flake has been re-worked. The tip is apparently crushed, perhaps by impact. None of these features preclude the explanation of its presence as any more than an isolated and casual loss. No prehistoric pottery has been recovered, and the only other artefacts that might be thought (by some) to be early Neolithic are the ground stone axes which have already been argued to be atypical and more probably Mesolithic. The chisel-ended arrowhead, of black unpatinated flint, may be of later Neolithic age (Green, 1980) and also a casual loss.

Although the sample for OxA-1498 comes from a trench separate from the main excavation (see Fig. 6.1) the artefacts from it are no less late Mesolithic in type than those anywhere else on the site: these include bevelled pebbles, narrow scalene triangles (Fig. 6.11), bladelet cores and debitage - some of which has been shown to re-fit. Charcoal was relatively abundant amongst this material, but, being on a slight knoll, the soil here was very shallow (15 - 20 cms). No features were present in the 4 sq m area excavated. These latter factors weigh considerably against giving this determination undue significance and serve only to illustrate the serious dilemmas aroused by attempting to date unsealed material from shallow soils. Perhaps the major dilemma so aroused in this case is whether or not the observed late Mesolithic technology survived later in some areas than the introduction of agriculture in others; or were the two co-existent? This debate can be approached in more detail at the end of the following chapter.

The remaining three determinations from Site II, although covering a range of about 1,860 radiocarbon years, fall well within the chronological extremes for British late Mesolithic activity (Fig. 6.21). The distinctive 'narrow blade' collection from Prestatyn has already been shown to be at the lower limit of this timespan, at c. 8,700 BP, substantially preceding the earliest date from The Nab Head II at 8,070 ±80 BP. If an hypothetical 'earliest' late Mesolithic assemblage-type, modelled on the Prestatyn material, was once present at The Nab Head at about this date, then one might argue that it is represented by the obliquely-backed points, larger scalene triangles, convex scrapers and steeply retouched flakes from there. Subsequent re-occupations of the headland might then have introduced a wider range of microlith types, particularly narrower scalene triangles retouched on all three sides, as well as other artefact types such as denticulates and various pebble tools.

Periodic re-occupations of the headland must now certainly be assumed to have taken place, but the available data does not allow for the confirmation or elaboration of such typological schemes as that speculated upon above; or, indeed, for the placement of the microlith 'assemblage' within any such seriation as that attempted for southern English sites (Jacobi and Tebbutt, 1981). Neither the horizontal nor the vertical artefact distribution allow of any convincing sequential segregation of the lithic material. Of the three Mesolithic dates only OxA-860 (7,360 ±90 BP) comes from a distinct feature, a shallow pit sealed by a possibly deliberately placed layer of angular stones. No diagnostic artefacts were found within it, however, and there is no means of relating its infilling to the artefacts found in the soil above.

Despite the dating evidence to the contrary, the spatial distribution of the artefact spread (Fig. 6.1) and the evidence of conjoining tools and debitage amongst it still provoke the impression of relatively short-lived activity within the specific area excavated. Other occupations must have taken place on the headland (as they certainly did on Site I, and also near Tower Point) and residues from these, including charcoal, may well have overlapped with or been introduced into Site II.

In summary, then, despite the promising typological and distributional coherence of most of the excavated artefact assemblage, this integrity must be considered more apparent than real. The range of dating obtained cannot be related to any particular episode of activity on the headland and it is now clear that the area was visited at different times during the late Mesolithic. Of the other dates for Wales, only that for Prestatyn falls outside the range represented at The Nab Head. As will be argued in the following chapter, The Nab Head appears to be typical of coastally located sites where occupation has recurred repetitively, leading to a palimpsest of artefact scatters. As demonstrated here, attempts to disentangle the characteristics and dating of the component parts of such aggregations present major methodological problems - especially in dry shallow soils. Despite the application of other dating techniques - thermoluminescence is currently being attempted at Site II - such problems are likely to persist until sites with waterlogged stratigraphy are fully investigated.

In the meantime, and despite these investigations at The Nab Head, almost the sole expression of late Mesolithic activity in Wales is provided by the distribution and composition of lithic collections from surface find-spots. It is a sample of the latter - mostly from north-west Dyfed - which are now to be described and assessed in the light of the data so far presented.

CHAPTER VII

SURFACE SITES IN NORTH-WEST DYFED

1. Introduction:

'The flint-working sites which occur in such numbers in the coastal areas of Wales are one of the problems of archaeology about which at the moment very little is known. The questions of date and culture connected with them can only be satisfactorily answered by scientific collecting which will provide a good body of material, and which will enable the distribution of such sites to be mapped and studied as a whole.' (Grimes, 1932, 179).

Only recently has it been possible to address the above objective set out by W. F. Grimes following his description of a local collection of mostly late Mesolithic surface material near Solva, Dyfed (ibid.).

The first part of this chapter will set out the results of fieldwork by the author which may go a little way towards providing the 'good body of material' required for a re-assessment of local Welsh 'surface industries'. In particular, it is now possible to review such artefact collections in the light of current knowledge of the late Mesolithic (Chapter V) and results of excavations at The Nab Head (Chapter VI).

Mapping of find-spots by Leach (1913) and Cantrill (1915) to the south and north of Milford Haven, respectively, can now be extended to the peninsular coast to the north of St. Brides Bay. Earlier comments on the latter area have been limited to brief notes by Bosanquet (1923) and to the short commentary by Grimes (1932), referred to above. Wainwright in his 1963 synthesis scarcely refers to the area.

Despite an overall similarity in character, a closer analysis of the artefact components of a sample of the many find-spots involved suggests that variability exists amongst them and that this may reflect functional diversity. In the second part of the chapter an attempt is made to interpret the character of the hunting, fishing and gathering livelihood responsible for these patterns. Finally, some speculation is made on the supposed 'transition' between late Mesolithic and agricultural activity in west Wales.

2. Fieldwork:

Much of the description to follow derives from fieldwalking by the author over very many years. Early inexperience has lead to many shortcomings and it should be admitted at the outset that much of the fieldwork falls short of the 'scientific collecting' demanded by Grimes (ibid.). Most to be regretted is a lack of any systematic gridded collecting, a technique prohibited for one person by the vast size of many of the find-spots. Despite such faults, however, it has been possible to examine some 48,000 artefacts from up to 37 locations. This information has been combined with that from other private and museum collections, together with published data, to compile the distribution map in Fig. 7.1.

The author's fieldwalking has been concentrated mostly around the coastal perimeter of the St Davids peninsula between Porthgain (SM 815 325) and Newgale (SM 848 224), with occasional excursions further afield along both coasts and inland. The construction of the 'Pembrokeshire Coast Footpath', skirting the clifftop in most places, and the erosion of the cliffs themselves, has allowed a fairly thorough examination of the immediate clifftop for lithic material. Wherever possible, the search was extended into adjacent ploughed fields and along the crests on either side of the small valleys which so commonly interrupt the coastline here. In this way, and despite the limitations imposed by uncultivated ground, the coverage of this coastal zone has been as thorough as possible, and the resulting distribution of sites is believed to be as complete as can be hoped for.

Scatters exposed on ploughed surfaces were walked on many occasions and usually all lithic material encountered was picked up and allocated a field number. The prodigious sizes of some of the scatters, however, means that the provenances of individual items from within them are often unknown.

'Inland' areas of the St Davids peninsula were also searched intensively in the hope of off-setting the potentially biased pattern provided by coastally oriented fieldwork. Although only a small percentage (approx. 0.5%) of the landscape was covered, with a bias towards valley and wetland margins, several lithic scatters were located.

Over half (56%) of the material was picked up over several years from one large site - Cwm Bach I. Of the remaining 36 sites, collections of over 1,000 pieces each are available only from Porthllisky, Penpant, Llanunwas, Pointzcastle and, inland, at Happy Valley and Tretio. The remaining find-spots are represented by anything from a few hundred pieces to those where only the presence of flints is recorded but no sample has been retained. Representative illustrations of artefacts from the main scatters are shown in Figs. 7.3 - 7.20

3. Site location:

The coastline of western Dyfed is everywhere indented by the selective erosion of interleaved hard and soft geology. Bays and small coves, usually cut into shales and weak

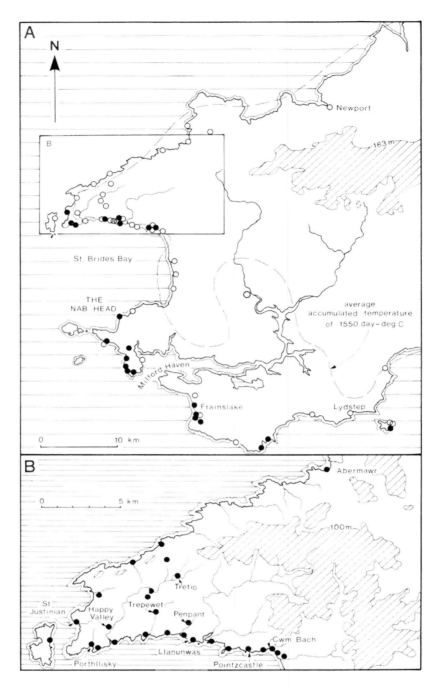

Figure 7.1: Distribution of late Mesolithic find-spots in western Dyfed.
Solid dots on plan A indicates finds of bevelled pebbles.

sedimentary rocks, are interspersed with more resistant headlands, often of igneous rock. The coastal plateau is drained by numerous streams, many of which have cut narrow valleys graded to a formerly lower sea level. The sea and the westerly Atlantic weather have therefore sculpted a ragged coastline which combines a multitude of coves, cliffs, islands and rocky promontories with a sharply undulating landscape. A rising sea level has in places further indented the coastline by drowning the mouths of small valleys and, in the case of Milford Haven, a substantial river system.

The siting of Mesolithic activity within such a landscape

therefore often seems to involve a relationship with both beaches and fresh water. Small streams, springs, streamlets and boggy patches are a regular feature of the clifftop, and more often than not lead down to small beaches or coves. Flint scatters seem to be almost invariably associated with these features and are nowhere more than a few minutes walk from one or the other.

The distribution of find-spots 'inland', within the St. Davids peninsula, is probably less realistic than that along the coast owing to the difficulty of searching a sufficiently large sample of the landscape. The few scatters that have been identified, however, are all located near sources of fresh

162

Plate 7.1: Aerial view of coastline near Solva, Dyfed.

water. Happy Valley, Trecenny and Penpant are all adjacent to streams in small valleys which only have a short distance to run before reaching the sea. Scatters at Rhodiad, Tretio and Maen-y-Groes are all located on the edge of cultivated land which skirts a central area of waterlogged moorland (Dowrog and Tretio Moors). Several small streams drain this area, which has never been fully cultivated, and it is probable that open water such as that still surviving on the Dowrog was more widespread in the past.

However, no part of the St. Davids peninsula is more than about 5 km., at the most, from the coast and the density of find-spots along its south side shows clearly the recurring and intimate association between flint scatters, streams and beaches. The southerly aspect of this coastline (Plate 7.1), overlooking the relatively sheltered and shallow St. Brides Bay, seems to have attracted settlement rather more than the northern coast of the peninsula which fronts deeper water from more barren and less hospitable clifftops.

The dense distribution of finds between Newgale and Ramsay Island is such that in places one scatter coalesces with another, resulting in agglomerations that can cover several hectares. Flints can be encountered along whole stretches of coastline, flanking valleys and adjacent clifftops, and concentrating about springs and beach heads.

It is no doubt the size of such 'spreads' and the density of patinated flint on ploughed surfaces which attracted the attention of early flint collectors. Superficial examination indicated an abundance of poor bladelet cores and cortical debitage with scarcely any finely finished tool forms. This gave to early commentators an impression of a somewhat crude and impoverished culture, 'decadent' by the standards of the Upper Palaeolithic and apparently without the technical achievements of the Neolithic and Bronze Age. A closer study of both site location and the more recently collected samples of artefacts considerably refines this picture.

4. Raw materials and cores:

As we have come to expect, the prevalent raw material is beach pebble flint, supplemented at nearly every find-spot by low percentages (<4%) of other stone such as Cretaceous chert or local conchoidally fracturing igneous rock. The very large quantities of flint debris at many spots certainly suggests that contemporary beaches were a prolific source of suitable pebbles. Early observers were right to note a certain profligacy in the use of this raw material: large primary flakes, unprepared and abandoned cores, and unused pebbles do suggest at least a reliable if not liberal supply.

Small-sized beach pebble flint is, however, an intractable material to work (as experimental knapping by the author has clearly shown) and the abundance of waste almost certainly results from expediency rather than simple wantonness. Cores usually have a single platform developed after the removal of one or more primary flakes,

163

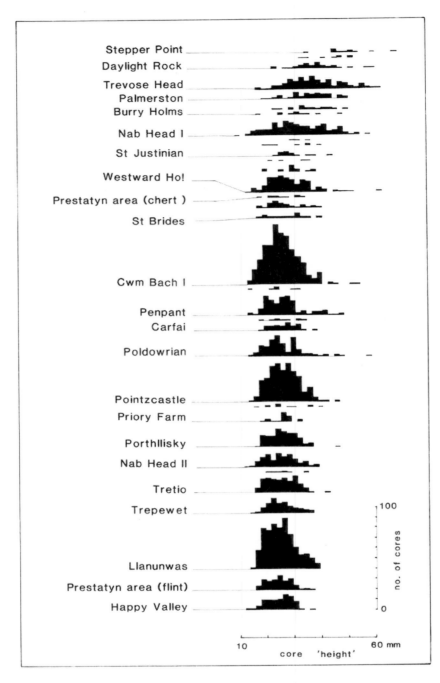

Figure 7.2: Bar charts showing core 'height' for samples from Welsh and Cornish Mesolithic find-spots.

but their final shape varies widely between amorphous lumps and the 'ideal' cylindrical or pyramidal forms. The original pebbles usually had a diameter of less than 5 cm., not allowing sufficient volume of flint for the core preparation and rejuvenation techniques often associated with larger raw materials. Beach pebbles are often flawed and in many cases repeated hinge terminations on the face of the core have rendered it useless. In the author's experience several pebbles can be worked out before a bladelet core can be developed capable of providing blanks suitable for transformation into microliths.

Core dimensions have already been used as an index of the character of raw material and its debitage, and it has been noted during discussion of material from The Nab Head that there is an apparent decrease in core size with advancing time (see Chapter IV). For comparison with the previous data, measurements have been made on samples from the surface collections and are illustrated in histogram form in Fig. 7.2 alongside those already discussed.

Amongst the surface collections, core dimensions appear to be weighted firmly within the smaller size range. Average values are all below 35 mm, and although there are some larger cores in each assemblage, these dominate only at Palmerston Farm and Daylight Rock, both find-spots already argued to be early Mesolithic in date and as possessing little or no admixture from later periods

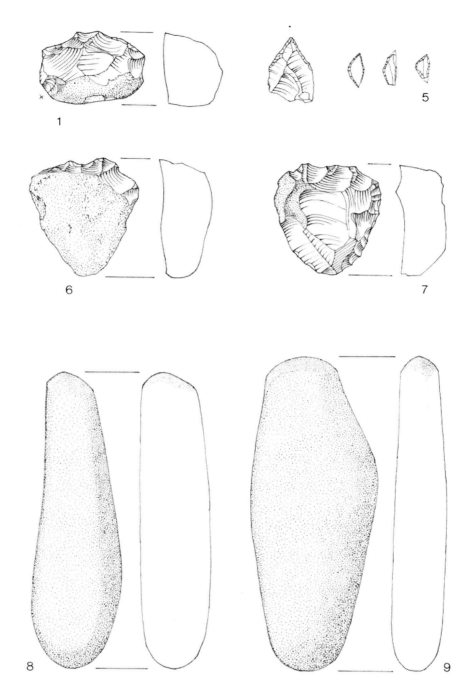

Figure 7.3: Artefacts from St. Justinian, Dyfed: - 1, 6, 7, denticulate; 2, "bec"; 3-5, Microliths; 8, 9, bevelled pebbles. Scale – 1:1.28.

(Chapter III). Amongst the collections dominated by the smaller cores only at Penpant, near Solva (see below) is there a significant proportion of larger pieces (18% of the total), and this coincides with the evidence from the retouched tools that here too there may be a distinct early Mesolithic component (Tables 3.11, 3.12). The distribution of core sizes from other sites, where samples are large enough to be meaningful, is statistically 'normal', and it could be argued that any variation to either extreme is only that which can be expected within a random selection of available raw material.

There is an implication in the last statement that the inhabitants of these 'later' sites made full use of the entire range of raw material available to them at the time. It would seem that only in the early Mesolithic was there a deliberate selection for the largest pebbles. It remains to be seen whether or not a rising sea level limited the availability of the latter and, by necessitating the use of smaller raw material, motivated the introduction of a 'narrow blade' technology. However, there seems no geological or geomorphological reasoning to support a significant differential distribution of grades of flint pebble. It seems unlikely therefore that the constraints of raw material were, on their own, responsible for the observed innovations in lithic products.

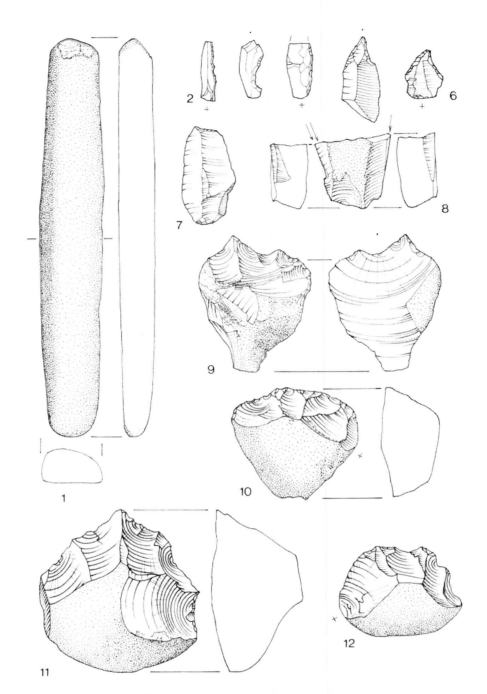

Figure 7.4: Artefacts from Porthllisky, St. Davids, Dyfed: - 1, bevelled pebbles; 2, 4, Microliths fragments; 3, micro-intermediate; 5, 6, "becs"; 7, truncated piece; 8, burin; 9, "nosed" piece; 10, scraper; 11, 12, denticulates. Scale – 1:1.31.

5. The surface collections and their retouched components:

The composition of early and late Mesolithic assemblages has already been detailed in previous chapters. Rather than duplicate this, it seems preferable to outline the composition of each of the main surface collections and to comment upon particular artefact types as necessary:

St Justinian (SM 7225 2520):

This scatter, like so many, is situated directly adjacent to the clifftop, and in this case faces westwards over the Sound towards Ramsey Island on which at least one similar flint

scatter has been noted. The cliffs here are steep and rocky, descending to small rock-strewn coves at low tide. The nearest freshwater, not abundant here, is about 150 m. away.

Of only 289 flints examined from an area of about 3,750 sq. m, most are debitage, but 'narrow blade' microliths are present, with denticulates, large convex scrapers and a 'bec'. Bevelled pebbles are also found (Fig. 7.3).

Porthllisky Bay (SM 7315 2385):

The scatter here, covering as much as 6000 sq. m., lies in

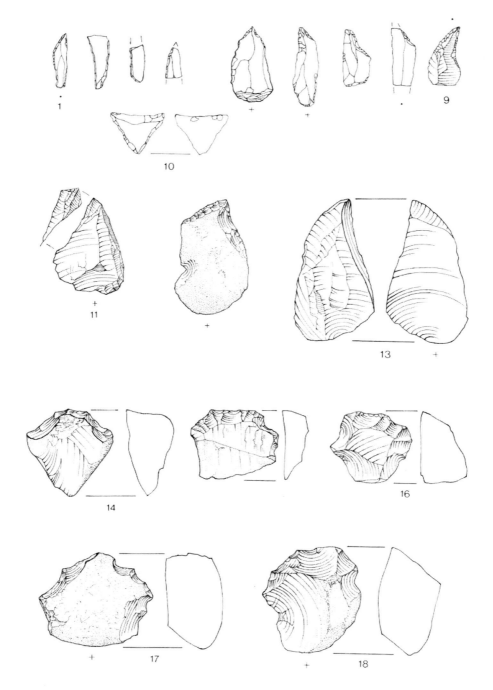

Figure 7.5: Artefacts from Happy Valley, St. Davids, Dyfed: - 1-4, Microliths; 5-9, "becs"; 10, transverse arrowhead; 11, 13, burins; 14-16, scrapers; 17, 18, denticulates. Scale 1:1.29.

ploughed fields immediately behind the south-west facing sandy and rocky beach of Porthllisky. Lithic debris is concentrated on the valley bottom alongside the small stream which drains onto the beach.

The same artefact range as at St. Justinian has been recovered here (Fig. 7.4), although the present collection of 1,826 pieces may have come from either this scatter or a rather smaller concentration (SM 7351 2361) situated on the clifftop to the south of Porthllisky Farm. Both locations have produced bevelled pebbles, although the latter has also turned up Neolithic and Bronze Age artefacts.

Happy Valley (SM 7417 2519):
This scatter is located in a small tributary valley of the River Alun on a north-easterly-facing slope adjacent to a small spring. The Alun drains much of the parish of St Davids, flowing through the city to the sheltered creek at Porth Clais. This is the nearest access to the sea from the site, which is thus about a kilometre 'inland'.

A late Mesolithic element within the collection of 1,276 pieces from this field is indicated by a 'narrow blade' microlith and fragments of other small microliths. Unusually, there is also a narrow *petit-tranchet* type arrowhead and a triangular chisel-ended arrowhead, both of

167

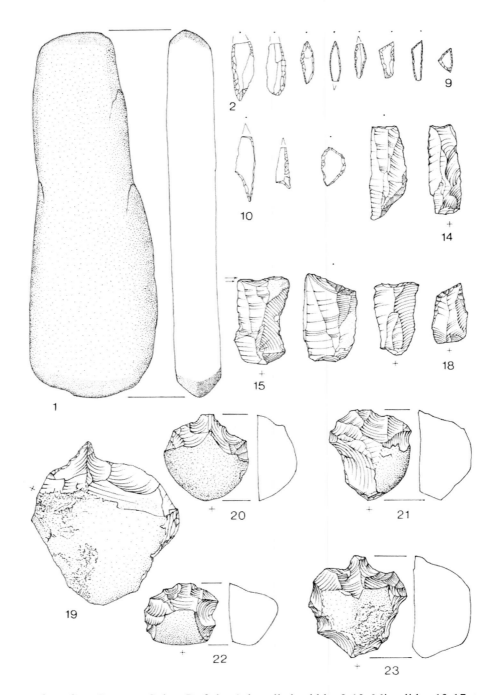

Figure 7.6: Artefacts from Penpant, Solva, Dyfed: - 1, bevelled pebble; 2-12, Microliths; 13-17, truncated pieces; 18, "bec"; 19, "nosed" piece; 20-21, scrapers; 22-23, denticulates. Scale – 1:1.32.

which are without parallel on Welsh Mesolithic or Neolithic find-spots. With these were found burins, large convex scrapers, denticulates and 'becs', all of which are also common to the clifftop sites (Fig. 7.5). The tip of a worn elongate pebble was found, as well as a hammerstone, but, significantly, no bevelled pebbles. A rather greater proportion of the flint material (26%) is unpatinated than is normal amongst the clifftop assemblages (averaging approx. 11%).

Carfai Bay (SM 7605 2441):
This is a fairly dense localization of flint material covering an area of about 2,500 sq. m. adjacent to a streamlet

descending the cliff to the sheltered beach at Carfai. No microliths are recorded from here, although denticulates and large convex scrapers are present, as well as bevelled pebbles. There is some confusion between records for this site and flints collected from ploughed fields on the headland to the east of the bay where there is also a large spread of apparently Mesolithic material. Some of the latter concentrates to either side of another small streamlet at SM 7632 2427 (Caerbwdi).

Penpant (SM 7869 2502):
This is a large multi-period scatter with a small but distinctive early Mesolithic element which has already been

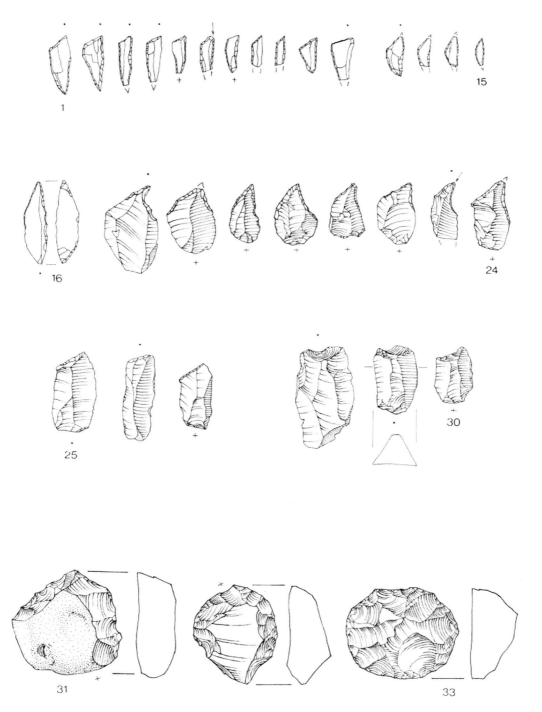

Figure 7.7: Artefacts from Llanunwas, Solva, Dyfed: - 1-16, Microliths; 17-24, "becs"; 25-30, truncated pieces; 31-33, scrapers. Scale – 1:1.2.

mentioned in Chapter III. The latter is confined to an area of some 5,000 sq. m. on a south-facing slope looking seawards down a small valley which leads to the sea at Porth-y-Rhaw some 800 m. away. Late Mesolithic material is found over an altogether wider area, and also at separate locations at Llanungar (SM 7916 2489) and to either side of the rocky beach at Porth-y-Rhaw (SM 7845 2423 and SM 7884 2423). At Penpant the presumed late Mesolithic elements of the assemblage (Fig. 7.6) include small microliths (with a micro-*petit-tranchet*), large convex scrapers, denticulates, 'nosed' pieces, 'becs' and bevelled pebbles. Burins and truncated pieces are also present.

Some 36% of the assemblage is unpatinated, probably a reflection of a later prehistoric contribution, indicated also by scalar cores, 'thumbnail' scrapers and surface-retouched arrowheads. The 4% of the flaked material which is not of flint consists of either Cretaceous chert, or more commonly a fine-textured green igneous rock of local origin. At least some of the latter may result from the manufacture of early Mesolithic core axes/adzes, testified by the fragment of a possible axe and a single sharpening flake (Fig. 3.16, No. 2), both of this material.

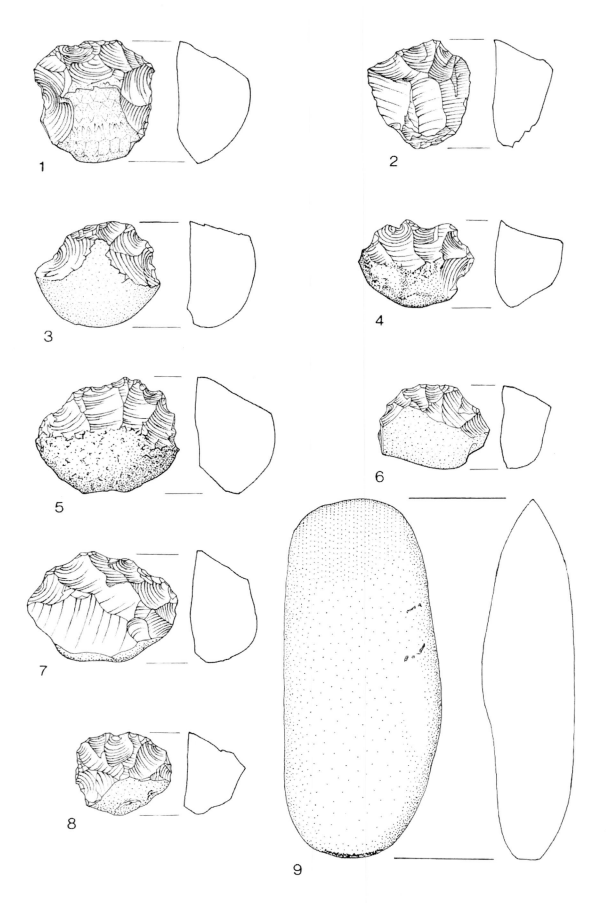

Figure 7.8: Artefacts from Llanunwas, Solva, Dyfed: - 1-8, denticulates; 9, sharpened pebble. Scale – 1:1.02.

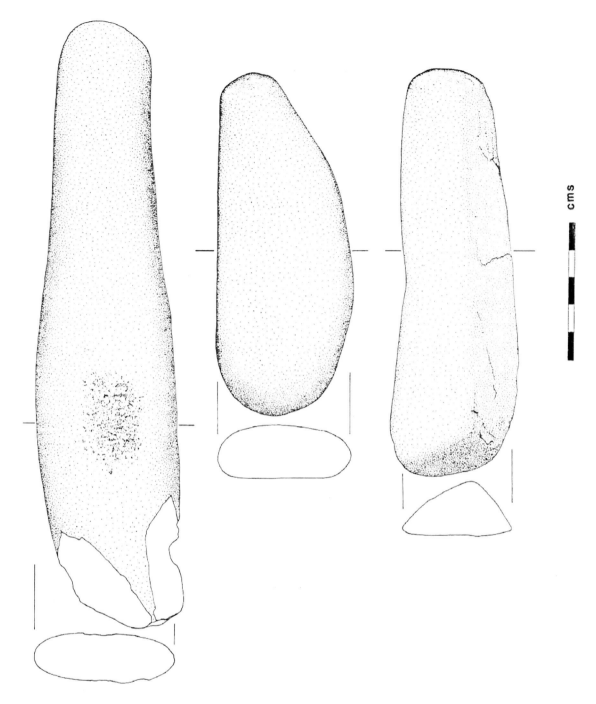

Figure 7.9: Artefacts from Llanunwas, Solva, Dyfed: - pebble tools.

cms

Llanunwas (SM 7034 2384):
This find-spot was well known before the writer made his own collection there (Grimes, 1932). It covers an area of some 10,000 sq. m. above steep shale cliffs between Porth-y-Rhaw and the drowned valley inlet at Solva (Plate 7.1). The flint and stone material is scattered on ploughed fields surrounding a small spring or boggy patch.

Intensive collecting has resulted in an assemblage of 5,991 pieces which is believed to represent a reasonably balanced sample of the available artefacts (Figs. 7.7 - 7.9). Of 358 flaked flint and stone tools, no less than 253 or 70% are denticulates. The remaining types are principally small

microliths, large convex scrapers, 'becs', and miscellaneous retouched pieces. Pebble tools include a hammerstone, five bevelled pebbles and a distinctive sharpened pebble or axe (see below).

Of only 16 classifiable microliths, 11 are small scalene micro-triangles, 4 are convex-backed pieces, and there is a single lanceolate piece. Amongst the 'late and decadent descendents of true microlithic types' from this site illustrated by Grimes (1932, fig. 3, 7-12) is at least one scalene micro- triangle (No. 7) and an oblique *petit-tranchet* form (No. 9).

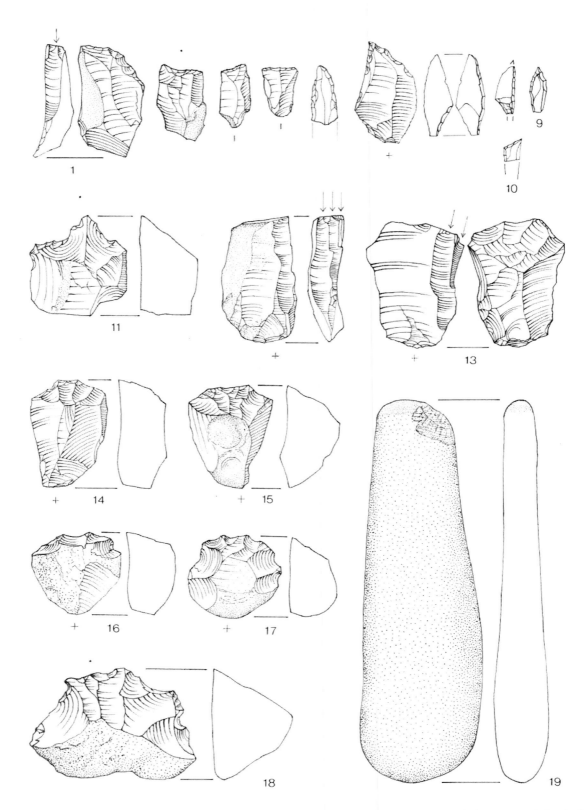

Figure 7.10: Artefacts from Pointzcastle, Solva, Dyfed: - 1, 12, 13, burins; 2-4, truncated pieces; 5, *mèche de forêt*; 6, "bec"; 7-10, Microliths; 11, "nosed" piece; 14-17, scrapers; 18, denticulate; 19, bevelled pebble. Scale - 1:1.13.

Average height in a sample of 339 cores is 27 mm., scarcely distinguishable from that at The Nab Head Site II (28 mm.). That there has been at least some admixture of later material is indicated by the presence of 15 scalar cores, 3 of which make use of formerly patinated flakes.

The sharpened pebble (Fig. 7.8, No. 9) is neither pecked and ground like the axes from The Nab Head, nor bevelled in the manner of the majority of the pebble tools from these sites. Its end has, however, been ground to an axe or chisel-shaped blade and it therefore finds its closest parallel with Irish Mesolithic axes.

Plate 7.2: Distant aerial view of Cwm Bach (at centre), near Solva, Dyfed.

Plate 7.3: Vertical aerial view of Cwm Bach. The limits of the flint scatter are indicated by the dots.

Pointzcastle (SM 8248 2326):
The 4.5 km. of coast between Solva and Newgale includes a great many find-spots and, indeed, there are probably few fields here that do not contain chipped flints. The clifftop fields in the small parish of St. Elvis, for instance, are known to contain rich flint scatters (Grimes, 1932; Rees, 1973), but these are not well recorded. The author's collecting has been concentrated instead to the west of these at Pointzcastle and Cwm Bach.

Springs and boggy ground to the south of Pointzcastle Farm feed a stream which reaches the sea at a small sandy beach 0.5 km. to the south-west. Its course is down a narrow valley broadening to a maximum of 450 m. at a point where it is fed by lateral springs. It then narrows as it breaches the higher ground which backs the cliffs. Worked flint and stone is scattered widely in the fields flanking the valley, especially on its west side and where subsidiary springs emerge. On this western side alone, these scatters can be estimated to coalesce into an overall area of some 6 hectares (60,000 sq. m.). Grouped with the rather more discrete scatters on the eastern side, this small valley would appear to support a considerable area of prehistoric activity.

Despite the very large areal spread of flint material, only 3,501 pieces were collected from the Pointzcastle fields (Fig. 7.10). The bulk of this is flint debitage (with 10 pieces each of Greensand chert and igneus rock, respectively). Some 7% of the material is unpatinated and a post-Mesolithic presence is again indicated by scalar cores (12), 'thumbnail' scrapers, a leaf- shaped arrowhead and a fragment of a plano-convex knife. A barbed and tanged arrowhead is also recorded from the area (Grimes, 1932, fig. 3, 18).

Four 'narrow blade' microliths include a scalene triangle fragment, two lanceolate-shaped pieces and an oblique *petit-tranchet* form. These are accompanied by denticulates (34), large convex scrapers (21), burins (3), truncated pieces (5), notched pieces (3), a 'nosed' piece, a 'bec', and a single bevelled pebble.

A large sample of 296 cores have an average height of 29 mm. and the majority are, in size and appearance, very like those from the other sites for which a late Mesolithic date is suggested. 12% of the cores are, however, over 35 mm. in height and this may be taken as a hint that early Mesolithic activity could be represented within the catchment of this small valley. This suggestion has some slight support from the presence of a possible tip fragment of a *mèche de forêt*.

Eastwards along the clifftop from the Pointzcastle valley there is a further scatter of flint, of about 10,000 sq. m. at SM 8321 2304 (Cwm Bach II).

Table 7.1: artefact composition at Cwm Bach I

i) Tools:

microliths:	
'broad blade'	6
'narrow blade'	82
Fragments	75
other tools:	
scrapers (including 17 'thumbnail' types)	48
denticulates	227
burins	82
truncated pieces	70
'becs'	16
'nosed' pieces	8
notched pieces	16
mèches de forêt	6
bi-facially flaked 'pebble chopping-tools'	6
retouched pieces	72
utilized pieces	42
other pieces	29

ii) By-products:

micro-burins	8
miss-hits	5
burin spalls	36
core rejuvenation flakes	242

iii) Debitage:

cores	2,612
core fragments	1,097
scalar cores	133
flaked flint pebbles	218
unmodified flint pebbles	22
flakes, blade fragments	21,758

TOTAL number of artefacts	**26,916**

of which 67 (0.2%) are of Cretaceous chert, and 47 (0.17%) are of igneous rock.

iv) Pebble tools:

bevelled pebbles	21
hammerstones	13
counter-sunk ('cupped') pebbles	2

Cwm Bach I (SM 8377 2326):
Continuing eastwards, in fields now to the south-west of Pointzcastle Farm, is a larger scatter (Cwm Bach I) of some 35,000 sq. m. The distribution of lithic debris, found in three separate fields, encircles a streamlet that descends to a small cove at Cwm Bach (Plates 7.2, 7.3). At low water, this forms the northern limit of a beach that runs southwards uninterrupted for 4 km.

This very large site, or aggregation of scatters, seems to have gone unrecorded by local collectors and was, therefore, particularly suitable for fieldwork, allowing

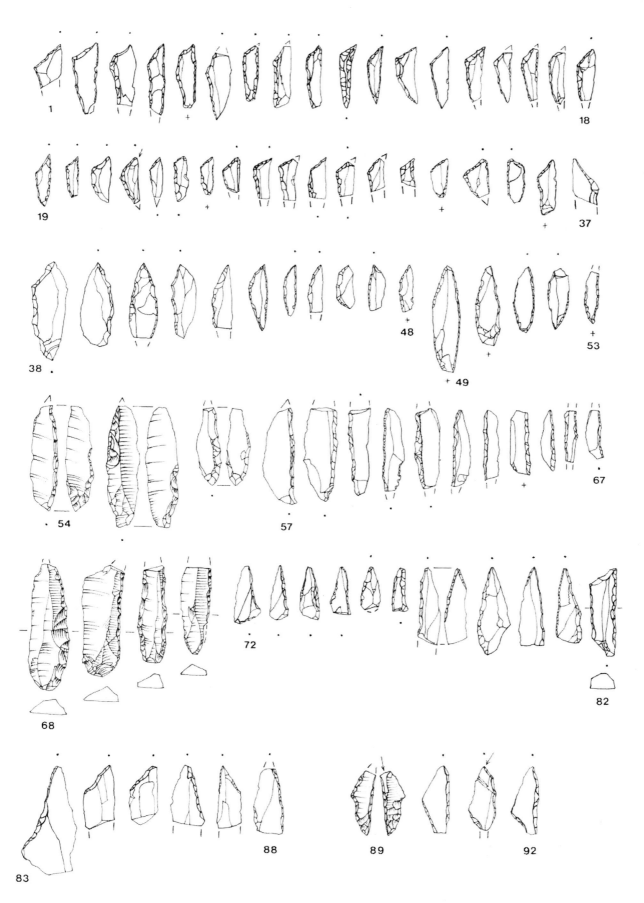

Figure 7.11: Artefacts from Cwm Bach I, Newgale, Dyfed: - 1-67, 72-92, Microliths; 68-71, retouched bladelets.
Scale – 1:1.

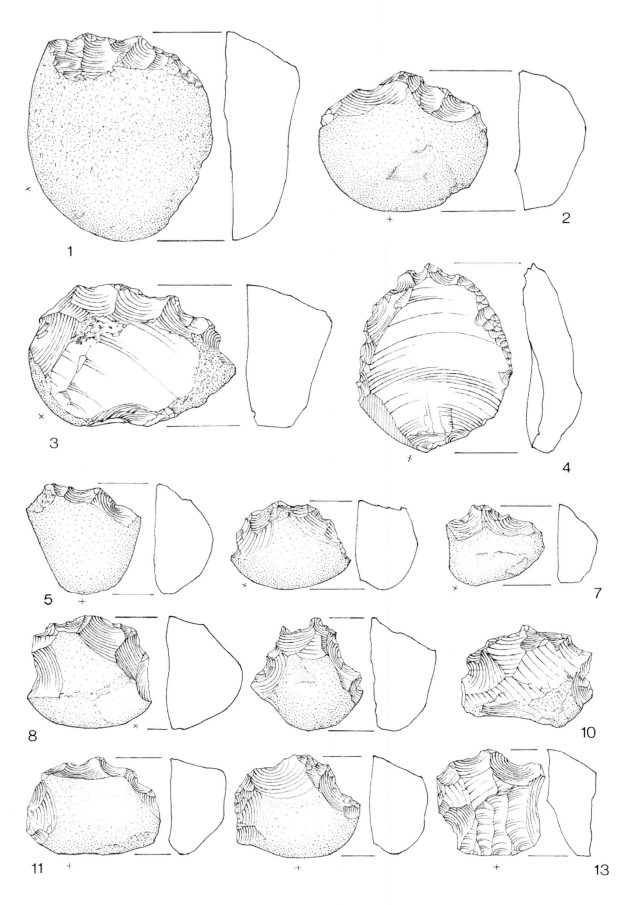

Figure 7.12: Artefacts from Cwm Bach I, Newgale, Dyfed. Denticulates. Scale – 1:1.

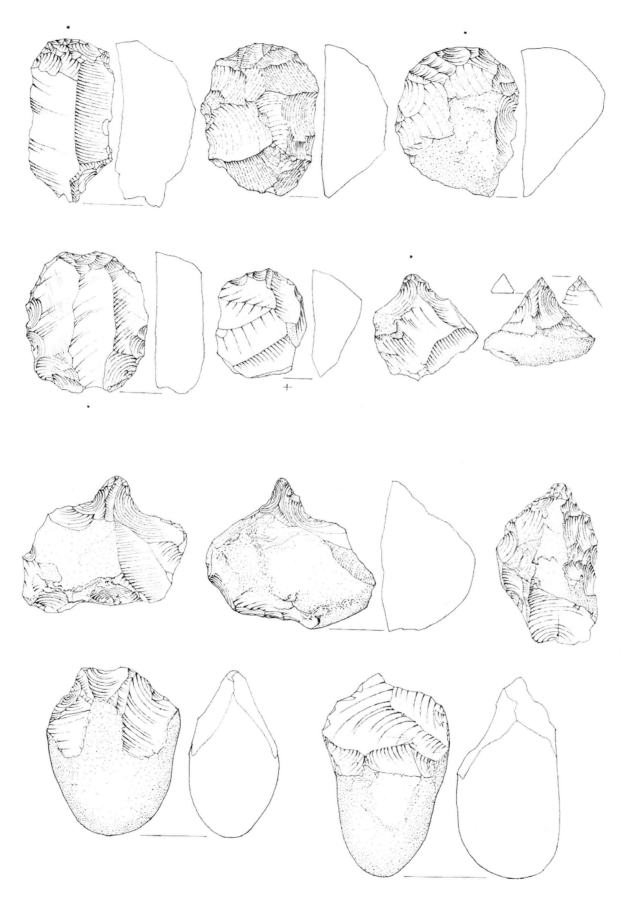

Figure 7.13: Artefacts from Cwm Bach I, Newgale, Dyfed: - 1-5, scrapers; 6-10, "nosed" pieces; 11-12, pebble "chopping-tools". Scale – 1:1.

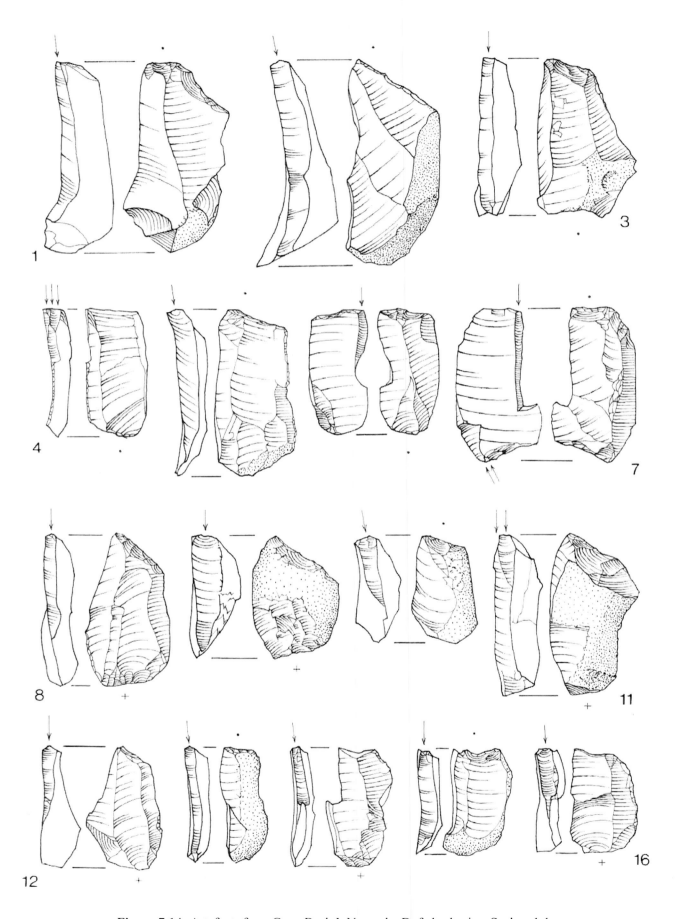

Figure 7.14: Artefacts from Cwm Bach I, Newgale, Dyfed: - burins. Scale – 1:1.

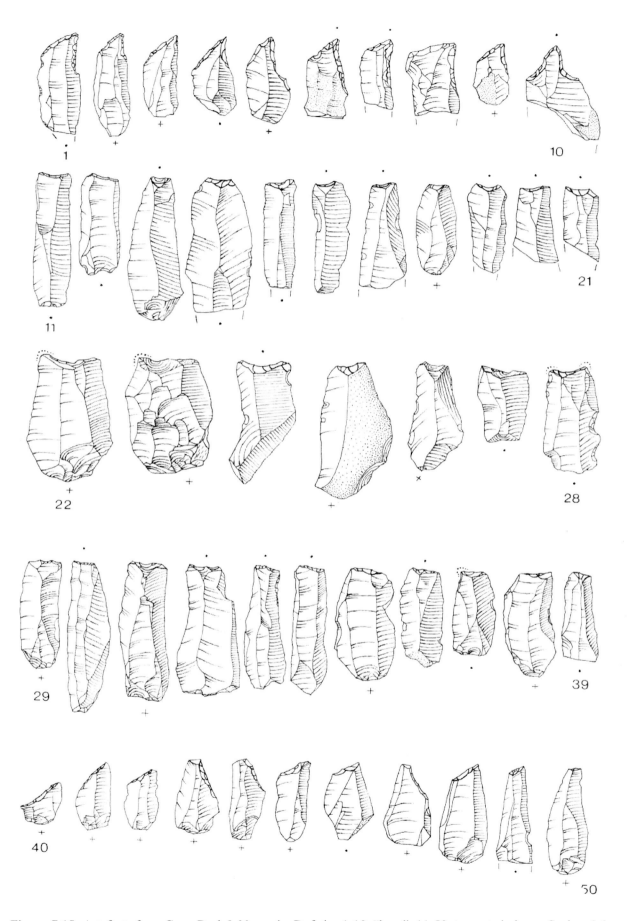

Figure 7.15: Artefacts from Cwm Bach I, Newgale, Dyfed: - 1-10, "becs"; 11-50, truncated pieces. Scale – 1:1.

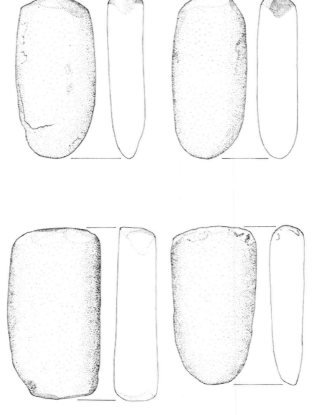

Figure 7.16: artefacts from Cwm Bach I, Newgale, Dyfed: - bevelled pebbles. Scale – 1:1.78.

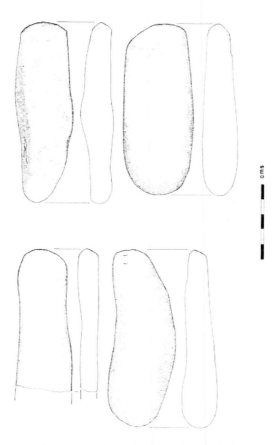

Figure 7.17: Artefacts from Cwm Bach I, Newgale, Dyfed: - bevelled pebbles.

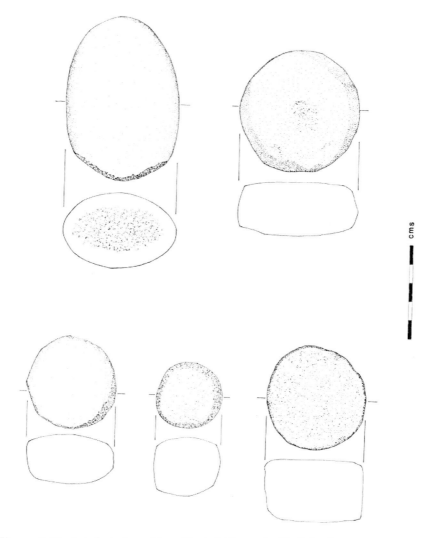

Figure 7.18: Artefacts from Cwm Bach I, Newgale, Dyfed: - hammerstones.

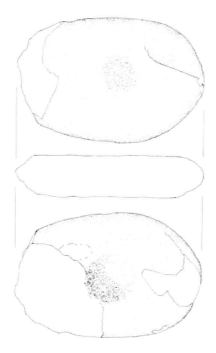

Figure 7.19: "cupped" pebble from Cwm Bach I, Newgale, Dyfed. Scale – 1:1.24.

recovery of no less than 26,916 artefacts. Such a large and (hopefully) representative sample of material in which contributions to the different tool categories are very much more numerous than for the other surface sites, warrants detailed description. The composition of the collection is detailed in Table 7.1 and artefacts from it are illustrated in Figs. 7.11 - 7.19.

Cores and raw materials: there are no significant differences between the character of the raw material and the cores at Cwm Bach I and that of cores and raw material from most of the other major clifftop sites so far described. The unmodified surfaces of flint pebbles and cores indicate the main source of raw material to have been shingle close to contemporary high-water mark, now overtaken by the advances of St. Brides Bay. Greensand chert and local igneus rock were also picked up, but together constitute only 0.4% of the collection. For a sample of 389 cores, an average value for 'height' is 30 mm.

Microliths: the representation of microliths from the assemblage is as follows:

Table 7.2: microlith composition at Cwm Bach I

obliquely-backed pieces	6
scalene micro-triangles	38
lanceolates	4
straight-backed pieces	14
convex-backed pieces	11
micro-*petit-tranchet*s	4
four-sided piece	1
other narrow-blade forms	10
unclass. microlith frags	75
TOTAL	**163**

This range of microliths (see Fig. 7.11, Nos. 1 - 53, 57 - 67, 72 - 92) is fully consistent with the proposed late Mesolithic attribution of the site, with the proviso that the small number of obliquely backed pieces (Nos. 83 - 88), and perhaps a very small number of other tools, may indicate a use of the area earlier in the Mesolithic. The relatively greater proportion (46%) of scalene micro-triangles (Nos. 1 - 18) over other 'narrow blade' types coincides with evidence from excavated samples from sites such as Prestatyn (66%) and The Nab Head II (68%). The association with smaller numbers of convex-backed (Nos. 38 - 48), straight-backed (Nos. 57 - 67) and lanceolate pieces (Nos.49 - 53) would also appear to be not unusual on the limited evidence available, although reading any further meaning into their presence in a surface assemblage would, at present, be unwise. The micro-*petit-tranchet*s (Nos. 89 - 92), 'points' (Nos. 72 - 77) and a four-sided piece may be noted as rare examples of microlith types which may be chronologically restricted, perhaps to the very end of the Mesolithic (Jacobi, 1980b, 175).

Denticulates (Fig. 7.12) and large scrapers (Fig. 7.13, Nos. 1–5), owing to their size, are perhaps disproportionately

represented in the collection, at 227 and 31 pieces, respectively. Morphologically, they are closely related and are recorded in one form or other from nearly every find-spot, and are therefore a far from unexpected component here at Cwm Bach I.

A striking change in the so far monotonous make-up of these surface collections is the large total for burins (82) at Cwm Bach I where they comprise 12% of the retouched component (see Fig. 7.14). Of these, 62 are angle burins, 14 are burins on breaks or unretouched surfaces, and 6 are double-ended. The burin facet (with an average width of 5.5 mm.) is usually on the distal left-hand edge of the blank and is clearly worn on some pieces.

Burins are encountered only very infrequently, if at all, at Welsh 'narrow blade' find-spots. Their numbers at Cwm Bach I set the collection apart, perhaps at some subsistence/functional level (see below), from its apparent contemporaries.

Also characteristic of Cwm Bach I are truncated pieces, of which there are 70 (eg Fig. 7.15, Nos. 11-50). The larger of these may be functionally related to burins (or represent burin blanks), and occasionally have their corners worn by use (eg. Nos. 22, 23, 28). The many much narrower truncations are sufficiently distinctive (with oblique, straight or slightly concave terminations) as to suggest a functionally discrete artefact type(s). The latter have been noted only very occasionally on some of the other sites discussed (eg. The Nab Head II, Llanunwas and Pointzcastle).

There are 16 'becs', or piercers (eg Fig. 7.15, Nos. 1-10). Those with a curved point (11) are already familiar from several of the other sites, and perhaps most notably at The Nab Head (6) and at Llanunwas (22). They are also recognized on some sites south of the Bristol Channel, for instance at Lands End (Jacobi, 1979, fig. 5, 40-45), and inland, at Broomhill, Hants (O'Malley and Jacobi, 1978, fig. 5, nos 25, 26).

The range of tools that have a possible piercing (or grooving) function, such as the 'becs', are supplemented by *mèches de forêt* and 'nosed' pieces in which large flakes have a pronounced projection defined by retouch or denticulation and which might be described as coarse piercers (Fig. 7.13, Nos. 6-10).

Notched pieces (16), crudely flaked pebbles resembling small choppers (6: eg Fig. 7.13, Nos. 11-12) and miscellaneous retouched and utilized pieces (122) complete the tool collection. A later prehistoric element is present, indicated by 17 'thumbnail' scrapers and 133 scalar cores, all but 5 of which are unpatinated, along with only 9% of the entire assemblage. That later occupants of the clifftop made use of earlier flint debitage on the site is indicated by at least 25 pieces (21 of which are scalar cores) where a previous patina is interrupted by later unpatinated working (see Plate 7.4).

Plate 7.4: Scalar cores on older flakes (from Cwm Bach I)

Pebble tools: these make a significant contribution to the artefact inventory from this find-spot. A special effort was made to recognize and collect pebble tools and it may therefore be significant that nothing resembling a pecked or ground stone axe has yet been recovered.

Whilst hammerstones and bevelled pebbles, arouse no special comment in this context (but see Figs. 7.16 - 7.18), counter-sunk or 'cupped' pebbles are encountered here for the first time in this account. Roe (1985) has recently summarized the state of knowledge concerning them, noting some 200 examples from Britain of which perhaps a dozen occur in contexts suggestive of a Mesolithic date. The determination of their chronological position is complicated by a lack of clear contextual data. An example that might occur early in this period comes from Dawes Heath, Essex (Jacobi, 1980c, fig. 8a), although this is amongst an old and selectively preserved collection (Jacobi, pers. comm.). Instances from later Mesolithic sites broadly analogous to Cwm Bach I have been recorded from Culverwell, Dorset (Palmer, 1976, 325) and Gwithian NE (Jacobi, 1979, fig. 13, 23). Also with probable late Mesolithic associations is the example from Lower Halstow, Kent (Burchell, 1927, pl. III). Although there are no specific Neolithic associations, counter-sunk pebbles appear to have endured into the Bronze Age where at least nine have been found associated with round barrows (Roe, 1985).

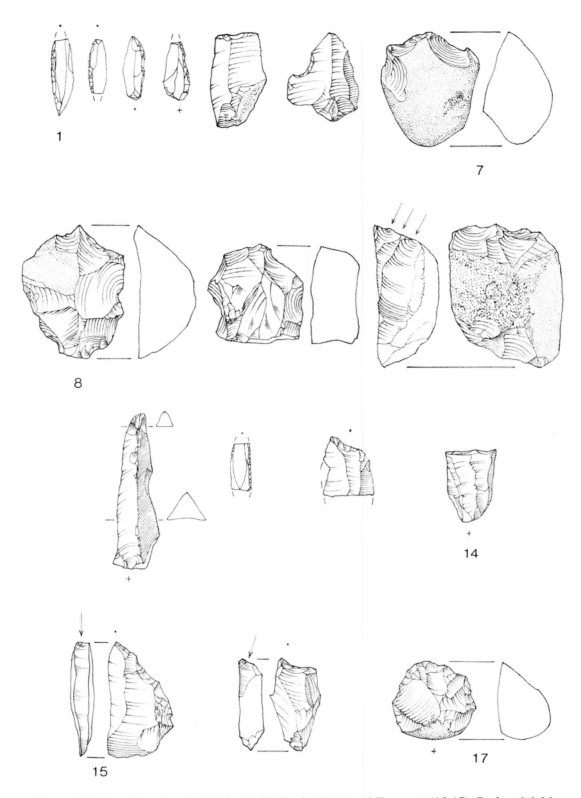

Figure 7.20: Artefacts from St. Brides (1-7), Tretio (8-14) and Trepewet (15-17). Scale – 1:1.14.

The specimens from Cwm Bach I, one of which is illustrated in Fig. 7.19, like most of the other known examples, are flattish oval or irregular cobbles on which opposing hollows have been pecked out. In many cases, although not here, the perimeters of the stones show signs of battering. About eight examples from Dyfed alone are known to the author. That there may be a relative preference for western areas is suggested by Roe's report of 22 examples from Cornwall, but only single examples from Devon, Somerset and Wiltshire. Finds from Culverwell (Palmer, 1976) add to the evidence that these artefacts may, like bevelled pebbles, have a predominantly coastal distribution. This may, of course, simply reflect a greater availability of suitable stones in these areas rather than any specifically cultural or economic phenomenon.

It is unlikely that counter-sunk pebbles were limited to any single function throughout the duration of their presence in the archaeological record. Rather than seeing them serve as anvils for breaking open hazel nuts (Roe, 1985), it may be that they are no more than incompletely perforated artefacts. The latter tools may have been abandoned at any stage of manufacture intermediate between unworked cobble and finished 'macehead' and, indeed, may also have served intermediary functions.

Other coastal sites:
Following the cliffs eastwards around from Cwm Bach, small numbers of flints of Mesolithic aspect have been found in the cliff section at Pen-y-Cwm (SM 8432 2285), and in ploughed fields at Newgale (SM 8479 2255 and SM 8489 2257). Between here and The Nab Head is a stretch some 16 km. of coast, much of which remains unexamined for lithic scatters. Limited fieldwork by the author has located artefacts at Nolton (SM 8629 1868), Haroldston (SM 8618 1478) and near St. Brides (SM 8065 1131). Cantrill (1915) has drawn attention to find-spots at Druidstone (SM 8625 1730 and SM 8639 1749). Although tool forms are scarce, these find-spots all share both a topographic situation and debitage characteristics indistinguishable from those already interpreted as of late Mesolithic date. Only at St Brides (Fig. 7.20, Nos. 1- 7) are there diagnostic 'narrow blade' microliths (4 convex-backed pieces: nos. 1 - 4), and these are supplemented by three denticulates (eg no. 7), a large scraper, a truncation (no. 5) and a notched piece (no. 6).

Leaving the coast, it only remains to describe three inland find- spots:

Tretio (SM 7767 2798):
This site covers some 5,000 sq. m. of relatively dry cultivated land surrounded by the often waterlogged moorland and rough ground of Tretio Common. The nearest sea is 2 km. to the north.

Amongst a sample of only 1,559 pieces, mostly of pebble flint, the most common tool form is the small convex 'thumbnail' scraper, one of which has been made from a scalar core. These, together with four other scalar cores, are unpatinated, as is 28% of the whole collection, indicating Neolithic or Bronze Age activity here.

Leaving aside such clearly later elements, one is left with four denticulates, three unclassifiable microlith fragments, and 165 bladelet cores as the sole evidence for possible Mesolithic usage (eg Fig.7.20, Nos. 8- 4). The large numberof platform bladelet cores, identical in size range to those from late Mesolithic flint scatters in coastal situations is certainly suggestive of microlith manufacture. It is puzzling, however, that despite meticulous searching, no complete microliths have been found, and no micro-burins. A possible explanation is that the scatter represents a bladelet manufacturing (or provisioning) site, providing blanks for hunting equipment which was then completed elsewhere. It may also be a possibility that bladelets were being manufactured and hafted without any retouched modification.

Trepewet (SM 7699 2582):
This flint scatter covers an area of about 2,500 sq. m. and lies adjacent to the stream which runs out to Caerbwdy Bay 1.5 km. to the south.

The lithic collection (eg Fig. 7.20, Nos. 15-17) has much in common with that from Tretio. Of 183 pieces 34% are of unpatinated pebble flint, and 1% are either of Greensand chert or local igneous rock. There are three scalar cores and a 'thumbnail' scraper. Despite many bladelet cores (93) there is again no confirmation of microlith manufacture. There are, however, denticulates (3), burins (3) and a large convex scraper which together hint at a late Mesolithic presence. Moreover, two of the scalar cores are worked on clearly earlier artefacts.

Priory Farm (SM 954149):
This find-spot, along with that on Palmerston Farm, was found by Miss Joan Rees. It lies on the southern outskirts of Haverfordwest and is included here as it is the only late Mesolithic find-spot from west Wales which can be said to be truly inland, being some 9 km. from the sea. The present tidal limit of the Western Cleddau does, however, reach to within a few hundred metres of the site.

A late Mesolithic attribution for at least a proportion of the 381 artefacts examined is suggested by three 'narrow blade' microliths (a small isosceles triangle, a convex-backed piece, and an oblique micro-*petit-tranchet*), and by three microlith fragments. A denticulate, three burins and a flake retouched to a point may also be of this age, as might 25 small bladelet cores with an average height of 28 mm. One of three convex scrapers is made on a scalar core and later activity at the site is again indicated by unpatinated scalar retouch on a patinated flake.

6. Surface sites - summary:
The foregoing account has described the more conspicuous of a total of 40 find-spots and lithic collections resulting from the author's fieldwork, mostly on the St. Davids peninsula. Often very substantial artefact scatters have been identified and these are repeatedly located on, or near, clifftops and within reach of beaches, springs and streamlets. Without exception, the collections from these find-spots are characterized by the use of beach pebbles and a bladelet core technology, the products of which are usually heavily patinated. Tools associated with many of these find-spots and which, on local analogy, are thought to be late Mesolithic, include 'narrow blade' microliths, denticulates, and bevelled pebbles. Of find-spots over a kilometre away from the sea, only two have produced microliths in confirmation of their attribution to the late Mesolithic.

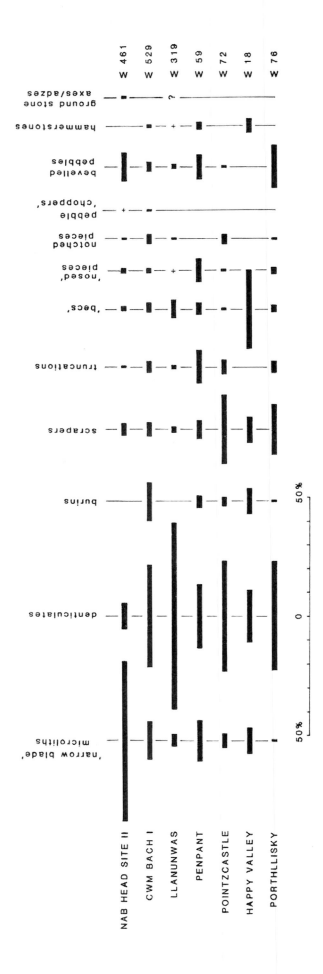

Figure 7.21: Chart of tool composition for selected find-spots from north-west Dyfed.

7. Functional variability

Now that the lithic components of some of the Welsh late Mesolithic 'sites' have been described one can note that, despite overall similarities, a low level of local diversity in the their composition is nonetheless detectable. Before any attempt to assess this apparent diversity it is again necessary to stress the shortcomings of the data.

Without recourse to the well-known and fundamental debate concerning archaeological variability (Binford, 1983), it is plain that the principal determinants of lithic diversity can be summarized in terms of either function and/or chronology. Cultural patterning or the influence of stylistic expression can be numbered amongst other underlying factors which are usually less accessible through the archaeological record but which may nevertheless be of some importance. None of these contributions can as yet be adequately assessed for the Welsh Mesolithic and any explanations must necessarily both be at a simplistic and highly speculative level. They must draw on scarcely less thin comparative data from outside the region.

Foremost amongst the shortcomings of the Welsh lithic data must be recovery. Surface retrieval can be expected to have favoured larger at the expense of smaller pieces, such as microliths. Many of the collections may be both chronologically mixed and internally undatable. Recovery by excavation, on the other hand, has been restricted to that at The Nab Head Site II, and even here the area sampled is only very partial. The site's chronology still remains to be more firmly established. Only in extremely rare cases has supplementary organic material been preserved, and these exceptional instances are capable of making only a minimal contribution towards the recognition of the potential range of 'soft' tools and utensils. Functional studies of the main lithic implements have yet to be made in order to determine task variability between and within the major typological categories recognized, and to identify those tools with multiple functions. Raw materials cannot be shown to depend on sources more exclusive than local beach shingle.

Despite these limitations and the absence of a coherent internal chronology for the late Mesolithic, it may still be worthwhile to document the observed variations between the lithic inventories. For ease of comparison, the lithic compositions of the larger collections discussed in this chapter and that for The Nab Head Site II are displayed in bar-chart form in Fig. 7.21. The main variation would appear to be between denticulates, 'becs', truncations, burins, microliths and ground stone tools (bevelled pebbles and axes). Preliminary statistical tests on both Welsh and Cornish data, whilst requiring considerable caution in any application to small and biased samples, nevertheless would seem to indicate a high level of positive correlation between microliths and 'becs', denticulates and 'becs', and burins with truncated pieces.

Denticulates have been recovered from every find-spot and are the commonest tool type in most of the collections. Only

at The Nab Head Site II are they outnumbered - in this case by microliths. This must partly or wholly be a function of retrieval by sieving at The Nab Head. Similar procedures would have to be applied at Llanunwas, for instance, to test whether the seeming dominance of denticulates over all other tool types is indeed genuine. At Cwm Bach I, where the very large sample of artefacts may perhaps comprise the least biased of the surface collections, denticulates are again the most common tool form.

It is at Cwm Bach I where the greatest divergence from any 'norm' is most clearly noticeable. This takes the form of significant numbers of truncated pieces and burins. Burins, as already noted, are only sparsely represented in the other collections, and no certain examples have been identified from The Nab Head Site II or at Llanunwas. Truncated pieces, especially on narrow blades, are a distinctive feature only at Cwm Bach I and the striking similarity amongst these is indicated by examples illustrated in Fig. 7.15. Observation of tool morphology and macroscopic wear patterns give a general impression of a persistence of a piercing or grooving function between many of the tools at Cwm Bach.

Amongst the group of sites at Gwithian, Cornwall, the artefacts of which display so many similarities to those in west Wales, it is perhaps relevant here to note the association of large numbers of bevelled pebbles (51) with truncated pieces (30% of 'essential tools') at Site NE (Jacobi, 1979, 78, table III). Denticulates are also significant on these sites but, unlike Cwm Bach, burins are scarcely represented.

Microliths, as already commented, have to be under-represented amongst surface collections. Their total and near-total absence from the two 'inland' locations at Trepewet and Tretio, however, may indicate the site of bladelet 'provisioning' in advance of microlith manufacture at other locations. A few denticulates are present at both find-spots, together with large numbers of small bladelet cores.

Bevelled pebbles have not so far been recovered from either of the two sites mentioned above nor from Happy Valley or Priory Farm. They are, however, recorded for all the larger clifftop flint scatters and at Penpant occur some 800 m. back from the present shoreline. Their most convincing context is at The Nab Head where they occur with microliths and small numbers of denticulates.

Ground stone axe-heads have yet to be identified from any other find-spot apart from The Nab Head, although isolated recoveries have been documented in the previous chapter. Perforated stone discs would also appear to be peculiar to The Nab Head, although a badly damaged example (Fig. 6.20, No. 2) may be represented at Porthllisky. Pebble tools from Cwm Bach I are numerous and, in contrast to the other sites, include several heavily-used hammerstones, short bevelled pebbles, and counter-sunk pebbles.

In the absence of any 'objective' assessment of function for these tool forms, interpretation of inter-site variability has to remain extremely basic. Involving least guesswork is the association of microliths with some form of hunting or fishing activity (as well as attacks on other humans). The use of at least some of the 'narrow blade' shapes as the tips and barbs of arrows, darts, spears, harpoons or knives seems highly probable. The likely association of small backed bladelet fragments with the wild pig skeleton found at Lydstep Haven is suggestive in this context, but there should be caution in relying only on the simple equation of microliths with hunting (Clarke, 1976). No interpretation has yet been offered on the role of the less common, but nevertheless persistently recurrent, geometric microliths such as tiny isosceles triangles and convex-backed pieces. Experimentation with composite projectile equipment, if this is relevant to these latter pieces, has yet to be attempted (Fischer, pers. comm.).

If it is conceded, then, that some hunting and/or fishing is indicated by the presence of microliths such as scalene triangles and straight-backed bladelets, it may follow that most of the other common tools, not obviously lethal in intent, were used in processing. Such processing, whether of animal, vegetable or mineral materials, has traditionally been seen as an indicator of 'domestic', or 'residence'-type activities, that might be expected at sites (sometimes 'base-camps') where an occupation has been of extended rather than merely fleeting duration (Mellars, 1976b). Such over-simplification may conceal the potentially very complex (and archaeologically indistinct) relationships between site function, and tool use, curation and deposition (eg Binford, 1979). However, until further evidence to the contrary is forthcoming we are left only with this very lowest level of interpretation.

In Mellars' study of the Mesolithic (1976b), his main index of industrial variability was the relative proportion of microliths to scrapers, and this was argued to have a broad correlation with site size, function and seasonality. Microlith-dominated assemblages were small, upland, and to be associated with summer hunting forays. Sites with relatively more scrapers and other tools were predominantly larger, lowland, and possibly of winter, multiple or residential occupation. A few assemblages which were dominated by scrapers were thought to indicate special-purpose skin-working sites.

The identification of scrapers as the archetype of skin-working throughout prehistory has yet to be seriously refuted. Amongst the Welsh lithic collections under discussion, though, the conventional convex scraper is relatively scarce and its structural place would appear to have been taken by the denticulate - by far the most regularly occurring tool throughout the collections. Whilst many of these might better be classed as 'denticulated scrapers', there are others which might be interpreted as small cores, and still more which are intermediate between these. The outline of such pieces varies between the convex (on large and steeply retouched scrapers) and the deeply indented, depending on the depth and coarseness of the peripheral flaking. Both the 'notched' and 'nosed' tools, when worked on stout flakes, can also demonstrate a denticulate-type morphology and may have shared related functions.

Once the techniques of microscopic analaysis of use-wear traces become fully established, it is to be hoped that the function(s) of denticulates and other tools will be confidently identified. Macroscopic wear is only rarely visible, but a preliminary microwear analysis of two unpatinated examples from Westward Ho!, north Devon, by Dr. E. Moss has revealed that one preserved traces like those produced experimentally by planing red deer antler which had been soaked in water (Moss, pers. comm.). Of five scrapers examined at the same time, only two preserved use- wear traces, but it was not possible to identify what material had been worked.

If, despite this lack of supporting evidence, denticulates and large convex scrapers are placed together as processing equipment then find-spots such as Llanunwas (where they seemingly represent 76% of all tools) might be classed at the 'scraper-dominated' end of Mellars' spectrum of variability. The nature of the processing activities cannot at present be determined, but might be argued to differ (at least in emphasis) from that represented by the significant numbers of truncated pieces and burins only 5 km. along the coast at Cwm Bach I. One can only speculate as to whether or not the working of bone, wood or antler was an important pre-occupation at any of these sites. One must also wonder whether sites were re-occupied on separate occasions for different purposes.

Of the pebbles, the bevel-ended tools represent a very distinct type, the possible functions of which have already been discussed at length (see chapter VI). Processing activities such as hide- or wood-working have been suggested, and the apparently irrefutable association of these pebbles with large numbers of microliths at The Nab Head Site II, and some Cornish sites, has to be accounted for. It seems reasonable to propose that, as the two implement types recur together regularly on coastal sites, they indicate a distinct hunting-processing sequence, but one which, without the preservation of associated organic data, we are still powerless to unravel.

Any discussion of lithic variability inevitably becomes inter-linked with the problems of attempting to assess the nature of late Mesolithic subsistence and how this may vary from season to season. Whilst admitting the poverty and pit-falls in deductions based on the lithic data alone, the level of supplementary information, for instance from environmental sources is also severely limited.

8. Seasonality and subsistence

'In Wales these industries are found on numerous chipping floors near the present sea shore; the associations suggest a poverty stricken folk, food-gatherers, living mainly on shell-fish. These characters are indeed fairly universal.' (Cyril Fox, 1933).

'...it may be well to regard these stations not as the pitiful hole-ups of a limpet-bashing minority but as stations receding before the rising sea, oriented specifically upon the presence of such splendid animals as the Borth Beast.' (P. Evans, 1975).

These two very differing views of our sites arose from an early emphasis upon a supposed technological impoverishment amongst their flint and stone industries, followed by the realization that their environmental setting implied instead a robust and varied level of subsistence.

The range of potential food resources at the interface between maritime and terrestrial environments can be expected to be wider than at any other type of location. The number of find-spots now recognized on the south-west coasts of Wales would therefore seem to add confirmation to the predictions offered by Webley (1976) and ApSimon (1976a) who both emphasized the special climatic and environmental attractiveness of this coastal strip.

The distribution map in Fig. 7.1 shows the position of a line to the south and west of which average accumulated temperatures for January to June are higher than 1550 day-degrees Centigrade (Rudeforth, et. al., 1984, 27, fig 8). It is most tempting to see in the latter a strong correlation between a maritime fringe of exceptionally mild climate and the quite remarkable density of evidence for late Mesolithic occupation in this same zone.

i) Terrestrial resources:

With optimal average annual temperatures being reached during the late Mesolithic, it may follow that the biomass in these areas attained corresponding proportions. The vegetational and faunal background has already been outlined in Chapter V, as far as the data available allow. Although dense deciduous and pine woodland together covered much of Wales, it has been argued (Jacobi, 1980b) that heavy shading species, principally lime, will have been less dominant here than in south-east England (Girling and Greig, 1977). Understorey species would therefore have been better able to compete in the lighter more westerly woodlands, and in turn may have attracted a greater density of ungulate browsers. Then as now, west Wales would have been both mild and exposed to occasionally severe westerly weather, which would have limited certain tree species such as oak and elm to more sheltered localities (Taylor, 1975; Donald, 1987). Coastal areas, at the forest-edge ecotone would have relieved the 'monotony' of closed woodland, and would consequently have encouraged the concentration of ungulates in these areas during parts of the year.

The principal dry-land mammalian prey species may be assumed to have been red and roe deer, elk, wild pig and aurochs, which will have contributed to a potential ungulate biomass, as calculated for temperate forest, of about 1,000 - 2,500 kg/sq. km. (Mellars, 1975). For the reasons outlined above, actual values for the coastal zones may be at the higher end of this estimated range and will have varied according to seasonal behaviour, especially of red deer.

As there is no evidence from Wales for the exploitation of red deer for anything but the odd antler tool, the construction of major economic and settlement models around the behaviour of this species is necessarily tenuous. However, given the argued importance of red deer throughout the Mesolithic on sites in England and abroad (but not Ireland), its influence on human strategies must be given some weight. Clark was the first to seek a correlation between the altitudinal distribution of artefact scatters, confined apparently to extremes of upland or lowland, with the seasonal movements of red deer between these two areas in summer and winter, respectively (Clark, 1972). That this bi- modal arrangement may have been seasonal is based on the fact that present-day red deer may congregate in winter 'yards' in lowland and often coastal areas, and then in summer disperse in smaller groups to higher ground (Ingebrigtsen, 1924: cited by Clark, 1972). Finds of hunting equipment at the highest altitudes are explained by the selective culling of stags and barren female deer which alone graze these higher areas. Jacobi has pursued such arguments further in separate considerations of northern England, the South-western Peninsula and Wales (Jacobi, 1977; 1979; 1980b).

In a recent reassessment of the faunal evidence from Star Carr, however, Legge and Rowley-Conwy (1988) have pointed out that the observed seasonal movement of red deer is in fact only a feature of their behaviour in open or mountainous terrains. In forested landscapes, red deer tend to be dispersed in small groups and any migration is minimal. For Wales, however, the sharp topographic division between upland core and surrounding lowland coastal plateaux contrasts significantly with the lower and much less accentuated topography of North Yorkshire. Taylor (1980) has stressed the exceptional contrasts amongst local Welsh environments: 'Wales witnesses the maximum climatic confrontation between the intensely maritime, early, west-slope environments along [Cardigan] Bay and the more extreme, cold, late habitats of the Cambrian Mountains which are succeeded eastwards by distinctly less maritime, harder climates of the Welsh borderland...' (ibid. 104). West Wales can demonstrate one of the most rapid temperature lapse-rates, per unit altitude rise, in the world (ibid. 111). Colder temperatures and wind exposure would ensure that upland plateaux would remain largely free of tree growth upwards of an altitudinal limit of about 610 metres (ibid. 117). Such contrasts between Welsh upland and lowland, and associated variations in forest density, would certainly seem, therefore, to increase the likelihood of seasonal movement amongst local red deer populations, although this remains to be demonstrated.

More information will be needed on the altitudinal extent and composition of forest cover across Wales before such arguments can be clarified in any detail. Certainly, mobility of some kind between upland and lowland is suggested by the archaeological evidence. As emphasized in the discussion of find-spots in south Wales, notably at Craig-y-Llyn and Waun Fignen Felen, there is an unmistakeable similarity between their small microlith-dominated artefact groups and the recoveries from find-spots which crowd upon certain watersheds of the Pennine and Cleveland Hills. Jacobi has proposed that, like these Yorkshire locations, the Welsh find-spots could represent the summer hunting activities of Mesolithic communities whose winter and spring encampments are to be found at lower altitudes and on the coasts. The use of beach- derived raw material on the uplands, and identical narrow-blade microliths, seems to add confidence to the supposition that the same communities were using both landscapes.

It remains to be seen whether or not such suppositions are plausible for the more subdued topographies of south-west Wales. It must be a priority for future fieldwork here and in central Wales, and particularly in central western areas such as the Prescelly Hills, to attempt to identify the traces of summer forays by hunters otherwise based along the clifftops and beaches of Dyfed. Such fieldwork may also be expected to find evidence for exploitation unrelated just to the pursuit of deer (see below).

Before moving on to cover alternative food resources, it is necessary to mention the increasing evidence for Mesolithic vegetation clearance. This is particularly relevant to upland ungulate exploitation and, by inference, its role in the model, described above, of movement between coastal and inland zones. Pollen and charcoal preserved in soil profiles has for some time now been thought to demonstrate intentional interference with vegetation, particularly by burning (Smith, 1970; Simmons, 1975; Mellars, 1976c). Lush regrowth after the intentional firing of woodland, particularly at its altitudinal limits, would attract game animals from surrounding areas and at the same time render them more vulnerable to hunting. The forest margin, already a 'fragile ecosystem' (Simmons, 1981), might even retreat in such circumstances, and repeated burning would favour fire-resistant shrubs such as hazel.

It has been pointed out (Rowley-Conwy, pers. comm.) that, despite the evidence for burning, it is still necessary to account for the extreme difficulty of setting light to mature deciduous woodland. This being the case, burning would have to have been selective, concentrating on marginal shrub growth and perhaps understorey vegetation. More susceptible to conflagration, however, would have been pine woodland (as it is today) - and one may wonder, perhaps, whether such woods were also deliberately selected for burning. Although this tree species was only a minor forest constituent in the Welsh late Mesolithic, it may

be significant that it survived as such in the uplands 'especially in the more sterile and more exposed locations where competition with other tree species was least' (Taylor, 1980, 116) - i.e. in just those areas where clearance and summer hunting have already been proposed. Burning of such areas, presumably during the driest conditions of late summer, might be expected to attract deer and other game from the denser forests of lower altitudes.

Just as it has been possible to parallel the location and character of Welsh with English upland late Mesolithic finds of flint and chert hunting equipment, so it is now possible to note a correspondence between them of evidence for clearance by burning. This new evidence is the result of biostratigraphic studies at Waun Fignen Felen, Powys, by A. G. Smith and E. W. Cloutman (1988), and has very fortunately been combined with the archaeological investigations already mentioned in Chapters III and V (Berridge, forthcoming).

This small upland bog, at about 480 m OD, overlying a Lateglacial lake basin, is mostly composed of an ombrogenous (blanket) peat overlying a thin basal mor - a distinct greasy amorphous humic layer, black with charcoal. Charcoal was also seen to form a distinct layer at the peat-mineral interface, even where a mor layer was absent, and was also detected in the basal peats. Pollen analysis and radiocarbon dating at 16 sampling sites in and around the bog indicates that the area was probably wooded prior to c. 8,000 BP, mostly with hazel. At about this time it is argued that a clearing was made nearby and was recolonised by birch and subsequently by hazel. The remnant of the Lateglacial basin was probably reedy and marshy. Outside this basin, the first organic (mor) deposits began forming at c. 7,900 BP and this was followed by the initiation of blanket peat from c. 7,600 BP, the growth of which continued for at least 3000 years.

Smith and Cloutman argue that the vegetational history of this site has been significantly affected by deliberate anthropogenic interference during the Mesolithic. After initial clearances within the hazel woodland, both charcoal and high values of heather pollen in the basal mor indicate burning and the conversion of at least some woodland to heath and scrub. The relatively impermeable mor deposit, itself associated with burning, is seen to have induced the growth of blanket peat which was further sustained by repeated but perhaps less frequent burning episodes. A very similar sequence has also been interpreted from pollen profiles at sites at Pen Rhiw-wen, also in the Black Mountains, where late Mesolithic burning is again implicated (Cloutman, 1983). It has also been suggested that the establishment and spread of alder, after an initial climatic change at the beginning of the Atlantic pollen zone, was encouraged by man's activities (Smith, 1984; Chambers and Price, 1985).

The lithic finds from Waun Fignen Felen have been suggested to be mostly early Mesolithic and, therefore, pre-date the vegetational succession described above. An early exploitation of this and other Welsh upland areas again finds its equivalent in northern England, where 'broad blade' sites are well known on the higher ground of the North Yorkshire Moors and the Pennines. At Waun Fignen Felen, an attraction at this time would have been the lake basin, which would still have supported some open water with attendant game and waterfowl. However, at some time after *c.* 8,000 BP, when the first evidence for clearance occurs, late Mesolithic hunting probably also took place, as suggested by the two separate finds of groups of 'narrow blade' microliths. At least one part of upland Wales might, therefore, be seen to provide evidence for the impact of late Mesolithic subsistence activity.

Apart from red deer it is assumed that roe deer, elk, wild pig and wild cattle were hunted and, equally, benefited from any opening up of the forest. Wild cattle in particular, which individually could supply more meat than any other contemporary land animal, may have been a much sought-after target. Their ecological preferences are not well understood, but the indications are that wild cattle were adaptable creatures capable of tolerating even forested habitats and were mostly unconstrained by topography (Evans, 1975). Their remains have been frequently recovered from foreshore deposits (see Chapter V), and include that of the post-cranial skeleton of a bull at Borth, Dyfed, notable for being the largest so far encountered in Britain (Taylor, 1973). Although there are no Welsh records of remains of wild cattle from higher ground, the finds of horn cores from widely disparate areas of the English uplands (Jacobi, pers. comm.) would suggest that their habitats were highly diverse.

Evans (1975) has argued persuasively that wild cattle may have been of some considerable importance to late Mesolithic subsistence. She suggested that their habitat and dietary requirements might have been most favourably met on Welsh lowland coastal fringes, and that both are likely to have been enhanced by any openings caused by the firing of these landscapes. The apparent density of late Mesolithic settlement on western coasts might, therefore, reflect the local abundance of wild cattle. It may even be relevant that finds of red deer bone and antler in Wales, when compared to those more numerous remains of wild cattle, are relatively rare, and perhaps reflect a significant scarcity of deer for exploitation at this time.

Evidence for widespread fires at lower altitudes has yet to be recognized. Recent palaeoenvironmental study of foreshore and adjacent organic deposits along the south-west Welsh coast (Lewis, forthcoming) has not identified satisfactory evidence for substantial clearance before *c.* 4,500 BP. There may have been slight disturbance at Abermawr, however, probably of valley-side woodlands, at *c.* 5,200 BP (ibid.), and temporary openings in lowland vegetation have been noted at Aberaeron on the coast of Cardigan Bay (Taylor, 1973) and some 10 km. inland at Abermad (SN 587 742: Taylor, 1987).

The wild pig found at Lydstep (see Chapter V), presents the only possible evidence for Mesolithic hunting from Wales. Pig has received rather less attention in the literature of the British Mesolithic, where discussion has perhaps been unduly focused on the red deer (eg. Jarman, 1972). Abroad, pigs may well have been a staple in Ireland (Woodman, 1978) and were the objectives of specialized hunting at Ertebölle sites such as Ringkloster (Rowley-Conwy, 1981). Wild boar would certainly have been very much at home in late Mesolithic woodland where they could have occupied territories of 20 - 200 hectares per animal (Bay-Petersen, 1978). Their mobility and territory sizes are both reduced in winter making them more vulnerable to hunting, and data from both Mount Sandel in Northern Ireland and from Danish sites suggest that they were taken at this time of year (Wijngaarden-Bakker, 1985; Bay-Petersen, 1978). All things considered, therefore, pig may well have proved a reliable and ubiquitous winter source of protein and fat.

Roe deer can also be expected to have made a contribution to diet and raw materials, but there is little or no evidence for this from Wales. The animal tends to be shy and solitary, preferring woodland cover in the earlier stages of forest growth or regeneration (Chaplin, 1975). It would therefore also have been attracted by forest margins and clearances although its relatively small meat yield might have warranted less effort in the chase than the larger ungulates. Roe deer have, however, been recorded from several British late Mesolithic sites (Jarman, 1972).

The contribution of vegetable resources to diet is particularly difficult to determine, but there can be no doubt that many plants, fruits and nuts were both edible and, in the cases of acorns and hazel nuts, extremely nutritious (Clarke, 1976). The charred shells of the latter are a frequent find on many Mesolithic sites, and in Wales have been noted at The Nab Head Site I, Trwyn Du, Prestatyn and at Brenig 53. Nuts and acorns are available in August and September and at this time might be expected to provide an optimal return on collection from only a small area of woodland (Rowley-Conwy, 1984; Jacobi, 1977). Such a return would be improved even further if burning off were to favour hazel in the subsequent regeneration. Jacobi (1980b, 194) has suggested that summer growth may have persisted longer in the uplands of Wales, where hazel was one of the main forest constituents, and therefore that the presence of hazelnut shells at Brenig might imply an autumn occupation. The possibility that nuts were stored might distort such predictions, but there is some doubt as to whether storage would have been very effective in the Mesolithic (Rowley-Conwy, 1984), or even necessary (but see Rowley-Conwy and Zvelebil, 1989).

Gathering of plant foods may therefore have played an important role only during brief moments of the year, and may otherwise have been of secondary importance (Lee, 1968). Such resources could at least have provided some starch and sugar (which are almost totally lacking in meat and fish), as well as variety, to the diet (Bonsall, 1981).

ii) Riverine resources:

There is no evidence from Wales for either the presence or exploitation of primary freshwater fish such as pike in the Mesolithic, but it is a safe assumption that the migratory salmonids and eels were available and could have provided a particularly abundant and predictable resource.

Although the present century has seen a sharp decline in productivity, the Welsh rivers and estuaries have been noted for their very rich fisheries. Vast quantities of salmon had been caught previously, and on the Severn, for example, netsmen and operators of fish traps caught 22,500 fish in 1870, 30,000 in 1883 and 20,950 in 1902. Even on a minor river like the Dwyfor in north Wales, the average catch in the 1880's amounted to over 1,300 fish annually, while on the Dee the annual catch varied from 12,000 to 16,000 (Jenkins, 1974). Rivers in west Wales were no less productive, and in the twelfth century the river Teifi was considered by Giraldus Cambrensis to be the finest salmon river in the country. There is no reason to believe that Mesolithic stocks need have been any less prodigious, or that the multitude of both simple and ingenious techniques of catching salmon were not thoroughly understood and practised at the time. Presuming this to be so, then any modelling of resources and settlement patterns during the Welsh Mesolithic should be able to accommodate salmon fishing no less than, for instance, deer hunting. In fact, salmon has a food value equivalent to deer, with less wastage (Watt and Merrill, 1963), and is a more predictable resource.

Runs of both salmon and sea trout take place throughout the summer, after an initial congregation at river estuaries from about May to June. They are perhaps at their most vulnerable whilst passing up-stream to spawn and then becoming confined to the narrower river courses and pools. Nets, weirs, basket traps, leisters and lures could have been used to capture them in great numbers and it would be surprising if at least some Mesolithic sites were not to be found at strategic points of interception along rivers such as the Teifi or the Cleddau. Modern data (Rowley-Conwy and Zvelebil, 1989) suggests, however, that peak salmon runs would have occurred variably at different locations, and at different times, even within the same river system.

Eels, too, either as elvers or as adults (silver eels) could have been an attractive and abundant food source. The adult skins can also be tanned and used in clothing and for other purposes. Elvers enter the rivers in countless numbers in March and April, and can be caught by the hundredweight with simple apparatus. Silver eels can be speared at any time of the year, but are particularly vulnerable to trapping during autumn floods when they migrate back to the open sea, never otherwise to be seen again.

iii) Marine resources:

Looking seawards and along the coasts, it is possible to enumerate a further series of prolific resources, both for foods and raw materials. Most importantly, too, coastwise ease of communication and transport may have been an additional determining factor in the patterning and distribution of settlement.

It is the potential availability of coastal resources that has understandably coloured the traditional interpretations of Welsh early prehistoric settlement:

'The fish of the pools and streams, the mammals and birds of the Morfa, the shell-fish and wet-fish of the coast, and even some of the seaweeds, would provide food, so that the shore near the pebble beaches, and the cliffs above the shore would be spots of special value on the ground of flint supply, as well as of food supply' (H. J. Fleure, 1913).

All these factors in combination are seen to be particularly relevant to explaining the density of find-spots along the coasts of west Wales, of which those listed earlier are just a sample. The use of flint and other rock types that occur locally in beach shingle does not now need further emphasis. If such gathering of lithic raw material is considered to be 'embedded' in the procurement of other resources (Binford, 1979), however, then it is necessary to consider what other attractions the shoreline may have had.

Sea fishing will have been a richly rewarded activity. The variety of coastal and off-shore marine habitats surrounding the Celtic and neighbouring seas, associated with favourable sea temperatures during the late Mesolithic, will have ensured a varied and numerous fish population. Early documentary sources indicate that, however poor Welsh fisheries may now be, they once supported an enormous range and quantity of fish:

'The fishinge of Pembrokeshire is one of the chiefest worldlie commodities, wherewithall god hath blessed this countrey, which fishing are of diverse sortes, taken at diverse times and that at diverse places' (George Owen, 1603: emphasis added).

The same author goes on to list turbot, halibut, brill, sole, plaice, flounder, ling, cod, hake, mullet, bass, conger, grey and red gurnard, whiting, haddock, shad, monkfish, horse-mackerel, smelt, sea bream, herring, dogfish and skate, amongst others. Many further types are now known, and include for instance sharks and sturgeon. Thus all the species of fish recorded from the Obanian (eg. wrasse, dogfish, mullet, skate, saithe, blenny, shanny) and the Morton (eg. cod, haddock, sturgeon, turbot and salmonid) middens of Scotland, and perhaps also those from Téviec and Hoëdic (unidentified), could also have been caught off the Welsh coasts.

Wales has been specially noted for its mackerel, herring and hake fisheries. Although the latter is caught in deeper water, the known ability of the inhabitants of Morton to catch large cod out at sea suggests that these two species could have been taken by boat from Irish Sea waters as well (Coles,

1971). Both herring and mackerel are minor components of some Danish Ertebölle middens. Herring used to congregate in vast numbers in Cardigan Bay, the Celtic Sea and the Bristol Channel during about March to July and was one of the staples of the fishing industry of Milford Haven and other ports. One of the most famous summer fishing grounds for mackerel is the area extending from St. Davids Head southwards around the coast into the Bristol Channel. The Bristol Channel acts as a vast funnel for the annual elver migration and also contained many other fish species. Its shores are well renowned for their flatfish, particularly sole.

A potentially very significant recent observation has been that the increasing numbers of intrusive warmth-demanding, even tropical, marine species recorded off the coasts of south-west Britain since the early 1980s (McCarthy, 1989; Gledhill, 1990). Devon and Cornwall lie close to a marine biogeographic boundary which can move northwards in response to only small shifts in water temperature with the subsequent substitution of warmer for cooler marine species, and the addition of others. Such changes affect a wide range of creatures, from plankton, worms and jellyfish to crustacea and large fish. Although these observations are thought to be symptomatic of a supposed modern 'greenhouse effect', they should perhaps alert us also to the possibility of similar fluctuations during the climatic optimum of the late Mesolithic.

Whether or not such fluctuations were significant for Mesolithic fishermen is unknown. A considerable abundance and variety of marine resources seems assured, however, although it has to be admitted that archaeological evidence for fishing from Welsh shores is entirely lacking (as it is also from rivers). No fish remains of significance (except perhaps skate: Jacobi, 1979) are recorded from the refuse accumulation at Westward Ho! In Wales, however, this lack of data undoubtedly reflects the bias in site preservation, and it would be surprising were sea fishing not a part of the late Mesolithic economy.

If so, then this would most likely have taken place in the spring and summer months when many fish species tend to move in-shore. Flat-fish and some other types could, however, have been taken throughout the year. As for river and estuary fishing, the technology required can vary from simple lures to the deployment of boats, traps, and nets. A primitive form of hook used into the present century in long-line fishing on the coasts of west Wales is made from thorns hardened by baking (Matheson, 1929). With this admittedly remote association in mind, one can note the presence of charcoal of *Prunus* and *Pomoideae* (possibly, therefore, of Blackthorn and Hawthorn) at The Nab Head Site II.

The role of sea fish in the Mesolithic economy is rarely visible in Britain, and may be limited to specialized task sites such as those on Oronsay (Mellars, 1987). The sporadic accumulation of shell-fish middens both here and abroad has, however, given rise to much speculation as to the importance of this food source. In Wales, in the absence of any substantial middens, the occurrence of 'limpet scoops' from exclusively coastal contexts has been cited as evidence for the exploitation of shell-fish. The only record of a possible Mesolithic shell accumulation from Wales is that made by Leach (1916) where both estuarine and rock mollusca were noted in Nanna's Cave, Caldey. Although the archaeological associations of this deposit are unclear, Jacobi (1980b) has tentatively placed the formation of its enclosing stalagmite to the Atlantic period, or at some time after *c.* 7,000 BP.

Some forty species of shell-fish were recorded from the midden at Morton on the east coast of Scotland, although the main types associated with such Mesolithic deposits are limpets, oysters, mussels and cockles. At Morton, 53% (by weight) of the mollusc sample was composed of the cockle (Coles, 1971). Using stable isotope analysis and growth-ring analysis of mollusc shells, Deith (1983, 1986, 1989) has been able to hypothesize that the site was visited at several times of the year and that the shellfish were collected only opportunistically whilst exploiting the local shore for lithic raw materials. Deep-sea fishing for cod was also taking place.

Nearer the present study area, oysters, mussels, limpets, winkles and Scrobicularia shells have been recorded from Westward Ho! (Jacobi, 1979) The recent examination of this midden (Balaam et. al., 1987) found no evidence for the presence of oysters noted by earlier authors (eg Rogers, 1946). It is possible that these came originally from Roman or medieval deposits which are now known to be present on the beach as well.

Cockles, mussels and oysters have featured strongly in recent Welsh fisheries, and most of the coastline is suitable for the growth of one type or other. 'Farming' has probably inflated the quantities collected in recent times but there can be little doubt that such fisheries were founded on prodigious natural shellfish beds, mostly in estuaries. Gathering and processing cockles was once a substantial local industry along the estuaries of Carmarthen Bay where up to 53,000 hundredweight could be collected annually (Jenkins, 1977). Mussels can be found on both 'hard' and 'soft' shores all along the coast, but have been cropped particularly vigorously on estuaries such as the Conwy in north Wales. Oysters also once flourished in Welsh estuaries, especially Milford Haven, and oyster beds were also known at Caldey and Stackpole. In the Swansea area alone up to 9,000,000 were taken annually in the late nineteenth century, before stocks declined. In about 1914 some 900 hundredweight of winkles could be picked from Dyfed beaches before being sent off to London (Matheson, 1929).

Relatively warmer winter and summer temperatures during the late Mesolithic will have been of advantage to shell-fish beds, particularly as these are susceptible to frosts. Cockles can be gathered throughout the year, although mussels are best picked in autumn and winter when they have put on most weight. Oysters are at their best and most accessible during the low spring tides of May and June (Walne, 1970).

Although the nutritional value of shellfish is low, their great productivity at certain places and times of the year may have occasionally exerted a control over subsistence strategies, especially if other resources were scarce. The economics of prehistoric shellfish gathering has been the subject of much discussion in the literature (eg. Bailey, 1975, 1978; Osborn, 1977; Rowley-Conwy, 1984; Erlandson, 1988). Bailey (ibid) has estimated that in terms of calorie return, one red deer is the equivalent of 52,267 oysters, whilst the mean calorific requirements of one person for a day can be met by about 700 oysters, 400 limpets, or 1400 cockles. For the predominantly rocky shores of Wales Jacobi (1980b) has argued that the demands made on local shellfish beds might in most cases have been too great for more than brief episodes of cropping. Whilst this would certainly seem probable on the coastlines considered earlier in this chapter - that is, around the St. Davids peninsula - any such proposition would require further testing before it is found to be applicable to the potentially very rich soft or estuarine shell-fish habitats of other parts of south-west Wales. The assessment of the role of all marine resources at this time is much hampered by the loss to sea level rise of just those sites which will have contained the relevant data. A more thorough reconstruction of contemporary coastal morphology will also be required before the contribution of shell-fish and other resources can be fully ascertained.

The list of other motives which might have influenced the observed coastal site distribution does not end with putative shell-heaps, and can be extended to include sea mammals, birds and their eggs, crustacea, seaweed and shoreline plants. With one exception, these can all be considered as probably ancillary to the more major food and raw material resources that have already been discussed.

Evidence for the exploitation of birds during the Mesolithic and later prehistoric periods is abundant, but mainly available only from Scandinavian sites (Grigson, 1989; Rowley-Conwy and Zvelebil, 1989). Most examples are of the exploitation of coastal migratory species and several sites are interpreted as specifically oriented towards bird capture. Such evidence is not limited just to coastal areas, however, or necessarily only to seasonal migrants, as demonstrated by avifauna from Danish inland sites (Grigson, 1989). In Britain, birds were apparently taken at Morton and other Scottish locations (Coles, 1971; Lacaille, 1954). The bird remains identified at the earlier site of Star Carr may be incidental to the human occupation there (Legge and Rowley-Conwy, 1988, 39).

Birds and their eggs are known to have been of importance historically, although the amounts quoted for St. Kilda in the north Atlantic are no doubt exceptional. Here, as many

as 40,000 puffins, fulmars and gannets might be taken in a single year, and about 60,000 eggs consumed in a week (Steel, 1977). Whilst these prodigious figures may be unrealistic for most other areas, it can safely be assumed that sea birds were taken for purposes such as food, oils, arrow fletches and clothing. Even today the cliffs and offshore islands of western Dyfed support large populations of seabirds - for instance, 60,000 pairs of gannets nest annually on Grassholm, making this small island the fourth largest such colony in the North Atlantic (John, 1976). Crustacea (Lacaille, 1954), seaweed (Clark, 1950) and shoreline plants (Bonsall, 1981) may only have played a minor part by comparison.

The exception referred to above, however, is that of sea mammals and above all, seals. Although whales, porpoises and dolphins may have been exploited as and when fortuitous strandings allowed, these occasions were not predictable and were probably infrequent. Seals, however, congregate in large numbers on rocky and sandy coastlines, and their breeding behaviour makes them very vulnerable to human predation. Clark (1946, 1952, 1975, 1983) has outlined much of the evidence for seal hunting in prehistory and has shown that this was significant on some later Mesolithic sites in Scandinavia, and intensified there in the Neolithic and Bronze Age. The evidence from Britain is poor, but this may in part be accounted for by the drowning of sites by eustatic sea level rise, and also by the fact that seal bones, do not preserve well in any case (Grigson, 1987). Their remains are known from Dalkey Island on the Irish coast (Woodman, 1978, Table X), and also from some of the Obanian sites. On Oronsay, faunal analyses of samples from the Cnoc Coig midden have shown the presence of grey seal and common seal amongst a total of 363 seal bones and teeth from the recent excavations (Grigson, 1987). Grey seals seem to have been the more frequent quarry and the minimum representation of 9 of these suggests that a wide range of age classes were taken, with a preference for breeding populations of adults and young pups.

Most of the present-day population of about 101,000 grey seals found off the British Isles occur around the Hebridean coastline. Outside Scotland, Wales supports the largest numbers of grey seal: some 150 around Anglesey and about 2,350 around the islands of Skomer and Ramsey, off west Wales (King, 1983). That so many remain here is an indication that at one time these coasts probably supported very many more of these creatures, which are otherwise so susceptible to human interference.

Although grey seals can be hunted at most times of the year, they are most easily taken during the few weeks in September and October when the pups are shore-bound and are being suckled by attendant adult females. A rocky coastline with cave and intermittent beaches for hauling out is ideal for this, and is typified by the shoreline below many of the sites under discussion. At a 5 or 2.5 km radius (Rowley-Conwy, 1983) many of the find-spots would have been within range of at least some sealing potential. The seals can be easily killed by bludgeoning when they are helpless and a great many can be dispatched at once. Clark (1950) notes that about 50 seals were often clubbed at a time in a single cave in the Faröes (citing Debes, 1676). Grey seal pups at only three weeks old can yield 12 - 18 kg of meat and 20 - 30 kg of blubber, in addition to excellent pelts. Any sizeable killing would therefore be highly productive of basic food and raw materials, and would necessitate a considerable investment in subsequent butchery and processing. Both the kill and primary butchering sites will have been lost to sea level encroachment, but it is legitimate to wonder whether many clifftop lithic scatters do not represent a major preoccupation with the secondary processing of seal products.

Quite apart from the high calorific return from seal meat and fat, their skins would have been much valued for any number of purposes of which incorporation into tents, ropes, clothing, harnesses, boots, bags, buoys and boats are just some. Movius was the first to suggest that 'rubbers' (bevelled pebbles) were 'probably for the preparation of seal skins for shelters or clothing' (1942, 183), and this has been reiterated by Jacobi (1979, 1980b) who has emphasized the apparent correlation between find-spots of such tools in Cornwall, Devon and west Wales with the present and probable past distribution of seal rookeries. This association may perhaps have been relevant to the Channel Islands as well, and is of course well documented for Scottish littoral sites.

The discussion in Chapter VI has already dwelt at some length on the possible function of bevelled pebbles and other ground stone tools, and it was proposed that amongst the foremost of these were roles in skin-working and perhaps also wood-working. They could have been effectively used on seal and other animal skins and might have been combined with wood-working in the construction of structures such as boats and living quarters. Sea-going boats, in particular, whether like kayaks, canoes or curraghs, would have been lined by hides or skins, and in the latter case seal skin is naturally well-adapted.

9. Summary
Owing to the limitations of the evidence this chapter has of necessity been largely of a descriptive nature, concerned firstly with lithic finds, and secondly with probabilities concerning the subsistence base for which these may have been adapted. Recent fieldwork, combined with excavation at The Nab Head, shows a remarkable density of large lithic scatters apparently confined on, or close to, the present clifftops. The retouched components of these artefact scatters demonstrate an overall similarity one to another which, in the absence of any detailed chronology, suggests that an assumption of approximate contemporaneity may not be totally unreasonable. Within this general framework of a local late Mesolithic, small-scale structural variability can be identified between collections. This can be seen most clearly in the relative proportions of burins, truncated

pieces, denticulates and microliths. A dependence on surface collection and only very restricted excavation does, however, severely limit any attempted interpretation of these data.

The area of many of these lithic scatters, frequently extending over thousands of square metres, and their location along a coastal lowland might, using the parameters defined by Mellars (1976b), suggest the existence of autumn-winter residential bases. Tool-kits would seem to suggest the manufacture and use of hunting/fishing equipment, alongside denticulates, scrapers, truncated pieces and bevelled pebbles used in a variety of unidentified, but perhaps specialist processing tasks.

The exploitation territories of these sites, of whatever radius, will include tidal strips and a substantial proportion of each catchment would extend over open sea. The indented character of western Dyfed's shore, accentuated by St. Bride's Bay and Milford Haven, means that many sites are peninsular locations which, at a radius of 10 km, would incorporate coastline well in excess of this distance. Llanunwas and The Nab Head Site II would, for instance, take in the entirety of the St. Davids peninsula and the Skomer peninsula, respectively; the sites at Dale and Castlemartin to the north and south of Milford Haven, would also incorporate large parts of the approaches and surroundings of this major inlet.

Insufficient data are available to choose whether or not these find-spots fell within some cycle of population movement which correlated with the differing seasonal availability of various food and raw material resources. Research on inland and upland sites seems to confirm that these areas were indeed exploited, and might suggest that the same peoples also made use of the coastal zone.

Consideration of food and raw materials available to human groups using this coastal zone reveals a wide spectrum of potential resources. A warming oceanic climate and the favourable westerly aspect of most coastlands would have provided optimum conditions for a range of flora and fauna already brought together at the interface of both marine and terrestrial environments. Whilst some resources could have been taken at any time of year, a period of relative dearth might have been during the mid-late summer months and it is perhaps then that inland and upland hunting and fishing sorties may have taken place. It is of course possible that major residential sites, dependant on land mammals, plant foods and salmon fishing, remain to be discovered inland. If this were so, the coastal find-spots might instead be peripheral task locations where inshore fishing, sealing, flint, or egg collecting were practised at appropriate seasons. The construction of boats to ease the transport of both people and materials may also have influenced site location. The very large size of the lithic scatters could perhaps be better explained as the overlap of debris from repeated re-use of the same locations where access to fresh water and the shore was most convenient.

Without any alternative, these arguments are necessarily deterministic in approach and cannot at present allow for any other influences on settlement patterns. Variables which cannot presently be accounted for are those hinted at by sociological, stylistic and 'psychic' factors. The database is at present too restricted, for instance, to allow interpretations of either raw material provenance or stylistic embellishment. The relevance of these to any 'social territories', population movements or exchange systems that could be superimposed on environmentally 'determined' patterns also has yet to be ascertained.

Least quantifiable of all are the 'psychic' (sensu Clark, 1975) influences on settlement and other activity, and it would be surprising if folk memory did not occasionally condition the use of sites over substantial timespans, when their original uses had been forgotten or abandoned in favour of others. It may, therefore, be no simple coincidence that The Nab Head appears to have been a distinctive site early in the Holocene and was then re-visited again and again throughout the Mesolithic, and later still. Similarly, the superimposition of Mesolithic scatters at Penpant, Pointzcastle and Cwm Bach may point to a continuity explicable not merely as the residues of itinerants who had been quarrying the shingle for flint. Perhaps such 'continuity' extended even further forwards in time when it is suggested that these same scatters were then quarried in their own right by the users of scalar cores. Is it even too far-fetched to imagine a correlation between certain Mesolithic flint scatters and later prehistoric burial and ritual sites?

10. The end of the Mesolithic
In Chapter V, it was suggested that a 'narrow blade' technology may have remained in use in Wales until *c.* 5,300 BP, a dating prompted by the apparent association of backed bladelets with a pig skeleton of that date found within forehore peat on Lydstep beach. Much more speculatively, the possibility was noted that, at two standard deviations, this dating overlapped with the still later determination of 4,950 ±80 BP for charcoal found with 'narrow blade' material at The Nab Head Site II. This latter association, if genuine, would therefore extend this technology even further into a time increasingly dominated by a food- producing economy and the trappings of the so-called 'Neolithic'. Indeed, the first appearance of a Neolithic archaeological record across the British Isles as a whole had already occurred by this time (Herne, 1988, 23).

The unfortunate Lydstep pig provides rare and very enigmatic evidence for possible interaction between hunters and husbandry. Because its dating falls close to instances of earliest Welsh Neolithic activity (at Llandegai and Coygan: see Fig. 6.21), one may conjecture with Lewis (forthcoming) that the animal was not wild, but domesticated. In apparent support of this suggestion is the size of the M3 molar (39.10 mm), rather smaller than would be expected in a wild specimen (Armour-Chelu, pers. comm. in Lewis, forthcoming). The pig might therefore conceivably be a Neolithic escapee fallen prey to, or even poached by, an indigenous hunter. Such incidents presumably happened. To be even more speculative still, one might wonder if the leaf-shaped arrowhead found with the microliths and pebble tools at The Nab Head might not be the ineffective shot of a farmer into an animal later brought down by hunters.

That such guesswork can be taken seriously highlights the level of ignorance with which we are equipped in approaching this crucial period in Mesolithic and Neolithic affairs. Much recent literature has been devoted to the challenging need to describe the background and mechanisms of the transformation from assumed highly mobile hunter/gathers to assumed sedentary pastoralists and agriculturists (for example: Clark, 1980; Dennell, 1983; Binford, 1983; Rowley-Conwy, 1983, 1984; Price and Brown, 1985; Zvelebil and Rowley-Conwy, 1984, 1986; Blankholm, 1987; Thomas, 1988; Williams, 1989; Edwards, 1988).

The lure of attempting to explain this 'most important transition of the history of the economic life of people' (Edwards, 1988, 255) has thus lead to the construction of a range of interpretative models. For Britain, much of this discussion is quite out of proportion to the available data (Kinnes, 1988) and none of the resulting interpretative endeavour has been directed specifically to Wales. Above all, it has to be stressed that the level of appropriate data is extremely poor. It is not intended here, therefore, to review these issues at great length, but instead to draw only on certain suggestive aspects which may turn out to have some relevance for the latter area.

The thread running through much of the discussion concerning the Mesolithic/Neolithic interface is a reaction against the idea of a nomadic lifestyle being interrupted or superseded by incoming 'Neolithic' peoples and/or practices: instead, the 'complexity' of some indigenous pre-agricultural societies has been stressed, leading to the suggestion that social and economic organization amongst these might have allowed for the independent and possibly precocious initiation of food production. An alternative suggestion has been that although sedentary hunter-gatherers were capable of absorbing a farming mode this may only have been adopted after prolonged contact with farmer groups, for instance at times of economic stress.

A pre-condition for sedentism in hunter/gatherer communities is the co-existence of many food resources whose successive exploitation throughout the year would prevent local depletion and allow permanent occupation of a base site. Coastal zones are frequently quoted as providing just these favourable conditions.

Once such a level of organization has become established it may then display several traits characteristic of sedentary behaviour which may be recognizable in the archaeological record. These include, for example, the use of storage facilities, substantial domestic structures, and burial in defined areas. Permanently settled groups might have little reason to adopt agricultural methods, although contact and exchange with farmers could well have taken place (Jennbert, 1984). Dependence on farming practice may only have become necessary if, for any reason, the sole reliance on natural resources came under stress. Such stress, either from failure of a food source, or in combination with population increase, may have stimulated social complexity still further. At whatever stage in the transition process, this has been argued to be expressed by increased territoriality, as marked by defined burial areas, and stylistic change. Throughout such a postulated transition the significance of technological change may be relatively slight, rendered so by the already versatile Mesolithic technology, perhaps leavened with exchanged 'prestige' items.

Most of the fuel for such model-building is derived from the relatively rich archaeological and economic data available from continental European sites, especially Scandinavia, and from ethnographic analogy. For insular Britain, there is as yet no specific evidence for sedentism, although circumstantial data would suggest that conditions in parts of the island were capable of supporting a settled Mesolithic population. Jacobi (1979) has already pointed to the optimal environmental conditions prevailing in the South-West Peninsula and has more recently (1987) confirmed that these could have supported a sedentary mode of existence. As earlier discussion has shown, no less a 'Garden of Eden' (Binford, 1983) exists in west Wales where like topography and environmental conditions also share an equivalent archaeological record to that of Devon and Cornwall (Berridge and Roberts, 1986).

The enormous potential resource base of the Welsh coastal ecotone needs no further stressing. If the distribution of resources within this system is examined in more detail it becomes apparent that their maximum coincidence is achieved in and around estuaries, fully in keeping with the view of Perlman (1980, 283) that:

'estuarine environments, particularly those above 40 degrees latitude provide a subsistence base that minimises mobility, maintains higher population densities by providing a number of high return rates and buffering resources, and involves less risk.'

Within west Wales, one's attention is drawn of course to Milford Haven which, even with a late Mesolithic sea level, would have been a substantial estuary. The many potentially available resources here will have included oyster beds (Matheson, 1929) which, as for the Ertebölle (Rowley-Conwy, 1984), could have been a substantial influence on the location of adjacent base sites.

Aggradation within this drowned valley system following the final adjustment of sea level and the increased sediment load induced by cultivation will, however, have obscured any suspected traces of Mesolithic sedentism within the estuary system. The lithic scatters which do survive, though, seem to concentrate by and large on clifftops and near beaches which are within range either of Milford Haven or smaller inlets. As already tentatively proposed, these locations may be peripheral task sites visited from more substantial permanent or semi-permanent residential sites inland, or, as might now be suggested, from estuarine areas such as Milford Haven. The use of boats in movement between sites would in this case seem a probable supposition. Various fish runs both in the estuary and off the coast are likely to have been sequential (Owen, 1603: quoted above) and, with other resources, could have been exploited in succession from both base and task sites. Observed lithic variability may, in turn, be a reflection of differing resource goals at specific task-oriented locations.

Given that communities indigenous to west Wales could have been in a 'complex' or sedentary mode, then, following Zvelebil and Rowley-Conwy (1986), one might suggest that the emergence of a farming economy might have been delayed relative to its adoption in other parts of the country. There is as yet no adequate chronology to support this notion, nor is there any economic data to suggest a possible trigger mechanism that might have necessitated the uptake of a more 'Neolithic' subsistence option.

That food resources were capable of unpredictable fluctuation has been emphasized by Rowley-Conwy and Zvelebil in their recent case study of salmon fishing records for north Wales (Rowley-Conwy and Zvelebil, 1989). One response to such uncertainty would be to resort to storage - a probable concomitant of which would, in turn, be frequent food surplus, itself a major factor capable of furthering both sedentism and social differentiation (ibid., 56).

Other unexpected depletions might be caused, for instance, by over-cropping of certain resources, or by frosts (Jacobi, 1979, 83). If a decline in salinity and oysters precipitated agriculture in the Ertebölle, then oyster-catchers (Haematopus ostralegus) could equally be invoked for Wales. These voracious eaters of several shellfish species were estimated to have devoured no less than 600,000,000 cockles in only four months (December-March) in 1961-2 in the Burry Inlet (Davidson, 1967). Even if these birds were present in the Mesolithic, and indeed even if there was any evidence for a dependence on shellfish, one might yet wonder if any one population crash would not be adequately buffered by alternatives other than agriculture.

The argument for a delay in the appearance of agriculture amongst settled hunter-gatherers must necessarily also be weighed against the alternative possibility that its uptake was, instead, early or precocious. Support for this is mainly derived from palynological data indicative of cereal cultivation and/or pastoral activity in contexts pre-dating the elm decline at c. 5,100 BP (Edwards and Hirons, 1984; Edwards, 1988). Both methodological and interpretative problems attach to the recognition of such pollen data, however, and firm association with cultural materials is still lacking (Kinnes 1988; Edwards, 1988). Actual cultigen remains (or grain impressions) have not certainly been recovered from contexts earlier than the Neolithic enclosure at Hembury, Devon, with dates of c. 5,280 BP - 5,100 BP.

In chronological terms, apart from the above suggestive palynological data, there are a number of early radiocarbon determinations for Neolithic remains (Zvelebil and Rowley-Conwy, 1986, fig 3; Williams, 1989, fig. 1; Edwards, 1988, fig. 1). Very few of these, however, stand up to critical examination (Kinnes, 1988, table 1.1). A possible exception is the series of four apparently unimpeachable dates for specifically Neolithic cultural material at Ballynagilly, Ulster (Smith et al., 1971; ApSimon 1976b). These range from c. 5,745 BP - 5,500 BP and are derived from two pits containing pottery and a hearth associated with pottery (plain shouldered ware, or Carinated Bowls). Such early dates for this type of pottery, however, are considered inexplicably anomalous - later dates from the same site being more appropriate - and are dismissed 'as currently unsupported and uninterpretable' (Herne, 1988, 22).

Whatever its timing, and whether or not indigenous sedentism prevailed, there can be no doubt that certain elements of the Neolithic 'package' were imported from overseas. Both the concept and the genetic means of animal husbandry and domestic crops probably arrived from the Continent, or indirectly from Ireland, by boat.

There is little doubt that late Mesolithic peoples could handle boats and that this may have been integral to coastwise settlement and exploitation (see above). The acknowledged later importance of the western seaways (Fox, 1947; Crawford, 1936; Bowen, 1977) could be projected backwards in time into our period and, with Clark (1977; 1980), one could also emphasize the attraction of deep sea fisheries in encouraging trans-marine contact. Clark (1977) has pointed out that hake and mackerel shoals could have been followed in their northward migrations, with the consequent transmitting of people and ideas to distant landfalls. Kinnes (1984) has emphasized the speed with which such transmissions can take place by coastal hopping.

The archaeological evidence for the appearance on western British coasts of certain apparently incipient Neolithic traits (such as burial in stone-lined cists), but combined with a Mesolithic seaside economy (middens sometimes with domesticates), is debated (Ashbee, 1982; Burenhult, 1984; Mercer, 1986; Woodman, 1986). Just as the Scilly Isles, with their 'entrance graves', project into the path of any northward sea movements toward the Irish Sea, so does the Dyfed peninsula, but there is as yet no clear indication from this latter area of any specifically trans-marine contact in either the late Mesolithic or the early Neolithic. This can hardly count as negative evidence for such contact, however, for lack both of relevant excavated sites and chronological data. Certainly, as for Bohuslän (Clark,

1977), the coastwise distribution of megalithic tombs such as the supposedly early portal dolmens (Herity, 1970, fig. 9) around parts of the Irish Sea is strongly supportive of marine contact, hinting at earlier ancestry. A coastal affluence engendered by fishery, and perhaps sealing, may have encouraged this quite as much as any 'megalithic missionaries' or adventurers.

It is much to be regretted, for instance, that most of the megalithic tombs that cluster in western Dyfed (Savory, 1980, fig. 5.4) remain unclassified and undated. The date of 5,240 ±150 BP (NPL-223: Houlder, 1976) from a settlement feature below the henge at Llandegai, Gwynedd, certainly implies that Wales had assimilated a Neolithic technology quite as early as its introduction into southern England. The distribution of Neolithic artefacts and monuments in Wales (Savory, 1980, fig. 5.2) illustrates that, despite the evidence for exploitation into interior valleys and uplands, activity still has a clear bias towards coastal lowland margins. One may wonder, with Savory (ibid.) and, in the allied case for Cornwall, with Mercer (1986), whether such a distribution reflects the uptake of animal husbandry introduced to societies in which transhumance and clearance were already a way of life. Such a proposal would, however, still require reconciliation with the lack of evidence for substantial forest clearance on western Welsh coasts (Donald, 1987; Lewis, forthcoming).

Also arguably within the sphere of influence of an hypothetical 'Irish Sea Province', but at its outermost northern limits, are the 'Obanian' middens such as those on Oronsay, formed at a time (c. 6,000 BP - 5,000 BP) coincident with Neolithic activity elsewhere in Britain (see Fig. 6.21). Without the excavation of more southerly shoreline sites, where organic remains are preserved intact, it will not be possible to detect satisfactory links with these Scottish sites (and their Irish counterparts). The scalar core technology by which the 'Obanian' is characterized, although it may have Scottish antecedants (Wickham-Jones, 1990), would appear to occur in Wales later than local 'narrow blade' technologies. The time interval between the use of these different stone-working techniques might have been relatively slight there, however, as lithic scatters deriving from the 'narrow blade' technology were still accessible as a source of raw material for scalar core reduction.

From all the foregoing it is apparent that there is little, if any, secure data on which to base anything more than guesswork concerning the timing and character of this critical transition. This is tantilizingly so for Wales where it has been argued that conditions favoured indigenous sedentism. What little evidence there is, and this includes the apparently late dating of 'narrow blade' technology at The Nab Head and Lydstep, possibly favours a retarded initiation of agriculture. It would be surprising, too, at a time when precise definitions of 'Mesolithic' and 'Neolithic' become blurred, if the two were not inextricably coeval and undetectable in current archaeological data. The puzzling presence of ground stone axes perfected at The Nab Head by *c.* 5,000 BP, if not much earlier, must raise the speculation that there was a level of technological advancement here, belied by the apparent 'decadence' of the clifftop chipped flint and stone industries - and also the 'impoverished ancestral technology' claimed for southern England (Jacobi, 1982). Local manufacture, or even 'invention', of axes from appropriately shaped pebbles would perhaps seem more probable in this case than any 'fertile gift' exchange from outsiders (Jennbert, 1984).

It would seem that 'the end of the Mesolithic' is presently indefinable. Perhaps now we are no better off, sixty years on, than that earlier explorer of The Nab Head, J. P. Gordon- Williams, who dismissed the problem thus:

'Theories of the hiatus or mesolithic and all the early neolithics are in a painfully chaotic condition' (Gordon-Williams, 1926, 110).

More positively, it seems reasonable to conclude, for the time being anyway, that the stimulus and means for rapid long-distance contact existed amongst potentially 'complex' littoral Mesolithic communities. Early colonisation and exchange of exotic items of 'Neolithic' type may well have taken place sporadically well in advance of establishment of a formal Neolithic. In parts of Wales this may have been rather later than elsewhere. The challenge is now to expand the archaeological record and to recognize within it when, where and how these crucial changes took place.

If the foregoing chapters have been justified, it is hoped that it has been so by their description of new data for parts of the Pleistocene and Holocene archaeological record for Wales. This new information has been integrated with a review of the pre-existing database and the whole presented in an attempt at an up-to-date assessment.

Within the Pleistocene, first appraisal of the total known lithic material from The Hoyle's Mouth has allowed recognition of an early Upper Palaeolithic component, identifying this cave as only third 'Aurignacian' find-spot in Britain. It is suggested, however, that the majority of the archaeological finds from here are Lateglacial in age. By analogy with similar material from Gough's (New) Cave, Somerset, occupation at The Hoyle's Mouth is believed to have taken place close to the thermal peak of the Lateglacial interstadial. The definition of a 'Creswellian' can now be restricted to artefact residues from this time.

Consideration has also been given to other finds of apparent Lateglacial age in Wales, with special attention to those from Caldey Island, Dyfed. Indeed, the early prehistory of Caldey, once of considerable richness, is given recurring emphasis and much material from the island is formally described and illustrated for the first time. As is the case for all Welsh caves, though, surviving data is inadequate for all but the most basic attempts at reconstruction. Further Lateglacial finds are identified, however, some of which - notably 'Penknife' points - have been tentatively allocated later than occupation at The Hoyle's Mouth.

The greater part of the thesis, though, has centred on the period after 10,000 BP. Most important in this has been a re- examination of the Mesolithic archaeology of Daylight Rock on Caldey and, on the mainland, of The Nab Head, and other areas. Over 120,000 artefacts from some 40 sites have been documented. Fresh samples of lithic material excavated from Caldey and The Nab Head have allowed a first definition of both early and late Mesolithic activity in this part of Wales. Not only have the original 'sites' been profitably re-investigated, but at The Nab Head Site II an entirely new and distinctive late Mesolithic find-spot has been sampled.

Most important of all has been the implementation of an AMS radiocarbon dating programme aimed at establishing a chronological framework for the Welsh Mesolithic. The earlier 'broad blade' technology has now been shown to date from at least c. 9,200 BP in south-west Wales. A further very significant result has been the secure dating of the first appearance of a 'narrow blade' technology for Wales to c. 8,700 BP, at Prestatyn, Clwyd. This dating

places the appearance of the late Mesolithic here as early as anywhere in Britain.

The late Mesolithic is further characterized following excavations at The Nab Head Site II. Lithic material from here has provided a foundation for the documentation and assessment of local surface collections most of which appear to be of 'narrow blade' type. Fresh distribution maps bring the pattern of find- spots up-to-date, and for the first time variability in artefact composition between lithic scatters has been identified. A disappointment, despite the application of AMS dating, has been the difficulty of establishing any developmental framework within the late Mesolithic and at its termination. At present little can be concluded about this save that isolated dates indicate some kind of activity throughout the period. Typological evolution at this time remains poorly understood and heavily dependant on speculations from elsewhere.

In the absence of preserved organic material and without much relevant palaeoecological research, discussion of Mesolithic subsistence still relies largely on extrapolation from historical and modern data. Examination of the latter suggests that, for the later period at least, western coasts may have been capable of supporting relatively affluent littoral communities and that these may therefore have been inclined towards social complexity and sedentism. Lack of appropriate field research, however, does not allow any real appreciation of inland settlement or of its relationship to that on the coast.

The inception of food production is viewed with circumspection, but that it was delayed in west Wales relative to other parts of Britain is cautiously suggested on the evidence of dating at Lydstep and The Nab Head. At present it is not possible to refute the longevity of a 'narrow blade' technology at the latter site, lasting to c. 5,000 BP. This time of economic and social, as well as technological, transition is acknowledged to be extremely complex, and demands clarification.

Indeed, rather than risk further repetition in summarising what has gone before, it might be preferable, as it is also customary, to offer in conclusion some thoughts on directions for future research.

A recurrent theme and one that often excites most interest is that of change, whether in terms of cultural transition, interface or hiatus. At least four diverse instances exist within the timespan covered by this thesis: at the Late Devesian glacial maximum (change from earlier to later Upper Palaeolithic), the Devensian/Flandrian boundary (change from Palaeolithic to Mesolithic), and within the Flandrian, the change between 'broad- and 'narrow blade' technologies and, finally, the Mesolithic-Neolithic transition. As the explanation of man's part in, and response to, the process of change is the raison d'etre of archaeology, it is perhaps in these four areas that research effort might seem most attractive. Change, by its very nature, is usually elusive in the archaeological record and the instances quoted above are no exception. Each is already the subject of at least some research initiative although the potential contribution from Welsh archaeology remains largely unexploited.

Leaving generality aside, a first priority would seem to be the construction of a more exacting chronological framework than has hitherto been possible. Undoubtedly, AMS radiocarbon dating should be more widely applied in all periods - utilizing the benefits of the technique (eg small sample size) yet with an awareness of pitfalls (eg poor sample integrity). The use of TL might be applied more often for the earlier periods, or when the radiocarbon record is especially misleading.

The advantages of AMS dating for the Upper Palaeolithic have been made clear following results now available from several English find-spots, including caves such as Gough's, Kent's Cavern and Pin Hole. This potential should be more fully extended to Wales, preferably allied to full multi-disciplinary investigation of new open air or cave locations. If appropriate sites cannot be found then renewed excavation of existing cave deposits, and analysis of museum archives, is needed. Such a programme is already under way for The Hoyle's Mouth but other caves such as Cathole and Priory Farm probably still contain intact deposits - although these are liable to remain sacrosanct and protected from destructive excavation.

Whilst AMS dating has already clarified something of the archaeological record for Paviland, more dates on human and artefactual material from this cave are required. It is time, too, for a reappraisal of the artefact collection in the hope that episodes of earlier Upper Palaeolithic occupation might now be more readily definable than formerly. As part of this and other lithic analyses, a more detailed research into the petrology and provenance of stone raw materials would benefit the understanding of exploitation patterns and inter-site relationships during periods of lower sea level.

Coming forward into the Holocene, AMS dating will be no less important. In contrast to the later Palaeolithic, it can be expected that more datable material will become available for sampling and that more fresh sites are likely to be found to supply this. Throughout the Mesolithic, there is an urgent need to extend fieldwork in Wales away from the coasts,

where most efforts have so far been concentrated. Only when inland sites have been investigated can models of seasonal movement be justified. In the earlier period, as for the preceding Lateglacial, a fuller chronological definition is required to allow a more confident placement of contemporary shorelines. The movement of lithic raw materials at this time will be of value in establishing at least local territorial relationships. One can only hope that the study of items such as beads and perhaps the discovery of early Mesolithic inhumations may, one day, widen perspectives towards the regional or European level to which this period in Wales appears to belong.

For whatever period, archaeological endeavour will be best served by the discovery and investigation of waterlogged sites, or sites where at least some fraction of their organic component survives. Wales has seen much palaeo-ecological research but a crucial failing of most of this work has been the lack of a direct juxtaposition with in situ archaeological material. Paramount must be the location and detailed examination of sites at which both artefacts, environmental and subsistence data are preserved together. Access to the full range of chronological and biogeographic data from even one well stratified site would be of very considerable advance on the present situation. More ideally still, such information is needed from a broad spectrum of locations.

Whatever hope there may be for understanding late Mesolithic society and economy and its relationship to the local emergence of agriculture must depend on such discoveries. 'The Irish Sea must have been an important means of communication in both the Mesolithic and Neolithic periods, *and research in this area, in Ireland, England and Wales, is clearly critical for an understanding of the whole process of the emergence and development of the Neolithic*' (Whittle, 1989, 281: emphasis added). The potential of foreshore deposits in this context has already been realized, although the practical difficulties of studying these are considerable. There is nevertheless scope for continuing effort in this direction and one should be alert and prepared to make use of sudden chance exposures at foreshore sites such as those now lost to us at Lydstep and Frainslake. In addition, coastlines need to be thoroughly searched and geomorphologically analysed to identify specific areas with potential. In particular, the depositional environments and associated taphonomies of local estuaries might well repay closer investigation in the hope that concealed sites can be detected. The discovery of cemeteries should not be considered too remote a possibility.

Allen, D.; 1975
Brenig Valley excavations, *Archaeology in Wales*, 15, 32.

Althin, c. A.; 1954
The chronology of the Stone Age settlement of Scania, Sweden. Acta Archaeologia Lundensia, 1.

Anderson, J.; 1895
Notice of a cave recently discovered at Oban, containing human remains, and a refuse-heap of shells and bones of animals, and stone and bone implements. *Proceedings of the Society of Antiquaries of Scotland*, 29, 211 - 30.

Anderson, J.; 1898
Notes on the content of a small cave or rock shelter at Druimvargie, Oban; and of three shell-mounds on Oronsay. *Proceedings of the Society of Antiquaries of Scotland*, 32, 298 - 313.

Atkinson, T. c., Briffa, K. R., Coope, G. R.; 1987
Seasonal temperatures in Britain during the past 22,000 years, reconstructed using beetle remains. *Nature*, 325, 587 - 592.

Andresen, J. M., Byrd, B. F., Elson, M. D., McGuire, R. H., Mendoza, R.G., Staski, E White, J. P.; 1981
The Deer Hunters: Star Carr reconsidered. *World Archaeology*, 13, 31 - 46.

ApSimon, A.; 1955
King Arthur's Cave section and plans, unpublished. University of Bristol Speleological Society Museum.

ApSimon, A.; 1976a
A View of the Early Prehistory of Wales., in G. c. Boon and J. M. Lewis (eds) *Welsh Antiquity*, National Museum of Wales.

ApSimon, A.: 1976b
Ballynagilly and the beginning and end of the Irish Neolithic. In de Laet, S. J. (ed) *Acculturation and Continuity in Atlantic Europe*. Bruges, 15 - 30.

Birks, H. J. B.; Deacon, J. and Pegler, S.; 1975
Pollen Maps for the British Isles 5,000 Years Ago, *Proceedings of the Royal Society*, London, series B.189.

Bailey, G. N.; 1975
The role of molluscs in coastal economies: the results of midden analysis in Australia. *Journal of Archaeological Science*, 2, 45 - 62.

Bailey, G. N.; 1978
Shell middens as indicators of postglacial economies: a territorial perspective. In Mellars, P. (ed) *The Early Postglacial Settlement of Northern Europe*, 37 - 63, Duckworth, London.

Balaam, N., Bell, M., David, A., Levitan, B., McPhail, R., Robinson, M., Scaife, R.; 1987
Prehistoric and Romano-British sites at Westward Ho!, Devon: archaeological and palaeo-environmental surveys 1983 and 1984, in Balaam. N., Levitan, B., Straker. V., (eds) *Studies in Palaeoeconomy and Environment in South-west England*. British Archaeological Reports, British Series, 181, 163 - 264.

Barker, H., Burleigh, R. and Meeks, N.; 1969
British Museum Natural Radiocarbon Measurements VI. *Radiocarbon*, 11, 2, 278 - 294.

Barker, H., Burleigh, R. and Meeks, N.; 1971
British Museum Natural Radiocarbon Measurements VII. *Radiocarbon*, 13, 157 - 188.

Barton, R. N. E., and Bergman, c. A.; 1982
Hunters at Hengistbury: some evidence from experimental archaeology. *World Archaeology*, 14 (2), 237 - 48.

Bateman, J.; 1973
Faunal remains from Ogof-yr-Ychen, Caldey Island. *Nature*, 245, 454 - 5.

Bay-Petersen, J. L.; 1978
Animal exploitation in Mesolithic Denmark. In Mellars, P., (ed) *The Early Postglacial Settlement of Northern Europe*, Duckworth, London, 115 - 146.

Becker, B. and Kromer, B.; 1986
Extension of the Holocene dendrochronology by the PreBoreal pine series, 8800 to 10,100 BP. *Radiocarbon*, 28, 2B, 961 - 967.

Becker, B. and Kromer, B.; in press
Dendrochronology and radiocarbon calibration of the early Holocene. In: Barton, R. N. E., Roberts, A. J. and Row, D. A. (eds), *The Late Glacial in NW Europe: Human adaptation and cultural change at the end of the Pleistocene*. Council for British Archaeology.

Behre, K. E.; 1967
The Lateglacial and early Postglacial history of vegetation and climate in north-western Germany. *Review of Palaeobotany and Palynology*, 4, 149 - 161.

Benson, D. G., *et al.*; in press, 1990
Excavations at Stackpole Warren, Dyfed. *Proceedings of the Prehistoric Society*, 56.

Berridge, P.; 1981
Waun Fignen Felen. *Archaeology in Wales*, 21, 20.

Berridge, P. and Roberts A.; 1986
The Mesolithic period in Cornwall. *Cornish Archaeology*, 25, 7 - 34.

Binford, L. R.; 1979
Organization and formation processes: looking at curated technologies. *Journal of Anthropological Research*, 35 (3), 255 - 273.

Binford, L. R.; 1983
In Pursuit Of The Past. London Thames and Hudson.

Bishop, A. H.; 1914
An Oransay shell-mound - a Scottish pre-Neolithic site. *Proceedings of the Society of Antiquaries of Scotland*, 48, 52 - 102.

Bishop, M. J.; 1975
Earliest record of man's presence in Britain. *Nature*, 273, 95-7.

Bishop, M. J.; 1982
The early Middle Pleistocene mammal fauna of Westbury-sub-Mendip, Somerset. *Palaeontology*, Special Paper.

Blankholm, H. P.; 1987
Late Mesolithic hunter-gatherers and the transition to farming in southern Scandinavia. In Rowley-Conwy, P., Zvelebil, M., and Blankholm, H. P., (eds) *Mesolithic Europe: Recent Trends*. University of Sheffield, 155 - 162.

Blore, J. D.; 1966
The excavation of Lynx Cave, 1962-4, a preliminary report. *Peakland Archaeological Society Newsletter*, No 21, March 1966, 17 - 19.

Blore, J. D.; nd
Lynx Excavations, Clwyd, 1962-81, second report. Privately circulated.

Bohmers, A.; 1960
Statistiques et graphiques dans l'étude des industries lithiques préhistoriques. V. Considérations générales au sujet du Hambourgien, du Tjongérian, du Magdélenien et de l'Azilien. *Palaeohistoria*, VIII, 15 - 38.

Bokelmann, K.; 1971
Duvensee, ein Wohnplatz des Mesolithikums in Schleswig- Holstein, und die Duvenseegruppe. *Offa*, 28, 5 - 26.

Bokelmann, K.; 1985
Duvensee, Wohnplatz 13. *Offa*, 42, 13 - 33.

Bonsall, c.; 1980
The Coastal factor in the Mesolithic settlement of Northwest England., *Veröffentlichungen des Museums für Ur- und Frühgeschichte*, 451-472.

Bosanquet, E. F.; 1923
Notes on the prehistoric flint chipping floors of the district. In Evans, H., *'Twr-y-Felin History and Guide to St. Davids*. St. Davids.

Bowman S. G. E., Ambers, J. c. and Leese, M. N.; 1990
Re-evaluation of British Museum dates issued between 1980 and 1984. *Radiocarbon*, 32, No 1, 59 - 79.

Bowen, E. G.; 1977
Saints Seaways and Settlements. Cardiff. University of Wales Press.

Bowen, D. Q. and Sykes, G. A.; 1988
Correlation of marine events on the northeast Atlantic margin. *Philosophical Transactions of the Royal Society*, B 318, 619 - 635.

Bowen, D. Q., Rose, J., McCabe, A. M., and Sutherland, D.G.; 1986.
Quaternary glaciations in England, Ireland, Scotland and Wales, *Quaternary Science Reviews*, 5, 299 - 340.

Bowen, D. Q., Sykes, G. A., Reeves, A., Miller, G. H., Andrews, J. T., Brew, J. S., Hare, P. E.; 1985.
Amino acid geochronology of raised beaches in south-west Britain. *Quaternary Science Reviews*, 4 (4), 279 - 318.

Boyd Dawkins, W.; 1874
Cave Hunting. Macmillan, London.

Boyd Dawkins, W.; 1880
Memorandum on the remains from the cave at Great Orme's Head. *Proceedings of the Liverpool Geological Society*, IV, ii, 156 - 159.

Bramwell, D.; 1963
Notes on some recent cave and gravel pit discoveries in N. Wales and the Peak District. *Peakland Archaeological Society Newsletter*, 19, 25.

Bramwell, D.; 1977
Bird faunas from Cathole, 1968, and Robin Hood's Cave, 1969. In Campbell, J. B., *The Upper Palaeolithic in Britain*, Oxford, Clarendon Press.

Breuil, H.; 1953
Statuette bisexuée dans le Microlithique de Nab Head, St. Brides, Pembrokeshire. *Congrès Préhistorique de France: Compte rendue de la XIVe Session*.

Brezillon, M.; 1968
La Denomination des Objets de Pierre Taillée. IVth Supplement of *Gallia Prehistoire*, published by Centre National de la Récherche Scientifique.

Britnell, W. J.; 1984
A barbed point from Porth-y-Waen, Llanyblodwel, Shropshire. *Proceedings of the Prehistoric Society*, 50, 385 - 386.

Britnell, W. J.; 1989
The Collfryn hillslope enclosure, Llansantffraid Deuddawr, Powys: excavations 1980-1982. *Proceedings of the Prehistoric Society*, 55, 89 - 134.

Britnell, W. J. and Savory, H. N.; 1984
Gwernvale and Penywyrlod: *Two Neolithic Long Cairns in The Black Mountains of Brecknock*. Cambrian Archeaological Monograph No 2. Cambrian Archaeological Association.

Broadbent, N.; 1979
Coastal resources and settlement stability. A critical study of a Mesolithic site complex in northern Sweden. *Archaeological Studies*, Uppsala University Institute of North European Archaeology, Aun 3. Uppsala.

Buckland, P. c.; 1984
North-west Lincolnshire 10,000 years ago. In: Field, N. and White, A. (eds), *A Prospect of Lincolnshire*. G. W. Belton Ltd., Gainsborough.

Buckland, W.; 1824
Reliquiae Diluvianae or Observations on the Organic Remains Contained in Caves, Fissures, and Diluvial Gravel, and on other Geological Phenomena attesting to the action of an Universal Deluge. London. John Murray.

Burchell, J. P. T.; 1928
A final account of the investigations carried out at Lower Halstow, Kent. *Proceedings of the Prehistoric Society of East Anglia*, 5, 3, 288 - 294.

Burenhult, G.; 1984
The Archaeology of Carrowmore. Theses and Papers in North European Archaeology, 14, Stockholm: G. Burenhults Förlag.

Burke, T. W.; 1966
Excavations at Pant Sychbant, Penderyn (Brecon). *Bulletin of the Board of Celtic Studies*, XXII, 78 - 87.

Burleigh, R., Hewson, A. and Meeks, N.; 1976
British Museum Natural Radiocarbon Measurements VIII. *Radiocarbon*, 18, No 1, 16 - 42.

Burleigh, R., Jacobi, E. B., and Jacobi, R. M.; 1985
Early human resettlement of the British Isles following the last glacial maximum: new evidence from Gough's Cave,Cheddar. *Quaternary Research Association Newsletter*, 45, 1 - 6.

Burleigh, R. *et al.*; 1982
British Museum Natural Radiocarbon Measurements XV, *Radiocarbon*, 24, 270.

Callow, W. J. and Hassal, G. I.; 1968
National Physical Laboratory Radiocarbon Measurements V. *Radiocarbon*, 10, 115 - 118.

Campbell, J. B.; 1977
The Upper Palaeolithic of Britain: a Study of Man and Nature in the Ice Age. Clarendon Press, Oxford.

Campbell, J. B.; 1980
Le problème des subdivisions du Paléolithique supérieur Britannique dans son cadre Européen. *Bulletin de la Société Royale Belge d'Anthropologie et de Préhistoire*, 91, 39 - 77.

Campbell, J. B.; 1986
Hiatus and continuity in the British Upper Palaeolithic: a view from the Antipodes. In: Roe, D., (ed) *Studies in the Upper Palaeolithic of Britain and Northwest Europe*, British Archaeological Reports, International Series, 7 - 42.

Campbell, J. B. and Sampson, c. G.; 1971
A new analysis of Kent's Cavern, Devonshire, England. *University of Oregon Anthropological Papers*, 3, pp I - VII and 40.

Caulfield, S.; 1978
Star Carr - an alternative view. *Irish Archaeological Research Forum*, 5, 15 - 22.

Cantrill, T. c.; 1915
Flint chipping floors in south-west Pembrokeshire. *Archaeologia Cambrensis*, LXX, 157 - 210.

Case, H.; 1986
The Mesolithic and Neolithic in the Oxford region. In: Briggs *et al.* (eds), *The Archaeology of the Oxford Region*. Oxford, 1986.

Celerier, G.; 1979
Inventaire morphologique de pointes aziliennes en Perigord. Un projet de rationalisation. In: de Sonneville Bordes, D.(ed), La Fin de Temps Glaciaires en Europe. *Colloques internationaux du CNRS*, 271, 461 - 466.

Chambers, F. M. and Price, S. M.; 1985
Palaeoecology of Alnus (alder): early postglacial rise in a valley mire, north-west Wales. *New Phytologist*, 101, 333 - 344.

Cherry, J.; 1982
Sea Cliff Erosion at Drigg, Cumbria: Evidence of Prehistoric Habitation, *Transactions of the Cumberland and Westmorland Antiquarian and Archaeological Society*, LXXXII, 1-6.

Childe, V. G.; 1931
The forest cultures of northern Europe: a study in evolution and diffusion. *Journal of the Royal Anthropological Institute*, LXI, 325 - 348.

Churchill, D. M.; 1962
The stratigraphy of the Mesolithic sites III and V at Thatcham, Berkshire, England. *Proceedings of the Prehistoric Society*, 28, 362 - 370.

Churchill, D. M.; 1965
The kitchen midden at Westward Ho!, Devon, England: ecology, age and relation to changes in land and sea level. *Proceedings of the Prehistoric Society*, 31, 74 - 84.

Clark, J. G. D.; 1932
The Mesolithic Age In Britain. Cambridge

Clark, J. G. D.; 1938
Microlithic Industries from Tufa Deposits at Prestatyn, Flintshire, and Blashenwell, Dorset. Proceedings of the Prehistoric Society, IV, 330-334.

Clark, J. G. D.; 1939
A further note on the tufa deposits at Prestatyn, Flintshire. *Proceedings of the Prehistoric Society*, V, 201 - 202.

Clark, J. G. D.; 1946
Seal-hunting in the Stone Age of north-west Europe: a study in economic prehistory. *Proceedings of the Prehistoric Society*, 11, 12 - 48.

Clark, J. G. D.; 1952
Prehistoric Europe: The Economic Basis. London: Methuen.

Clark, J. G. D.; 1954
Star Carr. Cambridge University Press.

Clark, J. G. D.; 1955
Notes on the Obanian with special reference to antler- and bone-work. *Proceedings of the Society of Antiquaries of Scotland*, 89, 91 - 106.

Clark, J. G. D.; 1972
Star Carr: a Case Study in Bio-Archaeology. Addison-Wesley Modular Publications.

Clark, J. G. D.; 1975
The Earlier Stone Age Settlement of Scandinavia. Cambridge University Press.

Clark, J. G. D.; 1977
The economic context of dolmens and passage-graves in Sweden. In: Markotic (ed), *Ancient Europe and the Mediterranean*, 35 - 49. Warminster: Aris and Phillips.

Clark, J. G. D.; 1980
Mesolithic Prelude. Edinburgh University Press.

Clark, J. G. D.; 1983
Coastal settlement in European prehistory with special reference to Fennoscandia. In: Vogt, E. von Z., and Leventhal R. M. (eds), *Prehistoric Settlement Patterns: Essays in Honour of Gordon. R. Willey*. Alberqueque, New Mexico: University of New Mexico and Harvard: Peabody Museum of Archaeology and Ethnology, 295 - 317.

Clark J. G. D. and Rankine, W. F.; 1939
Excavations at Farnham, Surrey (1937-38): the Horsham culture and the question of Mesolithic dwellings. *Proceedings of the Prehistoric Society*, 5, 61 - 118.

Clark, J. G. D. and Godwin, H.; 1956
A Maglemosian site at Brandesburton, Holderness, Yorkshire. *Proceedings of the Prehistoric Society*, 22, 6 - 22.

Clark, D. L.; 1976
Mesolithic Europe: the economic basis. In: Sieveking, G. de G., Longworth, I. H., and Wilson, K. E., (eds), *Problems in Social and Economic Archaeology*, 449 - 482. London, Duckworth.

Clarke, D. V., Gowie, T. G. and Foxon A.; 1985
Symbols of Power at the Time of Stonehenge. HMSO, Edinburgh.

Clarke, D. L.; 1968
Analytical Archaeology. Methuen & Co. London.

Cloutman, E. W.; 1983
Studies of the Vegetational History of The Black Mountains Range, South Wales. PhD. thesis, University of Wales, Cardiff.

Cloutman, E. W. and Smith, A. G.; 1988
Palaeoenvironments in the Vale of Pickering. Part 3: Environmental history at Star Carr. *Proceedings of the Prehistoric Society*, 54, 37 - 58.

Clutton-Brock, J. and Burleigh, R.; 1983
Some archaeological applications of the dating of animal bone by radiocarbon with particular reference to post-Pleistocene extinctions. In: *First International Symposium on C-14 and Archaeology. Groningen, Proc.*, 1981, Mook, W. G. and Waterbolk, H. T., (eds), PACT, 8, 409 - 18.

Coles, J. M.; 1971
The early settlement of Scotland: excavations at Morton, Fife. *Proceedings of the Prehistoric Society*, 37, 284 - 366.

Coggins, D, Laurie, T. and Young, R.; 1989
The Late Upper Palaeolithic of the northern Pennine Dales in the light of recent fieldwork. In: Bonsall, *c.* (ed), *The Mesolithic In Europe*, John Donald, Edinburgh, 164 - 174.

Cook, J. and Barton, R. N. E.; 1986
Dating late Devensian - early Flandrian barbed points. In: Gowlett, J. A. J. and Hedges, R. E. M., (eds), *Archaeological Results from Accelerator dating*. Oxford. Oxford University Committee for Archaeology.

Coope, G. R.; 1977
Fossil coleopteran assemblages as indicators of climatic changes during the Devensian (Last) cold stage. *Philosophical Transactions of the Royal Society of London*, B, 280, 313 - 340.

Coope, G. R., Morgan, A., Osborne, P. J.; 1971
Fossil Coleoptera as indicators of climatic fluctuations during the Last Glaciation in Britain. *Palaeogeography, Palaeoclimatology, Palaeoecology*, 10, 87 - 101.

Coope, G. R. and Brophy, J. A.; 1972
Late-glacial environmental changes indicated by a coleopteran succession from North Wales. *Boreas*, 1, 97 - 142.

Crawford, O. G. S.; 1936
Western Seaways. In: *Custom is King*, Oxford.

Currant, A. P.; 1986a
The Lateglacial mammal fauna of Gough's (New) Cave, Cheddar, Somerset. *Proceedings of the University of Bristol Speleological Society*, 17 (3), 286 - 304.

Currant, A. P.; 1986b
Pleistocene vertebrate remains from Little Hoyle. In: Green, H. S., Excavations at Little Hoyle (Longbury Bank), Wales, in 1984. In: Roe, D. A. (ed), *Studies in the Upper Palaeolithic of Britain and Northwest Europe*, British Archaeological Reports, International Series, 296, 113 - 115.

Daniels, J. E.; 1927
Excavations on the Kerry Hills, Montgomeryshire. *Archaeologia Cambrensis*, 82, 147 - 160.

Dansgaard, W., White, J. W. *c.* and S. J. Johnsen.; 1989
The abrupt termination of the Younger Dryas climate event. *Nature*, 339, 532 - 533.

David, H. E.; 1923-4
Culver Hole (Llangenydd). Report of the Council for the year 1923-4. *Royal Institution of South Wales*, Swansea, 25 - 30.

David, A. E. U.; 1989
Some aspects of the human presence in west Wales during the Mesolithic. In: Bonsall, *c.* (ed), *The Mesolithic In Europe*, John Donald, Edinburgh, 241 - 253.

Davidson, P. E.; 1967
The study of the oystercatcher (Haematopus ostralegus L) in relation to the fishery for cockles (Cardium edule) in the Burrey inlet, south Wales. *Fishery Investigations Series* II, XXV, 7, 27. HMSO.

Davies, M.; 1978a
Ogof Carreg Hir - excavations of 7th March, 1977. *Journal of the Cambrian Caving Council*, 4, 43 - 45.

Davies, M.; 1978b
Upper Kendrick's Cave. *Archaeology in Wales*, 18, 34

Davies, M.; 1979
Upper Kendrick's Cave, Great Orme: excavations of 1978. *Pengelly Cave Studies Trust Newsletter*, 32, 7 - 9.

Davies, M.; 1981
Worms Head cave. *Archaeology In Wales*, 21, 22.

Davies, M.; 1982
Archaeological caves of the south Gower coast. *William Pengelly Cave Studies Trust Newsletter*, 40, 1 - 8.

Davies, M.; 1983
The excavation of Upper Kendrick's Cave, Llandudno. *Studies in Speleology*, IV, 45 - 52.

Davies, M.; 1986
Worms Head cave, Rhossili. *Archaeology In Wales*, 26, 34.

Davies, M.; 1989a
Recent advances in cave archaeology in southwest Wales. In: Ford, T. D. (ed), *Limestones and Caves of Wales*, Cambridge University Press, 79 - 91.

Davies, M.; 1989b
Cave archaeology in North Wales. In: Ford, T. D. (ed), *Limestones and Caves of Wales*, Cambridge University Press, 92 - 101.

Deacon, J.; 1974
The location of refugia of Corylus avellana L. during the Weichselian glaciation. *New Phytologist*, 73, 1055 - 1063.

Debes, L. J.; 1676
Faeroe et Faeroa reserata: that is a description of the Islands and Inhabitants of Faroe (Transl. from the Danish). London.

Deith, M. R.; 1983
Molluscan calenders: the use of growth-line analysis to establish seasonality of shellfish collection at the Mesolithic site of Morton, Fife. *Journal of Archaeological Science*, 10, 423 - 440.

Deith, M. R.; 1986
Subsistence strategies at a Mesolithic camp site: evidence from Stable Isotope Analysis of shells. *Journal of Archaeological Science*, 13, 61 - 78.

Deith, M. R.; 1989
Clams and salmonberries: interpreting seasonality from shells. In: Bonsall, *c.* (ed), *The Mesolithic In Europe*, John Donald, Edinburgh, 73 - 79.

Delporte, H.; 1979
L'Image de la Femme dans L'Art Prehistorique, Picard, Paris.

Dennell, R.; 1983
European Economic Prehistory: A New Approach. Academic Press.

De Quincey, A. B.; 1969
Swanlake Bay. *Archaeology in Wales*, 8.

Devoy, R.J.; 1982
Analysis of the geological evidence for Holocene sea-level movements in south-east England. *Proceedings of the Geologists' Association*, 95, 65 - 90.

Devoy, R. J.; 1983
Late Quaternary shorelines in Ireland: an assessment of their implications for isostatic land movement and relative sea-level changes. In: Smith, D. E. and Dawson A. G. (eds), Shorelines and Isostasy. Institute of British Geographers Special Publication No. 16. Academic Press, London, 227 - 254.

Devoy, R. J.; 1985
The problem of a late Quaternary landbridge between Britain and Ireland. *Quaternary Science Reviews*, 4, 43 - 58.

Dickson, F. P.; 1981
Australian Stone Hatchets: a study in design and dynamics. Academic Press.

Dixon, E. E. L.; 1921
The Geology of the South Wales Coalfield Part III. The Country around Pembroke and Tenby. *Memoir of the Geological Survey of Great Britain.*

Dobson, M. R., Evans, W. E. and James, K. H.: 1971
The sediment on the floor of the Southern Irish Sea. *Marine Geology*, 2, 27 - 69.

Donald, A. P.; 1987
Aspects of Lateglacial and Postglacial Environments in South-west Wales. PhD thesis, University of Wales. Lampeter.

Dumont, J. V.; 1983
An Interim Report on the Star Carr Microwear Study., *Oxford Journal of Archaeology*, 2, 127-145.

Dumont, J. V.; 1985
A preliminary report on the Mount Sandel microwear study. In: Woodman, P. *c.* Excavations at Mount Sandel 1973-77, *Northern Ireland Archaeological Monographs*, 2. HMSO.

Dumont, J. V.; 1987
Mesolithic microwear research in North-west Europe. In: Rowley-Conwy, P., Zvelebil, M. and Blankholm, H. P., (eds), *Mesolithic North-west Europe: Recent Trends*, University of Sheffield, 82 - 92.

Emiliani, *c.*; 1966
Isotopic palaeotemperatures. *Science*, 154, 851 - 857.

Edwards, K. J.; 1988
The hunter-gatherer/agricultural transition and the pollen record in the British Isles. In: Birks, H. H., Birks, H. J. B., Kaland, P. E. and Moe, D. (eds), *The Cultural Landscape - Past, Present and Future.* Cambridge University Press, 255 -266.

Edwards, K. J. and Hirons, K.; 1984
Cereal pollens in pre-elm decline deposits: implications for the earliest agriculture in Britain and Ireland. *Journal of Archaeological Science*, 11, 71 - 80.

Evans, J. G.; 1972
Landsnails In Archaeology. London

Evans, J. G.; 1975
The Environment of Early Man in the British Isles. London, Elek.

Evans, P.; 1975
The intimate relationship: an hypothesis concerning pre-Neolithic land-use. In: Evans, J. G., Limbrey, S. and Cleere, H., (eds), *The Effect of Man on the Landscape; The Highland Zone*, Council for British Archaeology Research Report, No. 11.

Erlandson, J. M.; 1988
The role of shellfish in prehistoric economies: a protein perspective. *American Antiquity*, 53, 102 - 109.

Eskrigge, R. A.; 1880
Notes on human skeletons and traces of human workmanship found in a cave at Llandudno. *Proceedings of the Liverpool Geological Society*, IV, ii, 153 - 155.

Fairbanks, R. G.; 1989
A 17,000-year glacio-eustatic sea level record: influence of glacial melting rates on the Younger Dryas event and deep-ocean circulation. *Nature*, 342, 637 - 642.

Fairbridge, R. W.; 1961
Eustatic changes in sea-level. In: Ahrens, L. H. *et al.* (eds), *Physics and Chemistry of the Earth* 4. London, Pergamon Press.

Falconer, H.; 1868
Palaeontological Memoirs and notes of the late Hugh Falconer. Murchison, *c.* (ed). 2 vols. Hardwicke, London.

Fenton, M. B.; 1984
The nature of the source and the manufacture of Scottish battle-axes and axe-hammers. *Proceedings of the Prehistoric Society*, 50, 217 - 244.

Fischer, A., Hansen, P. V. and Rasmussen, P; 1984
Macro and micro wear traces on lithic projectile points. *Journal of Danish Archaeology*, 3, 19 - 46.

Fischer, A. and Tauber, H.; 1986
New C-14 datings of Late Palaeolithic cultures from Northwestern Europe. *Journal of Danish Archaeology*, 5, 7 - 14.

Fleure, H. J.; 1913
Welsh archaeology and anthropolgy. *Archaeologia Cambrensis*, XIII, 153 - 158.

Fox, *c.*; 1933
Presidential address to the Cambrian Archaeological Association. *Archaeologia Cambrensis*, LXXXVIII, part II, 153 - 184.

Fox, *c.*; 1947
The Personality of Britain, National Museum of Wales.

Froom, F. R.; 1972
A Mesolithic site at Wawcott, Kintbury. *Berks Archaeological Journal*, 66, 23 - 44.

Froom, F. R.; 1976
Wawcott III: a Stratified Mesolithic Succession., British Archaeological Reports, British Series, 27.

Garrod, D. A. E.; 1926
The Upper Palaeolithic Age in Britain, Oxford.

Gibbard, P. L. and Turner, *c.*; 1988
In defence of the Wolstonian Stage. *Quaternary Research Association Newsletter*, 54, 9 - 14.

Gillespie, R., Gowlett, J. A. J., Hall, E. T., Hedges, R. E. M. and Perry, *c.*; 1985. Radiocarbon dates from the Oxford AMS system: Archaeometry Datelist 2, *Archaeometry* 27, 2, 237 - 246.

Girling, M. and Greig, J.; 1977
Palaeoecological investigations of a site at Hampstead Heath, London. *Nature*, 268, 45 - 57.

Gjessing, H.; 1920
Rogalands Steinalder. Stavanger Museum.

Gledhill, R.; 1990
Warmer seas lure fish from tropics. Article in the *Times*, April 6, 1990.

Glenn, T. A.; 1926
Recent finds near Rhyl. *Archaeologia Cambrensis*, (7th. series) VI, 199 - 203.

Glenn, T. A.; 1930
Finds on the Rhyl foreshore. *Archaeologia Cambrensis*, LXXXV, 424 - 425.

Godwin, H.; 1975
The History of the British Flora. Cambridge.

Godwin, H. and Godwin, M. E; 1933
British Maglemosian harpoon sites. *Antiquity*, 7, 36 - 48.

Godwin, H. and Mitchell, G. F.; 1938
Stratgraphy and development of two raised bogs near Tregaron, Cardiganshire. *New Phytology*, 37:5.

Godwin H. and Willis, E. H.; 1959
Cambridge University Natural Radiocarbon Measurements I. *Radiocarbon*, 1, 63 - 75.

Godwin H. and Willis, E. H.; 1961
Cambridge University Natural Radiocarbon Measurements III, *Radiocarbon*, 3, 60 - 76.

Godwin, H. and Willis, E. H.; 1964
Cambridge University Natural Radiocarbon Measurements VI, *Radiocarbon*, 6, 116 - 137.

Gordon-Williams, J. P.; 1925
Nabs Head Chipping Floor. *Transactions of the Carmarthenshire Antiquarian Society and Field Club*, XVIII, part XLVI, 80.

Gordon-Williams, J. P.; 1926
The Nab Head Chipping Floor.2, *Archaeologia Cambrensis*, LXXXI, 86-110.

Gowlett, J. A. J.; 1986
Radiocarbon Accelerator dating of the Upper Palaeolithic in North-west Europe: a provisional view. In: Collcutt S. N. (ed), *The Palaeolithic of Britain and its Nearest Neighbours: Recent Trends*, 98 - 102. University of Sheffield.

Gowlett, J. A. J. and Hedges, R. E. M. (eds); 1986
Archaeological Results from Accelerator Dating. *Oxford University Committee for Archaeology, Monograph* 11.

Gowlett, J. A. J., Hall, E. T., Hedges, R. E. M., Perry, *c.*; 1986a.
Radiocarbon dates from the Oxford AMS system: Archaeometry Datelist 3, *Archaeometry*, 28, 1, 116 - 125.

Gowlett, J. A. J., Hedges, R. E. M., Law, I. A. and Perry, *c.*; 1986b.
Radiocarbon dates from the Oxfrod AMS system: Archaeometry Datelist 4, *Archaeometry*, 29, 1, 125 - 155.

Gowlett, J. A. J., Hedges, R. E. M., Law, I. A. and Perry, *c.*; 1987.
Radiocarbon dates from the Oxford AMS system: Archaeometry Datelist 5. *Archaeometry*, 29, 1, 125 - 155.

Gray, J. M.; 1982
The last glaciers (Loch Lomond Advance) in Snowdonia, North Wales. *Geological Journal*, 17, 111 - 133.

Gray, J. M. and Lowe, J. J.; 1977
The Scottish lateglacial environment: a synthesis. In: Gray, J. M. and Lowe, J. J. (eds), *Studies in the Scottish Lateglacial Environment*, Oxford. Pergamon. 163 - 181.

Green, H. S.; 1980
The Flint Arrowheads of the British Isles. British Archaeological Reports, British Series, 75.

Green, H. S.; 1981
A Palaeolithic flint handaxe from Rhossili, Gower. *Bulletin of the Board of Celtic Studies*, 29, 337 - 339.

Green, H. S.; 1984
The Palaeolithic Period. In: Savory, H. N. (ed), *Glamorgan County History, Vol. 2, Early Glamorgan.* University of Wales Press, Cardiff, 11 - 33.

Green, H. S.; 1986a
The Palaeolithic Settlement of Wales Project: a review of progress 1978-1985. In: Collcutt, S. N. (ed), *The Palaeolithic of Britain and its Nearest Neighbours: Recent Trends*, University of Sheffield, 36 - 42.

Green, H. S.; 1986b
Excavations at The Little Hoyle (Longbury bank), Wales, in 1984. In: Roe, D. A. (ed), *Studies in the Upper Palaeolithic of Britain and North-west Europe,* British Archaeological Reports, International Series, 296, 99 - 120.

Green, H. S., Bevins, R. E., Bull, P. A., Currant, A. P., Debenham, N. *c.*, Embleton, *c.*, Ivanovich, M., Livingstone, H., Rae, A. M., Schwarcz H. P. and Stringer, H. P.; 1989.
Le site Acheuleen de la Grotte de Pontnewydd, Pays de Galles: geomorphologie, stratigraphie, chronologie, faune, hominides fossiles, geologie et l'industrie lithique dans le context paleoecologique. *L'Anthropologie*, 93, 15 - 52.

Grieve, S.; 1885
The Great Auk or Garefowl (Alca impennis, Linn.): Its History, Archaeology, and Remains. London: Jack.

Grigson, *c.*; 1981
Fauna. In: Simmons, I. and Tooley, M. (eds), *The Environment in British Prehistory*, London. Duckworth, 110 - 124.

Grigson, *c.* and Mellars, P.; 1987
The mammalian remains from the middens. In: Mellars, P, *Excavations on Oronsay*, Edinburgh University Press, 243 - 289.

Grimes, W. F.; 1932
Surface flint industries around Solva, Pembrokeshire. *Archaeologia Cambrensis*, 87, 179 - 192.

Grimes, W. F.; 1933
Priory Farm Cave, Monkton, Pembrokeshire. *Archaeologia Cambrensis*, LXXXVII, 88 - 100.

Grimes, W. F.; 1951
Prehistory of Wales. National Museum of Wales, Cardiff.

Hall, R.L.; 1981
The Quartered Circle and the Symbolism of the Mississippian World. Ms on file, Dept. of Anthropology, University of Illinois at Chicago Circle.

Hallam, J. S., Edwards, B. J. N., Barnes, B., Stuart, A. J.; 1973
A Lateglacial elk with associated barbed points from High Furlong, Lancashire. *Proceedings of the Prehistoric Society*, 39, 100 - 128.

Hammond, N.; 1988
Early riverside footsteps for mankind. Article in the *Times*, August 19, 1988.

Harrison, *c.* J. O.; 1986
Bird remains from Gough's Cave, Cheddar, Somerset. *Proceedings of the University of Bristol Speleological Society*, 17, 3.

Harrison, S. J.; 1974
Problems in the measurement and evaluation of the climatic resources of upland Britain. In: Taylor, J. A. (ed), *Climatic Resources and Economic Activity*, Newton Abbot, David and Charles, 47 -63.

Hawkins, A. B.; 1971
The Late Weichselian and Flandrian transgressions of South-west Britain. *Quaternaria*, 14, 115 - 130.

Healey, E. and Green, H. S.; 1984
The lithic industries. In: Britnell, W. J. and Savory, H. N., Gwernvale and Penywyrlod: *Two Neolithic Long Cairns in The Black Mountains of Brecknock, Cambrian Archaeological Monograph* No. 2. Cambrian Archaeological Association, 113 - 132.

Hearne, A.; 1988
A time and a place for the Grimston bowl. In: Barrett, J. *c.* and Kinnes, I. A. (eds), *The Archaeology of Context in the Neolithic and Bronze Age: Recent Trends.* University of Sheffield, 9 - 29.

Hedges, R. E. M., Housley, R. A., Law, I. A., Perry, *c.* and Gowlett, J. A. J.; 1987
Radiocarbon dates from the Oxford AMS System: Archaeometry Datelist 6. *Archaeometry,* 29, 2, 289 - 306.

Hedges, R. E. M., Housley, R. A., Law, I. A. and Perry, *c.* 1987.
Radiocarbon dates the Oxford AMS System: Archaeometry Datelist 7. *Archaeometry,* 30, 1, 155 - 164.

Hedges, R. E. M., Housley, R. A., Law, I. A. and Bronk, *c.* R.; 1989.
Radiocarbon dates from the Oxford AMS system: Archaeometry Datelist 9. *Archaeometry,* 31, 2, 207 - 234.

Heinzelin de Braucourt, J. de.; 1973
L'industrie du site Paléolithique de Maisières-Canal. *Institut Royal des Sciences Naturelles de Belgique,* Memoire No. 171.

Herity, M.; 1970
The early prehistoric period around the Irish Sea. In: Moore, D. (ed), *The Irish Sea Province in Archaeology and History.* Cambrian Archaeological Association, Cardiff.

Heyworth, A. and Kidson, *c.*; 1982
Sea-level changes in south-west England and Wales. *Proceedings of the Geologists' Association,* 93, (1), 91 - 111.

Hicks, H.; 1886
Results of some recent researches in some bone-caves in North Wales. *Quarterly Journal of the Geological Society,* 42, 3 - 11.

Hicks, H.; 1887
On some recent researches in bone caves in Wales., *Proceedings of the Geologists' Association,* IX (1885), 1- 20.

Hicks, H.; 1888
On the Cae Gwyn Cave. *Quarterly Journal of the Geological Society,* 44, 562 - 577.

Hibbert, F. A. and Switsur, V. R.; 1976
Radiocarbon dating of Flandrian pollen zones in Wales and northern England. *New Phytologist,* 77, 793 - 807.

Houlder, *c.* H.; 1968
The henge monuments at Llandegai. *Antiquity,* 42, 216 - 221.

Houlder, *c.* H.; 1976
Stone axes and henge monuments. In: Boon, G. *c.* and Lewis, J. M. (eds), *Welsh Antiquity,* National Museum of Wales, Cardiff. 55 - 62

Hulle, W. M.; 1977
Die Ilsenhohle unter Burg Ranis/Thuringen: Eine palaeolithische Jagerstation. Gustav Fischer Verlag, Stuttgart, New York, pp I - XX and 203.

Ingebrigtsen, O.; 1924
Hjortens utbredelse i Norge. *Bergens Museums Aarbok* 1922-3. Naturvidensk. r. nr. 6.

Jacobi, R. M.; 1973
Aspects of the Mesolithic Age in Britain. In: Kozlowski, S. K., (ed), *The Mesolithic in Europe,* 237 - 265.

Jacobi, R. M.; 1976
Britain inside and outside Mesolithic Europe. *Proceedings of the Prehistoric Society,* 42, 67 - 84.

Jacobi, R. M.; 1978
The Mesolithic of Sussex. In: Drewett, P. L. (ed) *Archaeology in Sussex to AD 1500,* Council for British Archaeology Research Report, 29, 15-22.

Jacobi, R. M.; 1979
Early Flandrian Hunters in the South-west. In: Maxfield, V. A., (ed) *Prehistoric Dartmoor in its Context.* Devon Archaeological Society.

Jacobi, R. M.; 1980a
The Upper Palaeolithic in Britain, with special reference to Wales. In: Taylor J. A., (ed) *Culture and Environment in Prehistoric Wales.* British Archaeological Reports, British Series, 76, 15-100.

Jacobi, R. M.; 1980b
The Early Holocene settlement of Wales. In: Taylor J. A., (ed) *Culture and Environment in Prehistoric Wales.* British Archaeological Reports, British Series, 76, 131- 206.

Jacobi, R. M.; 1982
Later hunters in Kent: Tasmania and the earliest Neolithic. In: Leach, P. E. (ed), *Archaeology in Kent to 1500 AD.* Council for British Archaeology Research Report 48, 12 - 24.

Jacobi, R. M.; 1986a
The contents of Dr. Harley's showcase. In: Collcutt, S. N. (ed), *The Palaeolithic of Britain and its Nearest Neighbours: Recent Trends*. University of Sheffield, 62 - 68.

Jacobi, R. M.; 1986b
The Lateglacial archaeology of Gough's cave at Cheddar. In: Collcutt, S. N. (ed), *The Palaeolithic of Britain and its Nearest Neighbours: Recent Trends*. University of Sheffield, 74 - 79.

Jacobi, R. M.; 1986c
AMS results from Cheddar Gorge - trodden and untrodden 'lifeways'. In: Gowlett, J. A. J. and Hedges, R. E. M. (eds), Archaeological Results from Accelerator Dating, *Oxford University Committee for Archaeology Monograph* 11. 81 - 86.

Jacobi, R. M.; 1988
Towards a British Lateglacial archaeology. In: Otte, M. (ed), *De la Loire a l'Oder. Les Civilisations du Paleolithique final dans le nord-ouest europeen*. British Archaeological Reports, International Series, 444 (ii), 427 - 447.

Jacobi, R. M., Tallis, J. H. and Mellars, P.; 1976
The southern Pennine Mesolithic and the ecological record. *Journal of Archaeological Science*, 3, 307 - 320.

Jacobi, R. M. and Tebbutt, c. F.; 1981
A Late Mesolithic rock-shelter at High Hurstwood, Sussex. *Sussex Archaeological Collections*, 119, 1-36.

Jacobi, R. M., Gowlett, J. A. J., Hedges, R. E. M. and Gillespies, R.; 1986.
Accelerator mass spectrometry dating of Upper Palaeolithic finds, with the Poulton Elk as an example. In: Roe, D. (ed), *Studies in the Upper Palaeolithic of Britain and North-west Europe*, British Archaeological Reports, International Series, 296, 121 - 128.

Jacobi, R. M.; 1987
Misanthropic miscellany: musings on British early Flandrian archaeology and other flights of fancy. In: Rowley-Conwy, P., Zvelebil, M. and Blankholm, H. P. (eds), *Mesolithic North-west Europe: Recent Trends*. University of Sheffield. 163 - 168.

Jarman, M. R.; 1972
European deer economies and the advent of the Neolithic. In: Higgs, E. S. (ed), *Papers in Economic Prehistory*, Cambridge, 125 - 147.

Jelgersma, S.; 1961
Holocene Sea-level Changes in the Netherlands, *Mededelingen van de Geologische Stichting, Serie* C-Vi, 7.

Jenkins. D.; 1990
Pedogenesis and archaeology at Aled Isaf. In: Addison, K., Edge, M. J. and Watkins, R. (eds), The Quaternary of North Wales: Field Guide, *Quaternary Research Association*, Coventry.

Jenkins, J. G.; 1974
Nets and Coracles. David and Charles, London and Newton Abbot.

Jenkins, J. G.; 1977
Cockles and mussels: aspects of shellfish-gathering in Wales. *Folklife*, 15, 81 - 95.

Jennbert, K.; 1984
Den productiva gavan. Tradition och innovation i Sydskandinavien for omkring 5300 ar sedan. *Acta Archaeologia Lundensia*. Series in 4, 16. (English summary).

Jochim, M. A.; 1976
Hunter-gatherer Subsistence and settlement: A Predictive Model. New York, Academic Press.

John, B. S.; 1976
Pembrokeshire. David and Charles, London and Newton Abbot.

Johnson, N. and David, A.; 1982
A Mesolithic Site on Trevose Head and Contemporary Geography. *Cornish Archaeology*, 21, 67-103.

Jones, E. L.; 1882
On the exploration of two caves in the neighbourhood of Tenby. *Quarterly Journal of the Geological Society of London*, 38, 282 - 288.

Kennedy, R. A.; 1977
Nab Head, St. Brides, *Archaeology in Wales*, 17, 26.

Kidson, c.; 1977
The coast of south-west England. In: Kidson, c. and Tooley, M. J. (eds), The Quaternary History of the Irish Sea, *Geological Journal Special Issue*, No. 7. Liverpool. Seel House Press. 257 - 298.

Kidson, c. and Heyworth, A.; 1973
The Flandrian sea-level rise in the Bristol Channel. *Proceedings of the Ussher Society*, 2, 565 - 584.

Kinnes, I. A.; 1984
Microliths and megaliths: monumental origins along the Atlantic fringe. In: Burenhult, G., The Archaeology of Carrowmore, *Theses and Papers in North European Archaeology*, 14, Stockholm: G. Burenhults Forlag.

Kinnes, I. A.; 1988
The cattleship Potemkin: the first Neolithic in Britain. In: Barrett, J. c. and Kinnes, I. A. (eds), *The Archaeology of*

Context in the Neolithic and Bronze Age: Recent Trends. University of Sheffield, 2 - 8.

Kelly, R. S.; 1982
Mesolithic flints from Porth Ruffydd, Anglesey. *Transactions of the Anglesey Antiquarian Society and Field Club*, 141 - 142.

Kukla, G. J.; 1977
Pleistocene land-sea correlations 1. Europe. *Earth Science Review*, 13, 307 - 374.

Lacaille, A. D.; 1954,
The Stone Age in Scotland, London, Oxford University Press.

Lacaille, A. D.; 1961
Mesolithic facies in Middlesex and London. *Transactions of the London and Middlesex Archaeological Society*, 20, (3), 100 -150.

Lacaille, A. D. and Grimes, W. F.; 1955
The prehistory of Caldey. *Archaeologia Cambrensis*, CIV, 85- 165.

Lacaille, A. D. and Grimes, W. F.; 1961
The prehistory of Caldey, part 2. *Archaeologia Cambrensis*, CX, 30 - 70.

Lamb, H. H., Lewis, R. P. W. and Woodruffe, A; 1966
Atmospheric circulation and the main climatic variables between 8,000 and 0 BC: meteorological evidence. In: Sawyer, J. S. (ed) *World Climate from 8,000 and 0 BC*, Royal Meteorological Society, 174 - 217.

Lambert, c. A.; 1963
Report on peat samples from the submerged forest at Freshwater West. Appendix 2, in: Wainwright, G. J., A Reinterpretation of the Microlithic Industries of Wales, *Proceedings of the Prehistoric Society*, 4, 99 - 132.

Laville, H., Rigaud, J-P. and Sackett, J. R.; 1980
Rock Shelters of The Perigord. New York, Academic Press.

Laws, E.; 1880
Pembrokeshire earthworks. *Archaeologia Cambrensis*, 4th series, X.

Laws, E.; 1888
The History of Little England Beyond Wales and the non-Kymric colony settled in Pembrokeshire. George Bell & Sons, London.

Laws, E.; 1908
Priory Farm Cave. *Archaeologia Cambrensis*, 1908, 114 - 115.

Leach, A. L.; 1913
Stone implements from soil drifts and chipping floors etc., in south Pembroke., *Archaeologia Cambrensis*, LXVIII, 391-432.

Leach, A. L.; 1916
Nanna's cave, Isle of Caldey., *Archaeologia Cambrensis*, LXXI, 155-180.

Leach, A. L.; 1918
Flint working sites on the submerged land (Submerged Forest) bordering the Pembrokeshire coast. *Proceedings of the Geologists' Assosiation*, XXIX, part 2, 46-64.

Leach, A. L.; 1933
Stone implements from the Nab Head, St. Brides, Pembrokeshire., *Archaeologia Cambrensis*, LXXXVIII, 229-236.

Lee, R. B.; 1968
What hunters do for a living, or how to make out on scarce resources. In: Lee, R. B. and DeVore, I. (eds), *Man The Hunter.* Chicago, 1968.

Legge, A. J. and Rowley-Conwy, P. A.; 1988
Star Carr Revisited. University of London.

Legge, A. J. and Rowley-Conwy, P. A.; 1989
Some preliminary results of a re-examination of the Star Carr fauna. In: Bonsall, c. (ed), *The Mesolithic In Europe*, John Donald, Edinburgh.

Leroi-Gourhan, A.; 1968
The Art of Prehistoric Man in Western Europe, London, Thames and Hudson.

Lewis, J. S. c.; 1989
The Lateglacial/early Flandrian hunter-gatherer site at Three Ways Wharf, Uxbridge, Middlesex, England. *Mesolithic Miscellany*, 10, No 2, 7 - 9.

Lewis, J. S. c.; in press
Excavation of a Late Devensian and early Flandrian site at Three Ways Wharf, Oxford Road, Uxbridge: an interim report. In: Barton, R. N. E., Roberts, A. J. and Roe D. A. (eds), *The Late Glacial in NW Europe: Human adaptation and cultural change at the end of the Pleistocene.* Council For British Archaeology.

Lewis, M.; forthcoming
The Prehistory of Coastal SW Wales 7,500 - 3,600 BP: an interdisciplinary palaeoenvironmental and archaeological investigation. Unpublished PhD thesis, University of Wales.

Lister, A. M.; 1984
The fossil record of elk (Alces alces (L.)) in Britain. *Quaternary Research Association Newsletter*, 44, 1 - 6.

Lowe, J. J. and Gray, J. M.; 1980
The stratigraphic subdivision of the Lateglacial of north-west Europe: a discussion. In: Lowe, J. J., Gray, J. M. and Robinson, J. E. (eds), *Studies in the Lateglacial of north-west Europe*, Oxford, Pergamon. 157 - 175.

Lowe, S.; 1981
Radiocarbon dating and stratigraphic resolution in Welsh Lateglacial chronology. *Nature*, 293, 210 - 212.

Lowe, J. J. and Lowe, S.; 1989
Interpretation of the pollen stratigraphy of Late Devensian lateglacial and early Flandrian sediments at Llyn Gwernan, near Cadair Idris, North Wales. *New Phytologist*, 113, 391 - 408.

Mace, A.; 1959
An Upper Palaeolithic open site on Hengistbury Head, Christchurch, Hants. *Proceedings of the Prehistoric Society*, 25, 233 - 259.

Mangerud, J., Andersen, S. T., Berglund, B. E., and Donner,; 1974
Quaternary stratigraphy of Norden, a proposal for terminology and classification. *Boreas*, 3, 109 - 128.

Manley, J. and Healey, E.; 1982
Excavations at Hendre, Rhuddlan: The Mesolithic finds. *Archaeologia Cambrensis*, CXXXI, 18-48.

Marshak, A.; 1972
The Roots of Civilisation. New York, McGraw Hill.

Matheson, c.; 1929
Wales and the Sea Fisheries. National Museum of Wales, Cardiff.

Matheson, c.; 1932
Changes in the Fauna of Wales Within Historic Times. National Museum of Wales, Cardiff.

May, J.; 1976
Prehistoric Lincolnshire, History of Lincolnshire 1. History of Lincoln Committee, Lincoln.

McBurney, c. B. M.; 1959
Report on the first season's fieldwork on British Upper Palaeolithic cave deposits. *Proceedings of the Prehistoric Society*, XXV, 260-269.

McBurney, c. B. M.; 1965
The Palaeolithic. In: Foster, I. Ll. and Daniel, G. (eds), *Prehistoric and early Wales*. Routledge and Kegan Paul. London. 17 - 34.

McCarthy, M.; 1989
Greenhouse effect clues off the Cornish coast: sea change that may point to global warming. Article in the *Times*, August 7, 1989, pp 1 and 4.

Mellars, P; 1975
Ungulate populations, economic patterns, and the Mesolithic landscape. In: Evans, J. G., Limbrey, S. and Cleere, H. (eds), *The Effect Of Man On The Landscape: The Highland Zone*, Council For British Archaeology Research Report 11, 49 - 56.

Mellars, P.; 1976a
The appearance of 'narrow-blade' microlithic industries in Britain: the radiocarbon evidence. In: *Les civilisations de 8ieme au 5ieme millenaire avant notre ere en Europe*, Colloque 19, 9ieme Congres Internationale des Sciences Préhistoriques et Protohistoriques, Nice, 166 - 174.

Mellars, P.; 1976b
Settlement patterns and industrial variability in the British Mesolithic. In: Sieveking, G. de G., Longworth, I. H. and Wilson, K. E. (eds), *Problems in Social and Economic Archaeology*, London, Duckworth. 375 - 399.

Mellars, P.; 1976c
Fire ecology, animal populations and man; a study of some ecological relationships in prehistory. *Proceedings of the Prehistoric Society*, 42, 15 - 45.

Mellars, P.; 1987
Excavations on Oronsay. Edinburgh, Edinburgh University Press.

Mellars, P. and Reinhardt, S. c.; 1978
Patterns of Mesolithic land-use in southern England: a geological perspective. In: Mellars, P. (ed) *The Early Postglacial Settlement of Northern Europe*, London, Duckworth. 243 - 294.

Mercer, R.; 1986
The Neolithic in Cornwall. *Cornish Archaeology*, 25, 35 - 80.

Molleson, T. and Burleigh.; 1978
A new date for Goat's Hole Cave. Antiquity, 52, 143 - 145.

Moore, J. W.; 1950
Mesolithic sites in the neighbourhood of Flixton, north-east Yorkshire. *Proceedings of the Prehistoric Society*, XVI, 101- 108.

Moore, J. W.; 1954
Excavations at Flixton site 2. In: Clark, J. G. D., *Star Carr*, Cambridge University Press. 192 - 194.

Moore, P. D.; 1972
Studies in the vegetational history of mid-Wales III: early Flandrian pollen data from west Cardiganshire. *New Phytologist*, 71, 947 - 959.

Moore, P. D.; 1977
Vegetational History. In: Bowen, D. Q. (ed), Studies in the Welsh Quaternary, *Cambria* IV, 74-83.

Moore, P. D.; 1987
Tree boundaries on the move. *Nature*, 326, 545.

Mörner, N-A.; 1969
Eustatic and climatic changes during the last 15,000 years. *Geologie Mijnb.*, 48, (4), 389 - 399.

Morris, J. H.; 1923
Finds of Neolithic and Bronze Age antiquity from under the Submerged Forest Bed at Rhyl. *Archaeologia Cambrensis*, 78, 151 - 153.

Moss, E. H; 1983
The Functional Analysis of Flint Implements - Pincevent and Pont d'Ambon: Two Case Studies From The French Final Palaeolithic. British Archaeological Reports, International Series, 177, Oxford.

Moss, E. H.; 1986
New research on burin function suggests a reconsideration of functional typology. In: Collcutt, S. N. (ed), *The Palaeolithic of Britain and Its Nearest Neighbours: Recent Trends*, University of Sheffield, 95 - 97.

Movius, H. L.; 1942
The Irish Stone Age, Its Chronology, Development and Relationships. Cambridge, Cambridge University Press.

Musson, c. R.; 1975
Brenig valley excavations, 1974. *Denbighshire Historical Transactions*, XXIV, 1 - 25.

Myers, A.; 1987
All shot to pieces? Inter-assemblage variability, lithic analysis and Mesolithic assemblage 'types': some preliminary observations. In: Brown, A. G. and Edmonds, M. R. (eds) *Lithic Analysis and Later Prehistory*, British Archaeological Reports, British Series, 162, 137 - 154.

Myers, A.; 1989a
Lithics, risk and change in the Mesolithic. In: Brooks, I. and Phillips, P.(eds), *Breaking the Stony Silence*, British Archaeological Reports, British Series, 213, 131 - 160.

Myers, A.; 1989b
Reliable and maintainable technological strategies in the Mesolithic of mainland Britain. In: Torrence, R. (ed), *Time, Energy and Stone Tools.* Cambridge University Press.

Naroll, R.; 1962
Floor area and settlement population. *American Antiquity*, 27, 587 - 589.

Neaverson, E.; 1936
Recent observations on the Postglacial peat beds around Rhyl and Prestatyn (Flintshire). *Proceedings of the Liverpool Geological Society*, 17, 45 - 63.

Newell, R. R.; 1981
Mesolithic dwelling structures: fact and fantasy. In: *Mesolithikum in Europa*, Veröffentlichungen des Museums für Ur und Fruhgeschichte 14/15. Potsdam. 235 - 285.

Newell, R. R., Kielman, D., Constandse-Westermann, T. S., Gijn, A. van. and Sanden, W. A. B. van der.; in press
An enquiry into the ethnic resolution of Mesolithic regional groups: a study of their decorative ornaments in time and space.

Noddle, B.;
Cattle and sheep in Britain and northern Europe up to the Atlantic period: a personal viewpoint. In: Milles, A., Williams, D. and Gardner, N. (eds), *The Beginnings of Agriculture*, British Archaeological Reports, International Series, 496, 179 - 202.

Norman, c.; 1977
A flint assemblage from Constantine Island, north Cornwall. *Cornish Archaeology*, 16, 3 - 9.

Nygaard, S. E.; 1987
Socio-economic developments along the south-western coast of Norway between 10,000 and 4,000 BP. In: Rowley-Conwy, P., Zvelebil, M. and Blankholm, H. P. (eds), *Mesolithic North-west Europe: Recent Trends*, University of Sheffield, 147 - 154.

Oakley, K. P.; 1968
The date of the 'Red Lady' of Paviland. *Antiquity*, 42, 306 - 307.

Olsen, B. A. and Alsaker.; 1984
Greenstone and diabase utilisation in the Stone Age of western Norway: technological and socio-cultural aspects of axe and adze production and distribution. *Norwegian Archaeological Review*, 17, (2), 71 - 103.

O'Malley, M. and Jacobi, R. M.; 1978
The excavation of a Mesolithic occupation site at Broomhill, Braishfield, Hampshire. In: *Rescue Archaeology in Hampshire*, 4, 16 - 39.

Osborn, A. J.; 1977
Strandloopers, mermaids and other fairy tales: ecological determinants of marine resource utilisation - the Peruvian case. In: Binford, L. R. (ed), *For Theory Building In Archaeology*, New York, Academic Press. 157 - 205.

Otte, M.; 1976
Observations sur l'industrie lithique de Maisières et sur ses relations avec les autres ensembles périgordiens de Belgique. *BSPF*, Tome 73, 335 - 351.

Otte, M.; 1977
Donnees generales sur le Paleolithique Superieur Ancien de Belgique. *L'Anthropologie*, 81, No 2, 235 - 272.

Owen, G.; 1603
The Description of Pembrokeshire. Owen, H. (ed), *Cymmrodorion Record Series* No. 1, London (1892).

Palmer, S.; 1977
Mesolithic Cultures of Britain. Dolphin Press.

PAST, 1988
Photograph of Mesolithic footprints, Severn Levels, PAST: *Newsletter of the Prehistoric Society*, No. 5, p. 1.

Peake, D. S. and Osborne, P. J.; 1971
The Wandle Gravels in the vicinity of Croydon. *Proceedings of the Croydon Natural History and Science Society*, 14, (7), 145 - 176.

Pearson, G. W.; 1979
Belfast Radiocarbon Dates IX. *Radiocarbon*, 21, 279.

Pennington, W.; 1975
A chronostratigraphic comparison of Late-Weichselian and Late-Devensian subdivisions illustrated by two radiocarbon dated profiles from western Britain. *Boreas*, 4, (3), 157 - 171.

Pennington, W.; 1977
The Late Devensian flora and vegetation of Britain. *The Philosophical Transactions of the Royal Society of London*, B. 280, 247 - 271.

Pennington, W. and Bonny, A. P.; 1970
Absolute pollen diagram from the British Lateglacial. *Nature*, 226, 871 - 873.

Penny, L. F., Coope, G. R. and Catt, J. A.; 1969
Age and insect fauna of the Dimlington Silts, East Yorkshire. *Nature*, 224, 65 - 67.

Péquart, S-J. and M., Boule, M. and Vallois, H.; 1937
Téviec: station nécropole mésolithique du Morbihan. *Archives de l'Institut de Paléontologie Humaine*, 18.

Péquart, S-J. and M., 1954
Hoëdic Deuxième Station Nécropole Mésolithique du Morbihan. Anvers.

Perlman, S.; 1980
An optimum diet model, coastal variability and hunter-gatherer behaviour. In: Schiffer, M. (ed), *Advances in Archaeological Method and Theory, 3*. Academic Press. New York. 257 - 299.

Pitts, M.; 1979
Hides and antlers: a new look at the hunter-gatherer site at Star Carr, North Yorkshire, England. *World Archaeology*, 11, 32 - 42.

Pitts, M. and Jacobi, R. M.; 1979
Some aspects of change in flaked stone industries in southern Britain. *Journal of Archaeological Science*, 6, 163 - 177.

Preece, R. c.; 1980
The biostratigraphy and dating of the tufa deposit at Blashenwell, Dorset, England. *Journal of Archaeological Science*, 7, 345 - 362.

Price, T. D. and Brown, J. A. (eds),
Prehistoric Hunter- gatherers. The Emergence of Cultural Complexity. New York. Academic Press.

Radley, J.; 1970
The Mesolithic period in north-east Yorkshire. *Yorkshire Archaeological Journal*, 42, 314 - 327.

Radley, J., Switsur, V. R. and Tallis, J. H.; 1974
The excavation of three `Narrow Blade' Mesolithic sites in the southern Pennines, England. *Proceedings of the Prehistoric Society*, 40, 1 - 19.

Radley, J. and Mellars, P.; 1964
A Mesolithic structure at Deepcar, Yorkshire, England, and the affinities of its associated flint industries. *Proceedings of the Prehistoric Society*, 30, 1 - 24.

Rae, A. M., Ivanovich, M., Green, H. S., Head, M. J. and Kimber, R. W. L.; 1987.
A comparative dating study of bones from Little Hoyle Cave, south Wales, U.K. *Journal of Archaeological Science*, 14, 243 - 250.

Rankine, W. F.; 1956
The Mesolithic of Southern England. *Research Papers of the Surrey Archaeological Society*, 4.

Rees, J.; 1973
Palmerston Farm. *Archaeology In Wales*, 13, 29.

Reynolds, T. A.; 1983
Form, Function and Technology: A Test Case Of Limpet Scoops. Unpublished BA dissertation. University of Cambridge.

Roberts, A.; 1987
The later Mesolithic occupation of the Cornish coast at Gwithian: preliminary results. In: Rowley-Conwy, P., Zvelebil, M. and Blankholm, H. P. (eds), *Mesolithic North-west Europe; Recent Trends*. University of Sheffield. 131 - 137.

Robertson, D W.; 1988
Aspects of the Lateglacial and Flandrian environmental history of the Brecon Beacons, Fforest Fawr, Black Mountains and Abergavenny Black Mountain, South Wales (with special emphasis on the Lateglacial and early Flandrian periods). Unpublished PhD thesis, University of Wales.

Roe, D.; 1981
The Lower and Middle Palaeolithic Periods in Britain. London. Routledge and Kegan Paul.

Roe, F. E. S.; 1979
Typology of stone implements with shaft-holes. In: McKClough, T. H. and Cummins, W. A. (eds), *Stone Axe Studies*, Council For British Archaeology Research Report, 23. 23 - 48.

Roe, F. E. S.; 1985
Report on the cupped pebble from Lousey Barrow. In: Christie, P. M., Barrows on the Cornish coast: wartime excavations by *c.* K. Croft-Andrew 1939-44. *Cornish Archaeology*, 24, 23 - 121.

Rogers, E. H.; 1946
The raised beach, submerged forest and kitchen midden of Westward Ho! and the submerged stone row of Yelland. *Proceedings of the Devon Archaeological Exploration Society*, 3, 109 - 135.

Rogers, I.; 1908
On the submerged forest of Westward Ho!, Bideford Bay. *Transactions of the Devon Association*, 40, 249 - 259.

Rolleston, G., Lane Fox, A., Busk, G., Boyd Dawkins, W., Evans, J. and Hilton-Price, F. G.; 1878
Report of a committee ... appointed for the purpose of examining two caves containing human remains, in the neighbourhood of Tenby. *Report of the British Association for the Advancement of Science (Dublin)*, 48, 207 - 217.

Rose, J.; 1985
The Dimlington Stadial/Dimlington Chronozone: a proposal for naming the main glacial episode of the Late Devensian in Britain. *Boreas*, 14, 225 - 230.

Rose, J.; 1987
Status of the Wolstonian glaciation in the British Quaternary. *Quaternary Research Association Newsletter*, 53, 1 - 9.

Rowlands, B. M.; 1971
Radiocarbon evidence of the age of an Irish Sea Glaciation in the Vale of Clwyd. *Nature*, 230, 9 - 11.

Rowley-Conwy, P. A.; 1981
Mesolithic Danish Bacon: permanent and temporary sites in the Danish Mesolithic. In: Sheridan, A. and Bailey, G. (eds), *Economic Archaeology. Towards an Integration of Ecological and Social Approaches*. British Archaeological Reports, International Series. Oxford. 51 - 55.

Rowley-Conwy, P. A.; 1983
Sedentary hunters: the Ertebölle example. In: Bailey, G. N. (ed), *Hunter-gatherer Economy in Prehistory. A European Perspective*. Cambridge University Press, 111-126.

Rowley-Conwy, P. A.; 1984
The laziness of the short distance hunter: the origins of agriculture in Western Denmark. *Journal of Anthropological Archaeology*, 3, (4), 300 - 324.

Rowley-Conwy, P. A.; 1987
Animal bones in Mesolithic studies: recent progress and hopes for the future. In: Rowley-Conwy, P., Zvelebil, M. and Blankholm, H. P. (eds), *Mesolithic North-west Europe: Recent Trends*. University of Sheffield. 74 - 81.

Rowley-Conwy, P. A. and Zvelebil, M.; 1989
Saving it for later: storage by prehistoric hunter-gatherers in Europe. In: Halstead, P. and O'Shea, J. (eds), *Bad Year Economics Cultural Responses to Risk and Uncertainty*. Cambridge University Press.

Rozoy, J. G.; 1978
Les Derniers Chasseurs. Reims: *Société Archéologique Champenoise*. 3 Vols.

Ruddiman, W. F. and McIntyre, A; 1973
Time-transgressive deglacial retreat of polar waters from the North Atlantic. *Quaternary Research*, 3, 117 - 130.

Ruddiman, W. F. and McIntyre, A.; 1981
The North Atlantic during the last deglaciation. Palaeogeography, Palaeoclimatology, *Palaeoecology*, 35, 145 - 214.

Ruddiman, W. F., Sancetta, *c.* D. and McIntyre, A.; 1977
Glacial/Interglacial response rate of sub-polar north Atlantic water to climatic change: the record in ocean sediments. Philosophical *Transactions of the Royal Society of London* B, 280, 119 - 142.

Rutter, J. G. and Allen, E. E.; 1948
Gower Caves, Swansea.

Ryan, M.; 1978
Lough Boora excavations. *An Taisce*, 2, (1), 13 - 14.

Ryan, M.; 1980
An Early Mesolithic site in the Irish midlands. *Antiquity*, 54, 46 - 47.

Sahlins, M. D.; 1972
Stone Age Economics. London. Tavistock Publications (1974).

Salaman, R. A.; 1986
The Dictionary of Leather-working Tools c. 1700-1950. London.

Saville, A.; 1981
Mesolithic industries in central England: an exploratory investigation using microlith typology. *Archaeological Journal*, 138, 49 - 71.

Savory, H. N.; 1961
Levalloisian flake implement from Chepstow (Mon). *Bulletin of the Board of Celtic Studies*, 19, (3), 250 - 252.

Savory, H. N.; 1961-8
Recent excavation and discovery in Glamorgan. *Morgannwg*, vols. V (1961) - XII (1968).

Savory, H. N.; 1973
Excavations at The Hoyle, Tenby, in 1968. *Archaeologia Cambrensis*, CXXII, 18-34.

Savory, H. N.; 1980
The Neolithic in Wales. In: Taylor, J. A. (ed), *Culture and Environment in Prehistoric Wales,* British Archaeological Reports, British Series, 76. Oxford. 207 - 231.

Scott, K. 1986.;
Man in Britain in the late Devensian: evidence from Ossom's Cave. In: Roe, D. (ed), Studies in the Upper Palaeolithic of North-west Europe, British Archaeological Reports, International Series, 296. Oxford. 63 - 88.

Shackleton, N. J. and Opdyke, N. D.; 1973
Oxygen isotope and palaeomagnetic stratigraphy of equatorial Pacific core V28-238: oxygen isotope temperatures and ice volumes on a 10^5 and 10^6 year scale. *Quaternary Research*, 3, 39 - 55.

Shackleton, N. J. and Opdyke, N. D.; 1976
Oxygen isotope and palaeomagnetic stratigraphy of Pacific core V28-239, Late Pliocene to Late Holocene. *Geological Society of America Memoir*, 145, 449 - 464.

Shotton, F. W.; 1972
The large stone axes ascribed to north-west Pembrokeshire. In: Lynch, F. and Burgess, *c.* (eds), *Prehistoric Man in Wales and The West*. Adams and Dart, Bath. 85 - 92.

Shotton, F. W.; 1986
Glaciations in the United Kingdom. In: Sibrava, V., Bowen, D. Q. and Richmond, G. M. (eds), Quaternary Glaciations in the Northern Hemisphere. *Quaternary Science Reviews*, 5, 293 - 298.

Shotton, F. W. and Williams, R. E. G.; 1971
Birmingham University Radiocarbon Dates V. *Radiocarbon*, 13, no 2, 141 - 156.

Shotton, F. W. and Williams, R. E. G.; 1973
Birmingham University Radiocarbon Dates VII. *Radiocarbon*, 15, no 3, 451 - 468.

Sieveking, G. de G.; 1971
The Kendrick's Cave Mandible. *British Museum Quarterly*, 35, 230 - 250.

Simmons, I. G.; 1975a
Towards an ecology of mesolithic man in the uplands of Great Britain. *Journal of Archaeological Science*, 2, 1 - 15.

Simmons, I. G., 1975b
The ecological setting of man in the highland zone. In: Evans, J. G., Limbrey, S. and Cleere, H. (eds), *The Effect of Man on the Landscape: the Highland Zone*. Council For British Archaeology Research Report 11, 57 - 63.

Simmons, I. G., Dimbleby, G. W. and Grigson, *c.*; 1981
The Mesolithic. Chapter 3 in: Simmons, I. G. and Tooley, M. (eds), *The Environment in British Prehistory*. Duckworth. London.

Smith, A. G.; 1970
The influence of Mesolithic and Neolithic man on British vegetation: a discussion. In: Walker, D. and West, R. G. (eds), *Studies in the Vegetational History of the British Isles*. Cambridge University Press.

Smith, A. G.; 1984
Newferry and the Boreal-Atlantic transition. *New Phytologist*, 98, 35 - 55.

Smith, A. G., Pilcher, J. R. and Pearson, G. W.; 1971
New radiocarbon dates from Ireland. *Antiquity*, 45, 97 - 102.

Smith, A. G. and Pilcher, J. R.; 1973
Radiocarbon dates and vegetational history of the British Isles, *New Phytologist*, 72, 903 - 914.

Smith, A. G. and Cloutman, E. W.; 1988
Reconstruction of Holocene vegetation history in three dimensions at Waun-Fignen-Felen, an upland site in South Wales. *Philosophical Transactions of the Royal Society of London*, B, 322, 159 - 219.

Smith, F. G.; 1925
Some evidences of Early Man within and near to the northern portion of the Vale of Clwyd. *Proceedings of the Liverpool Geological Society*, XIV, (2), 117 - 122.

Smith, G.; 1926
Prehistoric remains at Bryn Newydd, Prestatyn. *Proceedings of the Llandudno, Colwyn Bay and District Field Club*, XIII, 62 - 67.

Smith, G.; 1982
The excavation of Mesolithic, Neolithic and Bronze Age settlements at Poldowrian, St. Keverne, 1980. *Cornish Archaeology*, 21, 23-62.

Smith, G. N.; 1862
On a successful search for flint implements in a cave called 'The Oyle', near Tenby, South Wales. *Report of the British Association* (Cambridge), 32, 95.

Smith, I. F.; 1965
Windmill Hill and Avebury - Excavations by Alexander Keiller 1925-39. Oxford. Clarendon Press.

Smith, R. A.; 1934
British Museum Quarterly, 8, 144 - 5.

Sollas, W. J.; 1913
Paviland Cave: an Aurignacian station in Wales. *Journal of the Royal Anthropological Institute*, 43, 325 - 374.

Stanton, Y. c.; 1984
The Mesolithic Period: early Post-glacial hunter-gather communities in Glamorgan. In: H.S.Green and Y.C.Stanton, The Old and Middle Stone Ages. In: Savory, H. N. (ed), *Glamorgan County History, Vol 2, Early Glamorgan*, University of Wales Press, Cardiff, 33-121.

Steel, T.; 1975
The Life and Death of St. Kilda. Glasgow. Fontana.

Stenger, c. and Williams, G.; 1980
Palmerston Farm. *Archaeology In Wales*, 20, 36 - 37.

Stevenson, A. c. and Moore, P. D.; 1982
Pollen analysis of an interglacial deposit at West Angle, Dyfed, Wales. *New Phytologist*, 90, 327 - 337.

Stringer, c. B.; 1986
The British fossil hominid record. In: Collcutt, S. N.(ed), *The Palaeolithic of Britain and its Nearest Neighbours: Recent Trends*. University of Sheffield. 59 - 61.

Stringer, c. B.; 1977
Evidence of climatic change and human occupation during the Last Interglacial at Bacon Hole, Gower. *Gower*, 28, 36 - 44.

Stuart, A. J.; 1982
Pleistocene Vertebrates in the British Isles. Longman. London.

Swanton, J. R.; 1946
The Indians of the South-eastern United States. *Smithsonian Institution Bureau of American Ethnology Bulletin*, 137, Washington DC.

Symonds, W. S.;
On the contents of a hyena's den on the Great Doward, Whitchurch, Ross. *Geological Magazine*, 8, 433.

Tauber, W.; 1968
Die Stielspitzen-Gruppen im nordlichen Mitteleuropa: ein Beitrag zur kenntnis der spaten Altsteinzeit. *Fundamenta Reiha* A, 5, (Koln, Bohlau).

Tauber, H.; 1970
Danske Kultsof-14 Dateringer af Arkaeologiske prover III. *Aaboger*, 120 - 142.

Tauber, H.; 1973
Copenhagen Radiocarbon Dates X. *Radiocarbon*, 15, No 1, 86 - 112.

Taylor, H.; 1928
Second Report on the excavations at King Arthur's Cave. *Proceedings of the University of Bristol Spelaeological Society*, III, No.2, (1927), 59-83.

Taylor, J. A.; 1973
Chronometers and Chronicles: a study of palaeoenvironments in West Wales. *Progress in Geography*, No.5. 250-334.

Taylor, J. A.; 1975
The role of climatic factors in environmental and cultural changes in prehistoric times. In: Evans, J. G., Limbrey, S. and Cleere, H. (eds), *The Effect of Man On The Landscape: The Highland Zone*, Council For British Archaeology Research Report 11. 6 - 19.

Taylor, J. A.; 1980
Environmental changes in Wales during the Holocene period. In: J. A. Taylor (ed), *Culture and Environment in Prehistoric Wales*. British Archaeological Reports, British Series, 76, 101-130.

Taylor, J. A.; 1987
Timescales of Environmental Change. University College of Wales, Aberystwyth.

Ters, M.; 1973
Les variations du niveau marin depuis 10,000 ans, le long du littoral atlantique francais: Le Quaternaire. Geodynamique, Stratigraphie et Environment. *Centre National de la Recherche Scientifique. Comité National Francais de l'INQUA*, 114 - 136.

Thomas, J.; 1988
Neolithic explanations revisited: the Mesolithic-Neolithictransition in Britain and south Scandinavia. *Proceedings of the Prehistoric Society*, 54, 59 - 66.

Thomas, R.; 1923
Pigmy flints found at Newport, Pembrokeshire. *Archaeologia Cambrensis*, 78, 324 - 326.

Thomas, R. and Dudlyke, E. R.; 1925
A flint chipping floor at Aberystwyth. *Journal of the Royal Archaeological Institute*, LV, 73 - 89.

Tooley, M. J.; 1974
Sea-level changes during the last 9,000 years in north-west England. *Geographical Journal*, 140, 18 - 42.

Tooley, M. J.; 1978
Sea-level Changes: North-west England During the Flandrian Stage. Oxford. Clarendon Press.

Tratman, E. K.; nd
Aveline's Hole, Burrington Combe. A Late Upper Palaeolithic-Mesolithic site. Unpublished MSc. University of Bristol Speleological Society's Archives, 12.

Van der Hammen, T., Wijmstra, T. A. and Zagwijn, W. H.; 1971
The floral record of the late Cenozoic of Europe. In: Turkian, K. K. (ed), *The Late Cenozoic Glacial Ages*. New Haven. Yale University Press. 391 - 424.

Vang Peterson, P.; 1984
Chronological and regional variation in the late Mesolithic of eastern Denmark. *Journal of Danish Archaeology*, 3, 7 - 18.

Van Nédervelde, J.; 1970a
Report of the latest archaeological findings from already known and new sites on Caldey Island (Jan 1970).*Unpublished*.

Van Nédervelde, J.; 1970b (nd)
Report of the discovery and excavation of 'Ogof-yr-Ychen' (Cave of the Oxen) on Caldey Island. *Unpublished*.

Van Nédervelde, J.; 1972
Ogof-yr-Ychen (Cave of the Ox), Caldey Island. *Archaeology in Wales*, 12, 19 - 20.

Van Nédervelde, J. and Davies, M.; 1977a
Nanna's Cave. *Archaeology in Wales*, 17, 24.

Van Nédervelde, J. and Davies, M.; 1977b
Potter's Cave, Caldey Island. *Archaeology in Wales*, 17, 25.

Van Nédervelde, J. and Davies, M.; 1979-80
Caldey Island (Nanna's Cave, Potter's Cave, Ogof-yr-Ychen). *Unpublished*.

Van Nédervelde, J. and Davies, M.; 1986
Caldey Island 1983-5 - Cave Archaeology. *Unpublished* report.

Van Nédervelde, J. and Davies, M.; 1987
Caldey Island Annual Excavation Report 1987. *Unpublished*.

Van Nédervelde, J., Davies, M. and John, B. S.; 1973
Dating from Ogof-yr-Ychen, a new Pleistocene site in west Wales. *Nature*, 245, 453 - 455.

Verhart, L. B. M.; 1988
Mesolithic barbed points and other implements from Europoort, The Netherlands. *Oudheidkundige Mededelingen uit het Rijksmuseum van Oudheden te Leiden*, 68, 145 - 194.

Wainwright, G. J.; 1963
A reinterpretation of the microlithic industries of Wales. *Proceedings of the Prehistoric Society*, XXIX, 99-132.

Wainwright, G. J.; 1967
Coygan Camp: A Prehistoric, Roman-British and Dark Age Settlement in Carmarthenshire, Cambrian Archaeological Association Monograph.

Wainwright, G. J.; 1969
Nab Head, St. Brides. *Archaeology In Wales*, 9, 13.

Wainwright, G. J.; 1970
Excavations at The Nab Head Mesolithic site, Pembrokeshire, 1970. *Bulletin of the Board of Celtic Studies*, XXXIV, 95.

Walker, M. J. c.; 1982
The Lateglacial and early Flandrian deposits at Traeth Mawr, Brecon Beacons, south Wales. *New Phytologist*, 90, 177 - 194.

Walker, M. J. c. and Harkness, D. D.; 1990 in press
Radiocarbon dating the Devensian Lateglacial in Britain: new evidence from Llanilid, South Wales. *Journal of Quaternary Science*, 5.

Walne, P. R.; 1970
The seasonal variation of meat and glycogen content of seven populations of oysters (Ostrea edulis) and a review of the literature. *Fishery Investigations*, Series II, 26, 3.

Watson, E.; 1977
The periglacial environment of Britain during the Devensian. *Philosophical Transactions of the Royal Society of London*, B, 280, 183 - 198.

Watt, D. K. and Merrill, A. L.; 1963
Composition of Foods; raw, processed, prepared. United States Department of Agriculture Handbook 8, Washington.

Webley, D. P.; 1976
How the West was won: prehistoric land-use in the southern Marches. In: G.C.Boon and J.M.Lewis (eds), *Welsh Antiquity*, National Museum of Wales.

Weissner, P.; 1974
A functional estimator of population from floor area. *American Antiquity*, 39, 343 - 350.

Welinder, S.; 1977
The Mesolithic age of eastern middle Sweden. Kungl. *Vitterhets Historie och Antikvitets Akademien*, 65.

West, R. G.; 1977
Pleistocene Geology and Biology. London. (2nd edition).

Wheeler, A.; 1978
Why were there no fish remains at Star Carr? *Journal of Archaeological Science*, 5, 85 - 89.

Wheeler, R. E. M.; 1925
Prehistoric and Roman Wales. Oxford.

White, R. B.; 1978
Excavations at Trwyn Du, Anglesey, 1974. *Archaeologia Cambrensis*, CXXVII, 16 - 39.

Whittle, A.; 1989
Review of Smith, *c.* A. and Lynch, F. M., (1987) Trefignath and Din Dryfol. The excavation of two megalithic tombs in Anglesey. In: *Proceedings of the Prehistoric Society*, 55, 281 - 282.

Wickham-Jones, *c.* R.; 1989
Recent work on the island of Rhum, Scotland. In: Bonsall, *c.* (ed), *The Mesolithic In Europe*. John Donald, Edinburgh, 156 - 163.

Wickham-Jones, *c.* R.; 1990 in press
Rhum: Mesolithic and later sites at Kinloch. Excavations 1984-86. Society of Antiquaries of Scotland, Monograph Series, No 7.

Wickham-Jones, *c.* R. and Sharples, N.; 1984
An interim report on the excavations at Farm Fields, Kinloch, Rhum, 1984. Artefact Research Unit. National Museum of Antiquities of Scotland.

Williams, E.; 1989
Dating the introduction of food production into Britain and Ireland. *Antiquity*, 63, 510 - 521.

Willkomm, von H.; 1981
14C-daten von Mesolithischen fundplatzen in Duvenseer Moor. *Offa*, 38, 37 - 40.

Willkomm, von H.; 1985
Kernphysikalische untersuchungen. *Offa*, 42, 32 - 33.

Winwood, H. H.; 1865
Exploration of The Hoyle's Mouth Cave, near Tenby. *Geological Magazine*, 2, 471 - 473.

Woodman, P. *c.*; 1973-4
Settlement patterns in the Irish Mesolithic. *Ulster Journal of Archaeology*, 36 and 37, 1 - 16.

Woodman, P. *c.*; 1978a
The Mesolithic in Ireland, British Archaeological Reports, British Series, 58.

Woodman, P. *c.*; 1978b
A reappraisal of the Manx Mesolithic. In: Davey, P. (ed), *Man and Environment in the Isle of Man.* British Archaeological Reports, British Series, 54. Oxford. 333 - 370.

Woodman, P. *c.*; 1985
Excavations at Mount Sandel 1973-77. Northern Ireland Archaeological Monographs No. 2. HMSO.

Woodman, P. *c.*; 1986a
Why not an Irish Upper Palaeolithic? In: Roe, D. (ed), *Studies in the Upper Palaeolithic of Britain and North-west Europe.* British Archaeological Reports, International Series, 296. Oxford. 43 - 54.

Woodman, P. *c.*; 1986b
Problems in the colonisation of Ireland. *Ulster Journal of Archaeology*, 49, 7 - 17.

Woodman, P. *c.*; 1987
The impact of resource availability on lithic industrial traditions in prehistoric Ireland. In: Rowley-Conwy, P., Zvelebil, M. and Blankholm, H. P. (eds), *Mesolithic North-west Europe: Recent Trends.* University of Sheffield. 138 - 146.

Wymer, J. J.; 1962
Excavations at the Maglemosian sites at Thatcham, Berkshire, England. *Proceedings of the Prehistoric Society*, XXVII, 329- 361.

Wymer, J. J. (ed).; 1977
Gazetteer of Mesolithic Sites in England and Wales. Council For British Archaeology Research Report 20.

Wymer, J. J.; 1981
The Palaeolithic. Chapter 2 in: Simmons, I. G. and Tooley, M. J. (eds), *The Environment in British Prehistory.* London. Duckworth. 49 - 81.

Wymer, J. J.; 1988
Palaeolithic archaeology and the British Quaternary sequence. *Quaternary Science Reviews*, 7, 79 - 98.

Wymer, J. J., Jacobi, R. M. and Rose, J.; 1975
Late Devensian and early Flandrian barbed points from Sproughton, Suffolk. *Proceedings of the Prehistoric Society*, 41, 235 - 241.

Yerkes, R. W.;1983
Microwear, Microdrills, and Mississippian Craft Specialization. *American Antiquity*, 48, No.3, 499-517.

Zvelebil, M.; 1986
Mesolithic prelude and Neolithic revolution. In: Zvelebil, M. (ed), *Hunters In Transition*. Cambridge University Press, 5 - 16.

Zvelebil, M. (ed); 1986
Hunters In Transition. Cambridge University Press.

Zvelebil, M. and Rowley-Conwy, P. A.; 1984
Transition to farming in northern Europe: a hunter-gatherer perspective. *Norwegian Archaeological Review*, 17, 104 - 128.

Zvelebil, M. and Rowley-Conwy, P. A.; 1986
Foragers and farmers in Atlantic Europe. In: Zvelebil, M. (ed), *Hunters In Transition*. Cambridge University Press, 67 - 94.

Additional sources

Aldhouse-Green, S.; 2000
Paviland Cave and the 'Red Lady'. Bristol: Western Academic Specialist Press.

Aldhouse-Green, S., Scott, K., Schwarcz, H., Grün, R., Housley, R., Rae, A., Bevins, R. and Redknap, M.; 1995
Coygan Cave, Laugharne, South Wales, a Mousterian site and hyaena den: a report on the University of Cambridge excavations. Proceedings of the Prehistoric Society 61, 37–79.

Barton, R.N.E., Berridge, P.J., Walker, M.J.C. and Bevins, R.E.; 1995
Persistent places in the Mesolithic landscape: an example from the Black Mountain uplands of South Wales. Proceedings of the Prehistoric Society 61, 81-116.

Barton, R.N.E. and Price, C.; 1999
The westernmost Upper Palaeolithic cave site in Britain and probable evidence of a Bronze Age shell midden: new investigations at Priory Farm Cave, Pembrokeshire. Archaeology in Wales 39, 3–9.

Bell, M., Allen, J.R.L., Buckley, S., Dark, P. and Nayling, N.; 2003
Mesolithic to Neolithic coastal environmental change: excavations at Goldcliff East, 2003 and research at Redwick. Archaeology in the Severn Estuary 14, 1–26.

Bell, M., Castledine, A., and Neumann, H.; 2000
Prehistoric Intertidal Archaeology in the Welsh Severn Estuary, Council for British Archaeology, Research Report 120, York.

Bell, M (ed).; forthcoming
Prehistoric Coastal Communities: the archaeology of western Britain 6000-3000 cal BC, Council for British Archaeology, Research Report 149, York.

Burrow, S.; 2003
Catalogue of the Mesolithic and Neolithic Collections in the national Museum & Galleries of Wales, Cardiff: National Museums & Galleries of Wales.

Caseldine, A.; 1990
Environmental Archaeology in Wales. Lampeter: Department of Archaeology, Saint David's University College, Lampeter.

David, A.; 1990
Palaeolithic and Mesolithic settlement in Wales with Special reference to Dyfed. Unpublished PhD Thesis, University of Lancaster.

David, A.; 1990
Lateglacial archaeological residues from Wales: a selection. In: Barton, R. N. E., Roberts, A. J., and Roe, D. A., (eds) The Lateglacial in NW Europe: Human adaptation and cultural change at the end of the Pleistocene. Council for British Archaeology Research Report No 77, 141-159.

David, A., and Walker, E.; 2004
Wales during the Mesolithic period, in Saville, A., (ed), Mesolithic Scotland and its Neighbours, Society of Antiquaries of Scotland, Edinburgh, 299-338.

Jacobi, R.; 2004
The Late Upper Palaeolithic lithic collection from Gough's Cave, Cheddar, Somerset, and human uses of the cave, Proceedings of the Prehistoric Society 70, 1-92.

Lynch, F., Davies, J. L., and Aldhouse-Green, S.; 2000
Prehistoric Wales, Sutton Publishing.

Schulting, R.J. and Richards, M.P.; 2002
Finding the coastal Mesolithic in southwest Britain: AMS dates and stable isotope results on human remains from Caldey Island, South Wales. Antiquity 76, 1011–1025.

Quinnell, H., and Blockley, M. R., with Berridge, P.; 1994
Excavations at Rhuddlan, Clwyd: 1969-73 Mesolithic to Medieval, Council for British Archaeology, Research Report 95.

Walker, E.A.; 2000a
Burry Holms (SS 4001 9247). Archaeology in Wales 40, 88–89.

Walker, E.A.; 2000b
Porthgain, Llanrhian (SM 81 32). Archaeology in Wales 40, 86.

Walker, E.A.; 2004
The Mesolithic: the final hunter-gatherer-fisher societies of south-eastern Wales. In M. Aldhouse-Green and R. Howell (eds), The Gwent County History Volume I: Gwent in Prehistory and Early History. Cardiff: University of Wales Press, 29–55.

Walker, M.J.C., Buckley, S.L. and Caseldine, A.E.; 2001
Landscape change and human impact in west Wales during the Lateglacial and Flandrian. In M.J.C. Walker and D. McCarroll (eds), The Quaternary of West Wales: Field Guide. London: Quaternary Research Association, 17–29.

Walker, E. A.; forthcoming
The Palaeolithic and Mesolithic hunter-gatherers of Pembrokeshire, in Kirk, T. (ed.) The Pembrokeshire County History Volume 1. Haverfordwest: The Pembrokeshire Historical Society.